E&G 蓝皮书 BLUE BOOK

2012中国城市科学发展综合评价报告

——城市与人

2012 Comprehensive Evaluation and Grading
Report on China Urban Scientific Development
(Chinese-English Bilingual Edition)
—— City and People

联合编著

中国城市发展研究院
中国房地产研究会
中国国际经济交流中心
中国战略文化促进会

中国社会科学出版社

图书在版编目(CIP)数据

2012 中国城市科学发展综合评价报告 / 中国城市发展研究院等
联合编著 . —北京：中国社会科学出版社，2012. 12
ISBN 978 - 7 - 5161 - 1858 - 0

Ⅰ. ①2… Ⅱ. ①中… Ⅲ. ①城市 - 发展 - 评估 - 调查报告 -
中国 - 2012 Ⅳ. ①F299. 2

中国版本图书馆 CIP 数据核字 (2012) 第 298583 号

出 版 人	赵剑英
责任编辑	任　明
责任校对	安　然
责任印制	李　建

出　　版	中国社会科学出版社
社　　址	北京鼓楼西大街甲 158 号（邮编 100720）
网　　址	http：//www.csspw.cn
	中文域名：中国社科网　　　010 - 64070619
发 行 部	010 - 84083685
门 市 部	010 - 84029450
经　　销	新华书店及其他书店

印　　刷	北京奥隆印刷厂
装　　订	北京市兴怀印刷厂
版　　次	2012 年 12 月第 1 版
印　　次	2012 年 12 月第 1 次印刷

开　　本	710 × 1000　1/16
印　　张	24
插　　页	8
字　　数	422 千字
定　　价	280.00 元

《中国城市科学发展综合评级
体系（E&G）设计》
著作权声明

《中国城市科学发展综合评级体系（E&G）设计》是中国城市发展研究院的重大研究成果之一，已经通过专家论证和中华人民共和国国家版权局的审核，"中华人民共和国国家版权局著作权登记证书"登记号为：2008 - A - 012255。

未经本院书面授权，严禁任何形式盗用、复制或仿造本《综合评级体系设计》，严禁任何形式使用本《综合评级体系设计》进行评价或其他活动。一经发现，本院将依法追究相关者的法律责任。

中国城市发展研究院

2012 年 9 月 15 日

目　　录

序 言

关 于 城 市

（十一届全国政协副主席　孙家正）

伴随着经济的发展、科技的进步，城市化进程明显加快。城市的发展，促进了人类社会现代化进程。目前，城市的数量和规模日益扩大，全世界城市人口在超过农业人口后迅速攀升，全球性的"城市时代"已经来临。

城市文明的发展是历史的进步，它广泛而深刻地影响着人们的生活方式和社会心理。城市的发展为人们带来了更多的舒适、便利和机会，也带来一些新的困扰和问题。我们赖以生存的城市家园不同程度地面临着记忆消失、面貌趋同、交通拥挤、环境恶化等诸多问题。城市的发展不断地满足并刺激着人们的物质需求，而精神上、心理上的慰藉和憧憬却在不同程度地失落了。人们在为城市日新月异的变化而兴奋的同时，应该保持一种忧患意识，冷静思考城市乃至整个经济社会如何科学发展。

我们究竟需要一个什么样的生存空间？我们究竟在追求怎样的生活？当人们试图以全新的、理性的眼光审视扑朔迷离的城市形态时，不约而同地选择了文化的视角。我认为，《中国城市科学发展综合评价报告》出版的意义在于，它的编辑和作者也试图从城市的个性差异，也就是从城市的文化角度去审视和评价每一座城市。

文化是什么？文化是一定历史、一定地域、一定人类群体的生存状态和愿望的反映，同时，又对人的生存和发展产生着广泛而深刻的影响。城市文化问题，可以说是当代备受关注的世界性话题。

城市是市民的安居之所和精神家园，城市建设应秉持以人为本的原则。城市的规划、建设、管理和服务都必须坚持面向最广大的普通民众，同时也要回应不同人群的诉求。创造人与自然友好相处的生态环境，形成亲切无碍的人际关系，构建和谐自然的城市空间，是民众的共同愿望和要求。面对现代生活的迅捷变化和市场经济下的激烈竞争，人们的物质需求需要不断地满足，而心理上的迷茫和困扰尤需抚慰。民众的生存状态、心理感受，需要更多的人文关怀。城市文化形态的变化和发展过程应该同时成为不断满足人们的精神需求、提高人的素质、促进人的全面发展的过程。城市建设和管理呼唤着深切的人文关怀。一个城市是否具有这种人文关怀的精神、环境和氛围，应成为考评城市建设水平高低、管理质量优劣的重要标尺。

形神兼备是文化城市的重要特征。所谓形，就是城市的建筑、街道、景观，表现为城市外在的风貌气度；所谓神，就是蕴含在城市历史和现实当中的文化内涵，闪耀着一个城市独有的内在品格和气质。物态景观和人类活动因共有的文化内涵而和谐统一。一个城市只有形神兼备，浑然一体，才能保持永不衰竭的魅力。一个对城市的科学评价体系，也应当从"形"和"神"两个角度去审视城市。我们感到欣慰的是，《中国城市科学发展综合评价报告》的编辑和作者在这方面做出了不懈的努力。

人创造了有形的城市，城市反过来又以无形的方式陶冶人、塑造人。市民的价值观念、思维方式、道德水准、社会风尚等因素是城市文化建设的综合反映，也是城市文化建设发挥作用的过程与结果。

无论是有形的城市面貌，还是无形的城市精神，都是一定的文化使然。文化如水，滋润万物，悄然无声。文化留存于城市空间的每一个角落，融汇于城市生活的全部过程和每一个细节。文化对城市的营造、演变，对市民的生活、行为都产生着潜移默化的作用，城市是文化的容器。城市中的街区、广场、建筑、雕塑、装置、绿化、小品等等构成了城市有形和外在的物态系统，作用于我们的视觉、听觉、嗅觉、触觉而直抵心灵；同时，它们又承载着在城市空间中发生着的人类活动，正是这些千姿百态、生动有趣的活动使城市富有了充沛的人气和旺盛的活力。

拒绝和防止趋同，保护和彰显个性，是当代城市建设中应该特别注意的问题。现代化、全球化无疑是一把双刃剑，其益处无需赘言，其弊端也显而易见。现代化对于传统的消解，全球化对于个性的抹杀已是不争的事实。正因为如此，近年来，保护文化多样性的声浪日趋高涨。尊重和珍惜城市的历史传统、地域风貌和民族特色，方能保持并彰显一个城市所独有的文化韵味。一个城市区别于另一个城市的，不仅在于它的规划布局、色彩基调、建筑样式，更重要的还在于其内在的气质、情感及其文化底蕴。城市的文化特色将是城市独特风貌和文化精神的完美结合。发现、界定、保护、传承和拓展城市的文化个性与特色，方可构建起轮廓清晰、结构完整、布局合理、神采独具的城市文化形象。

保护历史文化遗产是城市建设中的重大课题。历史文化遗产在城市建设中焕发着穿越时空的悠久魅力。一座城市就是一部历史，我们不能割断历史，割断历史就是在撕裂了现在。人类需要前瞻又耽于回忆，我们不能失去记忆，失去记忆也便失去了憧憬。城市中的物质与非物质的文化遗产见证着城市的生命历程，保持和延续着城市文化，并促进着城市肌体的健康发展，同时也赋予了人们真切的归宿感与认同感。我们必须坚守、传承、培育城市的优秀文化传统，尽可能避免因为盲目开发而对文化遗产、文化环境的破坏。精心呵护历史文化遗产，维系历史文脉，留住城市记忆，是人们生存发展的心理需求，也是当代人对祖先和子孙的责任。

城市不是钢筋、混凝土的堆砌物，而是一个有机的生命体。城市的演化和发展是一个生命体的成长发育和有机完善的过程。我们要尊重城市内在的遗传基因，顺应城市生成肌理和发展规律，在改造与完善中，有机更新，有序发展，使其生态环境不断优化、服务功能日趋完备、文化韵味更加浓郁。

城市建设不但要继承传统，同时也要适应时代的发展和生活的需要而不断地创造和更新。成功的城市必定是在保持自己文化传统基础上进行再创新的城市。坚守历史传统、适应时代需要的文化创新是城市发展的灵魂和活力。包括城市建设内在的文化创新，需要有坚定的自信和包容的胸怀。对外开放是中国的基本国策，和而不同是中国的哲学思维，追求和谐是中国人的价值取向。

城市从来就不是孤立的存在。追根溯源，是农村、农业和农民孕育并哺乳了城市。这一点，在中国城市化进程中尤为明显。反哺农村，善待农民，促进城乡协调发展是城市发展的应有之义。这不仅是道义上的必需，也是城市自身持续发展的必备条件。

对中国城市按遵循科学发展观进行综合评级，不但有利于促进中国城市社会经济的健康发展，而且也是对城市文化的总结和肯定。我衷心希望《中国城市科学发展综合评价报告》取得成功，为中国城市发展做出独特的贡献。

第一部分　2012 中国城市发展报告

第一节　城镇化内涵及特征

一、绪言

我国正处于快速城镇化的进程中。在这一过程中，既呈现出与世界各国城镇化类似的共性，也显现出自己的独有特征。其中最为重要的，就是**城镇化与市民化的严重不同步**。由于历史和国情因素，长期生活在城市尤其是大中城市中的城市居民，相当一部分不具有该城市的城镇户口，他们与本地居民相比，在就业、居住、教育、医疗、社会保障甚至交通等诸方面都存在着机会不均等，在收入、城市归属感和认同感等方面也都比本地居民低，二者间存在着显著差异。中国城市发展研究院于 2011 年所做的关于城市居民生活状态及主观评价的问卷调查结果清楚地显示了这一点。[①] 这些不具有本市城镇户口的城市居民，还不是完全意义上的市民，他们不仅在享受公共服务上受到限制，而且在意识、心理和行为上也都与完全意义上的市民有着很大的区别，譬如城市认同感和荣誉感、自律意识和行为。这种城镇化与市民化的不同步，对我国未来的城镇化和经济社会

[①]　白南风执笔（2012）中国城市居民生活状态及评价，比较，2，192—247
　　Bai Nanfeng（2012），Urban Residents'Living Condition & Assessment in China, *Compare*, 2，192—247

协调发展有着很大的影响，要求我们进一步致力于推进户籍制度改革和社会基本公共服务均等化。

中国城镇化过程所呈现出的特点和面临的问题，需要我们比较系统地梳理有关城镇化的研究，包括城镇化的内涵及特征、世界各国的城镇化理论及经验借鉴等，并在此基础之上分析中国城镇化的趋势、城镇化与城市发展要素的协调性、城镇化阶段与公共服务的关系等等，进而探索中国未来的城镇化之路。

二、城镇化内涵及特征

（一）城镇化的内涵

一般认为，城镇化的内涵主要包括四个方面：一是**人口城镇化**，指农村人口向城镇聚集，城镇人口数量不断增加、比重逐渐提高的过程；二是**地域城镇化**，指在地域空间上，农村地域逐渐转化为以人口的高度聚集为主要特征的城镇地域的过程；三是**经济活动城镇化**，指经济关系、经济活动在地理上聚集，以及生产方式日益趋向于城镇经济特征的过程；四是**生活方式城镇化**，指随着社会身份、职业、社会角色等的变化，人们在行为方式、思想观念、道德意识、社会交往、受教育程度、生活习惯、综合素质等方面，由农村向城镇转变的过程。

（二）城镇化基本特征

城镇化的核心是促进农村人口向城镇转移，实现基础设施和公共服务向农村的覆盖，优化城镇化的空间布局。

我国经过 30 多年的快速发展，城镇化已经接近世界平均水平。根据第六次人口普查资料显视，2010 年我国居住在城镇的人口为 66558 万人，城镇化率达到 49.68%，城乡几于各占半壁江山，城镇化已进入转型发展的新阶段。从世界城镇化发展轨迹中看，我国城镇化规模和发展速度前所未有，仅用了 20 年时间城市化率就从 20% 提高到 40%[1]。但实质上，**现行城镇化率统计口径中，城镇常住人口里包含总量接近 1/3 的大量农民工，在公共服务、社会保障等诸多方面都没有真正实现"市民化"，因此，城镇化的质量并不高。**

我国城镇化进入转型发展的新阶段时期，其主要特征可大致概况如下：

（1）城镇化从量的增长转入质的发展

城镇化的本质是生产方式和生活方式的转变，而不是城市空间粗放拓

① 姚士谋、陆大道、王聪等：《中国城镇化需要综合性的科学思维》，《地理研究》，2011 年第 10 期，第 75—77 页。

展与城市人口盲目扩张。当前国际金融危机的影响尚未消除，国际资源环境问题对宏观经济的约束增强，国内城镇化与社会发展的不均衡影响宏观经济增长，更影响城镇化质量的提升。在现行制度和规划体系下，**流动人口不能享受与城市对等人群的同等教育和培训，势必影响劳动力素质和城市竞争力的提升**。国内学者认为，我国城镇化过程将进入平稳发展的转型阶段，提升质量是重点[①]。"十一五"时期，我国每年GDP增长速度达16.56%，城镇化水平年均增长率实现了2.93%。无论是提升城镇化速度，还是提高城镇化质量，都给我国城乡规划与管理和公共服务均等化政策带来重大考验。

（2）城镇化空间诉求从产业区域转移进入基础设施和基本公共服务均等化

2010年统计数据显示，我国东部、中部和西部地区，社会经济要素呈现出巨大的区域性差异特征。东部地区城镇人口比重为45%，吸纳了近一半的全国城镇人口。其中，长江三角洲、珠江三角洲和环渤海三个地区主要城镇密集区的人口密度高达每平方公里739人、608人和481人；而同期全国每平方公里人口密度为140人，西部地区人口密度仅为53人。由于要素的实质性差异，使得东部沿海地区和以省会为代表的区域性中心城市仍将产生人口集聚与投资的吸引力，空间不均衡态势日趋加剧，反映在城市规划上，更普遍的表现为乡村基础设施低水平配置、低就业机会及教育、医疗等规划布局问题。经济转型与产业区域转移的新格局，的确增强了城镇对农村剩余劳动力的吸纳能力，但也在一定程度上导致对城镇化的曲解，进而引出了基础设施建设和基本公共服务均等化的诉求。

表1　　　　　　　　　2010年城镇人口在各地区的分布

	GDP（亿元）	城镇人口（万人）	常住人口（万人）	城镇化率（%）
东部地区	232030.7	30293.7	50645.75	59.8
中部地区	86109.4	15822.36	36208.76	43.7
西部地区	81408.5	14915.35	36056.29	41.4

资料来源：《中国统计年鉴（2011）》。

（3）城镇化发展模式从行政手段进入政府调控下的市场配置资源

过去几十年借助于行政管理体制和行政手段来进行资源配置，城市行政等级越高能分配的用地指标、专项公共资金越多，公共服务能力越强，

① 周一星：《关于中国城镇化速度的思考》，《城市规划》S1，第32—37页。

对投资和消费吸引力越大，人口越易集中。**行政手段会改变人口流向的空间布局，而在市场规律影响下，企业投资布局则受土地、劳动力和环境成本上升的影响，东部吸纳农民工的比重在持续下降。**现阶段以招商引资、推进城镇化为口号，违背城镇化发展规律，超前、超标准的进行城镇建设，导致经济发展的外部影响问题较多，亟需优质的城镇规划建设与科学的城市管理，根据区域实际情况，满足城镇化进程中城乡居民人居生活的客观需要，提升城镇公共服务水平，运用行政手段和市场配置资源方式共同引导城镇化的人口流向。

（三）中国城镇化研究展望

2010 年中国城镇化率已经达到 49.68%，城市人口约 6.66 亿。根据有关学者对 Northam 曲线的修正和发展，以及对城镇化饱和值的推断[1][2]，中国城镇化速度在 2005 年将达到峰值，且城镇化水平饱和值为 80% 左右，与现在美国的饱和值类似。类比推断，我国现阶段城镇化水平大致相当于美国 1920 年的中期阶段，呈现出"粗放式、混乱式"的发展形式。因此，**我国未来的城镇化速度应该逐渐放缓，由粗放式逐步转向内涵式发展，以提升城镇化质量**，否则有走向"过度城镇化"的危险。

尽管目前全国各地各种"新型城镇化"道路涌现，但无论从国外经验、历史发展，或者近期全国整体发展趋势来看，**工业化或者说产业化仍是推动城镇化的关键性因素，二者具有非常高的相关性。**在通过产业转型和结构升级推动城镇化的过程中，未来经济发展的速度放缓是十分正常的现象，同时也将带来城镇化速度的下降。

在全球化、信息化不断深入的今天，重要的大城市或特大城市由于占据信息网络的中心地位，会带来较大程度的发展，并可能升格为全国几大中心城市或世界城市。而对于许多小城镇来说，专业化经济仍是城市发展的主导因素，并不断推动产业结构转型，逐步向城市化经济转化，从而使经济焕发出新的活力。

对于刘易斯二元经济结构理论是否适用于中国，以及刘易斯拐点是否已经到来，学界目前仍有较大争议，需要通过进一步的经验研究验证和理论完善。同时，在空间上区域之间的差异是否在缩小，极化作用还是扩散作用为主导也需要未来进一步研究。

---

[1] 陈彦光、周一星：《城市化 Logistic 过程的阶段划分及其空间解释——对 Northam 曲线的修正与发展》，《经济地理》2005 年第 6 期，第 817—821 页。

[2] 陈彦光、罗静：《城市化水平与城市化速度的关系探讨——中国城市化速度和城市化水平饱和值的初步推断》，《地理研究》2006 年第 6 期，第 1063—1072 页。

第二节 城镇化理论及经验借鉴

一、城镇化相关理论

（一）城镇化阶段理论

Northam 曲线是城镇化发展研究中经常运用的理论模型。城镇化发展要经历低水平缓慢增长的起步期，然后进入城镇化的快速发展期，最终在高位进入稳定期。根据发达国家的经验，城镇化水平在 30% 以下为初期阶段，该阶段第一产业所能提供的生活资料不够丰富，国民经济总体实力薄弱，第二产业发展所需的社会资本短缺，所以城镇化的速度比较缓慢；30%—70% 为中期阶段，该阶段城镇化发展进入加速期，人口和经济活动迅速向城市集聚，城镇化水平大约每年提高一个百分点，城镇在外延扩大的同时也开始了向内涵发展；70% 以上为后期阶段，该阶段是城镇化发展进入的高级阶段，城镇人口比重的增长又趋缓慢甚至停滞，城镇化进入平稳阶段，城镇的职能更加复杂化和多样化，成为该区域的经济、科技、文化、商贸中心等①。

Northam 曲线在美国的城镇化发展过程中得到了较好验证。1790 年美国在第一次人口普查时城镇化水平仅为 5%，处于初级阶段。到 19 世纪中叶，随着美国内战的结束，美国城镇化快速发展，1920 年，美国人口突破了 1 亿大关，其中超过半数（51.2%）的居民住在城镇，这时城镇化水平达到中期阶段。1920 年以后，人口城镇化比例上升速度有所趋缓。进入 70 年代以来，城市人口占全国总人口的比例基本保持稳定，从 70 年代到 20 世纪末的 30 年时间里，城镇化水平稳定在 74%—77% 之间②。

---

① 王秀玲：《对国外城镇化发展的思考》，《河北师范大学学报》2006 年第 6 期。

② 湖南统计局：《国外城镇化发展经验对湖南省的启示》，《湖南统计局普查中心公报》2002 年第 4 期。

（二）城镇化动力理论

（1）工业化与城镇化

从发达国家的经验来看，大多数学者认为，工业化是城镇化的基本动力，二者具有高度相关性。伴随着工业化进入不同阶段，城镇化的水平也在逐渐提高。

英国是世界上最早开始工业化和城镇化的国家。在工业革命的推动下，英国的城镇化进程十分迅速，曼彻斯特、伯明翰、利物浦等一大批工业城市迅速崛起、成长。德国的鲁尔地区、法国北部地区、美国的大西洋沿岸等地区都是在工业革命中，随着资本、工厂、人口向城市的迅速集中而形成城市密集区。**从发展的速度看，城镇化的高速发展期一般处于工业化加速阶段，即从工业化初期向工业化中期迈进的时期。**

发达国家的城市化是一个逐步的人口转移与经济结构变化相适应的平滑过程，这就是经典的"戴维斯城市化曲线"。需要强调的是，西方发达国家150年相对渐增的城市化过程始终是与它们缓慢的城乡人口结构变化交织在一起的。从英、美等西方发达国家的城市化过程看，城市化与逐步的工业化和经济变化始终交织在一起。在这一时期，由于城镇的劳动力需求表现为稳定的增长，也就存在从农村到城市的稳定移民流。与此同时，农业技术进步和制造业发展也充分吸收了从农业部门中解放出来的剩余劳动力，并允许农村劳动力逐步转化为城市劳动力和居民。

而经济发展二元结构模型理论对发展中国家的城镇化过程进行了较好的解释。1954年，刘易斯（W·Arthur Lewis）创立了经济发展的二元结构模型，把发展中国家的经济结构概括为现代部门与传统部门，建立了两部门经济发展模型。他认为，在具有二元经济结构特征的社会里，由于传统农业部门存在着大量低收入的劳动力，所以劳动力供给具有完全的弹性。工业部门可以获得无限供给的劳动力而只需支付与传统农业维持生存部门相应的工资，这就促使农业劳动力源源不断地从农村流向城市，这一过程将一直延续到农村剩余劳动力被城市完全吸收，农村工资和城市工资趋向一致，城乡差别逐步消失，国民经济实现现代化为止。以此为基础，后来又发展出在乡村—城市人口迁移和人口城市化研究中产生重要影响的托达罗模型（Michael P. Todaro），并进一步解释了发展中国家普遍存在的农村人口向城市大规模迁移与城市高失业率持续并存的现象。

（2）全球化、信息化与城镇化

近几年全球化、信息化的迅速发展和深化是促进城市化的新经济因素之一，城市化不断创造就业机会，改变了城市的空间结构、人口结构及社会形态，对于发达国家如是，对于发展中国家也如是。

《信息工业、跨国公司及亚太国家城市化》（1989）一文认为，"技术，特别是那些与交通和通讯有关的技术，是城市转变的一个重要因素"，由于第三世界接受技术转让、开放国际贸易和交换，所以其城市化也与新技术密切相关。具体来看，这些新技术通过跨国公司——一种全球性的生产——实现了在全球范围内的流通，以亚太地区的国家为例，外国投资和跨国公司促进了当地信息业的发展。特别是它对于大城市或特大城市的发展，起着越来越明显的作用。因此在第三世界国家中，外资通过跨国公司使信息业—技术成为了城市化一种新的动力形式。如果把这种动力形式用基本力源——"拉力"和"推力"来衡量的话，很明显这是属于城市"拉力"的范畴，但它和传统的拉力又有区别，因为它并不来源于城市本身，而是外部资金和技术作用于城市后的产物。

（3）产业结构与城镇化

城镇化水平与第二、三产业的比重呈正相关关系，这一观点在很多文献里面都有过论述①。城镇化的依托是产业的发展、聚集和结构升级，因此，一个城镇除了要有主导产业外，还要积极发展为农业现代化和城市主导产业服务的二、三产业。

按产业结构的多样性差别，Hoover（1937）最早将集聚经济划分成地方化经济（或专门化经济）和城市化经济（或多元化经济）。地方化经济是指由于某一产业的地理集中而对生产效率的促进效应；城市化经济则是指由于地方经济体系的产业多样化而对生产效率的促进效应②。相对于城市化经济而言，地方化经济是最基本的单元，是低层次经济系统的聚集经济，而城市化经济则是高层次经济系统的聚集经济③。

从西方实证研究得出的结论是：随着城市规模的扩大和经济高密度的增加，生产率得到提高，表明存在着集聚经济。对于制造业来说，尤其是重工业和技术成熟的行业，地方化经济比城市化经济更为重要，相对于大企业，小企业更能从地方化经济中受益。一些不具备多元化功能的小区

---

① 郑菊芬：《关于城市化理论研究的文献综述》，《现代商业》2009年第11期。

② 吴学花：《西方城市化经济与地方化经济研究综述》，《科学与管理》2005年第6期。

③ 冯云廷：《聚集经济效应与我国城市化的战略选择》，《财经问题研究》2004年第9期。

域、小城镇也应该从专门化中获取更大的发展动力①。

国内的相关研究中，冯云廷（2005）计算了浙江省余姚等四城市行业的地方化和城市化弹性②，结果表明，浙江四个制造业集群相对成熟的城市，地方化效应较城市化效应显著，集聚经济极大地推动了城镇化进程。

（三）城镇化空间增长理论

城镇化是劳动力、资本等各种经济要素在空间上集聚的过程，因此是空间不平衡发展的产物。基于此发展出许多空间增长理论。

"增长极"理论③是由法国经济学家 F. 佩鲁（F. Perrous）提出的。"增长极"原来指对经济发展具有推动性作用的产业，后被推广到指空间上具有这种产业的地区。"增长极"理论指出经济增长并非同时出现在所有地方，它以不同的强度首先出现在一些"增长极"（Growth Pole）上。增长极形成的关键在于有创新能力的企业存在，这些企业往往处于支配地位，并使其所在的产业部门成为推进部门，在其经济聚集效应的作用下，推进部门和有创新能力的企业常常在某些地区或大城市聚集和发展，并使这些地区和城市成为经济活动的中心而具有支配和创新的特征，恰似一个"磁场极"，能够产生吸引辐射作用，促进自身并推动其他部门和地区的经济增长。

1957 年和 1958 年，K. G. 缪尔达尔（K. G. Myrdal）和 A. O. 赫希曼（A. O. Hirschman）分别在他们各自的代表作《经济理论与不发达地区》和《经济发展战略》中系统阐述了区域经济发展的不平衡理论。首先，赫希曼提出了"发展是一连串不均衡的锁链"的命题，指出"发展确实是按照主导部门带动其他部门增长，由一个行业引发另一个行业增长的方式进行的"。为论证此观点，他提出了产业关联效应概念，即"前向关联效应"和"后向关联效应"，用以说明国民经济中一个产业部门的发展会诱使其他产业部门发展的作用过程。其次，缪尔达尔和赫希曼分别提出了内容基本相同的"回波效应"（Backwash Effects）——"扩散效应"（Spread Effect）和"极化效应"（Polarized Effect）——"涓滴效应"。

"核心—边缘理论"是 1966 年由弗里德曼（J. R. Fridemna）在他的

---

① 吴学花：《西方城市化经济与地方化经济研究综述》，《科学与管理》2005 年第 6 期。

② 同上。

③ 刘辉煌：《西方城市化理论二元结构分析框架：一个文献综述》，《石家庄经济学院学报》2005 年第 1 期。

学术著作《区域发展政策》（*Regional Development Policy*）一书中正式提出的。1969 年，他在《极化发展理论》中又进一步将"核心—边缘"这个具有鲜明特色的空间极化发展思想归纳为一种普遍适用的、主要用于解释区际或城乡之间非均衡发展过程的理论模式。他认为，任何空间经济系统均可分解为不同属性的核心区和外围区。该理论试图解释一个区域如何由互不关联、孤立发展，变成彼此联系、发展不平衡，又由极不平衡发展变为相互关联的平衡发展的区域系统。

一是前工业化阶段：生产力水平低下，经济结构以农业为主，工业产值比重小于 10%，各地经济发展水平差异较小。城镇发展速度慢，各自成为独立的中心状态。区际之间经济联系不紧密，城镇的产生和发展速度慢，城镇等级系统不完整。

二是工业化初期阶段：城市开始形成，工业产值在经济中的比重在 10%—25% 之间，核心区域与边缘区域经济增长速度差异扩大。区域内外的资源要素是由经济梯度较低的边缘区流向梯度较高的核心区域。核心区域经济实力增大，必然导致政治力量集中，使核心区域与边缘区域发展不平衡进一步扩大。

三是工业化成熟阶段：快速工业化阶段，工业产值在经济中占比为 25%—50%。核心区域发展很快，与边缘区域之间存在不平衡关系。在工业化成熟期，核心区域的资源要素开始回流到边缘区域，边缘区域工业产业群开始集聚。

四是空间相对均衡阶段：后工业化阶段，资金、技术、信息等从核心区域向边缘区域流动加强。整个区域成为一个功能上相互联系的城镇体系，形成大规模的城市化区域，开始了有关联的平衡发展。

二、国外典型城镇化模式

（一）以西欧为代表的政府调控下的市场主导型

以西欧为代表的发达的市场经济国家，市场机制在城市化进程中发挥了主导作用，政府通过法律、行政和经济手段，引导城镇化健康发展。**城镇化与市场化、工业化总体上是一个比较协调互动的关系，是一种同步型城市化。**其特点是：首先，工业化与城镇化相互促进。城市化总体上来说是近代工业化的产物。近年来随着全球经济一体化和竞争的加剧，城市产业结构不断调整和重新分工，城市发展格局显现出新的态势，产业发展与城市发展更加密不可分。其次，政府在城镇化过程中发挥着不可替代的作用。各国在城镇化快速发展的过程中都不同程度地遇到了土地、住房、交通、环境和历史文化保护等方面的问题，政府公共政策涉及的范围越来越广。二战后，伦敦向外围的迅速扩展对农业用地产生了巨大的压力。1935年，伦敦郡通过了"绿带开发限制法案"，由伦敦郡政府收购土地作为"绿化隔离带"，引导城市建设开发，以减少对乡村环境和利益的损害。中央政府成立城乡规划部，规划成为地方政府的法定义务。

在西欧、日本的城镇化发展过程中，与城镇化相关的人口、土地、资本等经济要素能够自由流动和配置，首先得益于**市场机制发挥了主导作用**。同时，**各国政府强调对市场竞争和社会保障进行必要的国家干预**，通过健全法制、制定和实施国家城镇化战略和公共政策，开发建设区域基础设施，改善城市环境，提供公共服务设施，引导城镇化与市场化、工业化互动发展，积极推进区域结构调整，正确应对快速发展的城镇化进程。在此过程中，通过体制机制的不断完善，针对各个特定阶段出现的问题及时调整政府政策，用行政、财税、规划等手段来弥补市场机制的不足。

（二）以美国为代表的自由放任式

美国是当今世界最发达的资本主义国家，也是市场经济的典型代表，在其城镇化和城市发展的过程中，市场发挥着至关重要的作用。由于美国政治体制决定了城市规划及其管理属于地方性事务，联邦政府调控手段薄弱，**政府也没有及时对以资本为导向的城镇化发展加以有效地引导，造成城镇化发展的自由放任，并为此付出了高昂的代价。其突出的表现就是过度郊区化，城市不断向外低密度蔓延，城镇建设无序，空间和社会结构性问题日益突出。**由于20世纪上半叶美国城市的快速发展，城市中心交通拥挤、环境恶化、住房紧缺、犯罪率高等问题日益突出，富有家庭离开城市中心的高楼大厦到郊区居住，建造属于自己的独立院落式低层住宅。随着经济的发展和汽车的普及，广大中产阶级和普通居民也追随其后移居到郊区。在城市发展的空间格局上就表现为城市沿公路线不断向外低密度蔓延，城市发展为包含着若干连绵的市、镇的大都市地区。1970年美国郊区人口超过了中心城市的人口，也超过了非都市区的人口。

但是美国也为过度郊区化付出了沉重的代价：土地资源浪费严重、经济成本居高不下、生态环境破坏愈演愈烈、资源能源消耗量大以及加剧了贫富差距等一系列社会问题。20世纪90年代以来美国的政府官员、学者和普通百姓都开始意识到过度郊区化所带来的灾害，提出了"精明增长"的理念。其主要内容包括强调土地利用的紧凑模式，鼓励以公共交通和步行交通为主的开发模式，混合功能利用土地，保护开放空间和创造舒适的环境，鼓励公共参与，通过限制、保护和协调实现经济、环境和社会的公平。这是针对美国长期以来完全市场经济条件下，城市向郊区低密度无序蔓延所带来的社会和环境问题的反馈，是以可持续发展为价值取向、以科学管理为手段、有可操作性的管理理念和管理模式。

（三）受殖民地经济制约的发展中国家城镇化

由于历史传统和现实因素的作用，拉美和加勒比海及非洲大部分国家的城镇化与这些地区的国家长期沦陷为西方列强的殖民地直接相关，具有独特的发展模式。表现为在外来资本主导下的工业化与落后的传统农业经济并存，工业发展落后于城镇化，政府调控乏力，城镇化大起大落。其工业发展赶不上城市化进程，属于"过度城市化"。二战前夕，巴西、墨西哥、委内瑞拉、哥伦比亚和秘鲁五个处于半工业经济类型的国家，城镇化率和工业化率大致相等，都在 10%—15% 左右。到 1960 年，工业化比例没有发生太大的变化，仍维持在 10%—15%，而 2 万人以上城镇人口的比例却增至 30%—50%。这些地区的城市化道路崎岖不平，在乡村居民持续不断地流向城市的过程中，其经济却正在日趋衰落或停滞不前。主要问题是：正规就业水平持续下降，城市贫困人口空前增加。城市必要的基础设施严重短缺。城市环境恶化，贫民窟增多。

拉美、非洲国家的城市发展是典型的过度城市化，城市化水平与西方国家接近，但经济水平只是西方国家的 1/10—1/20，城市发展质量很低。造成这种结果的主要原因，一是城市发展与经济发展脱节。由于拉美国家早期的工业化发展源于宗主国的工业资本输入，政府没有利用好外资发展自身的民族工业。一旦宗主国工业资本撤出，本国将没有工业做支撑。二是忽视传统农业的改造与广大农村地区的发展，加剧了城乡差距，导致大量农村人口涌向城市，使城市就业、居住、环境和教育设施不足的问题进一步恶化①。

---

① 国家统计局：《中国统计年鉴》中国统计出版社 1983 年版。

第三节 我国城镇化趋势分析

一、我国城镇化发展总体趋势

建国以来，我国城镇化进程伴随不断的制度变迁，发展的总体趋势并未脱离客观规律，与"初期—中期—高级"的城镇化阶段理论吻合，并呈现出显著的阶段性特征[①]，其中，改革开放成为我国城镇化进程的最重要的转折点。改革开放30多年里，中国人口城镇化率从1978年的17.9%提高到2008年的45.7%。城镇化不仅带来了大规模基础设施和城镇住宅的投资需求，而且大规模的农村人口转移和生活方式变革还创造了巨大的消费需求，成为中国经济持续较快增长的强劲动力。在30多年的改革开放实践过程中，**中国城镇化发展经历了从支持小城镇到重点发展大城市，再到大中小城市与小城镇协调发展的一系列变化。这种变化实质上就是在城镇化进程中，中国的制度安排由限制农民进城到允许、引导农民进城，再到鼓励支持农民进城的过程**[②]。

具体来看，建国以来我国城镇化进程主要可以划分为七个阶段。

（一）城镇化发展的启动阶段（1949—1957年）

1949—1957年，我国的工作重心由农村转移到城市，城市经济得到健康发展，城市数量由1949年的132个增加到176个；城市市区人口比重由1949年的4.7%上升到1957的10.95%[③]；城镇人口占全国总人口的比重由10.6%提升到15.4%。该期间，除1955年城镇化率低于上年0.2个百分点外，其余年份城镇化率均比上年有所增长。

① 马晓河，胡拥军：《中国城镇化进程、面临问题及其总体布局》，《改革》2010年第10期。

② 王一鸣：《中国城镇化进程、挑战与转型》，《中国金融》2010年第4期。

③ 胡际权《中国新型城镇化发展研究》，西南农业大学，博士论文，2005年。

（二）城镇化发展的波动阶段（1958—1965 年）

1958—1961 年，"大跃进"运动的开展使得国民经济急剧膨胀、城镇人口盲目增长，城市数量由 1957 年的 176 个增加到 1961 年的 208 个；城镇人口由 1957 年的 9949 万猛增到 1960 年的 13073 万，增长了 31.4%，年递增率达到 9.53%。1961 年后又陆续撤销了 52 个城市，到 1965 年底城市总数为 168 个，比 1957 年减少了 8 个。

（三）城镇化发展的下滑与停滞阶段（1966—1978 年）

1966—1976 年，我国进入长达十年的"文化大革命"时期，工业布局上提出了"山、散、洞"方针，城镇建设不考虑自然、交通等条件，一味强调分散，经济社会发展遭受全面重创，城镇化发展缓慢。1972 年，城镇化水平一路下滑，一直跌落到 17.1%，形成了一个明显的"谷底"。1972 年以后，城镇化发展虽然有所提高，但较为缓慢。1972—1978 年的六年间，城镇化率总共提高了 0.8 个百分点。截至 1978 年底，我国城镇化率才回升到 1966 年的水平，即 17.9%。从城市数量上来看，到 1977 年全国城市总数为 190 个，比 1965 年仅增加 22 个。

（四）城镇化的恢复发展阶段（1979—1983 年）

1978—1983 年的改革开放起步阶段，我国城镇化发展迎来了新的契机。农村改革为城镇化的发展带来了巨大的推力；商品经济发展，投资渠道多元化，城镇基础设施建设步伐加快，城镇就业渠道拓宽吸引大量农民工进城，对城镇化发展产生拉力。1983 年 2 月，国务院发布《关于地市州党政机构改革若干问题的通知》提出地市合并，实行市管县，促进了小城镇的迅速发展。到 1983 年底，全国城市数达 289 个，比 1977 年增加99 个。1978—1983 年，城镇化率由 17.9% 上升至 23.5%。

（五）城镇化的平稳发展阶段（1984—1992 年）

1984 年 10 月，党中央在十二届三中全会上正式提出全面开展城市经济体制改革，实行有计划的商品经济新体制；同年 11 月，国务院批转《民政部关于调整建制镇标准的报告》；1986 年国务院又批转《民政部关于调整市标准和市领导县条件的报告》。随着市镇标准的降低，全国城镇数量迅速增加，城镇化水平随之提升。1984—1992 年，城市数目由 300个增至 517 个，建制镇由 6211 个猛增到 1.2 万个，城镇化率由 1984 年的23.0% 上升到 1992 年的 27.6%[1]。

---

[1]　杨风，陶斯文：《中国城镇化发展的历程、特点与趋势》，《兰州学刊》2010年第 6 期。

（六）城镇化的快速发展阶段（1993—2003 年）

以 1992 年春天邓小平南方讲话以及"十四大"的召开为标志，我国进入了全面建设社会主义市场经济体制时期，经济增长率年均在 9% 以上。随着新一轮的经济发展，城镇化步入快速发展期。这一阶段，中国城镇化率从 27.46% 提高到 40.53%，年均提高 3.97%。2003 年建制市达到 660 个，比 1991 年增加 181 个；建制镇达到 20226 个。以城市现代化建设、小城镇发展和建立经济开发区、工业园区等为标志，中国城镇化全面快速推进，城市综合承载能力与吸纳农村人口的能力得到明显提高。从国际比较看，中国城镇化率从 1981 年的 20% 提高到 2003 年的 40%，翻一番仅用了 22 年，而英国用了 120 年，法国用了 100 年，德国 80 年，美国 40 年，日本 30 年[①]。

（七）城乡统筹发展阶段（2004 至今）

2003 年以来，我国城乡关系进入新的发展阶段，城镇化发展方式也逐渐由快速城镇化向城乡统筹转变。在政策方面，我国加大了户籍改革的力度，从而推动城乡统筹发展。党的十六届三中全会明确指出，在城市有稳定职业和住所的农业人口，可按当地规定在就业居住地登记户籍，并依法享有当地居民应有的权利，承担应尽的义务。2010 年中央"一号文件"提出，深化户籍制度改革，加快落实放宽中小城市、小城镇特别是县城和中心镇落户条件的政策，促进符合条件的农业转移人口在城镇落户并享有与当地城镇居民同等的权益，多渠道多形式改善农民工居住条件，鼓励有条件的城市将有稳定职业并在城市居住一定年限的农民工逐步纳入城镇住房保障体系，采取有针对性的措施，着力解决新生代农民工问题。

2004—2010 年，城镇人口由 54283 万人增长至 66978 万人，年均增长 3.56%；城镇化率由 41.8% 上升至 49.68%，年均增长率达到 3.03%。到 2010 年底，全国地级及以上城市数已经达到 287 个，我国已经初步形成由 125 个市区总人口达到 100 万以上的特大城市、109 个 50 万到 100 万人口的大城市、49 个 20 万到 50 万人口的中等城市、4 个 20 万以下人口的小城市组成的全国城镇体系规模结构格局；形成了由珠三角大都市连绵区、长三角大都市连绵区、京津冀（环渤海）大都市连绵区和沿海城镇发展带等组成的全国城镇体系空间结构格局。

二、我国城镇化空间差异格局

近年来，城镇人口分布及人口城镇化水平的总体格局基本未变，人口

---

① 王一鸣：《中国城镇化进程、挑战与转型》，《中国金融》2010 年第 4 期。

城镇化水平的省级差异逐年缩小，差异主要存在于不同政策区域之间，并且其产生的影响有增强的趋势①。

本文根据 2011 年我国城市统计年鉴，收集全国地级市 2010 年的城镇化率数据，并采用五分法将各地级市的城镇化率分为五组（≤37.56%、37.59%—43.00%、43.00%—51.04%、51.12—62.75%、≥62.80%），通过空间数据库的构建，得出我国城镇化空间格局的差异，主要存在以下两个方面。②

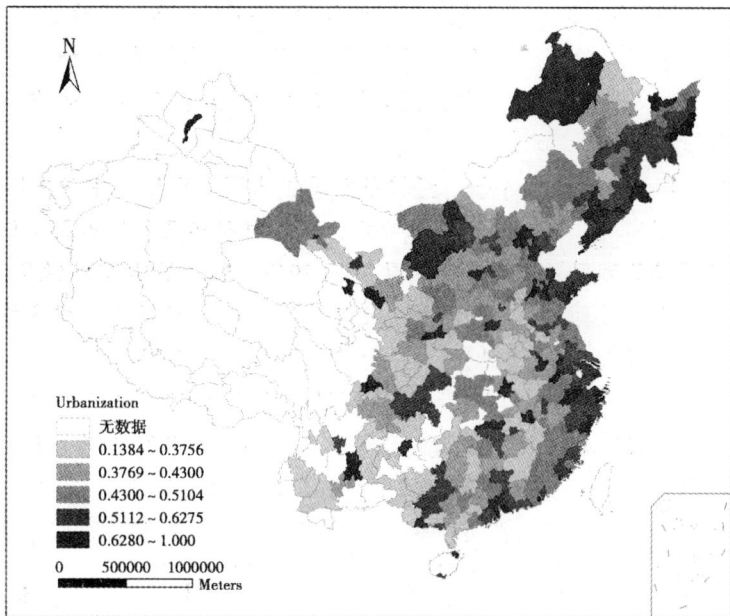

图 1 2010 年我国地级市城镇化率空间格局

（一）城镇化水平存在东高西低的分布特征

受改革开放以来中国东部地区快速工业化的影响，中国城镇化水平经历了从"北高南低"（北部地区城市化率高，南部地区城市化率低）向"东高西低"（东部地区城市化率高，西部地区城市化率低）的转变。到现阶段，中国城镇化水平的区域差异则呈现出"东高西低"的分布特征。根据 2010 年的东、中、西和东北部城镇人口比例计算，中国东、中、西、东北部的城镇化率分别为 56.7%、46.3%、44.7% 和 55.3%。上海、

---

① 林坚：《2000 年以来人口城镇化水平变动省际差异分析—基于统计数据的校正和修补》，《城市规划》2010 年第 3 期。

② 自本章节至第五节，采用的均是根据 E&G 评价体系分析所得数据及其结果。

北京、天津三大传统直辖市以及广东、江浙和部分自治区仍居全国前列；而西藏、贵州、云南、甘肃、四川等西部省区和人口大省河南仍在最后6位之列。

这种差异明显体现在城镇化空间格局中，如图1所示，东部沿海地区城镇化率普遍较高，尤其是东北老工业基地、京津冀都市圈、山东半岛、江苏沿海经济区、长三角都市圈、浙江沿海城市群、海西经济区、珠三角都市圈、北部湾地区所包含和辐射的城市，基本处于城镇化分组的第四、五组，属于高度城镇化，即城镇化率到达50%以上，增长率将逐渐减缓，并开始注重城镇化质量的提升。而中、西部地区的城市则主要处于城镇化率的第一、二、三组，属于中、低度城镇化，即不到50%，还将持续快速地增长。

（二）部分城镇化水平低、经济基础弱的省区出现超高速发展趋势

研究中也发现，**部分城镇化水平低、经济基础较薄弱的省区出现超高速的人口城镇化发展趋势**①。**特别是处于30%—50%的中度城镇化地区，如河北、河南、陕西、江西、安徽、湖南、湖北、重庆等地。城市化率高于50%以上的高度城镇化地区**，如北京、上海、天津三大直辖市（城市化率均超过75%）和东北三省，以及城镇化率低于30%的低度城镇化地区，则呈现出城市化率提升缓慢的特征。中国省级行政区也遵从着城市化发展"诺瑟姆曲线"规律。如我国中西部省份的省会城市、副省级城市，如石家庄、郑州、开封、西安、南昌、合肥、长沙、武汉等城市的首位度较高，城镇化率较突出，这种特征也能在图中清晰地看出。

2012中国城市科学发展综合评价报告

---

① 林坚：《2000年以来人口城镇化水平变动省际差异分析——基于统计数据的校正和修补》，《城市规划》2010年第3期。

第四节 我国城镇化与城市发展
要素的协调性分析

一、城市社会经济要素的协调性分析

（一）东部地区发展优势明显，地区间协调性有待加强

在全部 287 个地级及以上城市中，东部 87 个，占 30.3%；中部 81 个，占 28.2%；西部 85 个，占 29.6%；东北部 34 个，占 11.9%。区域划分情况如表 4.1 所示。

表 2   中国四大区域省份划分

区域	城市
东部	北京、天津、河北、上海、江苏、浙江、福建、山东、广东、海南
中部	山西、安徽、江西、河南、湖北、湖南
西部	内蒙古、广西、重庆、四川、贵州、云南、西藏、陕西、甘肃、青海、宁夏、新疆
东北	辽宁、吉林、黑龙江

按照三大系统（经济发展水平、公共服务水平、居民实际享有水平）指标综合分值进行排序，在进入前 50 名的城市中，东部 33 个，占 66%；中部 8 个，占 16%；西部 6 个，占 12%；东北 3 个，占 6%。

按照经济发展指标排序，进入前 50 名的城市中，东部 39 个，占 78%；中部 6 个，占 12%；西部 3 个，占 6%；东北 2 个，占 4%；

按照公共服务投入排序，进入前 50 名的城市中，东部 22 个，占 44%；中部 7 个，占 14%；西部 11 个，占 22%；东北 10 个，占 20%。

按照居民分享水平排序，进入前 50 名的城市中，东部 33 个，占 66%；中部 8 个，占 16%；西部 4 个，占 8%；东北 5 个，占 10%。

表 3　　　　　　　　　　　各指标前 50 名城市个数统计

指标名	东部	中部	西部	东北
指标综合分值	33	8	6	3
经济发展水平系统	39	6	3	2
公共服务水平系统	22	7	11	10
居民享有水平系统	33	8	4	5

从前 50 名的城市发展综合分值和各专项指标排序中可以看出，相较上一年度，东部地区的城市在其中的城市中仍然接近甚至超过半数，发展水平要明显高于其他地区；其中，经济发展指标差距最大，公共服务投入指标差距相对较小。而其他地区的城市发展水平相当，大多按中、西、东北部依次稍有递减。这种局面与我国的发展政策、当代经济全球化的背景以及我国产业的地域分工有关。

一方面，改革开放使我国东部沿海地区借助区位优势，发展外向型经济，发展水平和竞争力得到大幅度提高。但在国际化的背景下，东部地区由于自身产业结构不合理和缺少自主创新能力，高速的经济增长主要是依靠低成本的劳动力和土地崛起的粗放型的经济所维持。但这种经济在国际产业分工中尚处于产业链的末端，随着经济发展的环境资源成本日益上涨，这种优势正在被削弱，并且发展受国际经济环境的影响极大，整体经济结构的抗风险能力弱、稳定性差。

另一方面，我国目前尚未形成较为成熟的东、中、西、东北部互动发展格局。我国东北地区和中西部地区坐拥丰富劳动力和土地资源，但由于经济缺乏合理的地域分工，导致资源要素不能合理配置，东部地区向内陆地区的产业转移不能得到很好的承接，不仅制约了中西部地区的加速发展，也阻碍了东部沿海地区的产业转型升级。

（二）城市内部经济与社会发展水平协调性仍较低

为评价三类系统之间的协调性，我们在将 287 个城市按照综合分值进行排名的基础上，以 50 个城市为一个区段，分为 6 个排名区段，如果一个城市的三类系统排名都能进入与综合分值相同的区段内，则视为是相对协调的发展城市。

在综合水平进入前 50 名的城市中，三类系统都同时进入的有 14 个，占 28%；51—100 名中有 5 个，占 10%；101—150 名中 4 个，占 8%；151—200 名中 2 个，占 4%；201—250 名中 3 个，占 6%；251—287 名中 7 个，占 14%。排名相对协调的城市共有 35 个，仅占全部城市的 12.2%，与去年同比提高 0.7 个百分点，**但总体协调性仍旧不高。其中，第一区段的协调程度远高于其他区段，占全部协调性城市的 40%。**

在第一区段三类系统协调性较好的 14 个城市中，中部地区仅有太原，东北地区仅有大连，西部地区没有进入的，其余均为东部地区城市。除上海、天津以外，江苏 3 个、浙江 3 个、山东 3 个、广东 1 个、辽宁 1 个、山西 1 个，相对协调城市基本上都集中在沿海发达地区。**相较上一年度，区域格局并没有发生明显的转变，在现有城市体制的制约下，经济发展水平的高低仍在很大程度上左右着城市协调发展的可能。**

表4 城市排名协调性情况

排名区段	相对协调的城市
1—50 名	杭州、无锡、常州、苏州、珠海、绍兴、大连、上海、嘉兴、东营、威海、天津、淄博、太原
51—100 名	唐山、营口、莱芜、三明、黄山
101—150 名	焦作、蚌埠、葫芦岛、南平
151—200 名	吕梁、绵阳
201—250 名	自贡、来宾、益阳
251—287 名	贺州、定西、邵阳、巴中、昭通、贵港、拉萨

注：表中城市排名不分先后。

（三）直辖市、省会城市和计划单列市的综合优势依然显著

以综合指标排序为例，直辖市和省会城市进入前 100 名的城市有 22 个，占全部 31 城市个的 71%，其中进入前 50 名的有 14 个，占 45%；5 个计划单列市全部进入前 50 名。

以经济发展水平衡量，直辖市、省会城市处于前 100 名的 15 个，占全部 31 个的 48.4%。其中进入前 50 名的 10 个，占 32.3%；5 个计划单列市全部进入前 100 名，其中有 3 个进入前 50 名。

公共服务投入方面，直辖市、省会城市处于前 100 名的 26 个，占全部 31 个的 83.9%。其中进入前 50 名的 16 个，占 51.6%；5 个计划单列市全部进入前 50 名。

居民分享水平方面，直辖市、省会城市处于前 100 名的 21 个，占全部 31 个的 67.7%。其中进入前 50 名的 13 个，占 41.9%；5 个计划单列市全部进入前 100 名，其中有 3 个进入前 50 名。

显而易见，在目前中国这种自上而下的政府主导模式下，直辖市、省会城市和计划单列市所拥有的先天优势依然突出。

（四）经济转型成效仍未显现

我们继续采用经济发展类指标系统中的土地、水、劳动力以及能源的利用效率，科技信息等技术的投入水平，对外部产生的环境效应三组指标评价发展的质量。在经济发展水平进入前50名的城市中，发展要素利用效率能够进入前50名的有25个，占50%；外部效应较好的进入前50名的有10个城市，占20%；技术投入水平进入前50名的有22个城市，占44%。相较上年度有下降趋势，同样也没有一个城市的上述三项子系统能够同时进入前50名。**经济发展转型还没有进入实质阶段，城市在提高要素利用水平、降耗减污方面成效并不明显，仅仅依靠加大投入无法实现预期目的，能源对经济转型的"紧箍咒"仍在收紧。**

进一步比较经济增长效率进入前10名的城市中，发展要素利用效率进入前10的只有苏州、延安2个城市，但是经济增长效率进入前10名的城市也没有进入发展外部效应的前10名。**高速低效的粗放式增长给资源和环境带来的巨大压力日益凸显，反映出经济结构的不合理以及可持续发展观念、生产技术水平的落后。**

（五）公共投入有所提高，但经济发展与居民分享水平仍不协调

经济发展总水平进入前50名的城市中，财政公共投入同时进入前50名的达到15个，相较去年的7个城市增长了114%，但城市公共投入水平总体上与经济发展水平仍称不上协调。

经济发展总水平前50名的城市中，个人受益类项目，居民社保覆盖范围及水平进入前50名的有22个，占44%；居民生活环境水平进入前50名的有20个，占40%；居民就业水平进入前50名的有11个，占22%。三项均不过半，且较上年有所下降。

继续比较城市人均GDP和人均收入增长的同步性程度可以发现，在经济发展总水平进入前50名的城市中，人均收入增长进入前50名的有20个，占40%。同样，在经济发展总水平前50名的城市中，公共服务分享类项目规模进入前50名的有22个，占44%，其中就包括11个直辖市和省会城市。

可见，**城市在公共服务上的投入随着经济的发展确实有所提高，但在能使城市居民（包括外来居民）个人受益的服务项目上仍需进一步加大投入力度，完善分配路径，保障居民的享有权利。**

二、城镇化与城市经济发展协调性分析

（一）城镇化与城市经济增长水平

（1）城镇化与人均 GDP

不同城镇化阶段的城市在人均 GDP 上存在显著差异。城镇化水平较低的城市，随着经济发展水平的提高，城镇化水平提升的趋势较为明显；而城镇化水平较高的城市，其经济水平的差异则较大，如城镇化水平为 70% 的鄂尔多斯市，人均 GDP 达到 17.5 万元，而城镇化率 68.4% 的汕头市人均 GDP 仅为 2.36 万元，城镇化率 71.3% 的武汉市为 5.90 万元。

以全国城市城镇化与人均 GDP 的总体趋势相比，人均 GDP 明显高于平均水平的城市有鄂尔多斯、东营、大庆、榆林等，多为资源型城市；人均 GDP 明显低于平均水平的城市有鹤岗、防城港、潮州、汕头等。

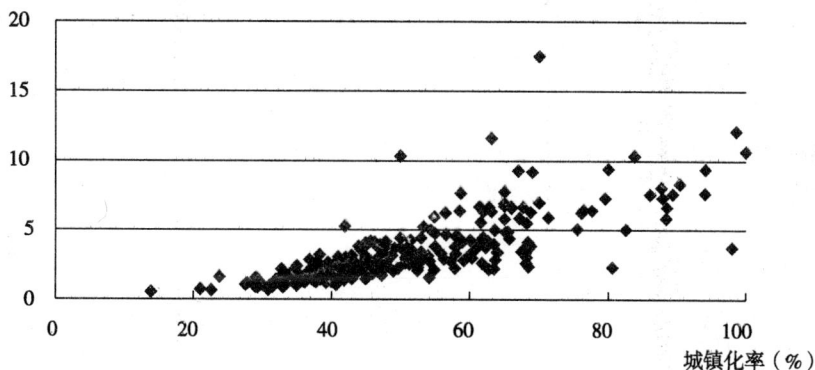

图2 城镇化与人均 GDP

（2）城镇化与人均收入增长率的关系

就全国而言，**人均收入增长率与城镇化水平不存在显著的相关性，相关性系数为 -0.0093。城镇化率较低和较高的城市人均收入增长率较为一致**，增长率均保持在 1% 左右；**城镇化率中等的城市人均收入增长率表现出较大的两极分化趋势**，承德市、邢台市城镇化率分别为 39.41%、42.5%，人均收入增长率为 -1.6%、-1.4%，但廊坊市、邯郸市城镇化率分别为 48.8%、46.5%，人均收入增长率分别达到 3.6%、2.6%。

人均收入增长率

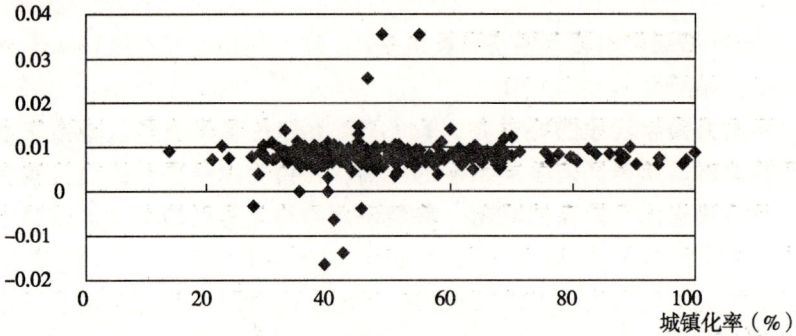

图3　城镇化与人均收入增长率

（3）城镇化与劳动报酬增长率

城镇化水平与劳动报酬增长率也基本无相关性，相关性系数为**0.0095**，全国城市劳动报酬增长率基本在0—0.2%之间。值得注意的是，低城镇化率的城市出现了几个劳动报酬增长率的高值，如定西市城镇化率仅13.84%，但劳动报酬增长率达到了0.4%，固原市城镇化率30.85%，劳动报酬增长率达到了0.5%。深圳市的劳动报酬增长率特别突出，达到1.2%。

劳动报酬增长率

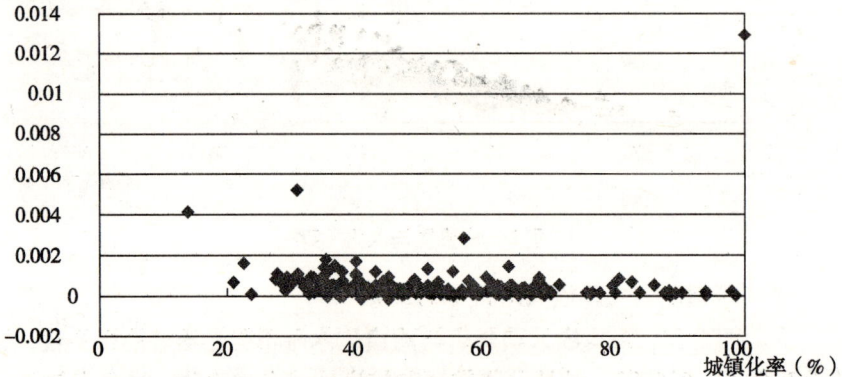

图4　城镇化与劳动报酬增长率

（二）城镇化与城市经济管理水平

（1）城镇化与单位土地面积产出率（亿元/平方公里）

城镇化与单位土地面积产出率不存在线性关系，相关性系数为**-0.0027**，大部分城市单位土地面积产出率在20亿元/平方公里以下。总体而言，低城镇化率的城市单位土地面积产出率也较低，但中等和高城镇

2012中国城市科学发展综合评价报告

化率城市内部单位土地面积产出率都存在较大极差，如城镇化率同在40%左右，沧州市单位土地面积产出率为47.9亿元/平方公里，蚌埠市单位土地面积产出率为6.1亿元/平方公里；城镇化率同在90%左右，东莞市单位土地面积产出率为46.15亿元/平方公里，嘉峪关市单位土地面积产出率仅为3.7亿元/平方公里。

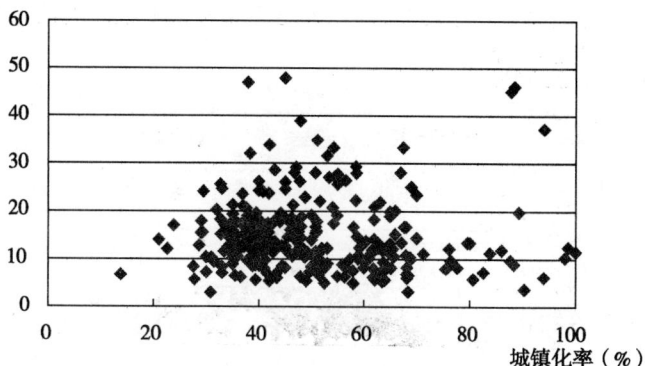

图5 城镇化与单位土地面积产出率（亿元/平方公里）

（2）城镇化与产出收益率

城镇化水平与产出收益率也不存在明显的相关关系，相关性系数为 **-0.0274**，无论城镇化率处于低、中、高阶段，大部分城市产出收益率均在0.05—0.1之间。其中，产出收益率比较高的城市有三亚市、北京市、上海市、厦门市等，说明经济产出效率较高。

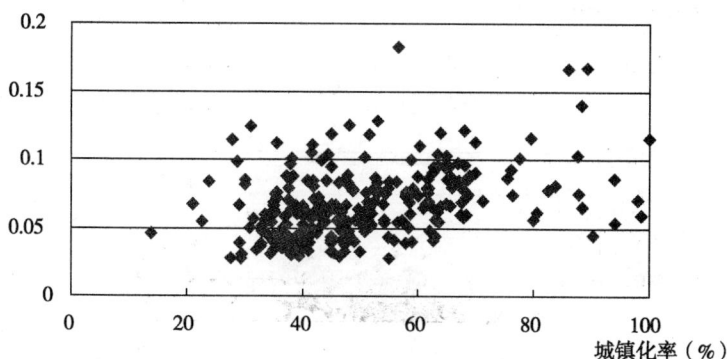

图6 城镇化与产出收益率

（3）城镇化与劳动生产率（亿元/万人）

城镇化水平与劳动生产率不存在显著的线性相关。城镇化水平处于较低水平的城市，劳动生产率差异较小：城镇化率在 40% 以下的城市，劳动生产率多分布在 100 亿元/万人以下；城镇化率 40%—70% 的部分城市，劳动生产率达到 200 亿元/万人左右。**城镇化水平较高的城市间劳动生产率差异较大，这与不同城市的发展特征有关。**

在城镇化率达到 70% 以上的城市中，东莞市劳动生产率达到 350 亿元/万人，佛山市达到 264.6 亿元/万人，也是劳动生产率最高的两个城市。

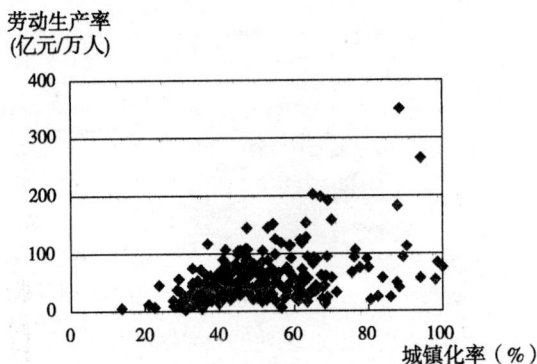

图 7　城镇化与劳动生产率（亿元/万人）

（4）城镇化与每万元 GDP 水耗（万吨）

城镇化率低的城市每万元 GDP 水耗都较低，但进入 **40%** 之后，平均单位 **GDP** 耗水量有所上升，并且各城市的单位 **GDP** 耗水量出现较大分化，尤其突出的为城镇化率在 **60%** 左右的城市，每万元 GDP 水耗最高达到 0.0055 万吨，最低为 0.00028 万吨。

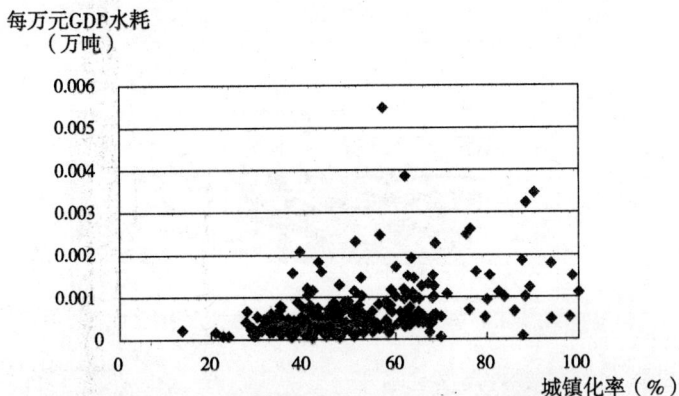

图 8　城镇化与每万元 GDP 水耗（万吨）

（5）城镇化与每万元 GDP 电耗（万千瓦时）

单位 GDP 电耗与城镇化的关系同水耗相似，**城镇化率低的城市单位电耗较小，但随着城镇化率的升高，特别是达到 40％以后，城市之间单位电耗的差异明显增加。**与城镇化水平相近城市相比，单位 GDP 电耗特别高的城市有白银、鄂州、石嘴山、嘉峪关、乌海，多为资源型重工业城市。

每万元 GDP 电耗
（万千瓦时）

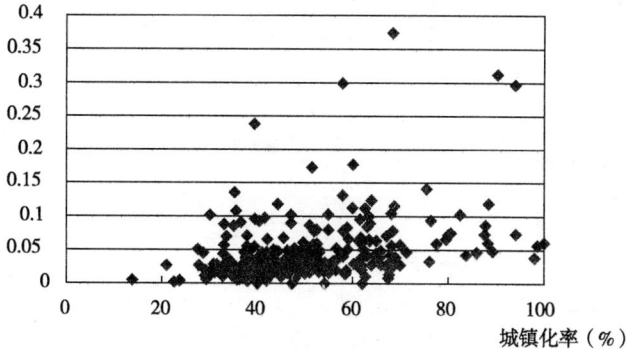

图 9　城镇化与每万元 GDP 电耗（万千瓦时）

（6）城镇化与每万元工业总产值电耗（万千瓦时）

大部分城市的每万元工业总产值电耗都在 0.1 万千瓦时以下，少数明显偏高的城市为贺州、来宾、白银、铜川、石嘴山、乌海。

每万元工业总产值电耗
（万千瓦时）

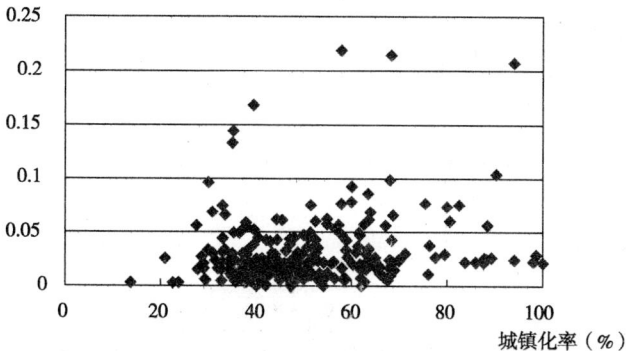

图 10　城镇化与每万元工业总产值电耗（万千瓦时）

（三）城镇化与城市科技信息水平

（1）城镇化与科学支出比重

城镇化率为 30％的城市平均科学支出比重仅占 0.57％，城镇化率

50%的城市平均科学支出比重占到1.57%，城镇化率70%的城市平均科学支出比重上升到2.57%，而城镇化率达到80%，平均科学支出比重则上升到3.07%。

科学支出比重

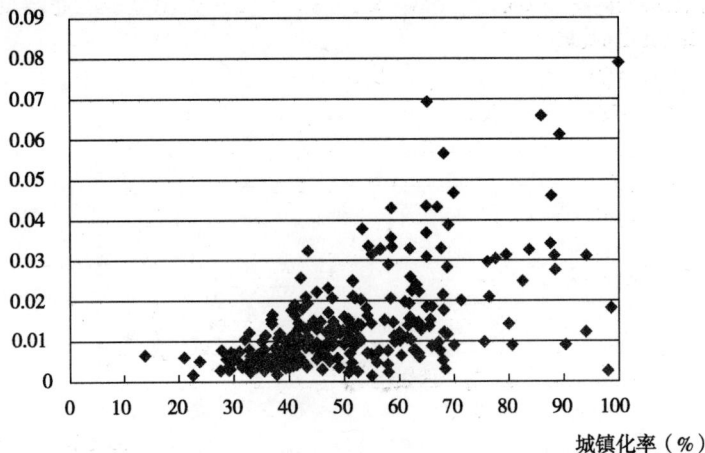

图11 城镇化与科学支出比重

（2）城镇化与国际互联网使用率（户/万人）

城镇化与国际互联网使用率之间存在微弱的正相关性，相关性系数为**0.0026**。特别是城镇化率达到50%左右的相当一部分城市，国际互联网使用率明显上升。宁德、泉州、福州、厦门、上海等城市的国际互联网使用率明显高于相同城镇化水平的城市，除上海外，均为福建省的城市。

国际互联网使用率
（万户/万人）

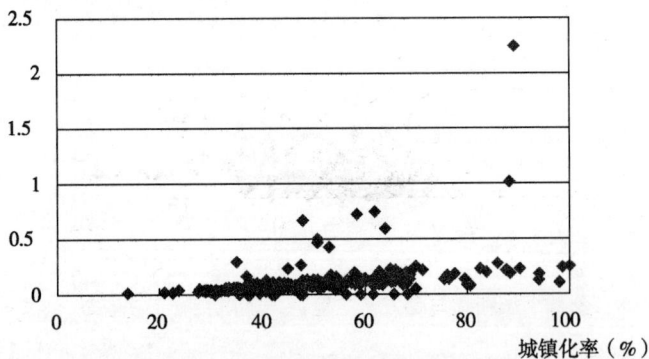

图12 城镇化与国际互联网使用率（户/万人）

（3）城镇化与信息业从业人员比重

城镇化与信息业从业人员比重的相关性不强，相关性系数为 **0.0152**。大多数城市的信息业从业人口比重都在 0—2% 之间。其中，信息业从业人员比重特别高的城市有广元、沧州和北京，均超过了 6%，**这也与城市的职能和专业化程度有关。**

信息业从业人员比重

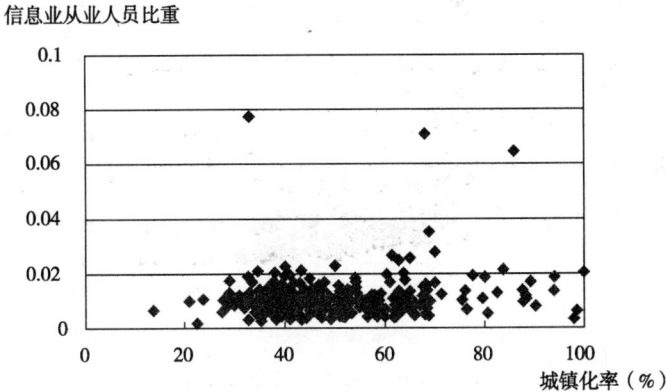

图 13　城镇化与信息业从业人员比重

（四）城镇化与城市发展外部效应

（1）城镇化与三废综合利用产品产值比重

随着城镇化水平的提升，三废综合利用产品产值比重呈现先升高后降低的趋势。城镇化率低和城镇化率高的城市，三废综合利用产品产值比重都较低，但城市化率在 40%—60% 的部分城市，则表现出三废综合利用产品产值比重较高的特点，典型的如鹰潭、金昌、贵港等城市。

三废综合利用产品
产值比重

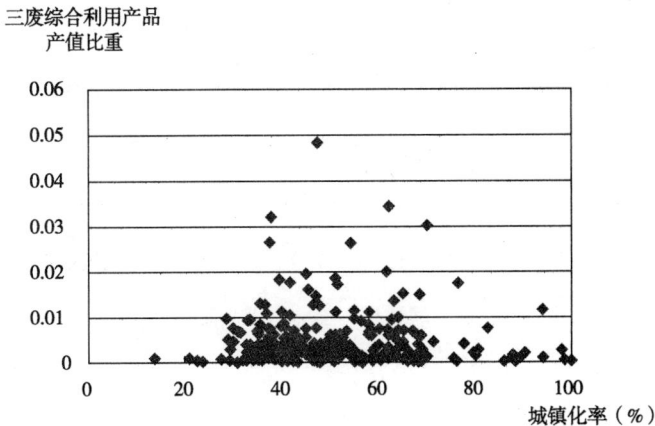

图 14　城镇化与三废综合利用产品产值比重

（2）城镇化与产出污染处理率

城镇化率与产出污染处理率呈微弱的负相关，相关性系数为－0.0638。一般而言，城镇化率越高，产出污染处理率则越低。

产出污染处理率

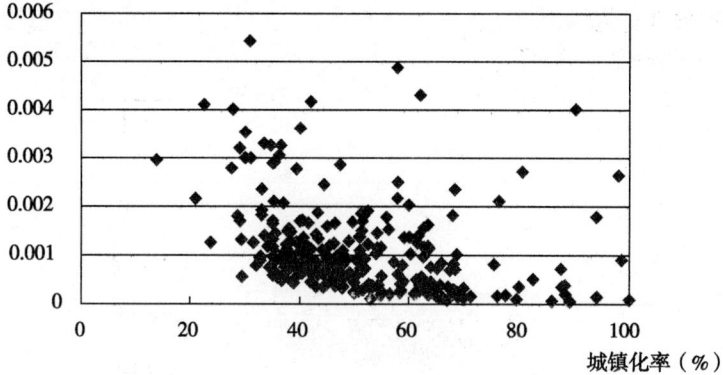

图15　城镇化与产出污染处理率

（3）城镇化与工业烟尘去除率

随着城镇化率上升，城市工业烟尘去除率也有相应上升，且城市间工业烟尘去除率的差异呈现收敛的趋势。工业烟尘去除率在60%以下的城市，城镇化率大多处于50%以下的中低水平。

工业烟尘去除率

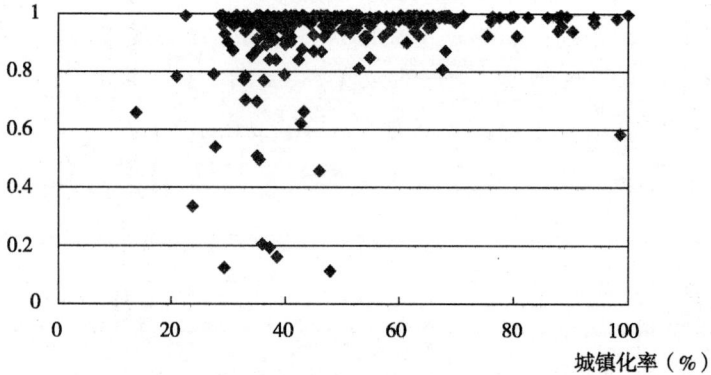

图16　城镇化与工业烟尘去除率

（4）城镇化与工业废水排放达标率

城镇化与工业废水排放达标率的关系同工业烟尘去除率相似，随着城镇化率上升，工业废水排放达标率也相应上升。在城镇化率达到80%及以上的城市中，工业废水排放达标率也都控制在90%以上。

工业废水排放达标率

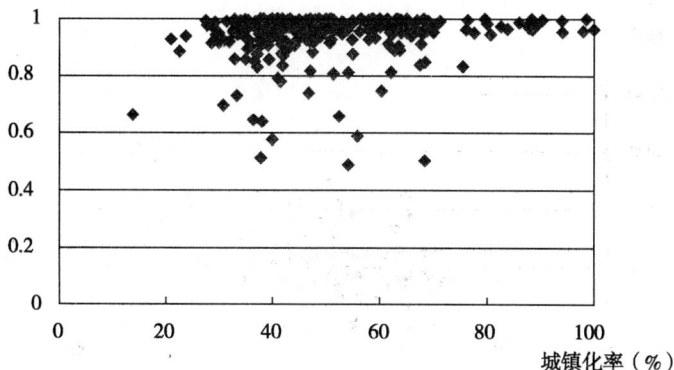

图17　城镇化与工业废水排放达标率

（5）城镇化与工业二氧化硫去除率

城镇化与工业二氧化硫去除率不存在明显的相关关系。全国各城市在工业二氧化硫去除率指标差别非常大，在0—1之间都有相当数量的分布。

工业二氧化硫去除率

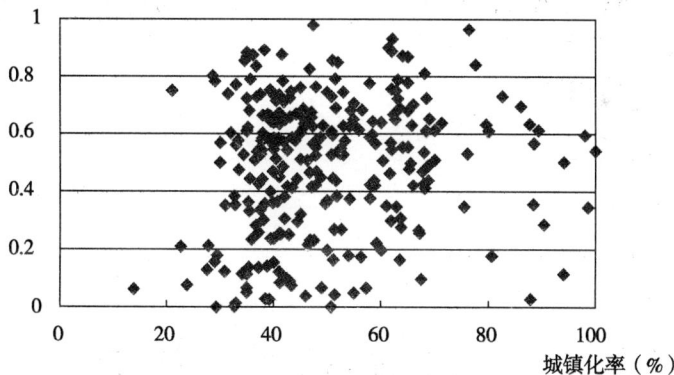

图18　城镇化与工业二氧化硫去除率

三、城镇化与城市公共服务协调性分析

（一）城镇化与财政公共投入水平

（1）城镇化与人均社会保障性支出（元/人）

城镇化与人均社会保障性支出的关系不明显，但在城镇化率达到**70％**以上的城市，平均人均社会保障性支出要高于其他城市的平均水平。

人均社会保障性支出
（元/人）

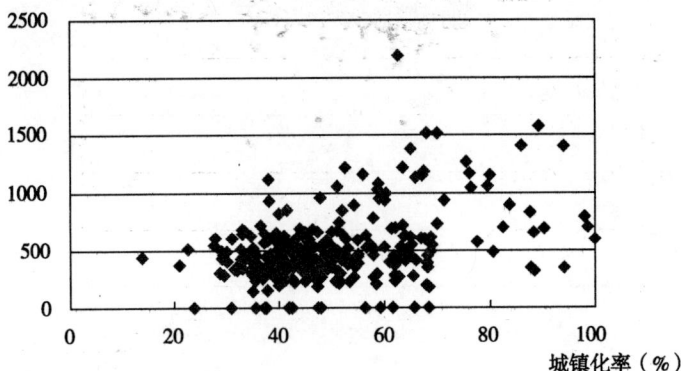

图19 城镇化与人均社会保障性支出（元/人）

（2）城镇化与人均公共服务财政支出（元/人）

城镇化率在60%以下的城市，人均公共服务财政支出大多在1000—2000元之间，**但城市化率60%以上的城市，人均公共服务财政支出水平明显提高，方差也增大**，最高的北京市人均公共服务财政支出达5567元/人，最低的东莞市人均公共服务财政支出近640元/人，二者差距甚大。

人均公共服务财政
支出(元/人)

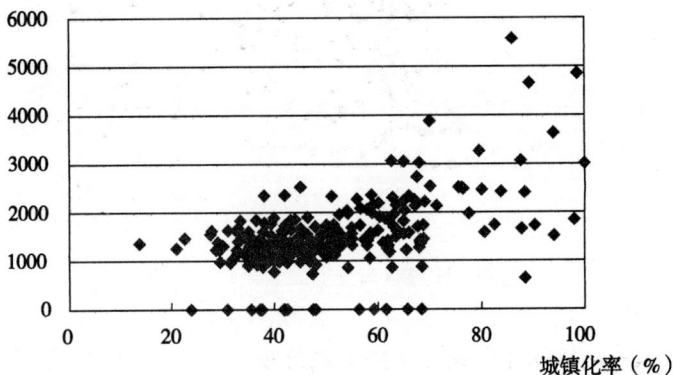

图20 城镇化与人均公共服务财政支出（元/人）

（3）城镇化与人均教育支出（元/人）

城镇化率中低水平的城市，人均教育支出相差不大，基本上在500—1000元/人左右，但城镇化率较高城市的人均教育支出水平差异则很大，比较高的如克拉玛依市达到2950元/人，比较低的如嘉峪关市仅654元/人。

人均教育支出
（元/人）

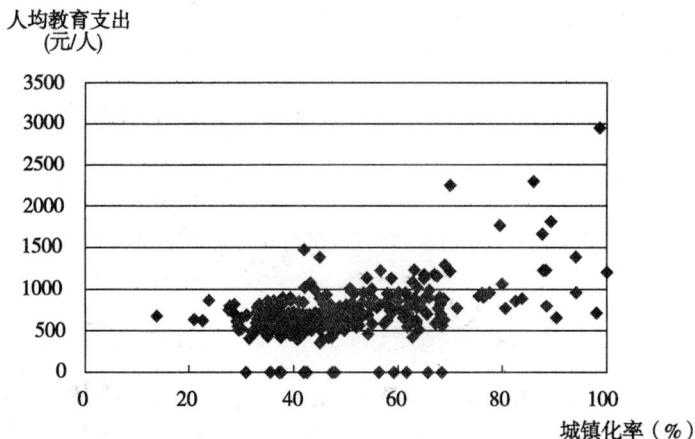

图 21　城镇化与人均教育支出（元/人）

（4）城镇化与人均医疗卫生支出（元/人）

与人均教育支出相似，以城镇化率**70％**为界，城镇化中低水平的城市，人均医疗卫生支出集中在 200—400 元/人左右，**各城市间差异较小**；**城镇化较高水平的城市，人均医疗卫生支出差异则比较大**，最高的克拉玛依市达到 1445 元/人，最低的东莞市仅 65 元/人。

人均医疗
卫生支出
（元/人）

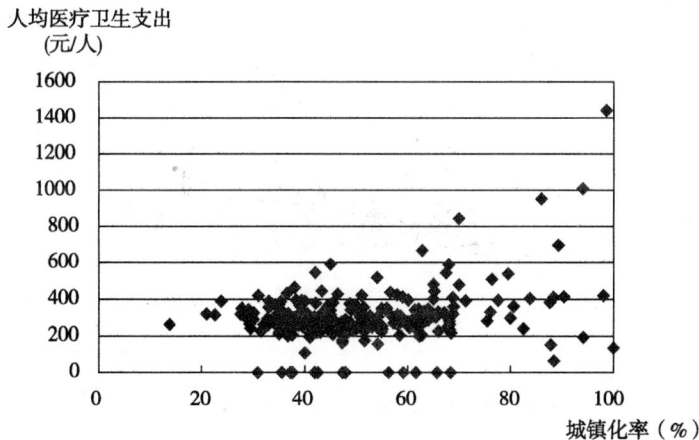

图 22　城镇化与人均医疗卫生支出（元/人）

（二）城镇化与城市公共项目规模

（1）城镇化与每万人拥有医院、卫生院床位数（张）

城镇化率与每万人拥有医院、卫生院床位数呈现"倒 U"型的趋势：城镇化率低于 80％的城市，基本上随着城镇化水平的提升，每万人拥有的医院、卫生院床位数呈现上升的趋势；但城镇化率高于 80％的城市，则随着城镇化水平的提升，每万人拥有的医院、卫生院床位数呈现下降的趋势。

每万人拥有医院、卫生
院床位数(张)

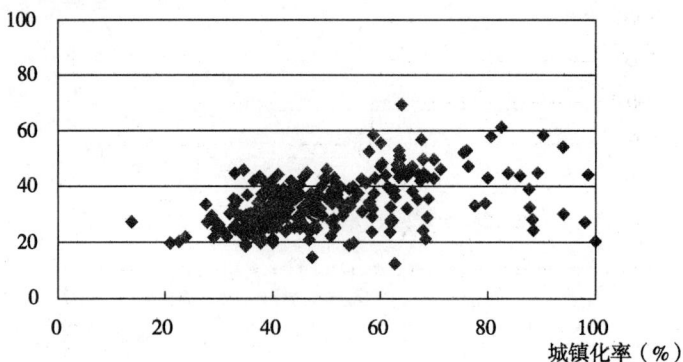

图23　城镇化与每万人拥有医院、卫生院床位数（张）

　　每万人拥有医生数也表现出相同的趋势，但存在一些指标较平均水平偏高较多的城市，典型如大庆、昆明、齐齐哈尔、黑河、乌兰察布等，主要为城镇化水平中等的城市。

每万人拥有医生数
（人）

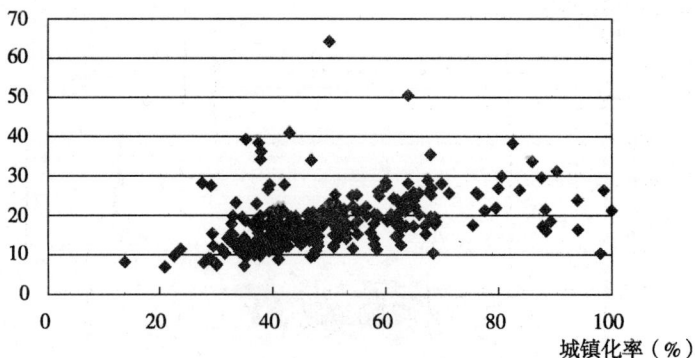

图24　城镇化与每万人拥有医生数（人）

　　（2）城镇化与每万人在校高中以上学生数（人）

　　城镇化与教育服务规模也呈"倒U"型的关系。城镇化率越高的城市，每万人在校高中以上学生数也越高，尤其在城镇化率低于70%的区段表现得特别明显。而城镇化率高于70%的城市间，则出现较多的偏高和偏低值。

2012中国城市科学发展综合评价报告

每万人在校高中以上
学生数（人）

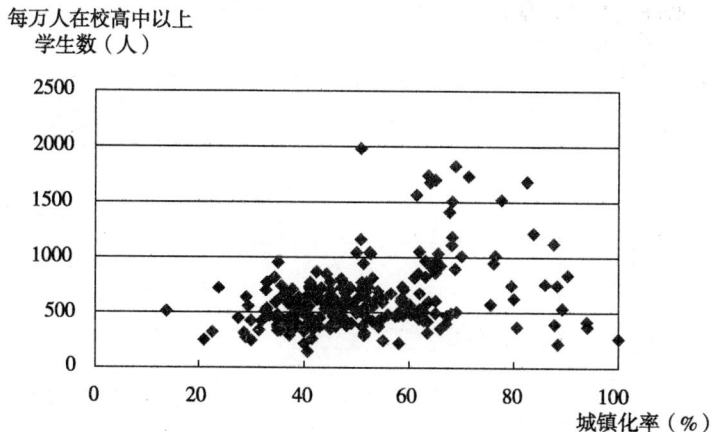

图25 城镇化与每万人在校高中以上学生数（人）

（3）城镇化与人均城市道路面积（平方米）

城镇化率越高的城市人均城市道路面积的数值也相应较高，但大多数都在建设部规定的指标范围内。鄂尔多斯（达到85.2平方米）、绥化、威海分别在城镇化率较低和中等组中处于高值，珠海和深圳则处于城镇化水平较高组的高值。

人均城市道路面积
（平方米）

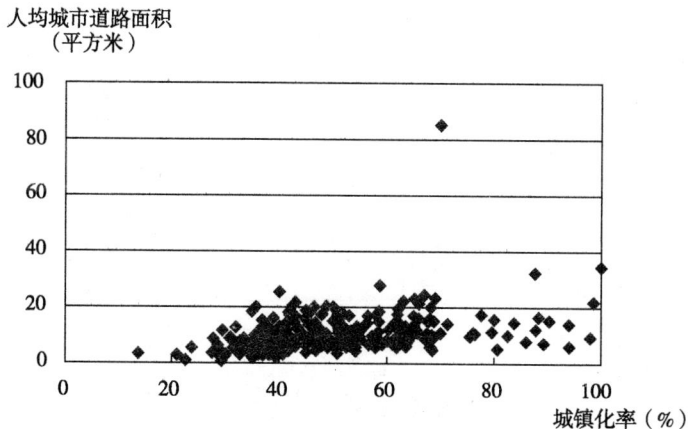

图26 城镇化与人均城市道路面积（平方米）

（4）城镇化与每百万人剧场、影剧院数（座）

不论城镇化率高低，各城市每百万人剧场、影剧院数（座）基本一致，均在0到10座之间，除了嘉峪关市、梅州市、镇江市明显偏高。

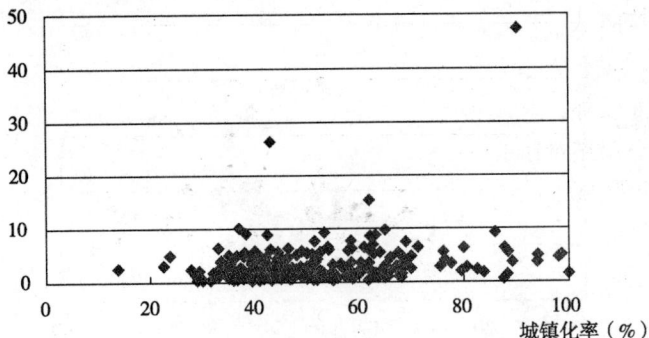

图27　城镇化与每百万人剧场、影剧院数（座）

　　（5）城镇化与每万人拥有公共汽车数（辆）

　　城镇化程度与每万人拥有公共汽车数呈弱正相关关系，随着城镇化率的上升，每万人拥有公共汽车数平均趋势也呈上升状态。其中邢台市城镇化率42.5%，每万人拥有公共汽车数12.38辆；汕尾市城镇化率54.18%，每万人拥有公共汽车数44.94辆；深圳市城镇化率100%，每万人拥有公共汽车数103.11，分别列不同城镇化水平公共交通配给量的前茅。

每万人拥有公共汽车数
（辆）

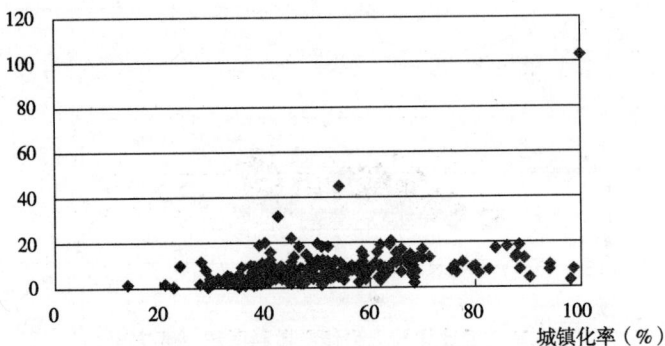

图28　城镇化与每万人拥有公共汽车数（辆）

　　（6）城镇化与每百人公共图书馆藏书数（册）

　　城镇化与每百人公共图书馆藏书数呈正相关，相关性系数为0.0186，总体而言，随着城镇化率的提高，每百人公共图书馆藏书数也有所增加，并且城镇化率大于70%的地区，指标差别也相应扩大。

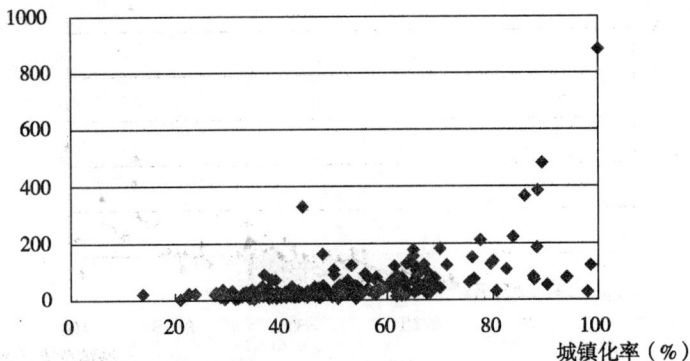

图29　城镇化与每百人公共图书馆藏书数（册）

（三）城镇化与城市社保水平

城镇化与养老保险参保覆盖率、医疗保险参保覆盖率、失业保险参保覆盖率三者均存在较强的指数型正相关性。城镇化率越高，三类社保参保覆盖率也越高，并且在高城镇化阶段，城镇化率每增加 **1** 个百分点，社保参保率上升的幅度也比低城镇化阶段显著增加。三类社保中，医疗保险参保覆盖率的上升速率最快。

养老保险参保覆盖率

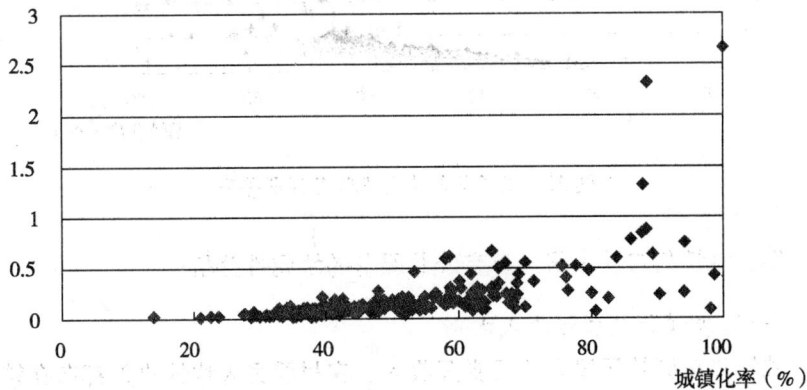

图30　城镇化与养老保险参保覆盖率

医疗保险参保覆盖率

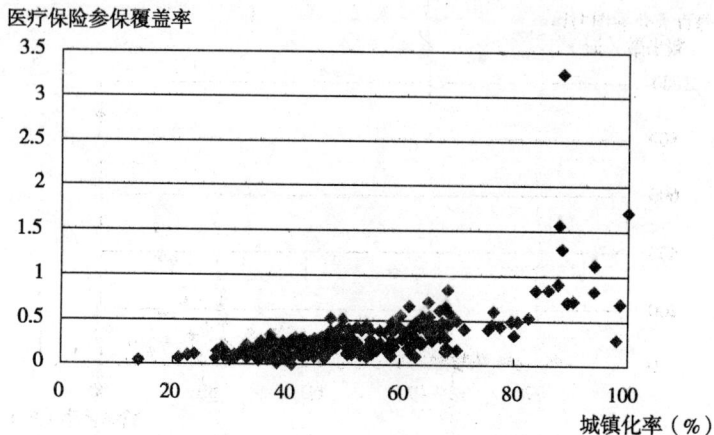

图31 城镇化与医疗保险参保覆盖率

失业保险参保覆盖率

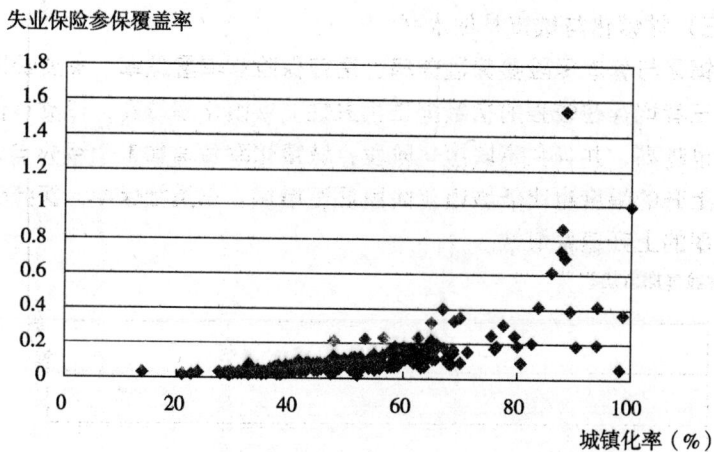

图32 城镇化与失业保险参保覆盖率

四、城镇化与城市居民享有公共服务的协调性分析

（一）城镇化与居民收入水平

城镇化与城镇居民人均可支配收入、农村居民人均纯收入都存在较强的正相关性。城镇化率越高，城镇居民和农村居民的收入也越高，说明城镇化对于提高城乡居民收入都起到了一定的作用。但相比而言，城镇化和城镇居民收入的相关性比农村居民要更大一些。

城镇居民人均可
支配收入(元)

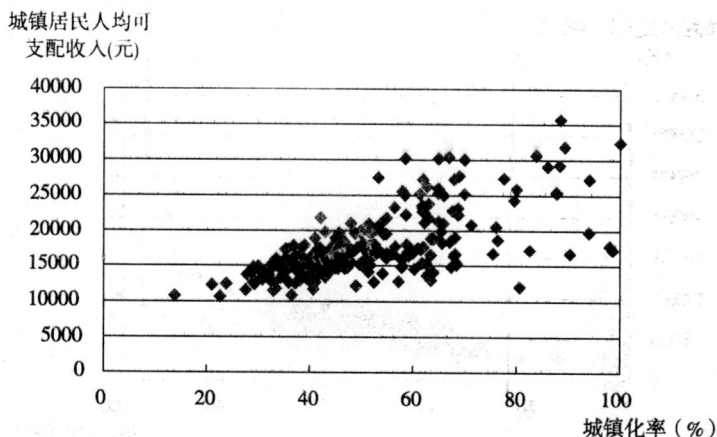

图 33　城镇化与城镇居民人均可支配收入（元）

　　城镇化与城乡居民收入比也存在弱正相关性。城镇化水平越高，城乡居民收入比越大，城镇居民收入增加快于农村居民，**说明目前城镇化阶段仍在持续拉大城乡间的差异**。

城乡居民收入比

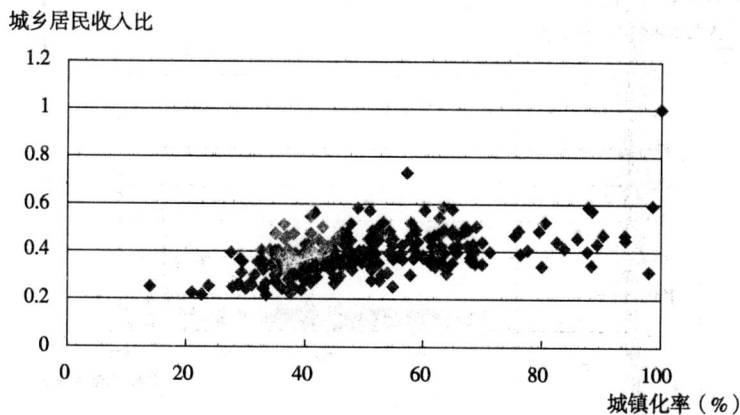

图 34　城镇化与城乡居民收入比

农村居民人均纯收入
(元)

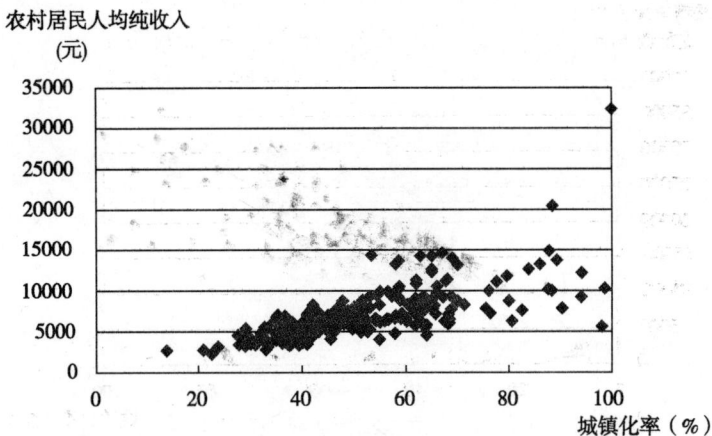

图35　城镇化与农村居民人均纯收入（元）

（二）城镇化与居民生活环境水平

城镇化水平与人均绿地面积不存在明显的关系，多数城市人均绿地面积在100平方米以下。人均绿地面积超过200平方米的城市有厦门、深圳、鄂尔多斯、黄山、十堰等少数城市。

人均绿地面积（平方米）

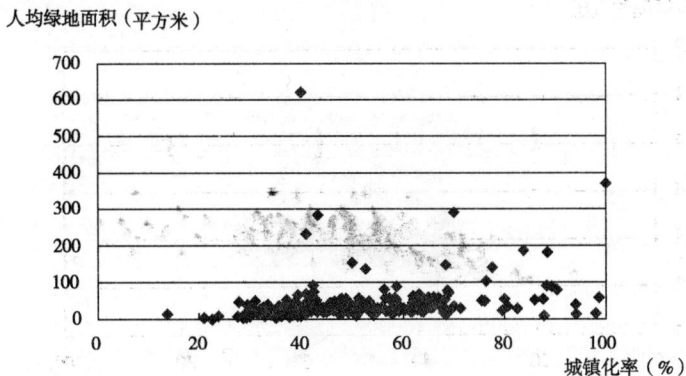

图36　城镇化与人均绿地面积（平方米）

城镇化水平较低的城市，平均生活垃圾无害化处理率较低，达州、宜宾、抚州三市甚至低于20％，但城镇化率在80％以上的城市，生活垃圾无害化处理率都达到80％以上。

生活垃圾无害化
处理率(%)

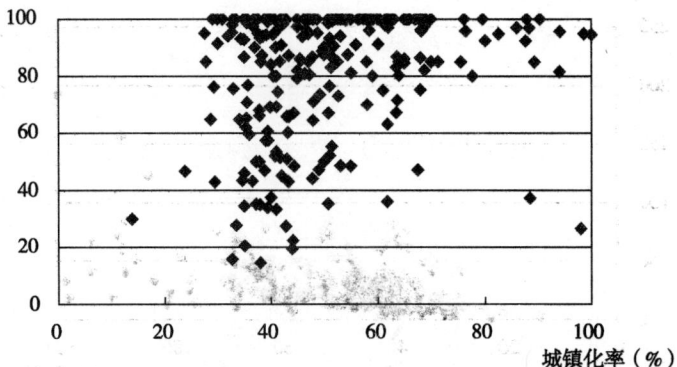

图37 城镇化与生活垃圾无害化处理率（%）

城镇化与生活污水处理率的关系同垃圾无害化处理率相似，但二者相关性更低。除了低城镇化率的城市，许多城镇化率在60%左右的城市，如丹东、七台河、攀枝花、潮州，生活污水处理率也在40%以下。

生活污水处理率(%)

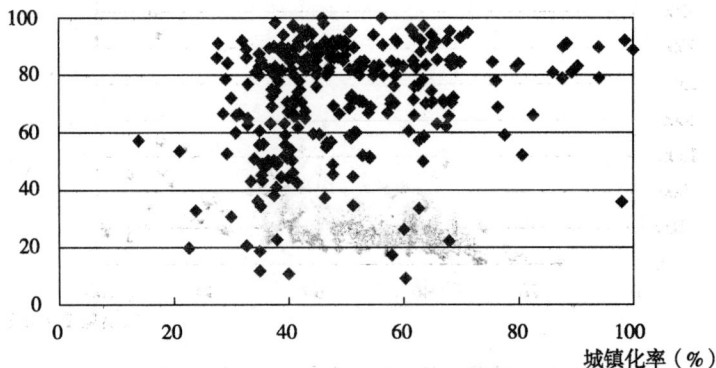

图38 城镇化与生活污水处理率（%）

城镇化与人均生活用水量呈正相关关系，相关性系数达到0.0194，城镇化率越高，人均生活用水量也越高，对城市供水系统的压力也越大。

人均生活用水量（吨）

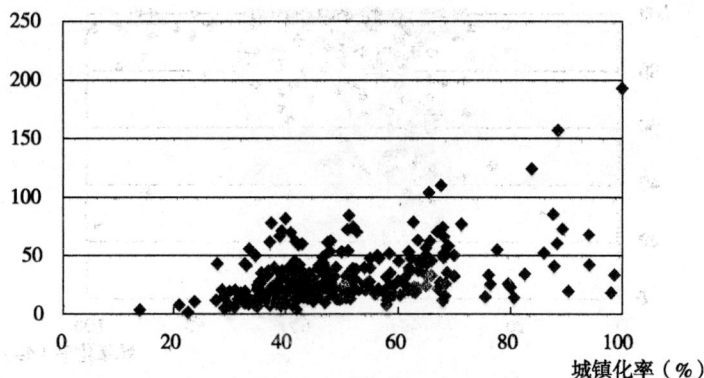

图39　城镇化与人均生活用水量（吨）

城镇化与人均生活用电量也呈正相关关系，相关性系数达到**0.0099**，城镇化率越高，人均生活用电量也越高，同样对电力资源需求也越大。

人均生活用电量（千瓦/时）

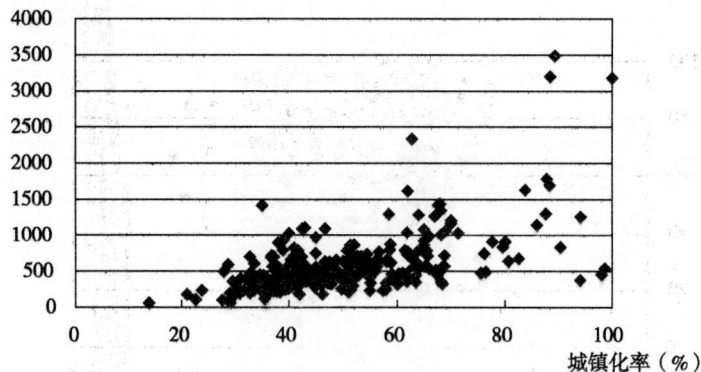

图40　城镇化与人均生活用电量（千瓦/时）

（三）城镇化与居民就业水平

城镇化率与城镇登记失业率的相关性并不显著。总体而言，低城镇化水平阶段的城镇登记失业率较高，到城镇化率40%左右有一个明显的过程，此后城镇化率中、高阶段的城镇，其登记失业率平均水平都比较低。

城镇登记失业率

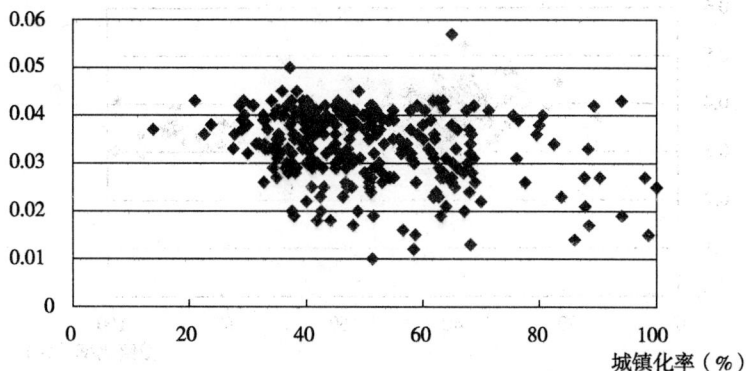

图41 城镇化与城镇登记失业率

城镇化与失业增长率的比值与城镇化率高低无相关性，比值基本稳定在1左右，说明二者保持同比例增长趋势。个别比值偏高的城市有商洛、曲靖、平凉、大同、海口。

失业增长率与城镇化
增长率的比值

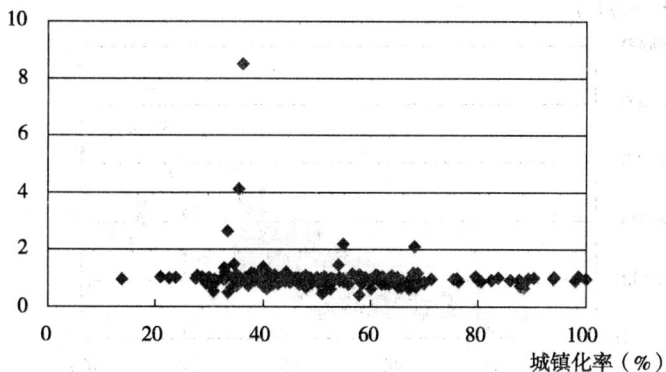

图42 城镇化与失业增长率的比值

（四）城镇化与居民消费水平

城镇化水平高的地区与城镇化低的地区相比，恩格尔系数略低，平均在0.3左右；但这种趋势并不十分明显。大多数城市城镇居民恩格尔系数都在 0.2— 0.5 之间，抚州市最高，达到 0.5226，朔州市最低，为 0.1181。

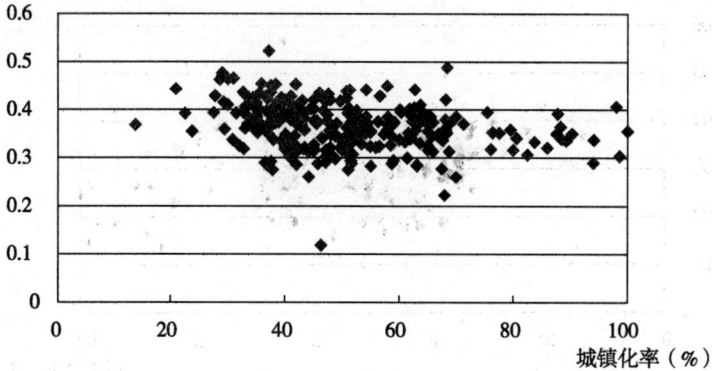

城镇居民恩格尔系数

图43　城镇化与城镇居民恩格尔系数

城镇化与人均年末储蓄余额呈较强的正相关趋势，相关性系数为**0.0127**。城镇化水平越高的城市，人均年末储蓄余额也越高，这跟城镇化带来居民收入提高的效应具有一致性。另一方面，随着城镇化水平的提升，城市间人均年末储蓄余额的差异性也越大。

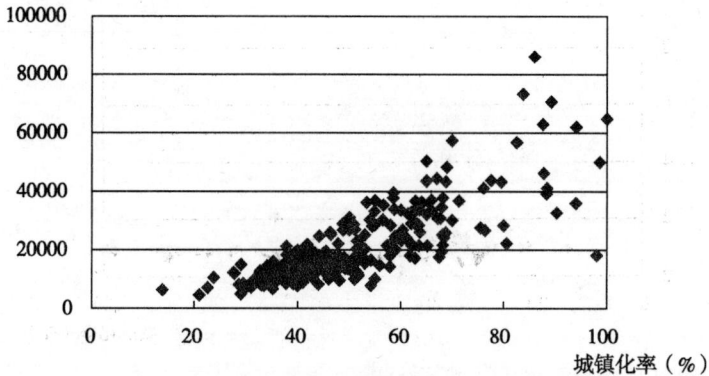

人均年末储蓄余额（元/人）

图44　城镇化与人均年末储蓄余额（元/人）

同样，城镇化与人均社会消费品零售额也存在较强的正相关性，相关性系数为**0.0332**。随着城镇化水平的提高，消费能力也相应增强，人均社会消费品零售额也显著上升。

人均社会消费品零售额
（元/人）

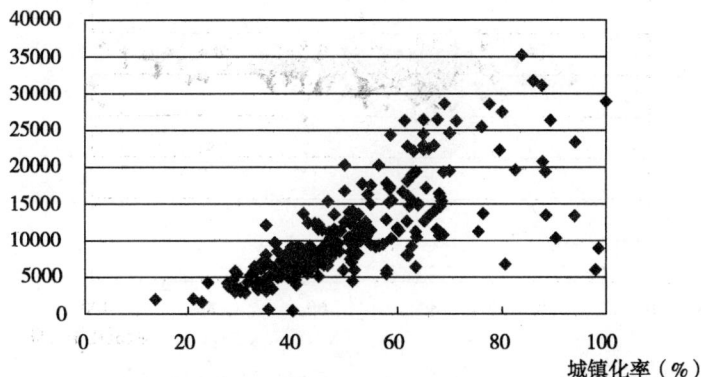

图45 城镇化与人均社会消费品零售额（元/人）

人均住宅建筑面积与城镇化水平不存在明显的相关性。各城市的人均住宅面积平均在30平方米左右，最高为东莞市，达到58.58平方米，最低为天水市，人均住宅建筑面积仅19.29平方米。

人均住宅建筑面积
（平方米）

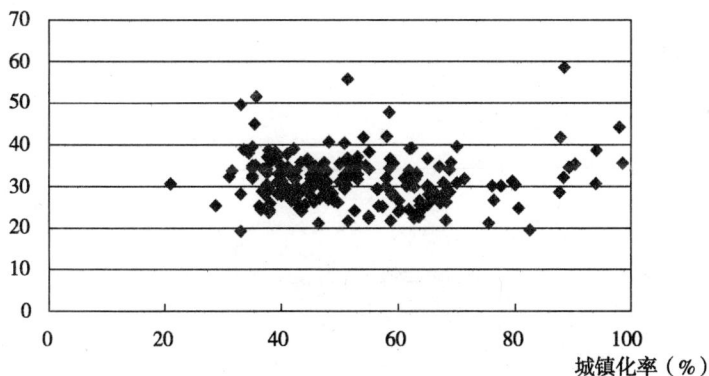

图46 城镇化与人均住宅建筑面积（平方米）

城镇化与居住支出占消费支出比重也不存在明显的相关性。各城市居住支出占消费支出比重的差别不大，平均在10%左右，最高的宣城市为12.64%，最低的白城市占7.80%。

居住支出占消费支出比重

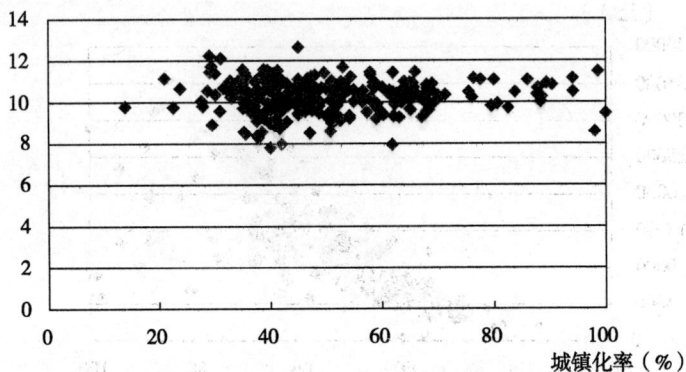

图47 城镇化与居住支出占消费支出比重

第五节　基于 E&G 评价体系的城镇化与公共服务分析

一、我国城镇化阶段划分

本研究采用五分位法①将我国地级市城镇化水平进行分组，不同城镇化阶段的区域差异明显。

（一）较低城镇化阶段（≦37.56%）

我国城镇化水平较低的城市主要集中在西部地区，占比达到 58.93%；其次，占比 28.57% 的较低城镇化阶段的城市集中在中部地区。

表 5 　　　　2010 年我国较低城镇化阶段地级市分布的区域差异

	东部地区	东北地区	中部地区	西部地区
较低城镇化阶段（≦37.56%）	8.93%	3.57%	28.57%	58.93%

（二）中低城镇化阶段（37.59%—43.00%）

我国处于中低城镇化阶段的地级市主要分布于中、西部地区，比重达到 75.00%；具体来看，中部地区城市所占比重高于西部地区。

表 6 　　　　2010 年我国中低城镇化阶段地级市分布的区域差异

	东部地区	东北地区	中部地区	西部地区
中低城镇化阶段（37.59%—43.00%）	14.29%	10.71%	41.07%	33.93%

（三）中等城镇化阶段（43.00%—51.04%）

我国中等城镇化水平的城市主要集中在东部和中部地区，占比分别为 42.86% 和 35.71%。

---

① 五分位法是统计学的一种分析方法。将全部数据从小到大排列，在 20、40、60、80 百分位处进行分段，将所有数据等分为五组。

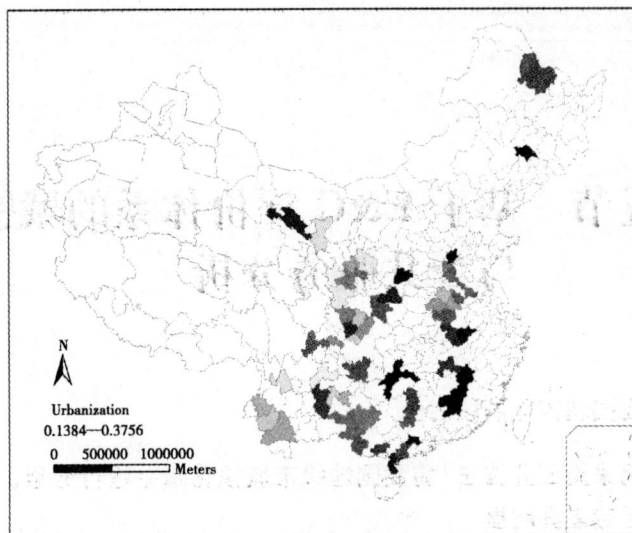

图 48　较低城镇化阶段地级市分布图

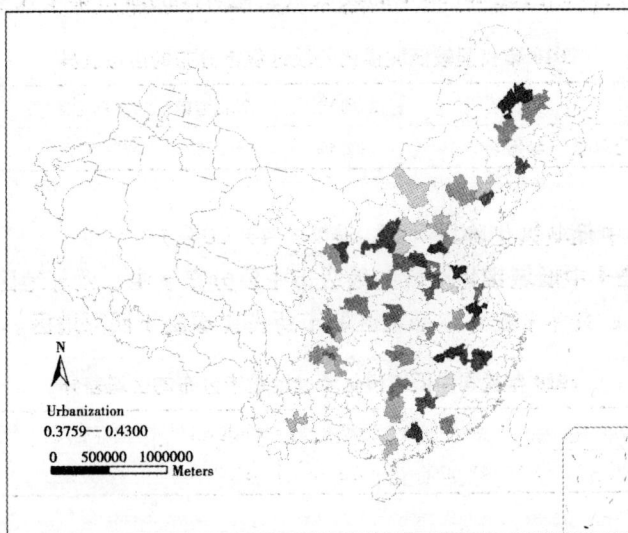

图 49　中低城镇化阶段地级市分布图

表 7　　　　　2010 年我国中等城镇化阶段地级市分布的区域差异

	东部地区	东北地区	中部地区	西部地区
中等城镇化阶段（43.00%—51.04%）	42.86%	7.14%	35.71%	14.29%

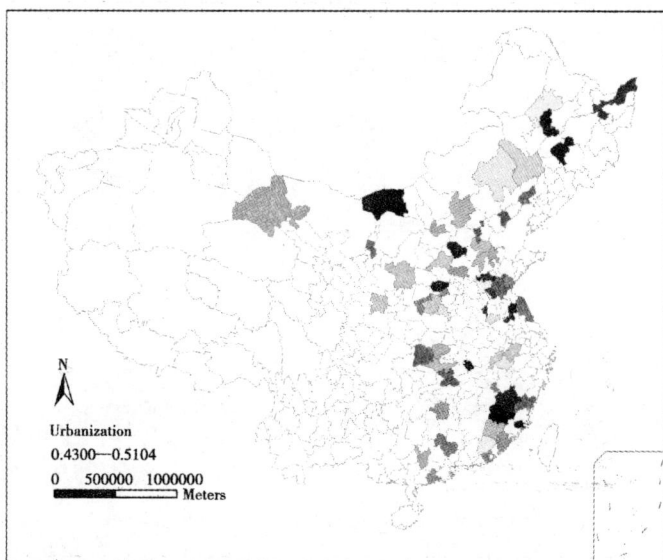

図50 中等城镇化阶段地级市分布图

（四）中高城镇化阶段（51.12%—62.75%）

在中高城镇化阶段，东部地区城市所占比重达到**46.43%**；东北地区位居第二，比重达到21.43%。

表8　　　　　　　2010年我国中高城镇化阶段地级市分布的区域差异

	东部地区	东北地区	中部地区	西部地区
中高城镇化阶段（51.12%—62.75%）	46.43%	21.43%	17.86%	14.29%

（五）较高城镇化阶段（≧62.80%）

我国较高城镇化水平的城市主要集中在东部地区，其比重达到42.86%；中部和东北地区均有9个地级市进入较高城镇化阶段；西部地区则有14个城市达到较高城镇化水平。其中，**西部地区的城市主要表现为省城或资源型城市**。

表9　　　　　　　2010年我国较高城镇化阶段地级市分布的区域差异

	东部地区	东北地区	中部地区	西部地区
较高城镇化阶段（≧62.80%）	42.86%	16.07%	16.07%	25.00%

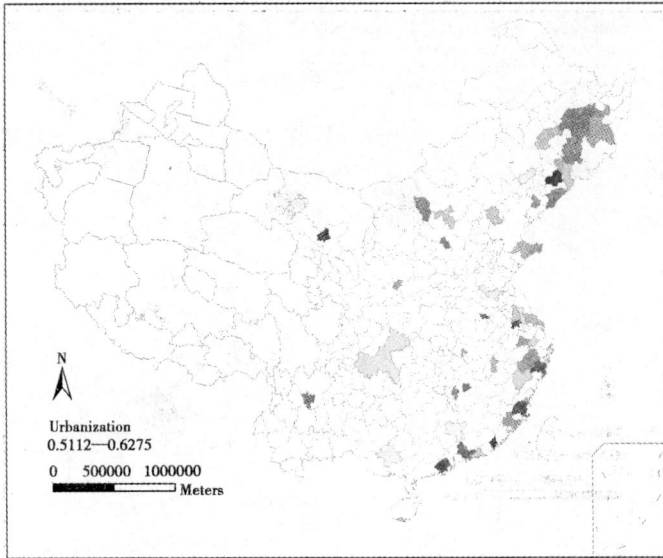

图 51　中高城镇化阶段地级市分布图

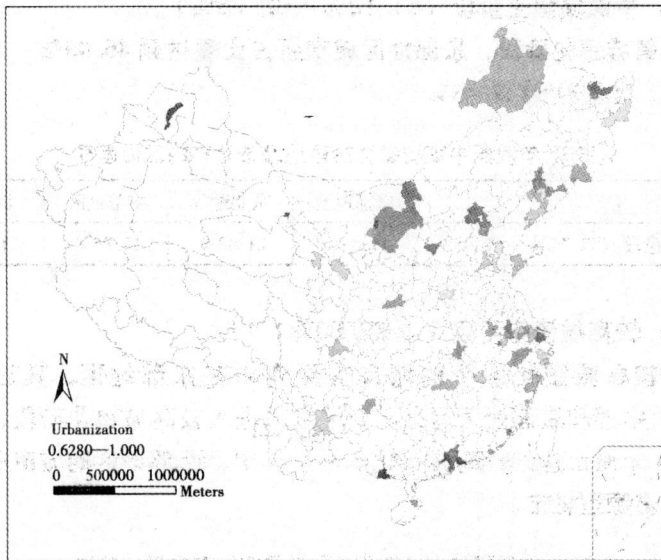

图 52　较高城镇化阶段地级市分布图

二、不同城镇化阶段公共服务的差异分析

（一）公共服务指标体系介绍

为了研究不同城镇化阶段公共服务种类和投入的差异，**本研究将公共服务划分为医疗、教育、交通、文化和社保五类子系统**。在医疗子系统中，选择每万人拥有医院、卫生院床位数和每万人拥有医生数作为衡量指标；在教育子系统中，选择中学和小学每万学生配备教师数作为衡量指标；在交通子系统中，选择人均城市道路面积和每万人拥有公共汽车数作为衡量指标；在文化子系统中，选择每百万人剧场、影剧院数和每百人公共图书馆藏书数作为衡量指标；在社保子系统中，选择养老保险、医疗保险和失业保险参保覆盖率作为衡量指标。

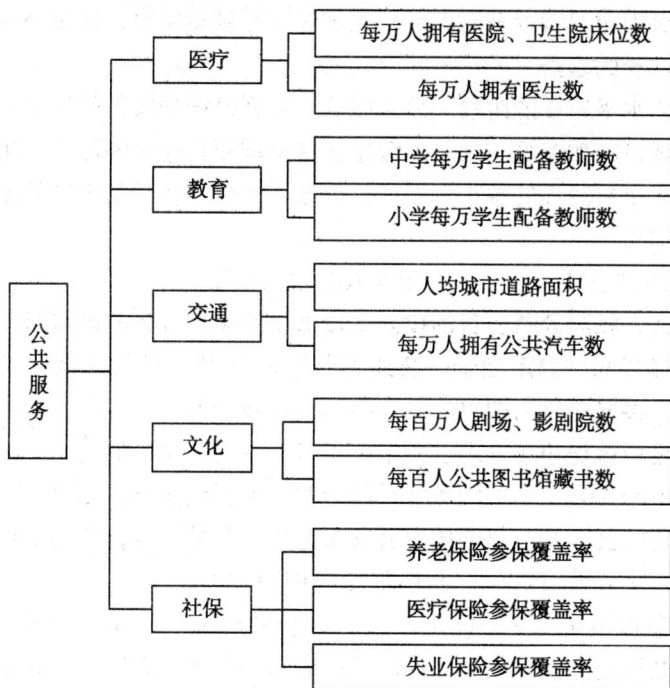

图53 公共服务的指标体系

在后续的分析中，为了消除量纲差异对指标贡献的不同，本文将各项指标采用规范化方法进行标准化处理，标准化的公式如下：

$$X_{STD} = \left(\frac{x_i - min(x_j)}{max(x_j) - min(x_j)} \right) \times 100$$

之后，默认指标权重相同，将去量纲处理后的指标相加，得到不同系

统的得分。为了消除不同系统下指标数量不同对得分的影响，对系统的得分再次进行标准化处理，处理方式相同。最终，得到的公共服务系统的得分阈值分布于0—100之间。

（二）不同城镇化阶段公共服务的描述性统计分析

本节对不同城镇化阶段的五类公共服务子系统进行描述性统计分析，并用单因素方差分析的方法检验各类公共服务对城镇化率的影响，从F检验的结果发现，各类公共服务均对城镇化率产生了显著影响。此外，统计分析发现，在我国地级及以上城市尺度上，公共服务和城镇化表现出以下三个主要特征：

（1）不同城镇化阶段公共服务投入的种类存在显著差异

在城镇化水平较低的阶段，公共服务中教育和医疗系统的投入最多，相对而言社保被重视程度严重不足。直至较高城镇化阶段，各类公共服务投入均呈现增长的趋势。

在城镇化水平较高的阶段，公共服务中教育系统的投入开始下降；且处于该阶段城市的教育系统投入均值低于中等城镇化阶段的城市。相比较而言，城镇化水平较高的城市在医疗、交通、文化和社保系统中的投入呈现飞跃式的增长。

（2）不同城镇化阶段公共服务投入的增长幅度不同

总体而言，我国公共服务的投入从较低城镇化阶段到较高城镇化阶段呈现出"快速增长—稳定增长—快速增长"的态势。究其原因，与不同城镇化阶段公共服务投入的目的差异有关：在较低城镇化阶段，公共服务更侧重于满足城镇化快速发展过程中公民对基本公共服务的需求；随着城镇化水平的不断提升，公共服务不足的问题逐渐得到缓解，相对而言，高品质、人性化的公共服务逐渐成为公共服务投入的关注点，从而推动了较高城镇化发展阶段政府对公共服务投入的快速增加。

（3）随着城镇化水平的提升，城市间公共服务投入的差距逐渐增大

从不同城镇化阶段公共服务标准差的分析结果可以看出，**随着城镇化水平的提升，城市间各类公共服务投入的差距在逐渐增大**。从城镇化阶段来看，**较高城镇化阶段的城市间公共服务投入差距最大**。从公共服务的类型来看，**不同城市间医疗和教育系统投入的差距最大**；相对而言，城市间**社保投入的差距最小**。

表 10 　　　　　　2010 年我国不同城镇化阶段公共服务的描述性统计

及单因素方差分析结果

		均值	标准差	极小值	极大值	F 值检验
医疗	较低城镇化阶段	21.31	14.15	1.59	69.71	
	中低城镇化阶段	27.60	11.93	5.95	58.36	
	中等城镇化阶段	32.27	14.63	0.00	100.00	
	中高城镇化阶段	36.51	14.08	0.45	72.98	30.49***
	较高城镇化阶段	50.19	18.16	8.60	91.10	
	总体	33.57	17.57	0.00	100.00	
教育	较低城镇化阶段	23.84	14.08	0.00	64.38	
	中低城镇化阶段	32.18	16.29	3.25	80.96	
	中等城镇化阶段	38.47	17.56	3.53	98.25	
	中高城镇化阶段	41.38	21.38	2.96	99.79	8.55***
	较高城镇化阶段	39.02	20.48	0.54	100.00	
	总体	34.98	19.11	0.00	100.00	
交通	较低城镇化阶段	6.65	4.38	0.00	17.97	
	中低城镇化阶段	10.81	6.77	2.03	36.01	
	中等城镇化阶段	13.56	6.71	2.76	29.62	
	中高城镇化阶段	14.49	6.10	5.48	33.95	18.15***
	较高城镇化阶段	20.03	15.08	4.29	100.00	
	总体	13.11	9.66	0.00	100.00	
文化	较低城镇化阶段	6.47	4.30	0.00	22.43	
	中低城镇化阶段	7.13	4.62	1.76	25.64	
	中等城镇化阶段	10.34	9.23	2.33	54.93	
	中高城镇化阶段	11.13	7.05	1.99	38.34	17.67***
	较高城镇化阶段	20.89	18.83	3.77	100.00	
	总体	11.19	11.45	0.00	100.00	
社保	较低城镇化阶段	1.83	1.16	0.00	5.02	
	中低城镇化阶段	3.07	1.33	0.51	6.32	
	中等城镇化阶段	4.57	2.04	1.70	13.02	
	中高城镇化阶段	6.78	3.30	1.67	15.63	33.67***
	较高城镇化阶段	16.87	16.83	3.90	100.00	
	总体	6.62	9.41	0.00	100.00	

　　F 检验又叫方差齐性检验。研究假设为总体内两部分方差不相等，虚无假设为这两部分方差相等。若计算所得的 F 值大于规定的某一显著水平下的临界值，则否定虚无假设，说明总体中两部分方差不相等，即无一致性或差异显著；反之，则接受虚无假设，即承认总体中两部分方差相等或具有一致性。

　　注：*** $p < 0.001$，表示均值的差异在 99.9% 置信水平上显著，即具备显著性差异的可能性为 99.9%。一般来说，$0.01 < p < 0.05$ 表示差异性显著，$p < 0.01$ 表示差异性极显著。下同。

三、城市公共服务与城镇化的实证分析

（一）模型设定与变量描述

本文选择分位回归模型对公共服务进行分析，以区分不同地级市、不同城镇化阶段各项因素对公共服务的不同影响。分位回归的思想最早由Koenker 和 Bassett（1978）[1] 引入经济学分析，它是对传统普通最小二乘估计（OLS）的一种扩展。OLS用来估计自变量对因变量条件平均数的效果，其假设是不同分布点自变量的效果是相同的。而分位回归则是一种更一般化的估计方法，以加权的平均绝对误差作为目标函数对回归系数进行估计，从而可以观察到分布中不同分位点上自变量的不同作用程度[2]。

与最小二乘估计相比较，分位数回归具有两个优点。其一，用最小二乘法进行估计，其结果反映的只是各种解释变量对应变量的条件分布的均值的影响；而分位回归允许所研究的回归参数依因变量的不同分布点（Quantiles）而变动，不再局限于较为简单的函数关系式，这有助于我们对现象之间的回归关系进行更为细致的分析。其二，它不对误差项分布做具体的假定，对非正态分布或异常值，具有较强的耐抗性。因此，其估计结果更加稳健[3]。

本文以城镇化率为自变量，以 GDP、工业化率为控制变量，分别对公共服务的 20%、40%、60% 和 80% 的分位数进行回归，从而可以对公共服务投入条件分布的不同位置进行分析。通过对公共服务不同分布点的差异做更详细的刻画，我们可以更加深入地了解公共服务与城镇化发展水平的关系。

其中，因变量公共服务的数值基于上文公共服务划分的医疗、教育、交通、文化和社保五类子系统得分加总的标准化结果，其得分阈值分布于0—100 之间。自变量城镇化率则继续沿用上文地级市城镇化率的结果；控制变量 GDP 和工业化率分别为各地级市的地区生产总值，以及第二产业产值占总产值的比重。其具体描述性统计分析结果见表12：

① Koenker, R. and G, Bassett（1978）Regression Quantiles, Econometrica, 46（3）：33—50.

② 陈珍珍、游家兴：《基于分位回归法的农民工收入影响因素分析》，《统计研究》2009 年第 26 期。

③ 张维迎、周黎安、顾全林：《高新技术企业的成长及其影响因素：分位回归模型的一个应用》，《管理世界》2005 年第 10 期。

表 12   变量的描述性统计分析结果

变量	样本量	均值	标准差	最小值	最大值
公共服务	280	29.13	14.60	0	100
城镇化率（%）	280	0.50	0.15	0.14	1
GDP（亿元）	280	1520	2010	104.028	17200
工业化率（%）	280	50.97	10.69	17.12	89.75

（二）模型结果分析

对公共服务的分位回归分析可以得到以下结论：

（1）在控制各城市 GDP 和工业化的影响下，城镇化水平仍对公共服务有显著的正向影响，即随着城镇化水平的提升，公共服务的投入呈现增长的趋势。这与之前的描述分析结果相一致。

（2）随着城镇化水平的提升，城镇化率对公共服务的拉动能力呈现"倒 U"型趋势。总体来看，我国地级市城镇化对公共服务的带动作用平均为 32.96，与不同分位回归的结果存在差异。其中，20%、40%、60%和 80%分位回归中，城镇化水平对公共服务的影响分别为 28.73、33.57、36.00 和 35.81。在公共服务 60%分位，即城镇化水平达到 51%前后呈现出公共服务投入的拐点。

表 13   公共服务的分位回归结果

	分位回归				OLS
	0.2 分位	0.4 分位	0.6 分位	0.8 分位	
Ln（城镇化率）	28.73 ***	33.57 ***	36.00 ***	35.81 ***	32.96 ***
Ln（GDP）	1.18	−0.15	−0.15	−1.18	0.46
Ln（工业化率）	0.30	1.39	−0.39	−7.74	−2.58
常数项	21.96	47.79 **	61.27 ***	112.3 ***	56.02 **
样本量	280	280	280	280	280
Pseudo R^2	0.25	0.28	0.29	0.30	0.45

注：* $p < 0.01$，** $p < 0.005$，*** $p < 0.001$。

四、城镇化发展新阶段对公共服务的新要求

（一）基本释义及现状概括

评价现代城市发展水平的一个通用标准，就是城市居民所能享受到的城市发展成果也即公共服务的数量和质量。联合国人类住区中心 2001 年在内罗毕发表的《城市管理》宣言中提出："完善的城市管理必须使男男

女女都能获取到城市公民的惠益……通过完善的城市管理，使市民有用武之地，充分发挥自己的才能，努力改善其社会和经济状况。"

前面章节中一直强调的公共服务，其实指的是狭义层面上的，是满足公民某种具体的直接需求的，如衣食住行、生产、生活、发展和娱乐等，不包括国家所从事的经济调节、市场监管、社会管理等广义公共服务中所涵盖的一些职能活动，因而更适用基本公共服务的概念。

"十二五"规划首次对**基本公共服务**做出了概念界定，指其是**建立在一定社会共识基础上，由政府主导提供的，与经济社会发展水平和阶段相适应，旨在保障全体公民生存和发展基本需求的公共服务**。同时，在此基础上提出，要"**逐步推进基本公共服务均等化**"，即全体公民都能公平可及地获得大致均等的基本公共服务。

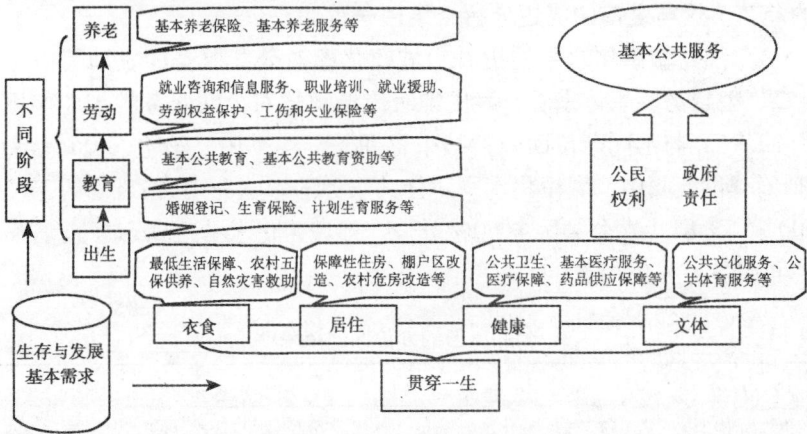

图54 "十二五"规划基本公共服务范围内涵

基本公共服务的实现，首先是基于现阶段经济社会的发展水平，其次是基于政府现有的基本财力状况和可提供的基本支持。从政府供给主体的角度理解，政府提供的公共服务范围和水平直接影响居民的福利水平和具体的生存状况。

在我国地级及以上城市尺度上，城市的综合发展水平，包括经济实力和城镇化速度等，在很多方面、很大程度上影响着政府对基本公共服务的投入。一方面，如前文分析，城镇化率达到60%—70%及至以上的城市，政府在社会保障、教育、医疗卫生方面的支出和建设规模都明显高于城镇化率较低阶段的城市。我们还发现，**在这些投入基本处于较高水平的高城镇化率城市之间，也有多项指标存在不少偏高值和偏低值，城市差异较为明显；但这种差异在城市道路面积、公共汽车数量等基础建设以及社会保**

险方面的表现却不明显，随着城镇化率的提高，基本都显示出不同程度的上升趋势。另一方面，经济增长（惯用人均 GDP 类指标）、经济发展（惯用城乡居民人均可支配收入指标）与基本公共服务之间，同样存在一种相互作用的关系，尤其是近几年来，前两者特别是经济增长与基本公共服务表现出了高相关性，相较而言，与经济发展之间的相关性则要弱一些。因此，三者之间并未简单遵从一种逻辑上的关系，即一个地区或城市的经济发展好了，公共财政能力随之增加了，则基本公共服务也就随之提升了；反推也同样如此。这也从侧面证明了，**经济的增长并不绝对代表着经济的发展。在我国现行政府主导模式和城市管理体制下，中央与地方政府在财政转移支付、基本公共服务事权和支出责任的界定与划分仍未明确**，要逐步缩小地区差异，实现经济增长与发展间、经济实力与公共服务间的协调发展，仍要走过一条漫长的道路。

（二）新阶段下的发展要求

事实上，我国的市场化、城市化进程早已对政府转型提出了客观要求，即从 20 世纪 80 年代后的"经济建设型政府"向现代"公共服务型政府"[①] 转型，这已成为我国新一轮政府改革的基本目标。服务型社会治理模式的出现，必然要求政府职能也随之发生变化，公共服务成为服务型社会治理模式中的核心价值，其内涵及外延也应当具备更为丰富的内容层次。

受西方公共产品理论的影响，我国早期对公共服务的界定，更多是基于物品性质的，认为公共服务就是提供公共产品和服务。现在的理论学界则更倾向基于行为方式加以界定，也就是**从公共管理的角度，把所有涉及为公众利益服务的事务及回应社会公众差异性需求的活动过程统称为公共服务**。从这一点来看，公共服务与公共管理的界线并不分明，在不同标准和角度的限定下，二者会表现出不同的关系。

美国行政学家登哈特提出**"新公共服务"理论，其核心思想是将公民置于整个治理体系的中心位置**，主张应对社会和民众的利益需求做出积极、及时和负责的回应；强调政府治理角色是服务而非导航；认为实现政策目标的机制，应致力于建立公共、私人和非营利机构之间的联盟，从而满足相互一致的需求，也即**建立起多中心的社会治理结构**。同时倡导和培

---

① "公共服务型政府"的概念是 1998 年在我国行政改革过程中提出的，以取代管制型政府模式。2004 年，温家宝总理在中共中央党校的一次讲话中正式提出服务型政府建设的问题，标志着服务型政府的理论探讨转向实践。与另一个中国式命题的"服务型政府"相比，它更突出政府提供公共服务的职能。

育积极的公民精神，强调公民应积极主动地介入公共事务。罗森布鲁姆则提出了一种多元行政观的思想，将新公共管理和新公共服务纳入其中，两者之间既存在对立又相互影响。他所谓的管理途径包括传统管理途径和新公共管理途径，并提出目前公共行政的迫切任务在于对政治、管理和法律三种不同研究途径所拥有的价值、结构与程序安排，以及技术方法进行整合。

　　世界各国的发展态势都已经表明，即便处于不同的国情和制度，公共服务同样都在国家化、市场化和社会化三个领域中出现了各自的缺陷，没有任何一个单独的主体或行动能拥有足够的资源和力量去解决一切公共问题。在信息化、全球化和政府统揽公共事务不可行的背景下，**公共服务应强调公共事务治理理念的民主性、治理主体的多元化和治理方式的多样性**，基本目的是为了解决任一独立的市场主体无法单独解决的公共问题，其隐含的价值观的判断，就是什么东西应该由也必须由政府提供，什么东西则应交由政府之外的主体完成。最终，**公共服务主体之间必须相互合作，从而形成一个复杂的、多元互动的社会治理结构。**

第六节　结语

　　无论公共服务或是公共管理，其本质都应是为公众利益服务的。政府的权力来自公众的让渡。这一让渡的前提，是政府要为更好地满足公众利益而提供更好的服务；这一过程同时要求公众服从政府根据公众利益制定的法律规章以及各项公共政策。两者从而形成一种社会契约关系，既相互制约又相互依存。政府作为最重要的公共部门，在公众为满足个人的需求而产生矛盾和冲突时，应当起到协调和规制的作用。①

　　我国政府近年来一直强调加快建立覆盖全体社会成员的基本公共服务体系，逐步实现基本公共服务均等化，正是为了实现上述目的，以期降低社会不公，缩小贫富差距。但是，**公共需求是随着经济社会的发展而不断发展变化的，即便是在同一时间截面上，也存在极大的城乡、区域、个体或群体差异，仅仅从物质生产和提供的角度去改善和推进，远远无法满足维护社会稳定的需要。**事实上，目前的公共管理和服务体系中仍存在大量有待改进和完善的方面，并且已经因此而暴露出各种社会问题。

　　进入 21 世纪以后，我国开始步入发展型社会，社会改革深化和经济结构的调整，引起了利益格局的剧烈变化。客观的讲，**我国目前公共服务尚未实现公共化。**这一期间，广大社会成员的公共需求的全面、快速增长，与公共产品短缺、基本公共服务不到位的矛盾日益突出。旧有的收入分配体制和资本占有不均，导致贫富差距不断拉大，部分群众缺乏相应的承受能力，引发社会心态失衡，从而产生了一系列社会问题。2004 年发生的重庆万州事件；2008 年 7 月 1 日，杨佳闯上海闸北警局连杀六人的惨案；同年发生的云南孟连事件及广东三江镇的警民冲突；2010 年 6 月的广州潮安县"古巷事件"；2011 年的"9·21 乌坎村事件"；2012 年 8 月 25 日，四川遂宁爆发的大规模冲突事件……这些充斥于各大媒体热点

---

　　①　薛澜：《公共管理的核心在服务》，《瞭望新闻周刊》2012 年。

版面的所谓社会群体事件，究其深层根源，就是在一系列的社会变革中，自身利益受损得不到补偿，应得利益因故无法获取，更多、更直接的因素正是相当一部分的群众认为自己应当享有的公共服务或利益没有充分得到甚至根本没有得到满足，这种不满的情绪自觉或不自觉地积淀下来，一旦碰触到任何一条导火索，都有可能酝酿成激烈的矛盾冲突。

我们国家现在面临的转型，从本质上说是政府的转型，公共管理（服务）则是这一重大转型的灵魂所在。从中央到地方，各级政府必须能够积极、有效地回应公众这种动态发展、各具差异的需求，大力推进公共管理和服务创新。通过对公共服务供给水平和能力的提升，增强公众的公民、公平意识，培养包容、自律、奉献的行为意识，从而真正实现社会公正。

有鉴于此，我们的年度《报告》特针对政府在公共管理与服务领域在转型过程中所面临的相关问题，编制了三份专题报告，期望以点带面，为各级政府在转型过程中的政策制定提供一些借鉴与参考。

（本报告参与人员：指导：杨旭、袁崇法、白南风；写作：郑樱、丁宇、项怡之、李燕、王婷、王璐、白南风；统计分析：李燕、郑樱、刘至贺、王婷；数据处理：刘至贺、郑樱、安顿、张文宁、田梅）

第二部分 评价体系编制及调整说明

《2012中国城市科学发展综合评价报告》体例编制及调整说明

自2008年首部《中国城市科学发展综合评级报告》（2009年始更名为《中国城市科学发展综合评价报告》）（以下简称《报告》）出版以来，每年都会根据当年的实际状况，针对编制体例的调整或变化作出必要的说明。

2011年起，《报告》在连续三年的研究探索基础上，综合社会各界，尤其是领域专家、行业学者的反馈与建议，对原有评价体系的架构组合进行了较大幅度的调整，《报告》本身的版块及内容也作出了相应的设计与变化。以上年度编制说明为基础，我们对本年度《报告》的编制体例再做一次全面、完整的梳理与说明，以使广大读者朋友们对《报告》始终保持一个清晰的脉络。

一、调整原则

《报告》是以中国城市发展研究院的重大成果之一，经多年深入研究设计，拥有自主知识产权的《中国城市科学发展综合评级体系（E&G）设计》为基础编写而成。E&G体系经过专家的多次论证和时间的反复检验，已被证明是科学、有效、务实的城市评价体系。

但是，随着我们关注主题、分析方向的逐渐明晰化和定向化，以及城市发展进程中逐渐呈现出的阶段性特征，必然要对原有的评价体系及其架构进行适应性调整，这种调整不是颠覆性的，而是在原有基础上作出的延续性的完善与优化。

《报告》的整套评价系统，依然采用国家统计部门等官方机构公布的权威数据，从最广泛公众的角度出发，设计最简单明了的代表指标来体现我们的研究理念，而不创建新的、复杂的模型，便于更多的人理解并接受。

二、指导思想

科学发展观，其核心是"以人为本"。自 2011 年起，《报告》将密切关注民生问题，始终围绕"城市与人"这一研究主线展开分析与评价，并据此选择各相关专项课题进行深入研究。为此，我们在沿袭原有评价系统的分类基础上，进一步优化了分类体系，主要是从指标的逻辑关系上，更加清晰地表述出城市与人的关系，更具针对性地完善判断与分析方法，从年度指标的评价排序上更为直观地发现城市与人的关系的趋势、特征和主要矛盾等。

三、调整说明

1. 体系结构图

➢ 原有体系结构：

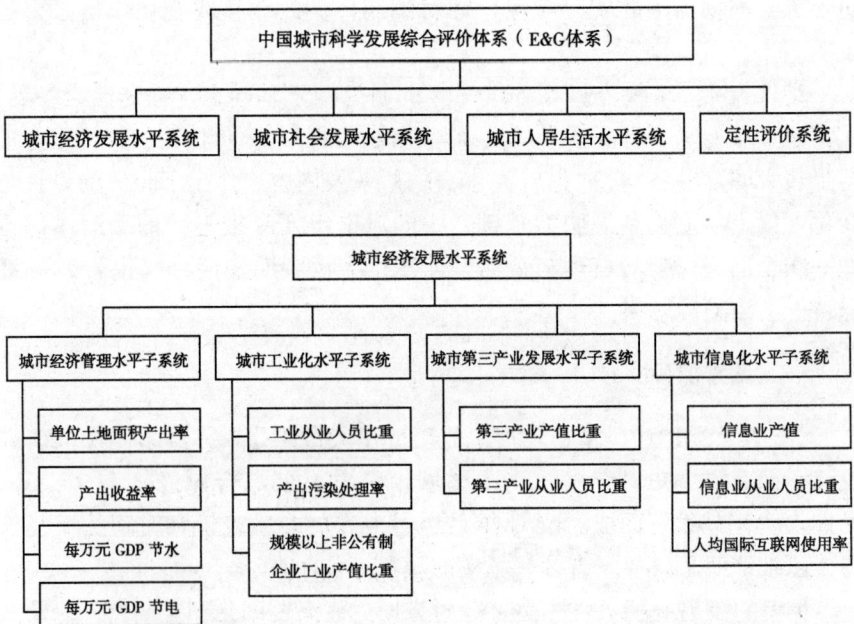

```
┌─────────────────────────────────────────────────────────┐
│         中国城市科学发展综合评价体系（E&G体系）          │
└─────────────────────────────────────────────────────────┘
   │              │                 │              │
┌─────────┐ ┌─────────────┐ ┌─────────────┐ ┌──────────┐
│城市经济发 │ │城市社会发展 │ │城市人居生活 │ │定性评价 │
│展水平系统 │ │水平系统     │ │水平系统     │ │系统     │
└─────────┘ └─────────────┘ └─────────────┘ └──────────┘
```

```
                ┌─────────────────────┐
                │   城市经济发展水平系统   │
                └─────────────────────┘
   │                │                 │              │
┌──────────┐ ┌──────────┐ ┌────────────────┐ ┌──────────────┐
│城市经济管理 │ │城市工业化水 │ │城市第三产业发展 │ │城市信息化水平 │
│水平子系统   │ │平子系统     │ │水平子系统        │ │子系统         │
└──────────┘ └──────────┘ └────────────────┘ └──────────────┘
   │              │                │               │
┌──────────┐ ┌──────────┐ ┌──────────────┐ ┌──────────────┐
│单位土地面积 │ │工业从业人员 │ │第三产业产值比重 │ │信息业产值     │
│产出率       │ │比重         │ └──────────────┘ └──────────────┘
└──────────┘ └──────────┘ ┌──────────────┐ ┌──────────────┐
┌──────────┐ ┌──────────┐ │第三产业从业人员 │ │信息业从业人员 │
│产出收益率   │ │产出污染处理 │ │比重            │ │比重           │
└──────────┘ │率           │ └──────────────┘ └──────────────┘
┌──────────┐ └──────────┘                      ┌──────────────┐
│每万元 GDP  │ ┌──────────┐                      │人均国际互联网 │
│节水        │ │规模以上非公 │                      │使用率         │
└──────────┘ │有制企业工业 │                      └──────────────┘
┌──────────┐ │产值比重     │
│每万元 GDP  │ └──────────┘
│节电        │
└──────────┘
```

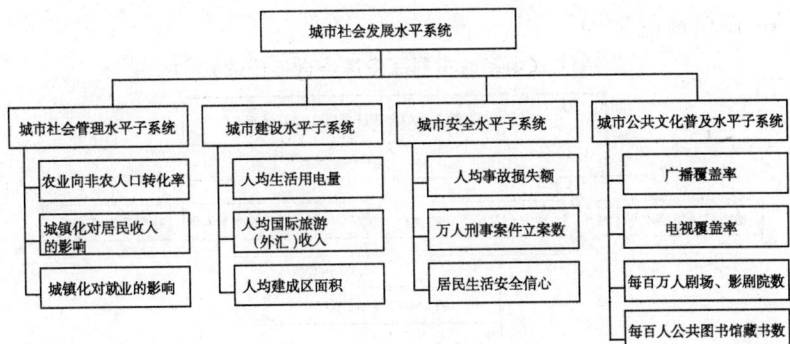

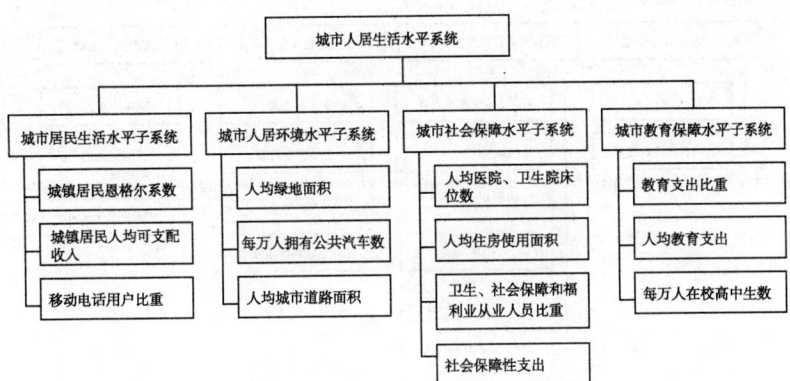

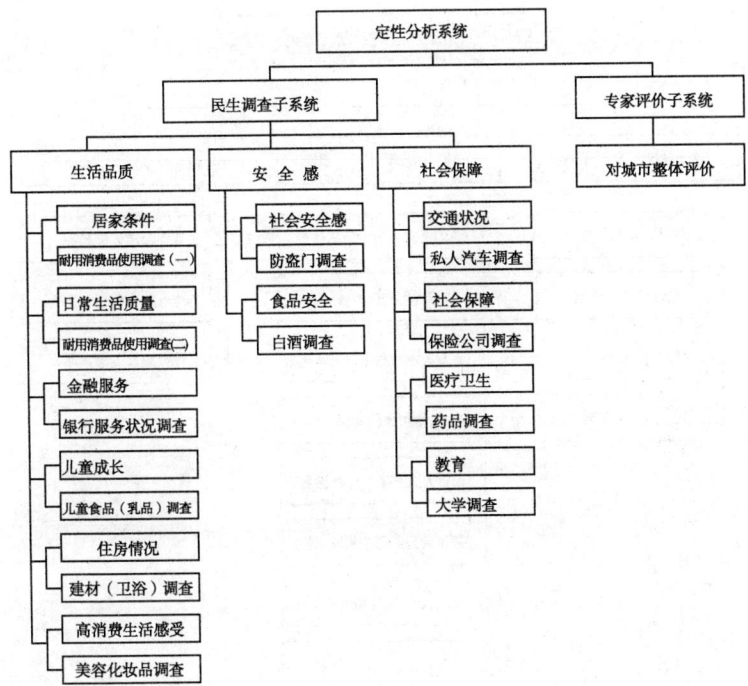

➢ 调整后的架构：

2011 年中国城市科学发展综合评价体系

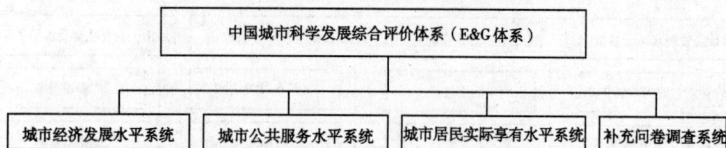

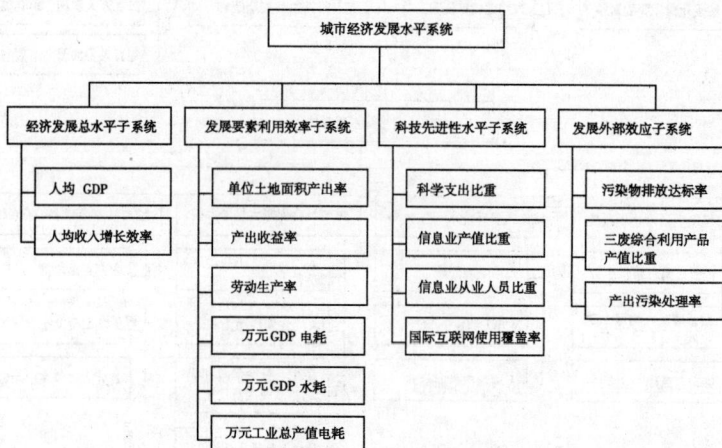

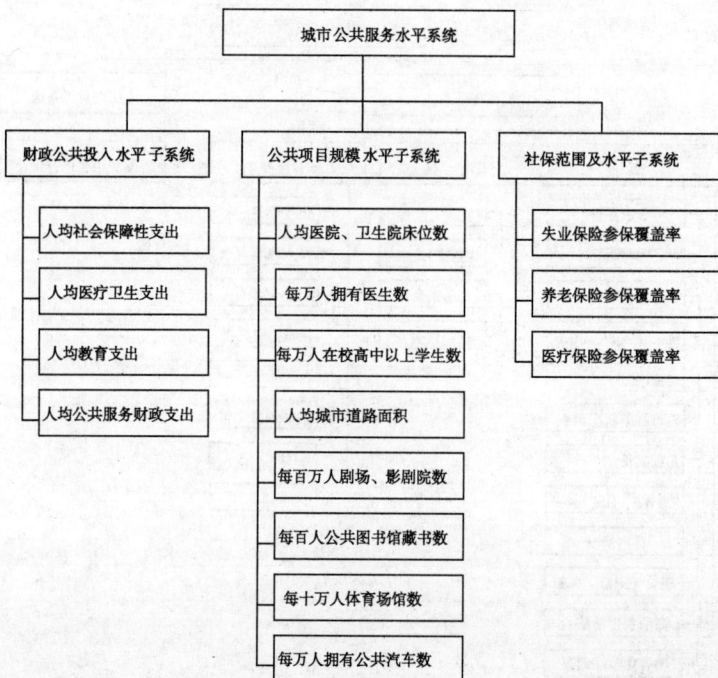

```
中国城市科学发展综合评价体系（E&G 体系）
```

| 城市经济发展水平系统 | 城市公共服务水平系统 | 城市居民实际享有水平系统 | 补充问卷调查系统 |

```
城市经济发展水平系统
```

| 经济发展总水平子系统 | 发展要素利用效率子系统 | 科技先进性水平子系统 | 发展外部效应子系统 |

人均 GDP	单位土地面积产出率	科学支出比重	污染物排放达标率
人均收入增长效率	产出收益率	信息业产值比重	三废综合利用产品产值比重
	劳动生产率	信息业从业人员比重	产出污染处理率
	万元 GDP 电耗	国际互联网使用覆盖率	
	万元 GDP 水耗		
	万元工业总产值电耗		

```
城市公共服务水平系统
```

| 财政公共投入水平子系统 | 公共项目规模水平子系统 | 社保范围及水平子系统 |

人均社会保障性支出	人均医院、卫生院床位数	失业保险参保覆盖率
人均医疗卫生支出	每万人拥有医生数	养老保险参保覆盖率
人均教育支出	每万人在校高中以上学生数	医疗保险参保覆盖率
人均公共服务财政支出	人均城市道路面积	
	每百万人剧场、影剧院数	
	每百人公共图书馆藏书数	
	每十万人体育场馆数	
	每万人拥有公共汽车数	

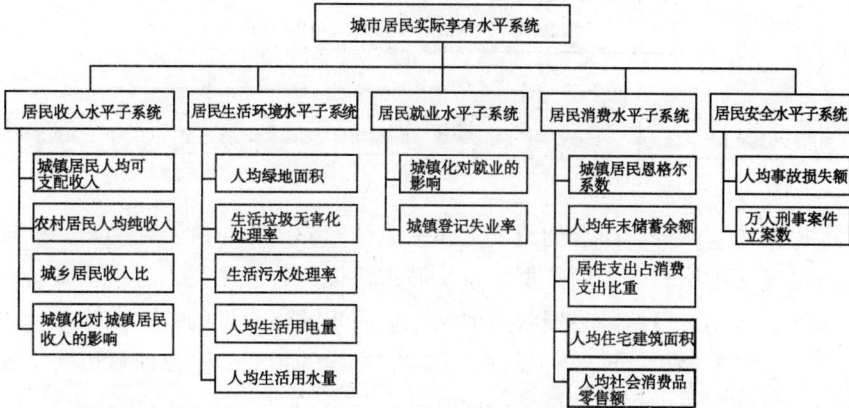

城市居民实际享有水平系统

居民收入水平子系统	居民生活环境水平子系统	居民就业水平子系统	居民消费水平子系统	居民安全水平子系统
城镇居民人均可支配收入	人均绿地面积	城镇化对就业的影响	城镇居民恩格尔系数	人均事故损失额
农村居民人均纯收入	生活垃圾无害化处理率	城镇登记失业率	人均年末储蓄余额	万人刑事案件立案数
城乡居民收入比	生活污水处理率		居住支出占消费支出比重	
城镇化对城镇居民收入的影响	人均生活用电量		人均住宅建筑面积	
	人均生活用水量		人均社会消费品零售额	

2. 母系统设计

《报告》采用的城市统计指标涵盖经济、社会、文化等各个领域，调整前，我们将这些定量的指标分为经济发展、社会发展、人居生活三大母系统。

调整后的评价体系仍分为三大定量母系统，分别是：

第一类经济发展水平，主要反映城市经济发展的规模、要素效益、科技先进性和外部影响效应，总体是属于体现完整性的生产类指标；

第二类公共服务水平，主要反映政府投入社会公共服务事业的财政、项目规模和范围，总体属于社会共享类的财富分配指标；

第三类居民享有水平，主要反映城乡居民在城市发展中分享到的各项实惠和机会，总体属于城市发展成果最终由居民收获的个人受益类指标。

三类母系统之间的逻辑关系为：一类指标反映的能力决定二类指标的规模和水平，二类指标的规模和水平则是影响三类指标可实现的基础；而三者间的协调程度就是判断城市是否形成了一套科学、有效的分配制度和技术路径以决定城市居民的受益程度。

由于上述统计指标只是反映可物化、可量化的方面，无法完全地、真实地反映出其背后存在的诸多隐蔽性现象与问题。而且，即便是精心设定的第三类母系统，其统计数据仍然是结果性的，不能反映城市居民的实际需求，也就不能以此作为判断居民实际感受的唯一依据。为此，我们设计了一类补充性的、定性类的母系统。

原评价体系中的定性分析系统包括民生调查和专家评价两项，但因为某些缘由尚未执行。调整后的体系取消了原有设定，对城市的定性评价，从 2011 年开始由问卷取代，这类问卷只做总体评价，不做评级排序，是对城市评价报告的有益补充。

```
                    中国城市科学发展综合评价体系（E&G体系）
        ┌───────────────┬────────────────┬────────────────┐
  城市经济发展水平系统   城市公共服务水平系统   城市居民实际享有水平系统   补充问卷调查系统
```

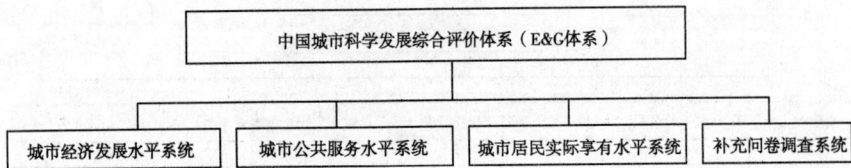

母系统是从分类组合的角度告知推演结论的出处、所发现问题的类别属性以及城市综合评价的依据，是从城市建设、管理角度，对反映城市和人全面、协调、可持续发展状态以及相应需求满足程度的各项系统的分类组合，包括了城市发展的主要方面。由它产生的指数，是推演城市科学发展综合指数，也即得出评价结论的基础。

3. 子系统设计

拥有标志性主题的母系统，反映的是整体的价值，其下分别设定有相应的各项子系统，反映城市发展中的局部现象。子系统是指标的基础集群，反映出指标设计和选择的走向，是进行科学评价的基础。

我们将各项子系统及其指标在原有基础上重新进行合理调整归类和增减。调整后的 E&G 体系，定量分析部分的三大母系统仍由十二个子系统组成，每个子系统下也包含对应的数个指标，其构成如下：

序号	子系统名称	子系统指标
1	经济发展总水平	人均 GDP
		人均收入增长效率（人均收入增长率与 GDP 增长率的协调性）
2	发展要素利用效率	单位土地面积产出率（单位建成区面积 GDP 产出）
		产出收益率（地方财政一般预算内收入与 GDP 比值）
		劳动生产率（职工人均工业总产值）
		万元 GDP 电耗
		万元 GDP 水耗
		万元工业总产值电耗
3	科技先进性水平	科学支出比重
		信息业产值比重
		信息业从业人员比重
		国际互联网使用覆盖率

序号	子系统名称	子系统指标
4	发展外部效应	人均GDP污染物排放达标率（包括工业废水、SO_2、烟尘）
		三废综合利用产品产值比重
		产出污染处理率（污染处理率与GDP间的比值）
5	财政公共投入水平	人均社会保障性支出
		人均医疗卫生支出
		人均教育支出
		人均公共服务财政支出（上述三项综合）
6	公共项目规模水平	人均医院、卫生院床位数
		每万人拥有医生数
		每万人在校高中以上学生数
		人均城市道路面积
		每百万人剧场、影剧院数
		每百人公共图书馆藏书数
		每十万人体育场馆数
		每万人拥有公共汽车数
7	社会保障范围及水平	养老保险参保覆盖率
		医疗保险参保覆盖率
		失业保险参保覆盖率
8	居民收入水平	城镇居民人均可支配收入
		农村居民人均纯收入
		城乡居民收入比
		城镇化对城镇居民收入的影响（非农人口转化率与收入增长率的协调度）
9	居民生活环境水平	人均绿地面积
		生活垃圾无害化处理率
		生活污水处理率
		人均生活用电量
		人均生活用水量
10	居民就业水平	城镇化对就业的影响（非农人口转化率与失业人口增长率的协调度）
		城镇登记失业率

序号	子系统名称	子系统指标
11	居民消费水平水平	城镇居民恩格尔系数
		人均年末储蓄余额
		居住支出占消费支出比重
		人均住宅建筑面积
		人均社会消费品零售额
12	居民安全水平	人均事故损失额
		万人刑事案件立案数

4. 权重设计

权重设计即构权,指在解决多指标之间的相互关系和主次程度时,用分解100%比例的方式,表现设计者对多指标之间关系或某一指标倾向的态度。

考虑到评价体系中每一项系统,甚至每一项指标,都对评价城市的实际发展状况具有重要的参考意义,因此,调整后的E&G体系不再设权重差别,也可以说,实质采取的是均权方式。

5. 综合指数设计

E&G综合指数由数值构成,每个城市都有不同的综合指数,所有城市综合指数的排序便成为评价活动完成的标志。

综合指数是由指标到子系统、再到母系统推演的最终结果,也是对该城市评价活动的最终结论。不同城市综合指数的对比,实质上构成了城市科学发展的相对标准,即处在发展过程中,线性动态运动选择某一静态时段,对这一时段城市发展所提出的标准。

四、名词释义

1. 中国城市 2012年度《报告》中涉及到的为全国287个地级及以上城市,因数据可得性等原因,暂未包括港、澳、台地区城市。

2. 科学发展 源于党中央、国务院提出的科学发展观及其内涵和外延。这是因为:科学发展观体现了中国特色社会主义的发展方向、模式和基本特征;体现了中国处于发展中国家和社会主义初级阶段的阶段性特点;体现了中国国情,代表着中国发展追求的目标。

科学发展的基本含义为:以人为中心的发展,包括全面发展,即以经济建设为中心,全面推进经济建设、政治建设、文化建设和社会建设,实现经济发展和社会全面进步；协调发展，即统筹城乡发展、统筹区域发展、统筹经济社会发展、统筹人与自然和谐发展、统筹国内发展和对外开放，推进生产力和生产关系、经济基础和上层建筑相协调，推进经济建设、政治建设、文化建设、社会建设的各个环节、各个方面相协调；以及可持续发展，即促进人与自然的和谐，实现经济发展与人口、资源、环境相协调，坚持走生产发展、生活富裕、生态良好的文明发展道路，保证一代接一代地永续发展。

3. 体系　由指标、子系统、母系统、数据及其计算、定量分析和问卷调查以及综合指数所构成的完整系统。

4. 城市评价　包括对城市的数据分析和综合评价，是建立在指标、子系统、母系统和推演方式基础上的分析与归纳。

五、补充说明

1. 2012 年度《报告》中，除特别说明外，所采用的数据均为国家统计部门、地方政府等官方机构公布的 2010 年度的统计数据。

2. 数据整理过程中，还发现个别城市统计数据仍存在疑点，在核对并参考各类城市年鉴、统计公报等资料后，我们进行了调整，其中包括云南省玉溪市城镇居民人均可支配收入的数据。

3. 《报告》中除国家统计部门直接公布的人均类指标数据外，我们设定的其他人均性指标均以常住人口为基数加以计算，其中包括国际互联网使用覆盖率，人均社会保障性支出，人均医疗卫生支出，人均教育支出，人均公共服务财政支出，每万人拥有医院、卫生院床位数，人均年末储蓄余额，人均社会消费品零售额等指标。

4. 在采集数据的过程中，国家统计部门公布的 2011 年各类统计年鉴（公布的即为 2010 年度的城市数据）中，相较上年度缺失了多项指标的统计，包括失业、医疗、养老保险参保人数，非农业人口，城镇居民人均住宅面积，城镇居民居住支出占消费支出比重等，为尽量保证研究与评价工作的延续性和一致性，我们采取了多种处理方式。一是花费大量时间翻阅、查找各类参考资料，包括各地方城市统计年鉴、统计公报、政府工作报告及各类官网等，补齐了大部分缺失的指标数据，但非农人口、城镇居民居住支出占消费支出比重指标则无法依靠扩增搜集渠道来获得更多、更可靠的数据。为保证每个城市得到尽量公平、客观的比较基础和环境，不因这一重要数据的缺失而大幅度影响评价成绩，我们采用插值法，补齐了全部城市的数据。如与实际情况存在出入，还请予以包涵和理解。

第三部分　中国城市社区发展初探

一、绪言

改革开放以来，除了在政府机关、事业单位和大型国企还有所保留之外，单位所有制已基本解体，中国迅速从单位社会向个体化社会转变。而随着中国的快速城市化进程，大量外来人口涌入城市，则加速了这一转变。在此种情况下，城市的公共服务和公共管理面临的问题日益突出，其中十分重要的方面，就是基层社会管理的困境与转型。可以说，公共服务及管理的良性发展，关系到城市化的前景，关系到社会和谐，关系到整个国家的经济增长和社会进步，是体制改革和城市化进程中不可忽略的重要环节。

新中国城市的公共服务和社会管理，改革开放前是单位制为主街居制为辅，随着单位所有制的解体，自然而然地转变为街居制。而街居制在快速城市化过程中显现出的不适应和局限性，促成了社区制的出现。目前，城市的基层社会管理正处于由街居制向社区制过渡的阶段。

每一次转变，都是一次制度创新。制度创新是一个过程，随着社会的发展和变革，原有制度的不适应日益突出，社会问题和矛盾不断积累，形成制度创新的需求。而在制度创新的过程中，由于试错机制、社会变化以及不同利益群体的多样性和复杂性，还会不断出现新的问题，这就需要一个在一定时期内持续不断的制度创新过程。在两种制度的过渡时期，尤其如此。

中国城市发展研究院的"城市社区发展研究"课题组，对中国城市基层社会管理制度创新现状进行了初步的调查研究，研究认为，原来只是作为单位制辅助管理手段的街居制，在单位制解体后被迫成为主流的社会管理制度，本就捉襟见肘，而随着城市化的进展，人口的水平流动激增，人户分离成为常态，街居制的基层社会管理日益困难，同时，商品房的兴起造就了大量的房屋业主，由产权派生出的财产权意识和自主意识日益强烈，这些都对传统的街居制构成了挑战。中央和地方政府为此进行了积极地探索并改革了基层社会管理体制，社区制应运而生。但由于传统制度和思维的惯性，目前的社区制仍存在诸多问题，很多方面仍在沿袭街居制的习惯做法，导致公共服务和管理效率低下，资源浪费严重，居民与政府的沟通渠道不畅，存在不安定因素。

只有继续制度创新，才能不断完善新的城市基层社会管理制度。我们认为，社区管理制度创新应该具有长远的战略眼光，不应头痛医头脚痛医脚，避免"水多了加面面多了加水"，为此，应该立足于服务管理一体化、市场化、居民自我管理、小政府大社会、与时俱进等基本原则。

二、中国城市基层社会管理制度变迁

新中国成立后，建立起强政府—弱社会的管理模式，导致政府对一切社会生活的包揽和控制。在此背景下，中国城市基层社会逐步建立了以单位制为主，以街道—居委会体系（以下简称街居制）为辅的"两条线"管理体制。一条线是政府—单位—职工；另一条线是政府—街道办事处—居委会。有工作单位的居民所需要的公共物品和服务大多由单位来提供，也就主要由单位来管辖；而社会闲散人员、家庭妇女、社会优抚对象和民政救济对象等无单位人员则被纳入街道办事处与居委会的管辖范围。单位制和街居制构成了城市社会管理体制的基本框架，通过对城市全体社会成员的分类管理，实现了国家政权对城市基层社会的强控制。随着公有化和计划经济体制的形成，以单位制为主、街居制为辅的基层社会管理体制在中国进一步普及和确立，成为中国城市社会管理制度的主要组成部分，并在城市经济社会生活秩序维护中发挥了重要作用。

改革开放后，中国经历了经济体制转轨和社会转型，单位制逐渐被打破。单位管理模式趋于失效。街居制也由于基层社会的巨大变化而面临众多现实难题，陷于管理的困境中。因此，城市基层社会迫切需要一种新的组织形态和制度安排来解决社会中出现的各种问题和矛盾，承担起重新整合社会的功能。社区制的出现，改变了传统的城市基层社会管理的理念和方法，将会在未来中国城市社会的发展中起到越来越大的作用。

（一）单位制的产生与历史终结

单位制是新中国成立后我国城市社会管理中一项重要的制度安排。单位是为适应计划经济体制而设立的一种特殊的组织形式，具有政治、经济

与社会三位一体的功能①。在计划经济体制下，单位制在资源配置、社会动员、满足人们的需求、实现社会的稳定等方面发挥了重要的功能。同时也严重制约了社会经济主体、社会组织和个人的自主发展空间，限制了社会流动，形成了高度依附型的社会结构（身份社会与单位社会二位一体），并使国家和经济体承担了沉重的社会负担。在改革开放后，所有制结构出现了变动，社会主义市场经济体制逐步建立，社会流动迅速加剧，单位制的功能及地位不断弱化，最终导致单位制基本解体。

1. 单位制的产生与发展

（1）单位制的发展阶段

单位制作为计划经济体制下中国城市管理的主要制度形式，其产生、建立和发展大体分为以下四个阶段②③：

①单位制的探索和初步形成时期（1948—1953 年）。革命战争时期，在农村革命根据地逐步形成了一套特殊的管理体制，即"公家人"管理，对以中国共产党为核心的公职人员，包括党群团体、军队、政府机构和公营企事业中的成员，一律实行供给制，这为新中国建立后单位制的形成积累了可资借鉴的制度模式。新中国成立后，工作重心由乡村转向城市，既要完成社会主义改造，建立新的社会经济体制，又要集中调度和使用有限的社会经济资源，迅速实现工业化。基于此，在借助根据地经验和苏联模式的基础上，结合东北解放初期的具体情况，率先在东北地区摸索出一套接收和管理城市和企业的模式及经验，形成了"国家—单位—个人"的单位社会体制，通过社会的再组织化，来改造旧社会，实现新的社会整合。

②单位制的形成时期（1953—1956 年）。随着新中国三大改造的完成，中国逐步建立了公有制占绝对主导地位的所有制结构和高度集中的计划经济体制，单位制以其高度的整合社会和资源控制功能逐步发展成为城市管理的主要形式，自此中国的"单位体制"在全国基本确立。中国形成了"国家—单位—个人"的社会组织体系和以大型国营企业为主体的经济体系，奠定了社会主义国家的基础。

---

① 何海兵：《我国城市基层社会管理体制的变迁：从单位制、街居制到社区制》，《管理世界》2006 年第 6 期。

② 田毅鹏：《"典型单位制"的起源和形成》，《吉林大学社会科学学报》2007 年第 4 期。

③ 周宇宏：《北京城市社区管理体制改革研究》，中国财政经济出版社 2010 年版，第 12 页。

③单位制全面推广时期（1956 年至改革开放）。随着社会主义改造的提前完成，特别是几亿农民快速地被组织进了合作社乃至人民公社，开始了单位制向农村地区的扩展，人民公社的生产大队或生产队是农村社会体制的基层单位，通过人民公社运动迅速地将农民组织到单位中来，实行类似于统一工资制的公分制。人民公社运动对当时的城市管理也产生了重要影响，通过区办、街办集体企业，公营企事业单位以外的职工家属和其他闲散人员陆续被纳入到单位体系中来，结果形成了城市社会完全单位化的格局。

④单位制的衰落和走向解体时期（改革开放后）。改革开放后，随着计划经济体制向市场经济体制的转变，单位制面临着巨大的冲击。单位的公共服务、福利和管理职能不断被弱化和剥离，单位对其成员的控制严重削弱。单位自身大量破产、改制、重组，单位体制外各种非公有企业和社会单元萌生，大量单位成员向体制外流动，新增就业人口进入体制内的比例日益缩小。外来人口涌入城市，无单位人员激增。这些变化，最终导致了单位社会的解体。

（2）单位制建立并发展的原因

单位制是建国初期所形成的一种独特的社会组织形式。它之所以出现在建国初期，究其根由，与当时政治、经济、社会的环境和体制以及中国传统的宗族文化有着密切的关系，正是政治上的高度集中化和组织化、经济上的计划经济体制、历史上的宗族制度，为单位制的形成提供了需求和基础①。

第一，单位制满足了当时以政治整合促成社会整合的要求。鸦片战争后，中国传统社会的控制和整合机制相继解体。清王朝推翻后，中国非但没有建立起强大、统一、以现代化为导向的中央政府和政治体制，反而陷入了军阀混战以及外强不断入侵的混乱境地。而与此同时，随着西方民主理念的传入，以儒家伦理为基础的传统社会整合机制不断受到冲击。面对当时国内外严峻的社会经济和军事形势，选择之一就是以政治整合促成社会整合，借助高度组织化和集中化的一元化政治体制，利用其极强的资源动员、配置和调度的能力，来改变当时一盘散沙的社会现状②，促成新的社会整合。社会整合和控制的需要，促使了单位制的产生，而自上而下等级排列高度集中的政治体制，则为单位制提供了政治基础。

① 张荣：《单位制的消解》，《社科纵横》2009 年第 8 期。
② 揭爱花：《单位：一种特殊的社会生活空间》，《浙江大学学报》2000 年第 5 期。

第二，计划经济体制是单位制存在的经济基础。多年的战争破坏，使得中国的经济秩序遭到严重破坏，尤其是新中国成立后，面临的问题众多：财政赤字、通货膨胀、大量失业和商业投机猖獗，现代化所需的资源稀缺且分散等①。当时政府必须考虑如何在这种满目疮痍、基础薄弱的情况下实现工业化目标。为了更好地集中社会资源，在苏联模式的影响下，中国建立了以公有制为主导、以国家强有力的垄断和控制为主要特征的计划经济体制，这为国家通过企事业单位这一组织形式实现资源的分配奠定了基础。

第三，中国传统的宗族制度是单位制产生和存在的社会基础和文化基础。长期以来，中国传统社会一直是依靠儒家提倡的宗族伦理关系来界定社会秩序的，这既为单位制提供了社会制度基础，也为其提供了文化心理基础。单位拥有全面管理单位成员的职责和全面负责单位成员生活服务的义务，因其具有的资源分配权力和等级秩序而使得单位成员对其有着很强的依赖和权威认同，这与传统宗族的功能和文化认同极为相似②。正是由于二者之间的这种继承性，使人们出于习惯心理，自然而然接受单位制的存在。

可见，单位制是应中国当时的政治、经济、社会、文化的需求，并在当时的政治、经济、社会、文化基础上生成的一种社会组织结构和制度安排，也必将会随着政治、经济、社会、文化的变化而发生变化。

2. 单位制的利与弊

单位制作为曾经长期存在的社会管理模式，为中国由乱到治立下汗马功劳，其整合和管理政治、经济、社会资源的能力超群。然而就像一枚硬币的两面，其优点就是其缺点。

首先，单位制将城市绝大多数的个人都纳入了单位管辖范围，保证了资源调度和分配的高效，也保证了管理和社会控制的有效性，使社会极为有序。然而这也使个人的发展和生活空间受到局限，人们的水平流动可能性很小，垂直流动在达到本单位高层领导之前，也大多局限在本单位之内。而每个人的政治地位、经济地位、社会地位的提升，主要取决于自己在本单位的上级。久而久之，人们便养成了只对自己的上级负责而不用对平级人员负责的心理特点和行为习惯，自律意识和自我管理能力较差，社会协商、互动意识和能力也受到很大影响。有些人在单位人格压抑，出了

---

① 张荣：《单位制的消解》，《社科纵横》2009 年第 8 期。

② 晋源军：《论单位制的社会功能对社区建设的负影响》，《山西青年管理干部学院学报》2003 年第 1 期。

单位就"无法无天"。这一点在单位制解体多年后的今天，仍然明显，也为新的建立在市场经济基础上的社会管理模式留下了难题。

其次，单位制中大多数公共服务和社会福利职能均由单位承担，人的生老病死，均由单位负责。在超大型国企，出生、托儿所、幼儿园、小学、初中、技校、工作、退休，直至去世，都不用出本单位。单位制全面包揽的公共服务及福利职能，和上述限制流动性的资源分配以及管理职能二位一体，保证了公共服务和福利在城市居民中的覆盖和平均化，也造成了很强的人身依附性，其结果就是严重弱化了人们的独立意识和独立生存能力。经济改革中一些大型国企不适应市场而停产或半停产，数万职工坐等政府救济和解决问题的事例，并不鲜见。因为保证职工生活是单位的义务，自然就要找单位解决问题，解决不了，就找政府，一些群体事件就是这样发生的。这种等靠要，甚至是会哭的孩子有奶吃的依赖心理，在单位制解体之后的社会管理中，也同样形成了遗留难题。

再次，单位制中单位是政府的化身和代表，除非告状等非常态事情，人们并不直接与政府打交道，使社会管理过于扁平，整个社会管理体制只有两个层级，就是个人与单位（政府代表）。同时，由于单位的大包大揽，整个社会管理体制又过于狭窄，对于就业人口来说，单位是政府唯一的腿，一切上传下达都通过单位来完成。这保证了社会管理的简捷高效和社会动员的全覆盖，但也严重妨碍了社会组织尤其是中间组织的发育。实际上，政府也不需要中间组织，一切都可以通过单位来完成，中间组织的社会协商和提供服务功能，在单位中均有专门的机构或人员负责。这造成了中国严重缺乏社会中间组织，在单位制解体之后，这也影响了新的建立在市场体制之上的社会管理制度的形成和发展。

成也萧何败也萧何，这并不是单位制的罪过，而是任何一个制度更替中旧制度的宿命。正是因为社会经济环境变化了，显现出旧制度的不适应，新制度才会应运而生。而旧制度过去的优点，恰恰就是造成不适应的原因，也是新制度要加以改变的对象，所以，对于新制度来说，旧制度的优点，往往就成了缺点。这完全不妨碍单位制在历史上的功劳。

3. 单位制的消亡与解体

随着改革开放和城市化，中国社会出现了剧烈的变迁，所有制结构发生变化，出现大量民营企业和个体经营者，非国有单位大量涌现，人们不再被束缚在原单位中，很多人从体制内走到体制外，其中不少人还去了其他城市。国有企业改制、重组或者破产，员工自谋生计，走向社会。大量农民工涌进城市，或者干个体，或者在非国有单位，或者在国有单位打临工。社会流动越来越频繁，无单位或者无长期固定单位的人越来越多，去单位化趋势日益明显，单位制失去了生存的土壤，其地位和职能日益弱化。

随着改革后的要素流动和组合日趋自由，国有单位失去了对资源的垄断和控制，尤其是对人的全面控制，就业双向选择逐渐成为社会常态。另一方面，企业改革和市场竞争使国企放弃了"企业办社会"的模式，将提供公共服务和福利的职能逐步交还给政府，国企逐步成为单纯的经济单元，向真正的企业靠拢，以盈利为主要目的。最终，除一些超大型国企和政府部门、事业单位还有所保留，就全社会而言，单位制基本解体，成为历史。

（二）街居制的发展与困境

政府—街道办事处—居委会所构成的街居制是我国城市社会基层管理体制的另一条线。计划经济时期，街居制主要是针对社会闲散人员、家庭妇女、社会优抚对象和民政救济对象等少数无单位人员进行管理和服务，作为单位制的辅助制度而存在。正是街居制的这种辅助性，使得街居制在单位制日渐衰落的情况下不得不成为主要社会基层管理制度之后，面临众多的不适应，陷于困境之中。

1. 街居制的发展历史

（1）改革开放前：街居制的建立和发展

1954年出台的《城市街道办事处组织条例》和《城市居民委员会组织条例》，基本确立了街居制。街居制是单位制的辅助性制度，所以，直至单位制衰落前，其发展过程与单位制基本一致，也经历了1949—1952年的最初探索阶段、1952—1958年的法定化阶段、1958—1978年的稳定发展阶段等。

（2）改革开放后：街居制的扩张

20世纪80年代初至90年代初，随着经济体制改革的持续深入和随之而来的社会转型，单位制逐渐走向了解体，取而代之的是街居制，它由原来的单位制的辅助性制度，变为主要的城市基层社会管理制度。

但是，这种转变是被迫的。单位制衰落后，由单位剥离出的公共服务和社会管理职能陆续移交给政府，相当一部分落在了街道—居委会的头上。失去了单位这条腿，政府只能利用剩下的那条腿街道—居委会来承接基层社会服务与管理。

随着社会流动和无单位人员的激增，很快就曝露出了街居制的不适应性。社会上出现了大量的个体户、私营企业主、失业下岗人员，农民工也大量涌入城市。住房改革和随之而来的商品房发售，老式小区中涌入大量外来租户，人户分离现象日益普遍。人手有限、建立在户籍管理基础上的街居制捉襟见肘。多由家庭妇女等无业人员以及退休人员组成的居委会，作为区政府派出机构管理本市户籍人口的街道办事处，无法满足基层社会剧烈变化带来的需求。这导致了街道办事处人员和机构的迅速扩张，但并不能从根本上扭转局面。

在这种形势下，民政部于20世纪80年代中后期提出了"社区"概念，要求开展社区服务，并逐步提出了社区建设的思路。然而这需要时间，这个时期的社区建设仍然是在街居制的框架下进行的。

2. 街居制的发展困境

街居制从成为主要基层社会管理制度之日起，就显得先天不足，这源于当初设立这个辅助性制度的目的和功能定位。

街居制设置初期，人员编制、机构职能定位明确，街道办事处是政府的派出机关，代表政府办理有关居民事宜，并不具有完全的行政机构性质，专职工作人员人数为3—7人，工作任务主要有三项：办理市、市辖区政府有关居民工作的交办事项，指导居民委员会的工作，反映居民的意见和要求。居民委员会是群众自治性居民组织，工作人员人数为2—4人，工作内容包括办理居民的公共福利事项、向当地政府或者它的派出机关反映居民的意见和要求、动员居民响应政府号召并遵守法律、领导群众性的治安保卫工作、调解居民间的纠纷。

这就决定了街居制在成为主要基层社会管理制度之后的不适应。

首先是街道本身的不适应。街道办事处虽然在日后的不断发展中，早已突破了最初的定位，不仅党政群组织齐全，部门增加，人员队伍扩大，甚至还有了经济管理职能，譬如街办企业，但其性质始终是一个政府的派出机构，而不是一级政府，只拥有事权，没有决策权，资源调度和分配能力也极为有限，对辖区内的各个单位也并无实质管理权限。这就是人们常说的责大权小。由它来接手单位制衰落后转移出来的公共服务和管理职能，有力不从心之处，更需要有一个适应、调整的过程。然而历史并没有给它充分的调适时间，在过渡性的街居制发展到社区制之后，这个矛盾依然存在，而且更加突出。

更重要的是居委会人员的不适应。在单位制负责对占城市居民绝大多数的就业人口提供公共服务、社会福利和进行社会管理的时期，街居制负责管理的对象人数很少，而且由于当时的政治社会环境，其主要职能是社会控制，服务职能很少，因为那时非就业人口能够享受的公共福利和公共产品本身就很少。因此，街居制中的居委会主要由家庭妇女等非就业人员或退休人员组成，由街道或作为房产所有者的单位指定人选，接受街道（有时也包括房产所有权单位）领导，由街道和相应辖区的派出所布置任务，除了上传下达，日常主要工作是监视、了解本区域社会动态、舆情和各家各户的家庭状况、人员状况、人际往来，巡视管理本区域的治安保卫，调解邻里纠纷，以及收卫生费、看管自行车等收费性生活服务。居委会是城市基层政权的腿，配合基层政权的社会控制工作。单位制解体后，众多公共服务和福利职能移交给街道，居委会人员的文化构成偏低，其中很多人从未在体制内工作过，自己都没享受过太多的公共服务和福利，从事这方面的工作配合有很大难度。因此，居委会在服务职能方面对街道的配合是很有限的，街道不得不扩充自己的人员，设立众多的专门机构，但仍然缺乏"腿"的配合。

街居制的困境注定了改革开放后街居制的过渡性质。加强居委会的功能，增加居委会的职能，提高居委会人员的素质，改变其人员构成，扩大居委会的"辖区"以减少街道服务、管理对象的数量和盲区，成为不得不做的事情。在这种情况下，社区制应运而生。

（三）社区制的发展与不足

不少研究指出，社区制管理模式是顺应各国社区建设社区发展之世界潮流的一种新型的社区治理模式，这种模式的建立标志着与发达国家基层社会管理模式的逐渐接轨。其实，社区制的产生首先是来源于改革开放后剧烈的社会变迁所带来的现实需求。市场经济的迅速发展打破了原有的社会基层管理制度，单位制解体后的过渡性制度安排——街居制不能适应市场经济和人口自由流动情况下的社会服务和管理需要，其中核心的问题和明显的弱项是居民委员会。于是，提升了级别的居委会—社区居民委员会登台了，社区制诞生。

1. 社区制的产生与发展

1991 年民政部提出了社区建设的概念。1996 年 3 月，江泽民在参加八届人大四次会议上海团的讨论时指出，"要大力加强城市社区建设，充分发挥街道办事处和居委会的作用"。上海市积极探索新形势下的城市管理体制，摸索出"两级政府（市、区县）、三级管理（市、区县、街道乡镇）"的新制度，全国推广后又发展出"四级网络（市、区县、街道乡镇、居委会村委会）"。1999 年，民政部制定了《全国社区建设试验区工作实施方案》。2000 年 11 月，中共中央办公厅、国务院办公厅联合下发了《民政部关于在全国推进社区建设的意见》。

2002 年，十六大报告明确提出，健全基层自治组织和民主管理制度，完善公开办事，保证人民群众依法直接行使民主权利，管理基层公共事务和公益事业，对干部实行民主监督。完善城市居民自治，建立管理有序、文明祥和的新型社区。

2. 社区制的特点

与街居制相比，社区制最明显的表面变化是将零星分散的居委会变成了社区居民委员会。社区居委会的辖区包括以往的多个居委会。根据宪法，居民委员会是城市居民的自治组织，由居民选举产生。现在的社区居委会在程序上仍然是通过选举产生，但在实际运作中，社区居委会的负责人是由街道安排的社会工作者（社工），这些社工是通过政府组织的考试获得任职资格的，往往并不是本社区的居民，而是有一定行政管理和社会协调能力的职业管理者，或者说职业社会工作者。他们的工资由街道发放，日常工作任务由街道安排，工作绩效由街道考核评价。他们从事的实际上是公务员的工作，但不具备公务员身份，不享受公务员的待遇和福利。他们的教育程度、工作经验、管理协调能力，都比传统居委会人员高出很多。

社区居委会与以往的居委会相比，最大的特点是承担了部分公共服务、社会福利和行政管理的职能，例如就业、社会保障、社会救济、计划生育、社会安全、文体娱乐和教育等工作，这是以往的居委会没有能力做到的，也是社区制区别于街居制的最大特点。之所以在单位制解体、街居制捉襟见肘的情况下社区制应运而生，最大的原因就在于此。

3. 社区制的发展现状

在各地政府的积极推动下，社区制有了很大发展，各地城市尤其是较大城市普遍建立了社区居民委员会，社区服务机构数量增加较快，社区从业人队伍迅速扩大。以北京为例：

截至 2011 年底，北京全市常住人口 2018.6 万人，常住外来人口 742.2 万人，占常住人口的比重为 36.8%。全市共有街道办事处 140 个，社区居委会 2773 个，社区服务机构 5411 个，其中社区服务中心 180 个，社区服务站点 5231 个。社区从业人员 27376 人，社区服务志愿者组织 8012 个，城市便民、利民服务网点 12490 个，社区服务机构建筑面积共计 123.8 万平方米。

4. 社区制的优点

（1）社区制提高了街道进行公共服务和管理的能力。社区制使街道办事处终于有了强有力的"腿"，有利于公共服务和福利的提供以及基层社会管理。社区制扩大了居委会的服务和管理区域，不仅使街道面对的服务、管理对象大大减少，而且可以集中使用资源，有利于资助、组织居民文体娱乐活动的开展。一些大城市的社区居委会有社区中心和活动场所，常年开办各种文体活动和教育活动，丰富市民的业余生活，提高居民的素质。

（2）社区制有利于消除社会管理盲点。

随着住房商品化和商品房小区的迅速增加，出现了大量的新式小区，不同于大多由单位建设分配管理或由房管部门管理的传统小区，新式小区是由房产商开发、物业公司管理的，大多没有建立居委会组织。其中少部分成立了业主委员会，但没有成立的更多。根据相关法规，业委会也不具备协助政府进行公共服务的职能，管理权限也很小，也不像传统居委会那样有配合街道行政工作的责任和义务。这就出现了基层社会管理的盲点。社区居委会成立后，不再需要每个小区都有居委会，社区可以与业委会、物业公司密切合作和沟通，这就将从未设过居委会的新式小区也纳入了社会管理和服务的范围。

（3）社区制有利于社会组织发育。由于辖区大，人口多，再加上有社区居委会或工作站的鼓励、组织、指导和资助，社区制更有利于社会组织发育，多种多样的居民团体和志愿者组织迅速发展起来，以自娱自乐、陶冶性情、锻炼体魄的文体娱乐性社团为主，还有为居民提供服务的服务性组织，例如浙江嘉兴市南杨社区的"邻帮邻工作室"、北京金宝街社区的"来京创业者俱乐部"北京天桥街道香草路社区的"阳光课堂"。尤为可喜的是，出现了一些立足于自我管理、自觉维护社会秩序的管理性组织，例如北京市东城区建国门街道居民自发成立的管理停车秩序的居民组织，浙江嘉兴市市民自发成立的维护市容市貌的"城市啄木鸟"义工组织，以及著名的反扒志愿者组织等。

（4）"社区共建"的指导思想为居民和社会组织参加社区服务与管理敞开了大门。在社区建设中提出了"社区共建"的指导思想，这与单位制和街居制形成了鲜明对比，使很多市民个人、居民团体和非政府组织投入了社区建设，为居民的自我管理和议事、监督以及积极参加社区服务与管理提供了前所未有的可能性。北京市东城区建国门街道，就有协和医院附近的社区居民自发组织了食品安全纠察队，配合城管和卫生部门巡视、制止有人在医院门口向通宵排队挂号的外地人兜售过期甚至假冒伪劣食品的行为，由于住得近，效果要比单纯的城管管理好得多。

4. 现阶段社区制的不足

（1）街道办事处在街居制被迫成为主要社会基层管理制度之后开始

暴露出的责大权小的弊病，在社区制中更加突出。

单位制衰落后，街道办事处在城市基层管理体制中的地位日益重要，客观现实需要它具有较强的权威性，能够在城市基层管理过程中对辖区内各个单位和不同利益群体的居民进行协调和组织。然而由于中国条块分割的管理体制和街道办事处自身的法律地位，使街道办事处陷入职能过度膨胀，什么都得管而什么又都管不了的权责不匹配怪圈①。

首先，街道办事处的职能过度膨胀。随着"两级政府，三级管理"体制的确立，街道办事处的职能迅速扩张，大量的行政、执法以及街道经济发展等各项任务都下放到街道办事处。单位制解体后，单位制所承担的大部分公共服务和管理职能剥离出来，相当一部分由街道办事处承载，而且随着经济发展和社会变迁，又增加了许多新的管理领域，譬如市容市貌、流动人口管理。上面千条线，下面一根针，各政府职能部门的服务与管理职能，大多下放到街道执行。行政、社会、经济，街道集各种职能于一身。

其次，街道办事处责大权小，权责不匹配。近年来，虽然街道办事处的行政管理、组织领导等权限大大加强，但实际上拥有的大多是事权而非决策权、审批权和处置权，主要工作内容是严格按照上级要求完成政府下达的指标和工作任务，在承担越来越多职责的同时，却没有相应的权力作为保证。街道作为行政权力链的末端，承担着日常行政管理和执法的职责，然而它缺乏各政府职能部门拥有的资源分配权力和调度能力，也就缺乏有效的约束机制和监督力度，加之在执行过程中缺乏必要的配套法规，行政执法现状不容乐观。处在城市基层管理第一线的街道办事处对很多问题往往是"看得见、无权管、管不好"，而政府职能部门则是"有权管、看不见、不担责"，造成"有责任管的无权管、有权管的无责任管"的局面。

最后，街道办事处组织法体系立法滞后，无法可依。1954 年制定了《城市街道办事处组织条例》，1979 年通过、2004 年修订的《地方各级人民代表大会和地方各级人民政府组织法》则规定："市辖区、不设区的市的人民政府，经上一级人民政府批准，可以设立若干街道办事处，作为它的派出机关。"1989 年的《中华人民共和国城市居民委员会组织法》则概要地规定了街道办事处与居民委员会的关系为指导与被指导、协助与被协助的关系。街道办事处组织法体系明显缺乏作为组织法基石的宪法依据②。当前

---

① 丁茂战：《我国城市社区管理体制改革研究》，中国经济出版社 2009 年版。

② 魏迪、厉旭宏：《我国"两级政府、三级管理"体制的法理质疑与完善选择》，《上海城市管理职业技术学院学报》2007 年第 2 期。

街道办事处的主要法律依据仍然是 1954 年的《城市街道办事处组织条例》，当时设立街道办事处的出发点是巩固政权，主旨是加强城市居民工作，密切政府和居民的联系，因此对其职能规定得十分简单。显然，当时对街道职能和管理权的界定以及执行层面的安排，已远远不能满足社会的巨大发展变化。

（2）社区居委会的行政化倾向严重，偏离了法律规定的居民自治组织性质，形成角色错位。

首先是社区居委会的行政化。在各地政府的积极推动下，社区居委会在社区建设中发挥了重要作用，形成了社区建设的大发展。但正由于中国社区建设的发展模式是政府推动、街道主导，更由于街道急需要将过度膨胀的公共服务与管理职能分解下移，社区居委会从诞生之日起，就承担着行政管理的使命。这保证了公共服务的覆盖面，加强了居民的便利性，提高了行政效率。这也是社区居委会与传统居委会的最大不同之处。社区居委会的经费来自于街道，日常工作由街道安排，行使街道给予的公共服务和管理权力，实质上是基层社会的"准政府"。

其次是居委会工作人员的准公务员化。为了保证行政管理质量和效率，社区居委会负责人的产生方式是"民选街聘"，形式上是选举，而候选人则是街道指定的社工，由街道发放工资，实质上是街道任命并派出的行政工作人员，是不享受公务员福利的"准公务员"，他们的利益来源和评价主要来自于其上级——街道，而不是居民，在对居民负责和对政府（街道）负责发生矛盾时，他们自然会更倾向于后者。

1982 年宪法明确规定城市居民委员会是基层群众性自治组织，随后的《城市居民委员会组织法》也规定"居民委员会是居民自我管理、自我教育、自我服务的基层群众性自治组织"。社区居委会目前这种实质上的行政管理性质以及实质上的负责人任命制，在很大程度上改变了居委会自治和居民自我管理的性质，削弱了居委会的议事、监督职能，减少了居民与政府沟通以及社会参与的渠道和平台，影响了居民参与社区建设的积极性，妨碍了市民个人和居民组织对社区共建的更多参与。

（3）对市场规律和利益调节规律缺乏重视，利用得不够。

由于传统制度和思维的惯性，社区制提供公共服务和进行社会管理仍然主要局限于行政手段，对通过市场手段有选择地外包、购买公共服务和通过利益调节手段进行公共管理认识不足，不利于进一步提高服务和管理效率、降低服务和管理成本、减少资源闲置和浪费，更不利于发挥全社会的力量和聪明才智来共建、共管社区。

同时，由于过于依赖行政手段和行政体系，对所有的服务和管理大包大揽，政府扮演永远的责任人角色，往往成为民众不满的矛头所向，既办了事，还挨了骂，出力不讨好。

（4）社区建设主体单一，缺乏多元化，社会组织尤其是业主委员会的作用发挥不够。

社区制的发展使社会组织发育取得了进展，但离社区建设的主体多元化还很遥远，仍然主要局限于街道—社区居委会主导，对与居民团体、志愿者组织、中间组织、非政府组织携手共建、共管社区认识不够。

特别要强调的是业主委员会和物业管理公司，前者是目前唯一的真正的居民自治组织，决定着居民的组织化程度和对后者监督、指导的水平；后者是小区居民日常生活服务的最重要提供者，保证着居民的生活质量。他们各自功能发挥的好坏以及二者的互动水平，决定着居民小区生活环境和生活质量的好坏。但目前很多商品房小区还没有成立业主委员会，老式小区更是空白，社区居委会对物业公司（和开发商）的监督管理也很薄弱，这些都影响了社区建设和管理。

三、中国城市社区发展面临制度创新

综上所述，中国的社区发展面临一些问题，也面临着一些机会，尤其是制度创新的机会。在这些问题面前，各地政府勇于探索、积极实践，摸索出了一些试图解决上述弊端的模式，在社会管理实践中进行着制度创新。

（一）社区制的改革探索

1. 社区制发展中的改革实践[①]

自 20 世纪 90 年代后期开始，上海、南京、沈阳、深圳、武汉等城市，陆续进行社区管理体制改革，积极探索适应现代社会发展需求的新型社区管理体制，在吸收各地改革经验的基础上，2000 年中共中央办公厅和国务院办公厅转发了《民政部关于在全国推进城市社区建设的意见》，社区管理体制改革在全国城市遂成燎原之势，并出现了几个典型的发展模式。

（1）上海行政引导型模式

在行政引导型模式中，政府是社区治理的主体，行政管理手段是社区

---

① 新华社：《城市社区管理体制改革的理论探讨和实践创新》，新华社 2012 年 7 月 13 日。

治理的主要方式。此种模式的主要特色是把社区建设与"两级政府、三级管理、四级网络"的城市管理体制改革相结合，不但加强街道办事处的权力、地位和作用，而且将社区定位于街道，把市、区两级政府的相当一部分管理职能分离出来，向街道层面集聚，注重政府在社区发展中的主导作用，构筑了社区管理领导系统、执行系统和支持系统相结合的街道社区管理体制。

上海行政引导模式在转变政府职能，建立街办"大部制"，打造专业化、职业化的社会工作队伍，建立决策、执行、监督相协调的行政运行机制等方面具有借鉴意义。

（2）沈阳自治型模式

以社区自治为主导的模式是现代新的治理模式的典范。沈阳市明确提出"以人为本、社区自治"的基本原则，社区党组织是社区的领导核心，社区成员大会或成员代表大会是社区最高权力机构，讨论决定社区重大事项；社区委员会由社区成员大会或成员代表大会选举产生，对它负责并报告工作、接受监督；社区协商议事会是社区协商议事机构，其人员主要由社区人大代表、政协委员、知名人士、居民代表以及驻区单位代表组成，设专职驻会主任 1 人（由社区党组织负责人兼任），副主任 2 人，委员若干人，实行义务工作制。

沈阳模式是城市基层民主自治建设的重大突破，体现了"社区自治、议行分离"的原则，从制度上保证了社区居委会的主体地位，使社区真正成为居民自治的共同体。

（3）深圳"一会二站"模式

2005 年深圳市盐田区根据"议行分设"理念，创立了"一会二站"的社区治理模式，把原来长期由居委会承担的行政、自治和服务三种功能进行分化，把政府行政职能和公共服务职能从居委会中剥离出来，转移给社区工作站。社区工作站是街道的派出机构，工作人员实行合同制，享有编制和财政工资；把服务职能交给社区服务站；同时由居民直选产生社区居委会，由其履行自治功能，以此理顺政府与社区的关系。社区居委会、社区工作站、社区服务站等社区组织都在社区党组织领导下，社区居委会与社区工作站是平行、合作的工作关系。社区居委会代表居民对社区工作站的工作进行检查、监督，社区服务站在社区居委会指导下开展工作，是为社区居民提供各种社会服务的功能性的民办非企业组织。

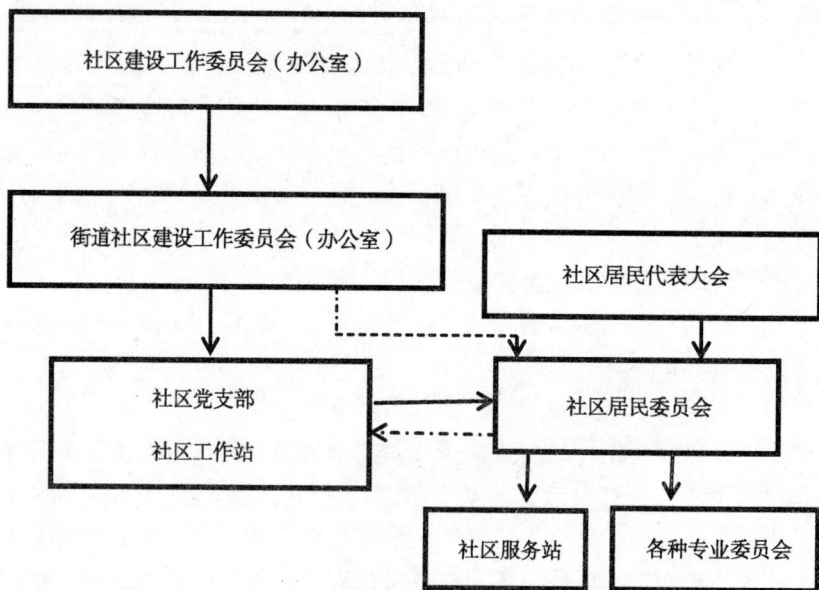

图 3-1 深圳盐田"一会两站"模式图①

注：实线表示领导与被领导的关系，虚线表示指导与被指导的关系

（4）撤销街道的铜陵模式

铜陵市先后撤销了铜官山区和狮子山区的 10 个街道办事处，把原来的 61 个社区整合为 23 个社区，从原来的"市—区—街道—社区"四级管理调整为"市—区—社区"三级服务，建立了以社区党工委为核心，社区居委会、社区服务中心、各类社会组织为支撑的整体架构。社区党工委直接隶属区委管理，主要承担社区范围内统揽全局、协调各方的职责。社区服务中心统一设置综合事务、民政事务、人口计生、综合维稳信访、文明创建、社会保障、经济服务等 7 个专业服务窗口，接受社区党工委和社区居委会的统一领导和管理，对进驻社区事项实行"一厅式"审批、"一站式"集中办理。将原街道办事处相关公共管理、服务、部门审批职能下放到社区，区直机关、原街道办事处人员沉到社区。同时，实行网格化管理，每 300 户居民配一名社区管理工作者，把居民满意度与社区管理工作者的工资直接挂钩，将社区各项工作都置处群众的监督之下。

① 汪波、苗月霞、梁莹：《城市社区管理体制创新研究——行政、统筹、自治之三元复合体制》，http://mzzt.mca.gov.cn/article/hxsqyth/zbkt/200810/20081000020653.shtml。

2. 社区工作站：改革中的亮点①

中共中央办公厅和国务院办公厅转发《民政部关于在全国推进城市社区建设的意见》，极大地刺激了地方政府的改革热情，社区工作站成为这一时期改革探索的亮点。尤其是进入 21 世纪后，许多城市相继设立了社区工作站。

（1）社区工作站的三种模式

① "议行分设"模式。2003 年北京西城区在社区中进行了居委会管理体制的改革，将社区居委会自治管理模式调整为"议行分设"的新型管理模式。议行分设的特点是实行"一会两站"，即在社区居委会下面设立社区工作站和社区服务站。居委会作为议事组织对社区重大事务和社区管理行使决策权、监督权；工作站、服务站作为居委会的"执行"机构，分别完成政府委托的行政工作、办理社区自治事务和为民服务。大连、广州、杭州、宁波、南京、常州和青岛等地的部分城区也实行"议行分设"模式。而深圳的"一会两站"，不是"议行分设"，而是"居站分设"模式。

② "居站分设"模式。2005 年深圳开始在社区管理中推行这种模式。"居站分设"是指在基层社区同时设立社区工作站和居民委员会，两者相互独立，前者承担行政管理和服务工作，后者从事居民自治事务。根据《深圳市社区工作站管理试行办法》，社区工作站是政府在社区的服务平台，协助、配合政府及其工作部门在社区开展工作，为社区居民提供服务。社区工作站在街道党工委、街道办事处的领导下开展工作，并接受市、区民政部门及其他政府工作部门的业务指导；工作人员的管理原则上参照深圳市机关事业单位普通雇员管理的有关规定执行。根据这些规定，社区工作站应该类似于政府全额拨款的事业单位。社区工作站与社区居委会之间的关系是政府工作机构和群众自治组织的关系，两者相互支持、相互配合，各司其职、各负其责。

③ "民非"模式。2005 年上海开始实行这种模式。所谓"民非"模式是指社区工作站的性质是民办非企业单位，它承接政府部门、街道办事处下放到基层的社会性事务工作，如社会救助，救济对象的调查摸底等；承接从居委会剥离出来的社会性事务，如协助调解民间纠纷，协助开展社会调查等；承接社区公益性服务，如社区服务和企业退休人员社区管理后的相关服务工作及各类敬老服务等。

① 徐道稳：《我国城市社区管理体制的改革和发展》，《海南大学学报人文社会科学版》2009 年第 3 期。

（2）三种模式的评价

① "议行分设"模式是对社区居委会传统的议行合一模式的改造。在议行合一模式中，城市社区的自治职能、管理职能和服务职能是三位一体的，而自治职能实际上付之阙如。在议行分设模式中，管理职能和服务职能相对分离，但是仍然接受社区居委会的领导。议行分设体制并没有改变社区居委会行政化的特点，只是为了完成社区越来越多的行政事务，而在居委会内部增设了机构和人员，因而在某种程度上还加重了社区居委会的行政化色彩。

② "民非"模式也完全符合现有法律规定，它与议行分设模式的区别在于，把社区服务职能从居委会中分离出来由民办非企业单位承担，这一做法与西方社会福利改革的民间化趋势是一致的，对打破中国的单一行政手段一统天下的局面有重要意义。然而，"民非"模式也没有触及到社区居委会自身的改革，它将居委会服务职能的履行方式非行政化了，但居委会的行政职能并未剥离。从这一点讲，"民非"模式其实是议行分设模式中的一种。

③ "居站分设"模式将行政职能、服务职能从社区居委会中剥离，交给街道的派出机构—社区工作站，居委会成为单纯的自治组织，行使议事、监督职能。这无疑最符合法律规定的居委会群众性自治组织的性质，也是解决前述社区制现阶段弊病的利器，是目前最值得重视的模式。但社区工作站作为街道的派出机构，却缺乏法律依据。

（二）社区制的制度创新

1. 制度创新的原则

根据社区制发展到今天的成绩，针对其目前存在的问题，我们认为，制度创新应该具有长远的战略眼光，不应头痛医头脚痛医脚，避免以往机构改革中"水多了加面面多了加水"的反反复复。为此，城市基层社会管理制度的创新应该立足于下列原则：

服务管理一体化原则。寓管理于服务之中，通过加强公共服务来加强公共管理，利用提供公共资源的权力，来达到管理和协调的目的。不应一味追求简单化的行政管理手段。

市场化原则。减少强制性行政手段，增加经济和利益调节手段。通过政府购买公共服务，有选择地将一部分服务和管理职能以公开、公平、公正的方式外包给经济主体，提高服务质量和管理效率，减少政府负担，同时避免因大包大揽而使政府永远作为直接责任人和民众的矛头所向。

居民自我管理原则。在街道—社区居委会—（小区业主委员会）—

居民组成的基层管理体制中，区分行政职能与监督职能，对二者进行相对剥离，通过将社区居委会分设为社区工作站、社区服务站、居民委员会（居民代表组织、居民大会）的方式，各自行使行政、服务和议事、监督职能。这样既可以加强居民对社区工作的监督，又可以加强居民的自我管理和自我约束，培养居民的自我管理水平和自律意识。在条件适宜的小区积极组建业主委员会，提升业主大会和业主委员会的管理、议事、监督职能，加强小区居民的自我管理。

小政府大社会原则。重视发挥居民的社区及周边区域服务热情，加强社会组织发育，鼓励居民成立健康、文明、有益于社会进步的居民团体和志愿者组织、中间组织，既要包括文体娱乐性社团，更要包括具有社会服务和管理功能的服务性组织和管理性组织，并对其加强指导和管理。通过政府及其派出机构、居民自治组织、志愿者组织、社会中间组织、非营利组织、非政府组织、居民等各方的协作和共同努力，进行社区建设和管理。

与时俱进原则。要研究互联网时代的社区服务与管理，如已经在大城市中推广的网格化管理、基于互联网和物联网并将商品服务和信息沟通互动有效结合的智慧社区理念及模式等。

2. 制度安排

（1）首先要将目前社区居委会的行政职能剥离，交给街道另设的社区工作站；将服务职能剥离，交给社区服务站等专门服务机构，专门服务机构最好是民办非企业单位。社区工作站的性质是街道办事处的派出机构。

（2）社区居委会由居民直选产生，行使议事、监督职能，并配合、协助社区工作站和专门服务机构的日常工作。社区居委会是与社区工作站平行设立的机构，没有相互的隶属关系。考虑到现在的社区都有一定规模，人口众多，在较大社区可以设立由热心公益的居民或有管理经验的退休人员组成居民代表机构、社区居委会顾问机构等配合、协助居委会工作的居民组织。

（3）有选择地将一部分服务和管理职能在社区居委会的监督下通过公开公平公正的方式外包，以政府购买服务的方式优化服务质量、提高管理效率、降低成本，同时减轻了社区工作站和服务机构的工作负担，也促进了社区建设主体的多元化。这方面，已有一些城市拥有了成功经验，如深圳将部分市容市貌监管等城管功能外包给企业，将政府接待用车任务外包给公司，北京推出了居家养老（助残）券等。政府购买服务的领域非常广泛，包括社会福利与救助、劳动就业、医疗保健、养老助残、残障康复、家政、老年餐饮、社区秩序、矛盾调处、权益维护、心理辅导、行为矫治、社区矫正、青少年教育、婚姻家庭等等。

（4）让居民团体等社会组织加入社区建设、公共服务与管理，提倡社区建设主体多元化，推进政府、居委会、居民、社会组织携手共建共管社区。部分服务、管理职能的履行可以与居民团体和志愿者组织协作。社会组织是对社会资源的重新组合和利用，社会中蕴含着大量的人力物力资源，过去政府单方面提供社会服务的方式忽略了发动、整合和利用散落在社会中的各种有生力量。

3. 配套性制度安排与政策建议

（1）加强业主委员会的功能。在居民小区积极推动成立业主委员会，加强业主自治管理，让业主有秩序地与物业公司、开发商合作和维权。现有关于业委会的法规已比较充分和清晰，要考虑进一步增加业主大会和业委会自我管理的范围和功能，以培养居民的自我管理能力、社会协商能力和自律意识。厘清业委会和社区居委会的关系，加强二者的协作。

（2）鼓励社会组织发育，加强对社会组织的管理和指导。重视、培养和发挥居民参与社区建设和管理的热情，支持、鼓励并扶持对社会有益的居民团体和志愿者组织，尤其要重视服务性组织和管理性组织的发育。目前服务性管理性团体最多的参与者是离退休人员，如退休医师免费为社区邻居传授保健知识，退休教师免费参与阳光课堂为打工子弟服务等。应将社会组织的覆盖面进一步拓宽。

（3）培养一支职业化、专业化的社会工作者队伍。通过培训、考核和资格认证制度的建立与完善，提高其专业化程度。通过激励制度的建立与完善，降低社工的频繁流动，减少人才流失。在制度建设中要正视目前社工收入低、地位低、职业期望低的现实，努力通过制度安排来加以改善。没有合格的数量足够的社工队伍，社区建设和制度创新就是一句空话。

（4）加强对社区制的立法工作。对街道办事处、社区居委会、社区工作站、社区服务机构、社会工作者、社会组织，应根据其发展和制度的成熟性逐步制定配套的法律体系，做到有法可依。目前政府的派出机构只有一层，就是街道，街道以下不设政权机关，而社区工作站这一新生事物的出现，目前没有法律依据可循，要在社会实践过程中根据需要和成熟度进行配套的法律建设。

四、结语

社会基层管理和社区发展，是随着时代的变革和进步而不断进步的。

人类已经进入互联网时代，社区公共服务和管理的理念及方式也会随着已经明显改变了人类生活方式的互联网时代的到来而继续进步。已经有人提出并研究了"智慧社区"这一互联网时代的社区生活服务和信息互动的构想，并已开发出相应的硬件设备和软件平台，通过这个整合了云计算、物联网、移动通信和多种智能控制的点对点平台，不仅可以让人们不出小区就可享受到快捷低价的生活服务、日用品购买以及健康保健等，而且可以帮助政府部门、街道、居委会、物业、业委会及公益组织实现与社区居民之间的无缝信息对接，解决城市社区的最后一公里信息化服务问题。这种将物流和信息流以点对点方式结合起来的设想，将为建立新型的社会服务体系，发展城市基层管理和公共服务的"智慧化"，提供一个可供选择的解决方案。

这些，都是我们面临的新课题。

（本报告参与人员：指导：杨旭、袁崇法；写作：白南风、田梅、张文宁、郎朗、项怡之、吴本健；调研结果汇总整理：张文宁）

参考文献

田毅鹏：《"典型单位制"的起源和形成》，《吉林大学社会科学学报》2007 年第4 期。

晋源军：《论单位制的社会功能对社区建设的负影响》，《山西青年管理干部学院学报》2003 年第 1 期。

吕方：《从街居制到社区制：变革过程及其深层意涵》，《福建论坛》（人文社会科学版）2010 年版，第 11 页。

张荣：《单位制的消解》，《社科纵横》2009 年第 8 期。

崔丽霞：《从单位制到社区制—对中国城市社区管理方式的探索》，《经济研究导刊》2009 年第 18 期。

夏建中：《从街居制到社区制：我国城市社区 30 年的变迁》，《黑龙江社会科学》2008 年第 5 期。

何海兵：《我国城市基层社会管理体制的变迁：从单位制、街居制到社区制》，《管理世界》2003 年第 6 期。

揭爱花：《单位：一种特殊的社会生活空间》，《浙江大学学报》2000 年第 5 期。

秦勃：《转轨时期单位制的嬗变——兼论社区制发展之必然性》，《甘肃理论学刊》2006 年第 6 期。

任学丽、李承：《建国以来我国国家与社会关系的嬗变——基于单位制度变迁的视角》，《湖北行政学院学报》2010 年第 10 期。

杨悦：《我国城市社区管理主体研究》，《南京师范大学硕士学位论文》2008 年。

丁茂战：《我国城市社区管理体制改革研究》，中国经济出版社 2009 年版。

纪乃旺：《当代中国单位制的形成及其特征》，《经济研究导刊》2011 年第 30 期。

何海兵：《我国城市社区管理体制的主要问题及其改革走向》，《上海行政学院学报》2007 年第 2 期。

吴俊明、高迪：《从转型期单位制的变化看我国社会组织结构的变迁》，《黑龙江教育学院学报》2005 年第 9 期。

王琼：《单位制的消解与政府治理模式的变迁》，《理论观察》2007 年第 2 期。

周宇宏：《北京城市社区管理体制改革研究》，中国财政经济出版社 2010 年版。

娄成武、孙萍：《社区管理学》，高等教育出版社 2006 年版。

潘小绢：《中国基层社会重构——社区治理研究》，中国法制出版社 2004 年版。

陈洁：《我国城市社区管理体制的演变历程》，《经营管理者》2011 年第 16 期。

新华社：《城市社区管理体制改革的理论探讨和实践创新》，新华社 2012 年 7 月 13 日。

潘小娟：《社区行政化问题探究》，《国家行政学院学报》2007 年第 1 期。

徐道稳：《我国城市社区管理体制的改革和发展》，《海南大学学报人文社会科学版》2009 年第 3 期。

魏迪、厉旭宏：《我国"两级政府、三级管理"体制的法理质疑与完善选择》，《上海城市管理职业技术学院学报》2007 年第 2 期。

王莲：《专业化的社区工作者队伍建设探析》，《湖北经济学院学报人文社会科学版》2010 年第 7 期。

王莹：《我国城市社区管理体制改革与创新探析》，《四川行政学院学报》2007 年第 6 期。

刘月平：《浅析城市社区管理体制改革中存在的问题和改革措施》，《新西部下半月》2008 年第 6 期。

汪波、苗月霞、梁莹：《城市社区管理体制创新研究——行政、统筹、自治之三元复合体制》，http://mzzt.mca.gov.cn/article/hxsqyth/zbkt/200810/20081000020653.sht-ml。

朱毅：《城市社区管理理论与实践研究》，《武汉理工大学博士学位论文》，2005 年。

黄燕：《我国城市社区管理模式研究》，《电子科技大学硕士学位论文》，2006 年。

刘昕：《中国社区管理模式创新初探》，《吉林大学硕士学位论文》，2006 年。

第四部分 现代服务型城管 转型问题研究

引　言

进入 21 世纪，我国的现代化、城市化进程再次进入一个高速发展阶段，城市（镇）化率由 1978 年的 17.92% 快速增至 2011 年的 51.27%，城镇人口首次超过农村人口，意味着中国社会结构出现了历史性转变，城市发展进入新的阶段。

但目前，我国仍处于社会转型、体制转轨的过渡期，现行行政管理体制与市场经济发展要求表现出很多不相适应甚至背离的地方，在城市化进程不断加速推进的同时，随之暴露出一系列城市管理中的困境和难题，比如流动商贩占道经营、城市环境治理不力、违章建筑屡禁不止、食品安全频现危机等等。与之相对的，在城市管理领域中，权力与利益挂钩、权利与责任脱钩的利益驱动色彩日趋明显且积重难返，根本无法有效应对不断增加并激化的各类城市管理问题。

这一背景下，2002 年 7 月，国务院法制办进一步明确了相对集中行政处罚权制度后，城市管理成为我国相对集中处罚权的先行试点领域，而担负起城市管理行政执法重要职责的城市管理行政执法机构（即我们常说的城管部门）则应运而生，并快速在全国推广。

经长期实践，城管执法确实在城市管理中产生了显著效用。但与此同时，城管执法从理论构想、体制机制设计到实践操作的缺陷与不足也逐渐暴露，并日盛一日地引发了社会与民众的质疑，尤其是执法中出现的诸如人员素质不高、执法程序不规范、方式不合理、暴力执法等现象更是屡遭指责和批评，社会对于加强城管执法监管甚至取缔城管部门的呼声越来越高。

取缔城管部门，还原多部门分别执法，是不是一种制度上的倒退？如果是，现行城管执法制度的改革方向又在哪里？国内多数学者仍主张重新构建较为完备的"城管"科学理论体系，设计更为规范的中国特色"城管"体制及其运行机制。无论中国城管的未来是什么，我们以为，任何判断的做出都需要建立在充分把握城管体制根源性问题的基础上，从内部到外部、从可逆到不可逆，对当前城管问题及其各影响因素进行系统的、多角度的分析后，才能得出尽可能科学、准确的判断。这也就是本研究的目的所在，我们将借助社会学、公共管理学、行政学、城市发展等多学科理论，从社会转型、城市发展与现代城市管理转型等视角，对城市管理行政执法体制的双重困境进行归类研究和论述。

第一节　研究背景

一、城管诞生源起

追根溯源，城管的前身其实可以归属至环卫部门。早在元朝时期，古临安因为城市人口聚居而产生大量垃圾，官府开始招募专人进行清除；晚清时，引入西方的一套城管制度，由警察机关负责城市的清洁管理工作；至近代（1929 年前后），各地政府颁布了有关清洁卫生的管理条例，开始设立专门的城市环卫机构。新中国成立后，各城市即建立环卫管理机构，此后，其隶属频繁变动，分别归属过公安、卫生、供销等部门；1988 年，国务院批转新组建的建设部的"三定"方案，"由建设部负责归口管理、指导全国城建监察工作"，随后，建设部设置城建监察办公室，也即全国城市管理相关队伍被叫做"城建监察"队伍的由来。

改革开放后，城市人口激增，城市环境遭受破坏，甚至严重影响到城市公用设施功能的正常发挥。但其时，长期形成的"条条"式管理模式使得包括行政处罚权在内的各项行政执法权分属不同部门，预埋下行政执法体制的诸多弊端，如政府部门机构林立，执法队伍庞大；职权重叠力量分散，边界不清；执法效率低下，经常出现执法疲软；管理、审批、处罚、监督权力集中而缺乏制衡；执法扰民现象极为突出等。随着改革的不断深入，特别是社会主义市场经济体制的进一步确立，转变政府职能，改革行政执法体制以完善行政管理体制的需求迫在眉睫。

为解决上述问题，经反复研究论证，1996 年 10 月 1 日开始实施的《中华人民共和国行政处罚法》，首次以法律形式确立了"相对集中行政处罚权"制度，提出综合执法的构想。于是，已经具备现实基础和条件的城市管理行政执法率先成为执法体制改革的突破口。1997 年，经国务

93

院批准，北京市宣武区作为"城市管理领域中试行相对集中行政处罚权"的改革试点区①，在宣武区的城市管理监察大队的组建并开展综合执法试点工作，被认为是全国第一支正式的城管队伍，它不再归口于建设部，而完全由地方政府管理，综合执行此前城建监察队伍的各项执法权，名称也从"城建监察"变为"城市管理"。在国办发〔2000〕63 号文件②发布前的试点扩大阶段，国务院先后批准的一批试点地方，名称都是城市管理综合行政执法；63 号文发布后的试点城市，名称逐步由综合行政执法试点工作改为相对集中行政处罚权试点工作；到国发〔2002〕17 号文件③出台后开始在全国推广。2003 年 2 月 21 日，中央编办和国务院法制办联合下发《关于推进相对集中行政处罚权和综合行政执法试点工作有关问题的通知》④，就推进相对集中行政处罚权和综合行政执法试点工作的衔接协调和贯彻落实问题做出了安排。

二、城管问题的社会性

现在，全国主要城市基本都已组建了城管行政执法机构，以开展相对集中行政处罚权工作。实事求是地说，城市管理综合执法实行 15 年以来，治理效果极为明显，城市面貌得到大幅改观，但也随之暴露出不少问题，例如暴力执法、越权执法、"钓鱼执法"等等，其中又以前者为民众诟病最甚，不仅导致公众对城管部门不满情绪日甚，也在很大程度上诱发了执法相对人的暴力抗法行为，从 2006 年的崔英杰案到 2008 年的魏文华案，再到 2011 年的夏俊峰案，几乎每一起城管与游商的博弈事件都会成为社会关注的焦点。普遍存在的民众不理解、不支持，处罚相对人抵触性大，执法纠纷不断等问题，反过来又加大了执法难度，城管执法领域出现执法"失灵"：执法力度不断加大，执法力量不断强化，执法手段不断变化，但大问题反复重现，小问题多增少减，执法成效如同进入"瓶颈"再难以推进，城市管理综合执法面临着"无论如何都是错"的尴尬局面。

从相对集中行政处罚到综合行政执法，正是行政执法体制改革理论研究不断深化的结果，从这个角度来看，城管部门本身就是为应对措手不及

① 国发函〔1997〕12 号文。

② 2000 年 9 月 8 日，国务院办公厅下发《国务院办公厅关于继续做好相对集中行政处罚权试点工作的通知》。

③ 2002 年 8 月 22 日，国务院颁布《关于进一步推进相对集中行政处罚权工作的决定》。

④ 中央编办发〔200314〕号文。

的社会突发、多发问题而加以行政体制改革的试验性产物，在理论和实践上都还具有极大的争议，其建立、试点到推广的实践过程相对较短，各地的具体运行模式又不尽相同，有关此方面的研究仍不完备，尚处于不断发展的变革中。

但学界在一个观点上似乎可以达成共识，那就是，以超乎预计的速度推进的城市化进程所引发的各类社会问题既是城管部门出现的根源性原因，同时也是它面临上述尴尬和难题的深层次原因。

第二节　城管发展概况

一、核心概念界定

城管并非单纯的"城市管理"的简称。它有着自己独特的理解内涵，同时又与城市管理密切相关。在对当前城管出现的各种问题进行分析之前，首先要对以下几个核心概念加以界定。

（一）相对集中行政处罚权与行政综合执法

这是与城管执法密切相关的两个概念：相对集中行政处罚权，即《行政处罚法》第16条规定，经国务院或者国务院授权的省、自治区、直辖市政府决定，一个行政机关集中行使其他行政机关的行政处罚权，它有其相对固定的内涵，仅指部分行政处罚权的相对集中。行政综合执法的内涵则相对更广，其实质在于对行政职能进行集中，将分散的执法职能集中于一个行政机构，包括执法行为的各个环节，如调查、取证、许可、强制、处罚等。由此可以判断，相对集中行政处罚权是行政综合执法的有机构成部分。

但实践中，常常混淆或者混用了两个概念，要么将相对集中行政处罚权作为独立于行政综合执法的一个事物，要么将其视为行政综合执法的代名词。这一情形自20世纪90年代末中央开始相对集中行政处罚权试点工作时就已出现，如《国务院办公厅关于继续做好相对集中行政处罚权试点工作的通知》（国办发〔2000〕63号），《国务院关于进一步推进相对集中行政处罚权工作的决定》（国发〔2002〕17号），《国务院办公厅转发中央编办关于清理整顿行政执法队伍实行综合行政执法试点工作意见的通知》（国办发〔2002〕56号），《中央编办、国务院法制办关于推进相对集中行政处罚权和综合行政执法试点工作有关问题的通知》（中央编办发〔2003〕4号）等文件。可以看出，中央编办主要是针对多头执法，从调整机构、精简人员的角度使用综合执法的概念，而相对集中行政处罚权是从行政法角度使用的法律术语。

由于长期以来在城市管理执法领域混用这两个概念已经约定俗成，本文继续沿袭实践中城管综合执法的惯用称呼，意指在城市管理领域由城管执法部门相对集中行使行政处罚权的行为和活动。

（二）城市管理与城管（城管管理综合执法）

现代城市是一个由经济、社会、环境几大系统组成的复杂巨系统，城市管理就是指以城市为对象，运用一系列机制和手段，通过政府、市场与社会的互动，围绕城市运行和发展进行的决策引导、规范协调、服务和经营行为。广义的城市管理是指对城市一切活动进行管理，包括政治、经济、社会和市政方面；狭义的城市管理通常就是指市政管理，主要指政府部门对城市的公用事业、公共基础设施等方面的管理。由于我国城市建设发展的阶段性局限，一度将城市管理与规划、建设并列，随着城市化进程的加快，越来越多的人意识到城市规划、建设和管理的密不可分，进而认识到城市管理是规划、建设、运行全过程的管理。

一般所说的"城管"，是城管执法机关中工作人员的通称，或者是指城市政府为维护城市市容市貌、经济秩序和社会秩序而尝试设立的综合管理执法的准行政部门，是城市管理中位于决策、执行之后的一个末端环节。习惯上将城市管理相对集中行政处罚权称作城市管理综合执法（有的地方为城市管理行政执法）或简称为城管执法，它属于一种城市管理方法，是为了将城市管理各专业领域的决策与执行通过一定程度的分离而强化相互监督，同时加强各专业执法间的协调，以提高执行效率。

实践中常说的城管执法的概念主要有两个：一是狭义上的，即执法与管理相分离，单纯指对违反城市基础设施管理方面法律、规章的行为进行处罚，纠正其违法行为，像北京、广州、济南就是执法与管理相分离；二是广义上的，即管理与执法一体化，城管执法部门既负责城市基础设施的管理，也负责涉及城市管理方面的执法处罚工作，例如，深圳、南京等市分别在城管办或市容局的基础上增挂了城市管理行政执法局（总队、支队、大队），德州市在原城市管理局的基础上增挂了城市管理行政执法局的牌子。①

（三）现代服务型城管

本文所强调的"现代服务型城管"，是相较传统意义上的"执法型城管"，指在社会化大背景，抛下"官本位"的特权观念，在"以人为本"

---

① 魏立路：《城管执法模式研究 ——以德州市为例》。

的大理念下，合理运用政府和社会资源，提供服务在先，加强管理在后，以服务治本、以管理治标，实现由"为城市管理人民"向"为人民管理城市"的转变，使城市公共空间管理与弱势群体利益达到平衡，其关键在于处理好"市容"与"民生"、"执法"与"服务"、"软手段"与"硬原则"、"疏"与"堵"之间的平衡关系。

二、城管综合执法机构发展现状

城管综合执法机构（以下统称城管机构）是我国体制转轨、社会转型时期的特殊产物，有区别于其他国家城市管理行政执法主体的特质，在国际上也没有现成的理论研究可供参考。经过近15年的发展，城管机构从无到有，从起初悄然试点到如今身处风口浪尖，有必要对其现状做一次简单的梳理。

（一）机构与模式设置

自开展相对集中行政处罚权制度改革试点工作以来，城管执法制度在全国迅速推广铺开。除经国务院批准开展相对试点工作的82个城市外，还包括193个市级政府和806个县级政府。全国656个城市中有266个，占总数的40.5%；287个地级及以上城市中有169个，占总数的58.8%；国务院批准的全部18个"较大的市"中有12个，占总数的66%；全部27个省会市中有26个，占总数的96%；全部15个副省级城市、4个直辖市都开展了此项工作。①

（1）机构设置情况

城管是地方政府推行各自城市管理理念和方式的执法机构，各地城管机构的设置并没有统一的标准或限定。

这种情形首先表现为城管机构没有统一的名称，有称"局"，也有称"支队、大队"的，北京为"城市管理综合行政执法局"，上海则叫做"城市管理行政执法局"，广州、大连、珠海称作"城市管理综合执法局"，武汉则是"城市管理局、城市管理执法局"；北京有"某某区城市管理监察大队"，广州则有"城市管理综合执法支队"。

其次，城管体制模式也不尽相同，各有各的挂靠部门。《关于进一步推进相对集中行政处罚权工作的决定》中强调："不得将集中行使行政处罚权的行政机关作为政府一个部门的内设机构或者下设机构，也不得将某个部门的上级业务主管部门确定为集中行使行政处罚权的行政机关的上级

① 青锋、江凌：《相对集中行政处罚权制度发展历程及实施情况》，载《城市法治管理》2010年第1期。

主管部门。"从各地来看，多数城市确实为独立设置，如大连市城市管理综合执法局就是市政府直接领导下的独立执法部门，北京市、厦门市城市管理行政执法也已由市政市管委下属二级局升格为市政府直属行政执法机构。但也有城市没有成立城管执法局，城管部门或挂靠在建设局（如济源市），或挂靠在规划局（如清远市）；有的城市成立了城管执法局，但挂靠在建设局（如青岛市）；有的是与政府其他部门合署办公，如长沙市城市管理综合执法支队就是与长沙市城管委合署办公，实行一套人马两块牌子，珠海城市管理综合执法局是与城市管理监督委员会合署办公。

有学者研究指出，城管机构的职能任务属于典型的政府职能，只能由政府机关执掌和行使，换言之，行使城管执法职权的机构应当是国家行政机关，而不是其他性质的机构和单位。因此，各地方将城管机构定性为事业编制的事业单位的做法，实际上是把典型的国家职能交由非国家机关的单位去行使，这既不符合国家职能应当由国家机关履行的基本要求，也不利于城管事业的改革和发展。①

（2）城管运行模式

试点过程中，因不同文化、历史和区位特质以及城市管理经验基础的不同，各地形成了不同的理念体系，呈现出不同的风格模式，概括起来主要有三种。②

以北京为代表的区管模式：北京最先开展试点工作，起始之处的承担机构——"××区城市管理监察大队"，是在市容监察大队的基础上建立起来的，为区政府所属职能部门，综合行使市容、园林、市政、公用等方面的全部处罚权及规划、工商、环保、公安交通等方面的部分处罚权。其管理体制和组织结构为：市一级不设相应的综合执法机构，但设城市管理监察办公室挂靠北京市市政管委，负责全市城市管理执法的指导、协调、监督和调度工作，市城管办设有一支约40人的直属督察大队，在各区组建由区政府领导、区市政管委或建委协调的"区城市管理监察大队"，区大队下设若干分队派驻街道办负责辖区的执法工作，分队受区大队和街道办的双重领导，街道分管副主任兼任监察分队分队长，对监察分队享有指挥调度权、日常管理权、经费使用权和人事建议权。城管监察人员实行执法专项编制，依照公务员管理，其待遇高于一般公务员。

---

① 杨小军：《城管执法机构性质与城管执法体制》，《行政管理改革》2010年第4期，第26页。

② 秦甫：《城市管理行政执法》，中国建筑工业出版社2004年版，第52—45页。

以大连为代表的市管模式：大连于1999年获批为试点城市，2000年初成立"市城市管理综合执法局"，为市政府直属机构，综合行使各方面的行政处罚权。其组织结构和管理体制是：市局下设规划土地、房地产、建筑市场、城建、公用事业等5个专业行政执法大队，各大队分设若干中队。市局不直接行使行政处罚权，大队具有独立的执法主体资格，在全市范围内行使各自职责范围的行政处罚权，中队以大队的名义负责辖区内的专业执法任务。全市城市管理综合执法实行垂直领导（大队受市局领导，中队由大队领导）。区大队为正处级单位，城市管理行政执法人员定为国家公务员，享受公务员待遇。

以广州为代表的市区共管模式：广州于1997年获批为试点城市，1999年9月正式组建"市城市管理综合执法支队"及各区"城市管理综合执法大队"，同时加挂"城市管理综合执法局"的牌子，综合行使行政处罚权。其组织结构和管理体制为：全市城市管理综合执法队伍按市、区两级设立，市设支队，区设大队，街道由区大队派驻中队。市支队和区大队对外独立行使处罚权，街道中队以区大队的名义行使处罚权，市支队由市政府直接领导，区大队受市支队和区政府双重领导，街中队受区大队和街道办的双重领导。其他如深圳、青岛、长沙、珠海等城市，基本也是遵照这一模式组建机构并开展工作的。

（二）执法职能范围

事实上，不仅各地行使城管职能的机构设置与管理模式各不相同，其承担的基本职能及范围也有较大差异。

按国发〔2002〕17号文件对"相对集中行政处罚权"的规定，同时对主要地方的城管执法范围进行归纳后发现，基本集中在工商行政、城市规划、园林绿化、交通管理和市容环境卫生的全部或部分职能。但实际中，各地执法的具体范围，因地方政治、经济、社会发展状况及其平衡程度不同，以及领导层的差异性而带有明显的地方特点。以执法权项来说，上述列举的城管执法权项目，各地方中较少的有100多项，多者如深圳市2010年新增9个执法项目扩展至总数21个执法项目；广州市城市管理综合执法局2011年新增29条细则后扩至232条；更如厦门，各类行政执法权已经达到384项。从执法内容来看，广州市有针对白云山风景名胜区范围的执法要求，包括砍伐林木、挖山采石等；深圳市也有森林分局对野生物植物资源实施重点保护；厦门市则成立了专门的养犬管理执法办公室。

（三）基本执法方式

综观各地城管机构的现行执法方式和手段，基本大同小异，从教育警告、书面整改、暂扣、罚款到申请法院强制执行、恢复原状、强拆等，形成了一个由轻到重、由简到繁的连续执法体系。这些方式中，申请法院强制执行在理论上具有普遍性和更有效性，但实际却存在执法成本高、程序繁琐、时间滞后、操作标的不明等问题，除大案要案或特殊案件外，一般很少使用。所以，暂扣、扣押方式，就因其直接、高效而成为最常采用的强制性执法方式。

（四）执法队伍构成

由于城管综合执法设立的渊源、执法范围、执法性质及进出门槛设定等因素影响，城管队伍构成相较其他部门机构而言更为复杂，人员素质差异也较大。一般包括以下几种：源于"联合执法"模式的探索，从工商、市政、环境等部门调来的在职人员；部门职能整合，分别承担专项职能的组织结构裁减合并，原有机构人员纳入新的综合执法机构；在全国实行综合执法人员考试后，又加入了考试进来的大学生和其他行业人员。北京市2010年、2011年的公务员招考中，城管职位始终是招录大户，其受追捧的主要原因在于该职位对学历和年龄要求较大多数岗位都低。以海淀城管监察员为例，要求任职者具备发现、处理城管执法权限内所有违法行为（24小时执法监控）的能力，学历仅需大专及以上，学位、专业、政治面貌不限，年龄35岁以下即可，岗位也不另设专业考试。

另外，各地城管机构大都存在人手严重不足的问题，如深圳全市配备的正式在编人员共1531人，与1500多万的实际人口相比，执法力量明显薄弱；厦门市在编与非在编人员共计1711人，其管辖范围从2004年的112平方公里增至2009年的300平方公里，但新增公务员仅4名。因此，一般除正式城管之外，各地都有一支协管员队伍，属各区和各街道管理。仍以北京为例，初期吸纳的人员成分相对复杂，除正式编制的7000多人外，还聘用协管员、保安等6500余名，其中相当一部分是街道乡镇自行聘用，不归城管局管理，流动性大。

三、城管效应及其评价

（一）良性效应

应该说，城管执法制度的确是对原有行政执法权过度分散的执法格局的革新和突破，也产生了一些积极的制度效应和社会效应。

其一，一定程度上实现了整合部分执法资源，优化执法体制的预期目的。具体来说，部分纠正了行政体制中职权交叉、机构林立、重条轻块的现象，减少了多头管理、多头执法的矛盾，实现部分执法重心下移，使执法开始主动适应城市管理综合化、区域化的发展趋势。同时锻炼和提高了执法队伍的工作能力，对提高执法效率和效能、减轻执法扰民现象等都起到了良性作用，用老百姓的话说，就是解决了"八个大盖帽，管不住一顶破草帽"的尴尬局面。

其二，城市的发展需要稳定有序的环境，城市建筑要依照规划施工建设，才能确保城市功能的合理匹配；取缔或规范无证商贩，才能保证公共场所的基本秩序，保护合法经营者的正当权益，维护正常的经济秩序……在面对超出预期的城市化推进速度所带来的各类问题时，城管及城管制度为城市发展和居民生活提供了一种更为稳定有序的经济和社会环境，居功至伟。

其三，城管机构从无到有，管理事项从少到多，民众对城管机构及人员的关注度也随之不断提升，民众认识城市管理、参与城市管理的积极性在某种程度上得以提高，社会共建的环境氛围开始形成。

无论对城管执法制度的评价如何众说纷纭，就某种意义而言，它已成为我国探索、尝试建立新的公共政策运行机制的一座重要里程碑。

（二）社会评价

如上所述，单论城管执法效果，由于执法力量的集中，市容环境得到明显改善，城管机构的效能和地位也随之确立。有一点难以简单评价的，那就是在全面城市化的持续推进下，城管机构俨然已经成长为一个职能繁多、权力宽广，日渐为地方政府所倚重的部门，同时，它也因为或主观或客观的问题不断引发社会热议，自诞生之日起就隐含其中的弊端与不足逐渐暴露，进而发酵为危机。

从各地建立城管执法制度以来，对城管执法权来源的合法性始终存在较大争议。一方是社会及学界的主流观点，坚持城管执法权有法律依据，即《行政处罚法》"第16条"；另一方认为城管执法没有法律依据，不具有正当性。后者首先就质疑了《行政处罚法》授权"国务院或者经国务院授权的省、自治区、直辖市人民政府"可以改变其他法律中有关行政职权的设定，并且没有一部法律专门对城管执法范围予以明确规定，现行职能基本上都是"借法执法"，因而城管执法主体资格和法律地位存在先天不足[①]。甚至有学者认为，城管执法是一种与法治行政原则相冲突的改革，违背了法治行政原则关于"职权法定"、"越权无效"的基本要求，

---

① 饶雷际、秦玮：《论城管执法权来源的非法性　江南大学学报》（人文社会科学版），2010年06期。

直言非理性狂潮极有可能导致既定的法治秩序遭受重创①。

在这些争议中，既有呼吁借鉴国外经验，改革现行城管制度弊端的，也不乏主张看清与国外的差距，取消城管机构彻底另寻他途者。我们在后文中还会进一步加以整理和探讨。

---

① 杨海坤、章志远：《中国行政法基本理论研究》，北京大学出版社 2004 年版，第 312—313 页。

第三节　问题及其产生的原因

对城管机构所取得的治理成效，社会层面大多持认可态度。但作为相对集中行政处罚权制度在城市管理领域的一次尝试，本就不可避免地存在一些先天不足，加之具体执法时持续暴露的问题，城管始终不能正名其应有的价值与地位。面对社会转型的大趋势和大环境，在服务型政府理念的指引下，离打造服务型城管究竟还有多远？要弄清楚这个问题，首先需要挖掘、梳理现行城管执法制度及城管机构本身到底存在哪些问题？这其中，有多少属于外部性，多少属于内部性？多少受客观因素制约，多少是主观原因影响？有多少是可逆性的，又有多少是不可逆转的？

一、城管执法面临的问题

（一）法律依据先天不足

在城管面对的所有问题或者说困境中，遭受最多质疑，引起最大尴尬的，就是前文一度提及的，城管执法机构始终没有获得明确的法律地位。

从执法依据来看，《行政处罚法》只规定了实施相对集中行政处罚权制度的原则，但因为没有《组织法》保障，导致相配套的、细化的城市管理行政执法的相关法规缺失。虽然部分拥有地方立法权的城市为之制定了地方法规①，但从 1997 年第一个综合执法试点建立至今，仍没有一部全国性的城市管理综合行政执法法规。城管执法依据颇为复杂，既有全国人大及其常委会通过的法律、国务院制定的行政法规及国务院部委制定的规章和省级人大、政府发布的地方性法规、规章及政策性文件，也有各地方政府出台的红头文件，或者是来自市容、市政、环保、工商、公安等部门的部分边缘性法律法规，甚至存在没有依据的执法行为。这些法律、法

---

① 截至 2007 年底数据，拥有地方立法权的 80 个城市中，仅有 38 个城市制定了《实施城市管理相对集中行政处罚权办法》，占总数 47.5%，包括北京、上海、天津、安徽、南宁、青岛等。

规、规章尚有不尽完善之处，相互不一致或只有禁止条款而无处罚细则，同一违法行为依据不同法规可能产生不同的法律责任，因而操作性差，无形中也增加了执法难度。

从机构设立来看，有人指城管机构的设立没有经过全国人大的立法程序，只是依据国务院有关文件，其法律地位不确定、不稳固，随时面临被取缔或与相关部门重新合并的可能。另外，中国行政机构体制的设置，一般遵循"区县等省市，省市看中央"这样一种自上而下的惯性：国务院设置一个新的部门，地方各级政府才对应设置独立的工作部门，所有行政机关中仅有行政（政务）审批服务中心和城管执法机构属于例外。许多地方根本没有给予城管机关行政主体资格，而是将其界定为事业组织，上海等地更是给予其第三种定性——一个介于行政机关和事业单位之间的行政事务执行机构。城管机构缺乏作为一个行政主体所应有的配置和功能，在中央、省级层面上都没有传统意义上的主管部门，也就处于没有足够的制度和体制支持的尴尬境地。①

（二）职能权限模糊不清

规范行政执法活动，首先应当规范其作为执法依据的法律规章。前文已指出，虽然中央和地方政府陆续出台了一系列文件，不断确立城管执法工作的法律地位，但期间探索与试验的色彩仍很浓郁，也就谈不上完善。

首先，权力配置不合理，执法位置处于"夹心层"。对于城管机构与其他行政执法部门间的行政处罚权的权利配置，相关规定笼统含糊，没有界定应该包括哪些领域的哪些事项，也缺乏具体明确的列举，导致城管成立之初的职能划分就缺乏严谨的科学论证，所谓相对集中，只是一些零散琐碎、繁杂无序的执法事项的简单归并。实际结果就是，各部门把最难管、最不愿管的事权和小权剥离出来，而依然保留实权和大权，城管机构则负担其那些"不该管、不好管、不能管"的事项，其执法对象必然主要集中于底层民众和社会弱势群体。

其次，权限规定不清晰，执法范围可随意增减转移。法规依据不统一客观上造成行政处罚实施范围难以规范，以至地方政府可随意为城管设定"执法"权限，执法范围不断膨胀，从驱逐小贩到拆除广告牌，从查处违建到拆迁，但凡属于"城市管理"范畴的，几乎被一网打尽。在某种意义上，城管机构已成为地方政府实施管理理念，执行管理意志最为便捷有力的"工具"。此时还没有接触的行政管理领域，彼时就可能因一纸红文

① 王仰文：《城市管理行政执法实践难题的化解之道》，《前沿》2011 年 15 期。

而被授权，反过来，取消某项权限也只需一纸红文。以北京为例，宣武区城管监察大队成立之始，城管仅承担市容环境、无照商贩、违章建筑等5项基本职能，此后每当城市管理中出现新的问题，城管的职能范围就可能面临扩张。2002年时扩大为8项职能105项行政处罚权，随后又增至13大类共285项行政处罚权。时至今日，北京城管机构已经集市容环卫、园林绿化、道路交通、停车、施工现场、城市河湖、黑车等共计14个方面、300余项职能于一身，几乎无所不包，无处不管。随着城市化的不断推进，地方城管机构的职能必然随之加强，执法职权也将相应增加。而且，各地方城管的职权范围差异较大，很容易形成对城管混乱定位的认知。

再次，职权分割仍有交叉，造成新的权力分散。分析中发现，城管执法行为涉及的职权类型，不仅包括行政处罚权的集中，还包括行政管理权、许可权、强制执行权、征收权、检查权、强制措施权、合同权、立法权等众多的行政职权。各地方政府还根据城市不同的管理强度和具体要求，将城管处罚权的内容扩大到了建筑业、国土资源、风景名胜等城市建设和管理领域，有的甚至延伸到文化稽查、卫生监督、爱国卫生、客运管理等方面，与卫生、规划、园林、工商、交管等部门均形成了"交叉地带"。

《国务院关于进一步推进相对集中行政处罚权工作的决定》（国发〔2002〕17号）规定：行政处罚权相对集中后，有关部门如果仍然行使已被调整出的行政处罚权，所作出的行政处罚决定一律无效，还要依法追究该部门直接负责的主管人员和其他直接责任人员的法律责任。但实际操作中，往往同一领域内的同一种权力，仍由多个行政执法部门行使。例如，对闹市各种噪声污染的处理目前仍由多个执法主体行使处罚权：户外噪声污染的处罚权由城管机构行使，但要由环保部门技术检测后再决定是否处罚，决定权在环保部门；室内噪声污染属工商、文化、环保部门；娱乐场所则属于公安部门管辖。又比如城市规划方面的处罚权，多按"以批为界"的原则划分，像对侵占城市道路的行政处罚权，就"以路沿石为界"，出现了"一房两拆"、"一路两治"的纠结局面，容易形成执法误区，出现新的执法交叉或执法真空（选择性执法）现象。如此，非但未能减少和归并执法主体，反而分裂出新的执法部门，不仅增加了部门间行政协调的几率和负担，提高了行政成本，同时也降低了执法效率。北京市政协完成的一份调研报告中显示，经过2002、2004—2005年的两次大规模扩权，北京城管的执法职权达到311项，管理的内容越庞杂，职责交叉的现象就越普遍，执法"力不从心"的感觉也就越强烈，仅街面上市容环境、工商管理、交通管理三项，就占用了城管工作量的近 90%，对于其他领域的履职精力明显不足。

（三）专业执法无法实现

现代社会各领域的发展都以专业化为趋势，按照这一原则，城市管理也应根据具体部门的专业特长划分执法职能，但作为改革先锋的城管机构，却恰恰未能做到这一点。

（1）缺乏独立运作的各项保障

在城管机构主体资格尚不明确的情况下，国办发〔2000〕63 号文件中对集中行使行政处罚权的部门的机构设置要求没有彻底实现，多数城市没有将城管机构设为本级政府的行政机关，而是以城市建设管理监察支（大）队名义运作，人员编制、经费预算等方面的需求也得不到有效满足，"不利于行政权的行使和行政权权威的体现"[①]。

行政执法工作是实行权力强制的管理工作，对人员素质要求较高，执法人员在某种程度上已成为政府形象的代言人。但各地城管执法队伍人员组成相当复杂，大多数地区城管人员属于事业单位编制，还有部分临时聘请的协管人员。如苏州市城管部门除局机关人员是公务员外，其余 420 名编制全部是"参照公务员管理的事业编制"；湖北天门市城管局机关只有 15 名行政编制的工作人员，属公务员，下属 80 余名执法人员全部属事业编制。城管机构编制不明确、人员资格规定不严格，导致人员素质整体过低，执法观念落后，在社会上造成了相当大的负面影响。

在经费上，城管机构也没有国家统一的财政保障，其经费供给体制实行的是"以块管理，分级负担"的地方财政管理体制。某些地区经费困难，造成城管执法装备不足，甚至办公用品和执法设施也相当缺乏。这既影响了本应是行政主体的城管机关所应享有的行政受益权，更直接导致国务院文件规定的收支两条线的约束失效，大多数城管实行收支一条线，执法队伍自行收支，以收费和罚没收入补充经费不足，形成"吃饭财政"、"自费财政"，权力寻租现象层出不穷。

编制、经费问题上的空缺，使原本就只有一个原则性规定的城管行政主体资格缺乏有力的物质保障。另外，某些专业性强的领域也会导致城管执法低效。各部门移交的部分执法权限中包含了一些对专业要求较高的领域，如环境保护、城市规划等，其审查和鉴别需要依赖专业技术鉴定，但"被划转处罚权的部门要将相应的编制、人员、经费、装备器材一并移交

107

---

① 关保英：《执法与处罚的行政权重构》，法律出版社 2004 年版。

城管监察组织"① 的要求实际上未曾实现，相关鉴定机构又大多隶属于行政职能机关，易引发行政相对人对鉴定结论的不信任感，也使得行政职能机关对城管执法仍有较大的主导性。在这些范围内，城管执法的主动性和专业性都必然大打折扣。

（2）与其他行政组织关系不顺

城市管理是一项复杂的系统工程，单纯依赖处罚无法保障其有序发展，相较行政规划、许可、指导等手段，行政处罚只是一种后置程序。按规定，城管机构仅相对集中了部分处罚权，在具体执法过程中，必然依赖于其他执法机关的配合与保障。举例来说，工商部门具有许可营业行为的行政许可权，所以原本被赋予了查处无照经营的权力，但被转移至城管机构后，查处无照经营经常需要工商部门的确认。诸如此类的情形大量存在于城管执法行为中，导致城管机构必然与其他部门频繁进行"联合执法"，才能确保其执法威慑力和有效性。

进一步分析，一项具体的行政管理活动，其行政管理权和处罚权多是相互依存、相互制约的，旧的行政管理习惯和管事职能的分散，客观上就存在协调难，加之缺乏必要的统筹规划和综合协调机制，事权、财权又过于集中在"条条"管理上，区、街往往责大权小，难以起到协调作用。另一方面，受目前机构设置所限，城管机构法律地位不被大众认可，在与其他部门的协调机制上处于相对弱势地位，有些部门对城管工作不支持、不配合，个别甚至采取不通报审批事项、不协同认定违法事实等手段予以抵制。因此，跨系统部门运作的难度极大。正如一位城管执法人员所说："比如占道经营屡罚难禁，店外归城管负责，店内由工商监管。城管来了，经营者搬进屋；工商来了，再搬到屋外。结果是城管、工商都没法管，店照旧开张。""再比如拆除违建，这边刚下达了《拆违通知书》，那边却以违建为营业地址发放了执照。各部门配合起来不容易，执法难度可想而知。"

（四）手段单一程序复杂

城管执法面对的违法行为一般具有几个特点。一是普遍性，指违法违章现象普遍存在，点多线长面广。二是不可预见性，指时间、空间上都具有不确定性，几乎无规律可循，随时随地都可能发生。三是反复性，也是最重要的特征，在多种因素的影响下，违法行为常表现出多发性、反复性和经常性，大多无法彻底解决。这一点集中表现在几个方面：一是流动摊

① 《北京市人民政府关于进一步推进城市管理领域相对集中行政处罚权工作的决定》［2002］24 号文。

点难禁止，众多无证商贩适时流动设摊，因大多使用三轮车、农用车等，机动性强，逃逸方便，执法人员不追难以达成执法效果，追则易酿成社会问题；二是违章建筑难拆除，与前者同属城管执法的老大难问题，违法建筑的投入与拆除难度成正比，投入越多，拆除难度越大，且认定、拆除的程序复杂，耗时长；三是五小行业难治理，餐饮、加工、洗车、修理、娱乐等行业，存在规划滞后、卫生差、污染重、投诉多、安全隐患等问题，从业者流动性大，法律意识淡薄，也难以实现长效管理。

与执法对象的复杂性问题相比，城管机构现行的执法方式体系，经过多年实践也逐渐显现出一些弊端。

（1）方式单一，存在操作真空

其他政府职能部门如公安、工商、交通等，法律赋予了其行政许可、强制、处罚、指导、给付等综合性职权帮助履行某一方面职能，与之相对的是，城管机构履行的是综合职能，行使的却是单一职权，甚至还不完整。单处罚权就包括行为罚（吊销执照、驾驶证等）、声誉罚（批评教育）、财产罚（罚款）和人身自由罚[①]，最后一项只能由公安机关和法院执行，而另一项最有效、最有针对性的行为罚也没有移交城管部门。城管常用的执法方式有教育、整改、暂扣、罚款、申请法院强制、恢复原状等，要通过行使有效手段迫使执法对象服从处罚，必须获得公安机关和行政许可、审批部门的实质性配合，但实现概率极小。违法者不执行处罚决定时，城管机构也无强制执行权，案件办结周期长，难以达到及时纠正违法行为的要求，甚至会助长违法者的持续违法行为。

权力没有随职能进行调整转移，现行执法方式不能适用所有管理任务，造成执法效率低下，甚至存在操作真空。比如，执法相对人没有暂扣物或相对人消失的，相对人或违法行为具有隐蔽性不便于巡查的，都构成了城管执法的死角。

（2）程序繁琐，成本高效率低

规范执法程序的必要性不容置疑，但实际过程往往是程序与实践脱节，手续步骤繁杂而徒耗精力，制式化管理偏于封闭和理论化，无形中将执法主体与执法对象推向了二元对立的局面。

举例来说，在店铺外堆放杂物，根据《广州市市容环境卫生管理规

[①] 《行政处罚法》规定的行政处罚种类包括："（一）警告；（二）罚款；（三）没收违法所得、没收非法财物；（四）责令停产停业；（五）暂扣或者吊销许可证、暂扣或者吊销执照；（六）行政拘留；（七）法律、行政法规规定的其他行政处罚。"

定》的要求，执法人员发现违规行为后，第一步：对店主说明情况，进行教育提出要求。第二步：开出《责令限期改正通知书》限期清理，要求相对人在文书上签字；如拒签则找证人签字证实。第三步：如相对人拒不改正，就对物品实施暂扣处理，开出《暂扣物品通知书》和《财务收据》，要求相对人签字；如不签字，仍需找证人签字；相对人不配合甚至暴力抗法，理论上要对相对人进行法律制裁，但实际能执行的极少。第四步：相对人凭暂扣单前往接受处理，执法人员确认后开出处罚单，相对人交完罚款（简易程序个人 50 元以下，单位 1000 元以下可直接交；一般程序到银行交）后，签字确认拿回暂扣物品才算结案。如相对人不来接受处理，执法人员只能申请法院强制执行。① 但如前文所说，这种方式同样难以实现。

专栏案例：人行道违规停车处理权交接对执法方式的启示

1999 年 9 月 5 日，广州市政府发布《关于整治市区人行道违章停放车辆的通告》，决定由城管执法部门负责人行道违章停放车辆的执法工作。而从 2005 年 7 月 10 日凌晨零点起，该职能又移交回广州交警部门。

分析其原因：一为法律依据不足，《中华人民共和国道路交通安全法》没有明确规定城管对人行道车辆乱停放具有拖车执法权，城管拖车的合法性受到质疑；二是按《道路交通安全法》规定，城管要自行承担拖车费用：行人道车辆乱停放处罚 200 元，拖车费用接近 100 元，执法成本太高；三为执法方式落后、效率低，一个班组一上午只能拖几台车，而人行道停车一个辖区一天有几十甚至上百台，无法及时全部处理。交还给交警部门后，再做一下对比：城管能采用的执法方式是暂扣——拖车，一个班组一班次只能暂扣几台次；交警则是对乱停放车辆拍照取证，填发《违章通知书》，也可现场免填，车主自动到相关部门接受处理，一个班组一班次可现场拍摄成百上千台。

同一案例，执法主体或方式不同，执法成本、执法效率的差别极为明显。但其实，城管部门只需与政府相关部门达成一致，由其执法人员拍照取证后，将违章车辆照片交给交警部门，其后按照交通违规正常程序处理即可。

---

① 林启迪：《城市管理执法方式变革研究——以广州城市管理综合执法为例》2009 年 4 月。

（五）暴力执法与柔性执法的困境

因暴力执法、暴力抗法导致的重大恶性案件，是直接影响社会各界对城管机构及执法人员主观印象和评价的关键因素，我们将其单独抽离加以分析说明。

（1）城管执法中的暴力行为

城管执法中的暴力行为一般有两种表现形式，即暴力执法行为和暴力抗法行为，最常出现在城管执法人员与无证流动摊贩的博弈现场。

治理流动摊贩是城管的重要职责之一，但由于摊贩群体"弱势"的特性使得城管在执法时往往有所顾虑，而且摊贩的流动特性也极易造成"你进我退，你退我进"的游击战局面。2011年5月9日，小贩夏俊峰因刺死城管以故意杀人罪被判处死刑，裁定一经公布，城管再次被推向舆论的风口浪尖。而在此之前，城管人员暴力执法、执法对象暴力抗法的事件早已屡见报端，从数量到影响程度一度有不断增长的趋势，甚至有些个体事件还演变为群体事件，导致社会矛盾进一步激化。北京市政协的调研报告显示，2008年至2010年间，全市共发生阻碍执法、造成城管队员人身伤害案件198起，其中无照游商158起，占总数的79.8%。

这里就以无照游商为例概括一下，除大众接受的相关法律机制不健全、城管执法程序不规范、执法人员素质低下、舆论偏颇误导等原因之外，导致暴力事件不断发生的其他因素。

（2）导致暴力行为出现的原因

首先，流动摊贩的存在有其必然性。改革开放后，二元分隔对立的社会结构逐渐被打破，城市的财富聚集效应不断显现，吸引着农村剩余劳动力不断向城市转移。与此同时，随着市场经济的形成，城市中也出现了大量失业人口。二者基本都属于就业弱势群体的范畴，且数量远超过城市对劳动力的吸纳能力，无法进入正规就业部门，只能转向非正规就业部门寻求机会。摊贩经营以其独特的经营特点吸引着越来越多的人加入其中，于是城市流动摊贩的数量逐年增加。他们其实是经济、社会和文化发展处于转轨、转型期的必然产物：一方面与市民生活息息相关，为市民购买廉价物品和享受便利服务提供了条件，另一方面也缓解了部分下岗工人、外来务工者的就业压力，减轻了社会负担。对于多数流动摊贩来说，生存是其最迫切的需求，一旦其权益有可能遭受较大的损失，不论城管是以哪种方式执法，都必然遭遇到强烈的阻力和反抗。

其次，执法方式赋予不足。暂扣执法相对人的物品和工具，是目前城管所能采用的最主要、最有效的执法方式。但这几乎是唯一带有强制性的执法手段，却成为暴力事件不断出现的重要原因之一。一方面，暂扣方式实施的前提，是决定对同一种违法行为采取不同执法方式。城管执法人员只有对物的暂扣权，而没有对相对人争抢违法行为物品和工具甚至暴力抗法的拘留权，易于形成双重标准，如力量足够控制现场就实施暂扣行为；如不能，就采用教育和整改方式，于是形成城管队伍"欺软怕硬"、"主观执法"的负面形象。另一方面，暂扣方式本就容易导致争抢。一般执法人员会做出前期的教育和整改，但相对人少有主动配合，大部分选择躲避或争抢物品和工具甚至暴力抗法。其结果有二：一是执法人员占上风，经争抢后把物品搬上车，二是执法人员力量不够，在争抢中失去暂扣物导致行为失败。无论哪种结果，暂扣方式从本质上就离不开争抢的过程，这也是导致执法暴力的直接诱因。

（3）柔性执法的失效危机

城管制度自登上历史舞台以来，一方面面对政府和公众对良好城市环境秩序的需求，一方面是社会公众对弱势群体的同情，政府对社会稳定的重视。城管在政府内部各种压力以及社会舆论的"夹板"中左右为难。在学者提炼、媒体渲染和社会偏见等多重作用下，迫使不少地方较为仓促地推出了又一波改革举动，文明执法、柔性执法的呼吁似乎开始成为现实。我们在城市街头的调研中也确实验证了这一点，流动商贩大多承认，"城管最近好像是文明多了，不怎么追赶，也很少查抄东西了"。于是，大家欢欣鼓舞，认为已经找到城管执法制度改革的方向。

但事实果真如此？恐怕也不尽然。不知什么时候开始，柔性执法又被冠之以"不作为"的标签。那么，症结究竟在哪里？

暴力抗法根源于社会矛盾的复杂化和城管执法强制力的缺陷，而违法成本低、处罚力度弱则是暴力抗法行为漫延的重要推手。无照商贩与城管执法人员的摩擦频繁发生，暴力抗法出现的频率较高，城管执法人员没有拘留权，可依靠的警察部门又只能处理城管部门与相对人发生的治安事件，导致执法程序常因暴力抗法而被迫终止，结果助长了执法相对人的抗法行为。再有，公安执法遭遇暴力事件有袭警罪一说，而城管遭遇的暴力抗法行为往往被定性为民事纠纷。在目前公众法制观念仍较淡薄，信用体系尚未建立，公民社会意识没有真正形成的社会大环境下，一味压缩执法空间而不赋予其更丰富有效的执法手段，必然造成城管执法的"束手束脚"，面对"游击经验"丰富的"钉子户"和有恃无恐的反抗者，不仅无法遏止违法行为，反而进一步影响了城市形象和政府威信。因此，单向式"柔性执法"的强力推进，使得此消彼长之下，城管执法又陷入了新的尴尬境地。

当然，文明执法确是时代的要求和大势所趋，摒弃粗暴简单的执法手段和方式，依法文明执法是所有行政执法部门必须做到的基本准则，文明也不代表软弱和放纵，而是一种态度，尊重他人也尊重自己的态度。但现实中，任何一种执法行为，或者说文明执法行为，都需要满足两个前提条件，一是理论层面上，要尽可能消减违法行为萌芽、传播的环境和途径，二是实践操作中，必须有具体可行的处罚细则和强而有力的执法手段。后者也是实施城市管理工作最直接、最有效的保障，失去它，文明执法只能沦为空谈。

二、地方创新及其效果

（一）地方创新与尝试

近两年，各地方除推行"柔性执法"重塑城管形象外，各种或大或小的创新与尝试也"生生不息"，大致归纳后，主要可分为以下几种类型：

（1）设立城市管理警察

西方学界普遍认为城市管理行政执法的任务应主要由警察承担，因此西方国家警察的职能几乎包括了我国城管的大部分职责，例如法国城市管理就是由警察和宪警依照法律进行。

早在几年前就有某市人大代表提出，应借鉴国际主流模式，由警察从事城市管理工作。持这一观点的人认为，增加城管警察不仅能有效减少暴力抗法，执法人员在暴力抗法中被动挨打的尴尬局面也能得到根本解决，从而提高执法效率。对此，一些地方城市尝试让城管接受军训，也有地方想把城管纳入警察序列。如长沙市设立了城管公安队伍，专门处理暴力抗法问题；广州市出台了"大部制"改革方案，在市公安局治安管理支队设立城市管理特勤大队，配合、协助城市管理执法，还给队员配备了防刺背心和手套；2012 年 8 月 1 日，号称中国首个"城管武装部"在武汉汉阳区城管局成立，而此前，浙江省宁波市海曙区城管局、江苏省高邮市城管局、河北省张家口市桥西区城管局、江西省南昌市安义县城管局、浙江省宁波市北仑区城管局等都早已相继成立了武装部。相关人士认为，成立武装部有利于执法队伍素质进一步提升，组织纪律性、身体素质、应急能力均会强于一般城管队员，出现急难险重等特殊情况时，他们是民兵抢险队伍中的尖兵；城管工作出现难题时，他们又是执法者中的突击队，能应对复杂局面。

（2）服务外包，物业进城管

公共服务外包，是近年来颇为流行的一项新的制度尝试。2007 年，深圳市宝安区西乡街道首创城管服务外包模式，初始目的是为解决综合执法中人手不足的问题，以民间力量充当"城市保姆"，购买社会服务，其后逐步形成"政府主导、企业协同、公众参与"的格局并在全市推广，至今已有 35 家公司参与城管服务外包，共雇用了 3204 名协管员。目前，有不少城市开始尝试将某些城市管理服务外包给物业公司，实行市场化运作、社会化管理的"物业进城管"模式，如安徽宣城市、郑州市金水区花园路等地将市政道路清扫保洁、市容环境维护等工作"外包"。这其中，物业公司的职责是依合同约定提供城市管理服务，服务购买方——城市管理部门对服务提出质量要求并加以监督规范。这一模式的出现，源于越来越多的人已经意识到，政府公职部门的单维度管理方式，已无法适应中国日趋复杂、多变的社会现状，政府职能转型，权力下放、部分剥离甚至将职能有规划地转至社会力量完成，这也是构筑现代型政府的基本趋势。

城管外包对提高服务效能的确能起到一些积极效果，一是城管机构转任"裁判者"角色，可以避免与商贩间的直接对立冲突，减少暴力行为的出现；二是将部分职能剥离后，可以将释放出的力量投入到其他社会化管理职能中，弥补以往无力顾及的执法领域。同时，运用得当的话，在促进就业、压缩成本等方面也有不小的助益。

（3）标准化执法模式

标准化执法模式，是由西安市莲湖区城管执法局首先提出并在全市推广的，意图以程序法规范执法行为，用细化的标准压缩自由裁量权的"弹性空间"，通过司法的最终强制力和违法成本的付出实现长效管理。[①]

其一，标准化探索执法不公的解决之道。2009 年初以来，莲湖区城管局对城管涉及的 40 多部法律、法规和规章进行全面梳理、整合，制定了《城管执法行政处罚自由裁量权细化标准》，对工作中常见的 72 种违法行为在法定裁量幅度内细化成 2—4 个档次，细化处罚标准 620 条，最大幅度地压缩了行政处罚权的"弹性空间"。同时，依靠综合信息管理系统进行案件质量监控，处理过程中各执法关键点上能做到类似案件相同处理，较好地解决了处罚中的不公与不合理问题。

其二，实行"四权分离"，即检查权、调查权、处罚权、强制权相分

---

① 杨小军：《城管执法制度创新与分析 》，行政管理改革》2011 年第 4 期。

离，改变过去随意执法的现象。具体包括：立案督办中心履行检查权，统一搜集案源线索；中队根据督办的任务依法行使调查权，不得随意对督办外内容进行选择性检查；三级审查行使处罚决定权，中队法制员、案件审理中心和分管领导按照权限对各环节进行审查；法院行使最终强制权，进行前置司法审查。

为保证行政处罚的执行力，莲湖区还引入"司法强制"程序，依托莲湖区法院成立全国第一家城管巡回法庭，实行非诉案件申请法院强制执行，其极大地提高了城管处罚决定的执行力。

（4）"大城管"模式

由住建部提倡的"大城管"模式，是在地方政府机构改革和大部制改革背景下产生的一种综合管理体制，由市长任"一把手"，统筹各职能部门成立城管委，打破部门界限，把城管的管理权和执行权统一在一起。近年来，这一改革方案逐渐在包括北京、南京、广州、武汉在内的城市推行开来。

2007年，北京市崇文区城管就开始推行"大城管"和"综合执法机制"。全区7个街道办事处分别成立综合行政执法组，城管、公安、工商、民政、劳动和社会保障等25个执法部门派专人到各街道办事处上班，街道办主任担任执法组组长，"全权、全责、全时"处理辖区内的所有城市管理问题。同时联合劳动保障、民政等部门，通过一系列措施解决弱势群体的生存难题，包括设立便民服务临时市场，让无照商贩"合法"、规范经营；采取岗位支持、适地安置、联合救助、就业帮助等措施，推出"创业者俱乐部"模式等等。

相较之下，顺义模式更具有"大监察"的特征。2009年，顺义城管大队升格为"顺义区城市管理监察局"，将监察作为工作重点。一是对政府等各管理层级主管人员履行职能的监察，将存在的问题向相关主管领导发送《告知书》，规定期限内未解决的发送《责令改正通知书》，直至按行政不作为移交区监察局进行处理。二是出台《顺义区委顺义区政府关于加强违法建设查处工作的实施意见》，区长担任工作组组长，城管牵头协调各部门履行查处违建的监察职能；供水、供电、供气、供热、电信等部门切断对违建的服务；公安、工商等部门不办理从事生产、经营活动的相关手续。三是实行24小时不间断管控，主要大街每30分钟巡查不少于一次，发现问题后成立案件处理组，实行巡查和处理问题相分离。

（5）其他尝试

联合国《经济、社会、文化权利公约》明确规定，"人人应有机会凭其自由选择和接受的工作来谋生的权利"。保障小商贩的经营权是很多国家的通行做法。英国地方政府把摊贩的经营街道分为三类：严格禁止经营的、同意经营的和可颁发经营许可证的街道；法国巴黎对跳蚤市场（flea-market，旧货地摊市场的别称）的管理，是将市区在一周时间内分别辟为举办跳蚤市场的地点，相关的交通管制提前公布，定时、定地、轮流举办。

打击"无照商贩"一直就是中国城管的主要职责，针对这一顽疾，各地也都做了一些尝试。湖北宜昌、山东聊城等市的城管局长出任了由市长为主任的"城市规划委员会"委员，有助于避免城市基础设施规划的先天不足，从源头上减少社会矛盾。除此之外，各地也在尽力为小商小贩拓展生存空间。比如，厦门市城管局对占道经营者进行集中宣传劝导，并采取"疏堵结合"的办法，划出一些场所设立临时"摊归点"，采取"定点、定时、定范围、定责任"的管理模式；淮安市城管局设置了遍布城区的定时定点便民摊点，重点关照残疾人、下岗工人、低保户、失地进城农民等弱势群体；保定市城管局对进城售卖自产自销农产品的农民实行"不扣、不罚、疏导、指导、服务"五项惠民管理原则；宜昌市城管局对菜市场进行标准化改造，建夜市城便于摊点集中规范经营等。

（二）实际效果评估

上述方式，由于这样或那样的原因，如执法成本高、执法漏洞多、可持续性差等，均未能在全国范围内加以推广。甚至可以判断，直至目前，也还没能真正形成一套高效、实用、彻底解决城管执法难题的制度或模式。

首先是城管警察模式面对的质疑和阻力：一是城管人员列入警察编制会导致警察队伍过分膨胀，甚至成为"警察国家"，包括个体商户在内的市民的权利诉求更可能被城管的话语霸权压制。二是有人指出，城管不少职权是从其他部门划分出来的，很多不属于传统警察的职权范围，如淄博市在市、区分别设立城市管理警察支队、大队，但其职责只是"处理以侮辱、威胁或者暴力方式妨碍、阻挠城市管理行政执法的行为"，并不直接行使城管职权。甚至有人主张，国外没有城管一说，公安警察才是城市管理执法的真正主体，设立"城管公安"授予其权力之后，大可取消城管机构，让公安配合、协助城管执法是本末倒置，多此一举。

其次是外包模式同样陷入两难境地，"一包了事"、"不如不包"的对立情绪又有蔓延之势。曾被视为革新之举的这一模式，就在其发源地深圳遭遇了一波接一波的攻击：涉黑人员利用制度漏洞，借城管外衣肆意敲诈勒索、非法执法，加之越权执法、"山寨执法车"等多起恶性事件，使得城管形象再次受到损害。以至一度有消息称，在深圳运行5年之久的城管外包制度将退出历史舞台。市城管局法制处针对开展的调研发现，服务外包领域缺乏准入、退出和监督机制，管理部门对此类外包企业的资质要求没有明确规定，外包协议不规范、不透明，对外包企业或协管员违规行为也缺乏监管和强制性的惩罚措施。

再如"大城管"改革，在正视城管合法性问题上有其进步意义，也产生了客观效果，但仍存在一些隐忧。像"崇文模式"，其整合执法力量所能达到的效果远高于救助就业生存。弱势群体面临的困境各不相同，其需求内容和层次也有差异，绝非某个区级政府或部门就能轻易解决的。如执法力量增强，救助效果却流于形式，又会出现什么局面？至于"顺义模式"，则因为现实中各地城管队伍与部门、街道在人财物方面的牵绊而难以复制，正如一些前往参观学习的城管大队队长所说，"没有可操作性"。更本质的问题是，在没有真正明确部门职能和权力界限的情况下，大城管格局只能是对原有职能进行适当归并，甚至可能诱发更加激烈的法律冲突。

因此，尽管各地政府在体制、机制、设置等方面都进行了诸多的创新与尝试，但似乎都是走一条"曲线救国"的改良式推进道路，而非根源上的改革，因而始终只能治标而非治本。城管执法面临的深层次矛盾依然清晰，没有从根本上摆脱管理危机和信任危机。每当发生负面事件，舆论在强烈谴责过后，几乎又无一例外地将矛头指向了城管机构的合法性问题上。

三、城管执法困境的深层次原因

（一）城市化速度与城市管理矛盾

"城管问题是中国在城市化进程中所遇到的特有问题。"

城管问题不仅是一个体制改革的问题，甚至也不仅是一个城市管理的问题，更是一个应当考虑的社会改革问题。

自20世纪八九十年代开始至今的中国社会转型是重大的时代命题，这一场在速度、广度、深度、难度和向度方面都是前所未有的转型，带来了全面、快速的变革。尤其自20世纪90年代中期以来，社会结构出现急剧变化，利益格局分化日趋明显，"全国一盘棋"的区域格局被打破，以地方行政机构为代表的地方社区开始成为利益主体。利益的再分配趋势和意识观念的多元冲击，使得社会意识和结构都处于一个相对多元化的阶段。

　　基于这样的背景下，中国的城市发展日新月异，但市场经济和计划经济接轨期固有的矛盾和遗留问题，导致由之而来的社会冲突和社会问题频现，其中，城市管理领域遭受的冲击尤为突出，局面日趋复杂。比如流动人口激增、下岗失业工人增加、农民工大量涌进城市、交通堵塞、环境恶化，城市区域迅速扩大，形成大批"城市里的村庄"，城中村、城乡结合部等区域基础设施不完善、功能不健全，脏乱差难以有效治理等等，这都是城市管理者无法回避的问题。

　　"行政执法体制改革的契机来自政府与市场、政府与社会的关系的深度重构。"① 城市管理综合执法体制改革，一方面是顺应社会转型的要求，试图通过集中各专业部门的相关职能来解决政出多门、重复执法的弊端，精简机构又能提升效率；另一方面，这场改革其本身就是一个急剧分化与多元并存的试验过程，随着社会转型的逐步深入，明显表现出应对失措、准备不足，因而暴露出许多预料中和意料外的问题。正如有学者②所言，在推进城市化和市场经济建立的过程中，农村和城市的分界线被打破，行政管理体制表现出不适应，城管综合执法应运而生，且处于矛盾高发期，"难免要代人受过，代其他部门受过"。

　　城管执法人员面对的执法对象大多是农村进城务工人员或者其他失去生活来源的"弱势群体"。针对这一难题，"大城管"理念的设计者——《中国城市管理体制及其运行机制研究》课题组也曾提出，"城管应该管也只能管城市基础功能和城市公共空间，而衍生功能即人类各种政治、经济、社会活动，则不应当由城管去管理"，"化解城市公共空间管理矛盾的关键点，在于给予弱势群体尽可能多的实际可分享空间"。《中国青年报》2007年初做的一项调查也显示：43.5%的公众"经常在街边小摊买东西"，51.2%的公众"偶尔买一些"，"从来不买"的只有5.4%；此外，70.6%的公众明确表示反对城管部门查抄小摊贩——因为"小摊贩给市民生活提供了极大便利！"③

　　法律的本质是协调社会关系，执法的目的是缓释社会矛盾。我们需要一个相对规范、有序的市场和生活环境，这就必然需要严格、规范的城市

---

　　① 张吕好：《城市管理综合执法的法理与实践》，《行政法学研究》2003年第3期。

　　② 张耘：北京市社会科学院管理所所长。

　　③ 王俊秀：《市在城先民为邦本——民意推着城管往前走》2008年12月4日。

管理执法。但在国家层面尚未做出全盘化考虑和完整的制度化设计的情况下，城管作为与百姓接触最多、最直接的政府部门，其工作难度之大自然可想而知。

（二）理念方式与体制机制问题

从某一角度来看，城管问题本质上是城市化、市场化、现代化过程中政府该做什么、不该做什么的问题。

（1）本位思想严重

我国一直实行政府对社会高度集中的管理模式：政府把对社会公共事务的管理与对政府内部的管理等同起来，也就是常说的"大政府、小社会"。再由于特定时期财税、干部体制以及中央与地方关系的设置，政府地方利益的形成并逐步强化已经成为现实。在一厢情愿的"为民做主"观念影响下和"官本位"思想的阻碍下，城市似乎脱离了发展的本质追求，往往以执政者为中心，出于各种意愿，按照个人或团体诉求施政执政，距离实际需求越行越远。从利益视角来看，政府作为公共权力机关，谋求的应当是社会公共利益，而不是自身的特殊利益。但是，按照公共选择理论，政府同样存在自利性：政府一旦形成，也是一个"经济人"，不仅其内部的官僚集团会有自己的利益，会追求自身利益的最大化，政府组织同样拥有自身的特殊利益，如特殊的政治地位、经济待遇和精神文化特权等。随着社会分工的发展，政府管理工作成为一种特殊的专业化、专门化工作，政府组织的特殊利益也就日益突出。这种自利性冲动碰撞到未改革到位的行政执法体制，导致行政执法队伍过度膨胀，管理部门职权交叉、执法分散、效率低下。

"城管的兴起是权力为了规避法律而催生的一种组织。可以这样理解，城管正是'单位人'思维在新社会中的形态化，人们试图用单位的管理模式（非法治模式）来管理'自由人'的城市，他们将城市当成了他们原来管理的单位。"[①] 虽然稍显偏激，但可谓一针见血地指出了城管制度产生的根本目的。

（2）管理理念滞后

与西方城市管理理论相比，我国城市管理理论的发展相对滞后，这也是城管执法实践久陷困境的一个重要原因。

城市管理必须不断满足和适应社会经济发展的需要。但是，受传统计划经济体制影响，对城市管理学的理解一直比较狭窄，把城市管理等同于

---

① 周永坤：《城管吓死人的制度性反思》。

市政管理，对地方政府职能和城市管理范畴都不能准确界定，城市管理行政执法缺乏宏观上的协调和统一，仍停留在各自为政的松散发展阶段，出现了"重经济扩张、轻社会管理"，"重建轻管"或"建管不分"等现象，越来越跟不上现代城市发展的节奏。

现代城市管理理论认为，"三分建设，七分管理"，城市管理不仅指市政管理，它贯穿于城市规划、建设和运行管理的全过程，城市规划和建设时离不开管理，规划、建设完成后同样离不开管理。前述流动商贩问题的根源之一，就是因前期城市规划视角狭隘、城市基础设施建设缺失而直接引发的。城市快速发展的过程中，一些地方热衷于见效快、政绩大的城市形象工程，在前期的城市规划忽视或者干脆无视对很多便民利民的基本设施的布局安排，或放任原有的设定在利益博弈中被强势集团侵占，不能满足不同层次民众的需求，导致民众生活不便、小商贩顺势而生。而城管机构，则无奈地成为了直接承担这一后果的委屈部门。

（3）体制机制不适

城管执法体制一些体制机制上的根源性问题，很多在前文中已经分别提及，这里再做一次补充和梳理。

首先，综合多家观点，认为目前城管体制的首要缺陷在其合法性不足[1]，主要表现为：权力来源上，其设立的法律依据与法治精神相冲突；权力主体上，城管行政主体资格缺乏法律保障；权力内容上，职权范围界定模糊；权力行使的程序和方式上，缺乏严密的法定规范。除此之外还需要指出的一点是，这一制度设定中，权力监督与救济形同虚设。

在我国，对行政权力的监督与救济主要有行政系统内部监督和司法监督两类，但城管法律地位的不明确使得监督制度难以落实，导致基本形同虚设。第一，行政系统内部的监督形同虚设：一是各地城管的领导体制各异，其上级机关也缺乏统一性，使得行政机关系统内部的监督机制难以发挥作用，行政复议更无法执行；二是原职权行政机关的监督也难实行。如果说城管职权出于行政授权，那原行政职权机关就没有监督权；如果定位为行政委托，又缺乏行政委托的合法依据和自主权。第二，表现在司法监督方面，同样由于城管机构法律地位不明确，导致行政相对人提起行政诉讼十分困难，司法监督成为口号。目前城管机构受到的监督主要来自于党的监督、新闻舆论监督和社会监督，但欠缺系统性和严密性，也缺乏相应的制约手段，不仅收效不高，且容易形成偏颇。

---

① 章志远：《相对集中行政处罚权改革之评述》，《中共长春市委党校学报》2006 年第 1 期，第 76—78 页。

其次，城管执法制度与现行的行政管理体制之间不协调。

城管机构属于地方政府，而不是省政府和中央政府，这导致很多人认为，城管执法事务应当属于市（县）地方事务、城市事务。但从立法规定的内容看，城管事务更符合行业管理事务的特征，即从中央到地方的事务。这样就出现了一个矛盾：城管机构管理着从中央到地方的事务，体制归属上却没有与之相协调。其他执法机构如规划、建设、道路交通、工商管理等，都可以自下而上地反映诉求，唯独城管机构一直存在着诉求难达上级政府和中央的困难，一般只能到达所在城市政府。这样一来，省政府和中央政府及其他部门决策时就可能忽略掉城管机构的利益，如编制、身份、执法手段、机构协调等。

近代以来西方国家行政改革成功的经验说明：行政改革必须在法治理念的指导下，先行立法，通过制定相应的改革法或组织法来规范行政改革，以保障改革的顺利进行。当前，我国城管执法领域出现的各种问题已经充分表明，从体制上解决城市管理行政执法领域中的实践难题迫在眉睫，甚至关系到社会稳定与发展的改革大局。

第四节　结语

　　"城管"只是城市管理体制中的一个方面，应该放在大环境中去研究，而不只是就城管来说城管。

　　城管执法是一个复杂的社会系统工程，包括城管执法的主体制度、程序制度、责任制度、监督制度、救济制度、评价制度等多个制度环节。为了解决城管执法中遇到的难点问题，大家开出的药方无非两种，要么取消城管，要么改革制度。但问题在于，在多个领域同时大转型的时代，如何才能设计出合理的制度，以保证精细化执法、制度化执法成为可能并具有可持续性？可以肯定的是，解决城管问题的方向，其实在城管制度之外。要破解城管执法过程中积累的诸多问题，就必须依法深化行政综合执法体制改革，探索建立与社会主义市场经济体制相适应的行政执法机制，提高行政执法的效率和水平。

　　简单地说，就是在城管仍将长期持续存在的前提下，给城管该有的权，让城管做能做的事，所谓的服务型城管才可能成为现实。

　　（本报告参与人员：指导：杨旭、袁崇法、白南风；写作：郑樱、田梅、安颀、刘至贺）

参考文献

周向阳：《城市管理行政执法制度的发展困境及解决对策》，《行政论坛》2011 年第 5 期。

第五部分 城市排行榜及部分城市数据

第一节 中国城市科学发展典范城市

排 名	城 市	排 名	城 市
1	杭州市	11	嘉兴市
2	无锡市	11	东营市
3	常州市	13	威海市
4	苏州市	14	沈阳市
5	珠海市	15	天津市
6	绍兴市	16	深圳市
7	大连市	17	厦门市
8	北京市	18	烟台市
9	上海市	19	青岛市
10	宁波市	19	武汉市

上述城市即为"中国城市科学发展综合评价（E&G）体系"综合排名前 20 位的城市。

第二节 中国城市科学发展典型城市

一、综合实力典型城市

排　名	城　市	排　名	城　市
21	长沙市	35	金华市
22	舟山市	37	芜湖市
23	马鞍山市	38	湖州市
24	鄂尔多斯市	39	铜陵市
24	淄博市	40	呼和浩特市
26	太原市	41	包头市
27	镇江市	42	乌海市
28	昆明市	43	唐山市
29	南京市	44	廊坊市
30	福州市	45	佛山市
31	济南市	46	辽阳市
32	中山市	47	龙岩市
33	广州市	47	克拉玛依市
34	晋城市	49	扬州市
35	南通市	50	阳泉市

　　上述城市即为"中国城市科学发展综合评价（E&G）体系"综合排名第21—50位的城市。

二、系统发展典型城市（三大母系统排名前50名城市）

经济发展水平系统

排　名	城　市	排　名	城　市
1	东营市	26	泰州市
2	苏州市	27	铁岭市
3	无锡市	28	宣城市
4	宁波市	29	淄博市
5	延安市	30	威海市
6	常州市	31	武汉市
7	泰安市	32	天津市
8	南通市	32	徐州市
9	青岛市	32	济宁市
10	台州市	35	龙岩市
11	扬州市	36	玉溪市
11	昆明市	37	大连市
13	沧州市	38	滨州市
13	潍坊市	39	邯郸市
15	晋城市	40	太原市
16	嘉兴市	41	朔州市
17	上海市	42	连云港市
18	绍兴市	43	湖州市
19	杭州市	43	许昌市
20	济南市	45	盐城市
21	廊坊市	46	丽水市
22	镇江市	47	石家庄市
23	金华市	48	福州市
24	聊城市	48	珠海市
25	烟台市	50	南京市

公共服务水平系统

排 名	城 市	排 名	城 市
1	北京市	26	呼和浩特市
2	杭州市	27	本溪市
3	广州市	27	济南市
4	珠海市	29	舟山市
5	大连市	30	抚顺市
6	沈阳市	30	长春市
6	克拉玛依市	30	常州市
8	上海市	33	太原市
9	铜陵市	34	马鞍山市
10	乌海市	35	东营市
10	厦门市	36	绍兴市
12	南京市	37	青岛市
13	天津市	38	深圳市
14	武汉市	39	西安市
15	包头市	40	鄂尔多斯市
15	无锡市	41	长沙市
17	威海市	42	白山市
18	宁波市	43	丹东市
18	攀枝花市	43	昆明市
20	嘉峪关市	45	淄博市
21	苏州市	46	阳泉市
22	烟台市	46	西宁市
23	呼伦贝尔市	48	辽阳市
23	芜湖市	49	鞍山市
25	盘锦市	50	嘉兴市

居民实际享有水平系统

排 名	城 市	排 名	城 市
1	东莞市	26	镇江市
2	杭州市	27	廊坊市
3	长沙市	27	韶关市
4	深圳市	29	佛山市
5	厦门市	30	江门市
6	鄂尔多斯市	31	广州市
7	中山市	32	长治市
8	绍兴市	32	芜湖市
9	珠海市	34	温州市
10	常州市	35	威海市
11	泉州市	36	晋城市
12	南通市	37	克拉玛依市
13	北京市	38	嘉峪关市
13	惠州市	39	淄博市
15	嘉兴市	40	漳州市
16	成都市	41	湖州市
17	鞍山市	42	盘锦市
18	沈阳市	43	太原市
19	福州市	43	合肥市
20	舟山市	45	东营市
21	大连市	46	长春市
22	马鞍山市	47	天津市
23	郑州市	48	肇庆市
24	苏州市	49	上海市
25	无锡市	50	莆田市

第三节　中国城市特色发展优势城市

一、经济增长效率优势城市

即经济发展总水平子系统排名前 10 名的城市：

城市	城市
杭州市	榆林市
唐山市	延安市
绍兴市	太原市
上海市	深圳市
呼和浩特市	西安市
淄博市	

二、居民收入统筹优势城市

即居民收入水平子系统排名前 10 名的城市：

城市	城市
深圳市	大连市
嘉兴市	南通市
杭州市	东莞市
广州市	天津市
盘锦市	绍兴市

三、要素利用效率优势城市

即发展要素利用效率子系统排名前 10 名的城市：

城市	城市
榆林市	铁岭市
泰州市	吉安市
延安市	吕梁市
盐城市	苏州市
金华市	宁德市

四、人居生活环境优势城市

即居民生活环境子系统排名前 10 名的城市：

城市	城市
河源市	厦门市
九江市	深圳市
景德镇市	杭州市
长沙市	青岛市
无锡市	银川市

五、外部效应调控优势城市

即发展外部效应子系统排名前 10 名的城市：

城市	城市
鹰潭市	日照市
铜陵市	曲靖市
莱芜市	铜川市
黄石市	鄂州市
阜阳市	昆明市

六、发展速度提升优势城市

即相较 2008 年排名增幅速度前 10 名的城市：

城市	城市
银川市	鹰潭市
石嘴山市	承德市
景德镇市	南昌市
邢台市	岳阳市
衡水市	汕尾市

第四节 2012年中国城市科学发展综合数据分析表（部分）

（综合指数排名为 1—50 位的城市）

一、城市经济发展水平母系统

1. 城市经济发展总水平子系统

二级指标		城市经济发展总水平子系统									
三级指标		人均GDP			人均收入增长效率			分值小结
城市	数值（万元）	排名	分值	比值	排名	分值	
杭州市	69828	20	0.924	0.012304	8	0.972	1.896
无锡市	92166	10	0.964	0.008243	127	0.496	1.46
常州市	67327	22	0.916	0.008103	137	0.456	1.372
苏州市	93043	9	0.968	0.008789	85	0.664	1.632
珠海市	80697	12	0.956	0.008556	101	0.6	1.556
绍兴市	63770	31	0.880	0.011129	12	0.956	1.836
大连市	77704	13	0.952	0.007885	152	0.396	1.348
北京市	75943	17	0.936	0.008479	107	0.576	1.512
上海市	76074	16	0.940	0.010061	30	0.884	1.824
宁波市	69368	21	0.920	0.008603	98	0.612	1.532

二级指标				城市经济发展总水平子系统			
三级指标	人均GDP			人均收入增长效率			分值小结
城市	数值（万元）	排名	分值	比值	排名	分值	
嘉兴市	52143	45	0.824	0.008259	125	0.504	1.328
东营市	116448	3	0.992	0.008694	89	0.648	1.64
威海市	76778	14	0.948	0.008271	124	0.508	1.456
沈阳市	62357	35	0.864	0.007914	149	0.408	1.272
天津市	72994	19	0.928	0.007763	166	0.34	1.268
深圳市	106880	4	0.988	0.008790	84	0.668	1.656
厦门市	58337	40	0.844	0.007912	150	0.404	1.248
烟台市	62254	36	0.860	0.007262	205	0.184	1.044
青岛市	65827	28	0.892	0.009115	65	0.744	1.636
武汉市	58961	38	0.852	0.008958	73	0.712	1.564
长沙市	66443	26	0.900	0.008212	130	0.484	1.384
舟山市	66581	25	0.904	0.007937	147	0.416	1.32
马鞍山市	62942	34	0.868	0.009053	69	0.728	1.596
鄂尔多斯市	175125	1	1.000	0.007990	141	0.44	1.44
淄博市	63397	32	0.876	0.009456	45	0.824	1.7
太原市	50225	47	0.816	0.009617	41	0.84	1.656
镇江市	63280	33	0.872	0.007801	160	0.364	1.236
昆明市	33550	102	0.596	0.010306	21	0.92	1.516

二级指标			城市经济发展总水平子系统				
三级指标	人均GDP			人均收入增长效率			分值小结
城市	数值（万元）	排名	分值	比值	排名	分值	
南京市	64037	30	0.884	0.008393	115	0.544	1.428
福州市	44667	55	0.784	0.008448	111	0.56	1.344
济南市	57966	41	0.840	0.009042	70	0.724	1.564
中山市	73348	18	0.932	0.007070	218	0.132	1.064
广州市	103625	5	0.984	0.008363	118	0.532	1.516
晋城市	32337	106	0.580	0.010553	15	0.944	1.524
南通市	47419	52	0.796	0.009309	52	0.796	1.592
金华市	39897	74	0.708	0.007322	198	0.212	0.92
芜湖市	48306	51	0.800	0.006496	240	0.044	0.844
湖州市	45323	54	0.788	0.008137	135	0.464	1.252
铜陵市	64496	29	0.888	0.006699	234	0.068	0.956
呼和浩特市	66929	24	0.908	0.009763	35	0.864	1.772
包头市	94269	7	0.976	0.007506	184	0.268	1.244
乌海市	76653	15	0.944	0.006107	253	-0.008	0.936
唐山市	59389	37	0.856	0.035444	2	0.996	1.852
廊坊市	31844	110	0.564	0.035535	1	1	1.564
佛山市	93983	8	0.972	0.007588	178	0.292	1.264
辽阳市	39686	75	0.704	0.008589	99	0.608	1.312
龙岩市	38698	78	0.692	0.007968	143	0.432	1.124
克拉玛依市	121387	2	0.996	0.007093	217	0.136	1.132
扬州市	49786	49	0.808	0.009431	47	0.816	1.624
阳泉市	31898	109	0.568	0.014065	5	0.984	1.552

2. 城市发展要素利用效率子系统

二级指标	发展要素利用效率子系统																		
三级指标	单位土地面积产出率			产出收益率			劳动生产率			万元GDP水耗			万元GDP电耗			万元工业总产值电耗			分值小结
	数值	排序	分值	数值	排序	分值	数值	排序	分值	数值	排序	分值	数值	排序	分值	数值	排序	分值	
杭州市	144047.668	123	0.512	0.112846	15	0.944	579146.4	101	0.6	0.000533	172	0.316	0.057471	214	0.148	0.023317	167	0.336	2.856
无锡市	250792.208	29	0.888	0.088359	44	0.828	1917664	5	0.984	0.000553	177	0.296	0.038911	160	0.364	0.014647	96	0.62	3.98
常州市	199012.418	51	0.8	0.093987	39	0.848	2024661	3	0.992	0.000608	193	0.232	0.063775	224	0.108	0.022736	165	0.344	3.324
苏州市	280513.982	17	0.936	0.09758	31	0.88	1985316	4	0.988	0.000382	113	0.552	0.025853	98	0.612	0.00773	46	0.82	4.788
珠海市	97467.4032	211	0.16	0.103035	23	0.912	490795.2	128	0.492	0.001872	275	-0.096	0.073339	236	0.06	0.021867	152	0.396	1.924
绍兴市	279520.29	19	0.928	0.069129	112	0.556	686168.7	74	0.708	0.000299	87	0.656	0.015501	46	0.82	0.005252	21	0.92	4.588
大连市	132260.567	144	0.428	0.097095	32	0.876	892552.5	41	0.84	0.000648	199	0.208	0.034153	145	0.424	0.017367	120	0.524	3.3
北京市	119001.518	172	0.316	0.166785	3	0.992	237481.6	240	0.044	0.000663	204	0.188	0.046425	192	0.236	0.022006	155	0.384	2.16
上海市	198221.478	52	0.796	0.1674	2	0.996	937005.1	34	0.868	0.001229	257	-0.024	0.04172	198	0.212	0.026121	187	0.256	3.104
宁波市	189816.239	59	0.768	0.102833	24	0.908	822648.2	48	0.812	0.000596	190	0.244	0.044469	181	0.28	0.018258	124	0.508	3.52
嘉兴市	270612.082	22	0.916	0.076876	85	0.664	665647.1	80	0.684	0.000328	92	0.636	0.029525	123	0.512	0.011521	76	0.7	4.112
东营市	218512.963	41	0.84	0.044443	225	0.104	1536742	8	0.972	0.000333	94	0.628	0.041704	171	0.32	0.015469	105	0.584	3.448
威海市	147325.758	118	0.532	0.060817	155	0.384	1129345	20	0.924	0.000234	59	0.768	0.019494	62	0.756	0.006856	34	0.868	4.232
沈阳市	121785.017	165	0.344	0.092745	40	0.844	931897.8	36	0.86	0.000704	212	0.156	0.032854	140	0.444	0.011025	70	0.724	3.372
天津市	134271.616	141	0.44	0.15867	12	0.956	911068.4	38	0.852	0.000522	168	0.332	0.065908	228	0.092	0.029386	199	0.208	2.88

二级指标							发展要素利用效率子系统													
三级指标	单位土地面积产出率			产出收益率			劳动生产率			万元GDP水耗			万元GDP电耗			万元工业总产值电耗			分值小结
	数值	排序	分值	数值	排序	分值	数值	排序	分值	数值	排序	分值	数值	排序	分值	数值	排序	分值	
深圳市	115439.881	181	0.28	0.115516	13	0.952	757588.2	54	0.788	0.001109	250	0.004	0.060622	220	0.124	0.021451	148	0.412	2.56
厦门市	89568.4217	223	0.112	0.140371	4	0.988	407573.6	166	0.34	0.001009	241	0.04	0.060405	219	0.128	0.024354	180	0.284	1.892
烟台市	264149.091	23	0.912	0.05456	186	0.26	1190082	16	0.94	0.000256	68	0.732	0.019899	64	0.748	0.007093	39	0.848	4.44
青岛市	200928.723	50	0.804	0.07988	74	0.708	902101.1	39	0.848	0.000395	120	0.524	0.028329	116	0.54	0.011296	72	0.716	4.14
武汉市	111318.6	189	0.248	0.070103	108	0.572	323445.1	206	0.18	0.001076	246	0.02	0.046389	190	0.244	0.029782	201	0.2	1.464
长沙市	16171.224	88	0.652	0.069118	113	0.552	410629.9	165	0.344	0.000436	140	0.444	0.013183	32	0.876	0.005368	23	0.912	3.78
舟山市	123907.115	157	0.376	0.094735	38	0.852	595892.7	100	0.604	0.000454	146	0.42	0.041722	172	0.316	0.020291	137	0.456	3.024
马鞍山市	103976.256	200	0.204	0.086164	52	0.796	944076.4	32	0.876	0.002277	278	-0.108	0.115371	269	-0.072	0.065835	260	-0.036	1.66
鄂尔多斯市	233914.159	37	0.856	0.090449	42	0.836	1587371	7	0.976	5.83E-05	2	0.996	0.027505	108	0.572	0.024192	178	0.292	4.528
淄博市	127411.111	152	0.396	0.056648	173	0.312	1287387	12	0.956	0.000753	219	0.128	0.084482	246	0.02	0.029352	198	0.212	2.024
太原市	72573.6286	251	0	0.077883	83	0.672	246131.9	236	0.06	0.00112	251	0	0.102777	264	-0.052	0.075403	268	-0.068	0.612
镇江市	182352.294	65	0.744	0.06948	110	0.564	1184403	17	0.936	0.000634	197	0.216	0.038936	161	0.36	0.016446	114	0.548	3.368
昆明市	77104.3636	246	0.02	0.119711	9	0.968	270051	228	0.092	0.000969	238	0.052	0.027569	109	0.568	0.023995	176	0.3	2
南京市	82886.1066	235	0.064	0.101118	26	0.9	752710.2	57	0.776	0.001603	270	-0.076	0.059424	217	0.136	0.02667	191	0.24	2.04
福州市	141973.145	127	0.496	0.079343	76	0.7	461322.6	141	0.44	0.000478	159	0.368	0.02027	66	0.74	0.007225	40	0.844	3.588
济南市	112695.305	187	0.256	0.068055	116	0.54	371140.8	182	0.276	0.000397	121	0.52	0.040797	168	0.332	0.02619	188	0.252	2.176
中山市	451378.561	4	0.988	0.075311	91	0.64	1822798	6	0.98	7.88E-05	7	0.976	0.086707	249	0.008	0.025667	185	0.264	3.856

二级指标	发展要素利用效率子系统																		
三级指标	单位土地面积产出率			产出收益率			劳动生产率			万元GDP水耗			万元GDP电耗			万元工业总产值电耗			分值小结
	数值	排序	分值	数值	排序	分值	数值	排序	分值	数值	排序	分值	数值	排序	分值	数值	排序	分值	
广州市	112902.13	186	0.26	0.081189	72	0.716	577794.6	102	0.596	0.001007	240	0.044	0.042303	175	0.304	0.022088	156	0.38	2.3
晋城市	178181.171	72	0.716	0.075956	88	0.652	324114.4	205	0.184	8.98E-05	9	0.968	0.02079	70	0.724	0.014975	98	0.612	3.856
南通市	277253.6	20	0.924	0.08391	66	0.74	1256709	13	0.952	0.00037	111	0.56	0.027988	114	0.548	0.011359	74	0.708	4.432
金华市	293061.681	13	0.952	0.073897	98	0.612	686753	72	0.716	0.000159	26	0.9	0.014	36	0.86	0.006514	31	0.88	4.92
芜湖市	82117.9556	241	0.04	0.085547	56	0.78	935582.9	35	0.864	0.000959	237	0.056	0.041819	174	0.308	0.017276	119	0.528	2.576
湖州市	166888.385	90	0.644	0.07472	94	0.628	755391.7	55	0.784	0.000408	127	0.496	0.040326	167	0.336	0.016524	115	0.544	3.432
铜陵市	97229.1667	214	0.148	0.074424	96	0.62	1062782	25	0.904	0.002608	282	-0.124	0.093747	256	-0.02	0.037452	221	0.12	1.648
呼和浩特市	112392.265	188	0.252	0.067943	118	0.532	373161.6	181	0.28	0.000478	158	0.372	0.062974	222	0.116	0.036721	220	0.124	1.676
包头市	134470.492	140	0.444	0.05656	174	0.308	754297.1	56	0.78	0.000938	235	0.064	0.072338	235	0.064	0.073649	265	-0.056	1.604
乌海市	62083.0952	268	-0.068	0.086068	53	0.792	571015.7	105	0.584	0.001805	273	-0.088	0.296684	279	-0.112	0.207156	280	-0.116	0.992
唐山市	190989.692	57	0.776	0.043821	230	0.084	987699.1	29	0.888	0.000457	148	0.412	0.102659	263	-0.048	0.057409	251	0	2.112
廊坊市	228999.695	38	0.852	0.078354	81	0.68	702519.8	69	0.728	0.000197	42	0.836	0.023718	89	0.648	0.011417	75	0.704	4.448
佛山市	371810.678	6	0.98	0.054154	190	0.244	2646169	2	0.996	0.000483	160	0.364	0.073681	237	0.056	0.024202	179	0.288	2.928
辽阳市	75043.8265	248	0.012	0.103995	21	0.92	943548	33	0.872	0.00193	276	-0.1	0.099978	260	-0.036	0.033143	211	0.16	1.828
龙岩市	260762.447	26	0.9	0.067361	121	0.52	419131.3	162	0.356	0.000364	105	0.584	0.029401	121	0.52	0.020619	139	0.448	3.328
克拉玛依市	124798.789	156	0.38	0.059647	161	0.36	840427.6	47	0.816	0.001503	266	-0.06	0.056443	212	0.156	0.028636	195	0.224	1.876
扬州市	271888.829	21	0.92	0.075256	92	0.636	1517232	9	0.968	0.00042	133	0.472	0.023296	84	0.668	0.007086	38	0.852	4.516
阳泉市	82572.5769	239	0.048	0.087785	47	0.816	239036	239	0.048	0.001018	242	0.036	0.112638	268	-0.068	0.078463	271	-0.08	0.8

3. 城市科技先进性水平子系统

二级指标				城市科技信息水平子系统						
三级指标	科学支出比重			国际互联网使用率			信息业从业人员比重			分值小计
城市	数值	排序	分值	数值	排序	分值	数值	排序	分值	
杭州市	0.0468	6	0.98	0.25031	16	0.94	0.027889	5	0.984	2.904
无锡市	0.038825	11	0.96	0.207768	26	0.9	0.009885	151	0.4	2.26
常州市	0.030942	28	0.892	0.170359	41	0.84	0.010482	137	0.456	2.188
苏州市	0.043251	9	0.968	0.180023	35	0.864	0.008329	193	0.232	2.064
珠海市	0.034243	15	0.944	0.213828	24	0.908	0.013935	57	0.776	2.628
绍兴市	0.043047	10	0.964	0.156573	47	0.816	0.004574	259	-0.032	1.748
大连市	0.043507	8	0.972	0.173165	37	0.856	0.02569	7	0.976	2.804
北京市	0.065843	3	0.992	0.278179	13	0.952	0.064535	3	0.992	2.936
上海市	0.061169	4	0.988	2.246928	1	1	0.017079	30	0.884	2.872
宁波市	0.036863	13	0.952	0.225989	21	0.92	0.006563	226	0.1	1.972
嘉兴市	0.037858	12	0.956	0.173362	36	0.86	0.005597	247	0.016	1.832
东营市	0.014229	89	0.648	0.150878	49	0.808	0.012718	86	0.66	2.116
威海市	0.033437	17	0.936	0.160103	46	0.82	0.006009	239	0.048	1.804
沈阳市	0.029711	30	0.884	0.167654	43	0.832	0.013766	58	0.772	2.488
天津市	0.031415	25	0.904	0.133949	62	0.756	0.010892	122	0.516	2.176
深圳市	0.07891	1	1	0.252121	15	0.944	0.020512	15	0.944	2.888

二级指标	城市科技信息水平子系统									
三级指标	科学支出比重			国际互联网使用率			信息业从业人员比重			分值小计
城市	数值	排序	分值	数值	排序	分值	数值	排序	分值	
厦门市	0.031266	26	0.9	1.013877	2	0.996	0.011854	102	0.596	2.492
烟台市	0.032826	21	0.92	0.12566	68	0.732	0.004201	271	-0.08	1.572
青岛市	0.018548	58	0.772	0.215961	23	0.912	0.004996	254	-0.012	1.672
武汉市	0.020056	53	0.792	0.216658	22	0.916	0.01244	88	0.652	2.36
长沙市	0.033043	18	0.932	0.128934	66	0.74	0.015286	44	0.828	2.5
舟山市	0.023222	40	0.844	0.203717	27	0.896	0.01369	61	0.76	2.5
马鞍山市	0.028268	32	0.876	0.137201	58	0.772	0.00454	261	-0.04	1.608
鄂尔多斯市	0.008956	155	0.384	0.047447	226	0.1	0.016753	35	0.864	1.348
淄博市	0.023962	39	0.848	0.11888	81	0.68	0.005884	242	0.036	1.564
太原市	0.024792	38	0.852	0.228095	19	0.928	0.012996	77	0.696	2.476
镇江市	0.032941	19	0.928	0.138739	57	0.776	0.006173	235	0.064	1.768
昆明市	0.012807	106	0.58	0.593528	6	0.98	0.017785	26	0.9	2.46
南京市	0.030453	29	0.888	0.1845	33	0.872	0.019341	19	0.928	2.688
福州市	0.015913	70	0.724	0.744905	3	0.992	0.011283	114	0.548	2.264
济南市	0.018449	59	0.768	0.172045	39	0.848	0.013537	68	0.732	2.348
中山市	0.046108	7	0.976	0.212872	25	0.904	0.009642	161	0.36	2.24

二级指标	城市科技信息水平子系统									
三级指标	科学支出比重			国际互联网使用率			信息业从业人员比重			分值小计
城市	数值	排序	分值	数值	排序	分值	数值	排序	分值	
广州市	0.032679	22	0.916	0.196798	28	0.892	0.021472	11	0.96	2.768
晋城市	0.014265	87	0.656	0.078889	148	0.412	0.00884	178	0.292	1.36
南通市	0.031546	24	0.908	0.113925	90	0.644	0.009666	160	0.364	1.916
金华市	0.035706	14	0.948	0.17041	40	0.844	0.01181	106	0.58	2.372
芜湖市	0.069302	2	0.996	0.11143	91	0.64	0.007113	216	0.14	1.776
湖州市	0.028893	31	0.88	0.167671	42	0.836	0.00765	204	0.188	1.904
铜陵市	0.020941	47	0.816	0.135471	60	0.764	0.006855	220	0.124	1.704
呼和浩特市	0.010861	126	0.5	0.098469	107	0.576	0.026667	6	0.98	2.056
包头市	0.01426	88	0.652	0.084404	131	0.48	0.018717	23	0.912	2.044
乌海市	0.012225	109	0.568	0.125234	69	0.728	0.013655	63	0.752	2.048
唐山市	0.014357	83	0.672	0.117808	85	0.664	0.007736	203	0.192	1.528
廊坊市	0.013103	102	0.596	0.120314	79	0.688	0.010681	131	0.48	1.764
佛山市	0.0312	27	0.896	0.181322	34	0.868	0.018727	22	0.916	2.68
辽阳市	0.014615	81	0.68	0.116075	87	0.656	0.009031	175	0.304	1.64
龙岩市	0.013397	99	0.608	0.097266	109	0.568	0.00982	153	0.392	1.568
克拉玛依市	0.018154	60	0.764	0.241877	17	0.936	0.006345	232	0.076	1.776
扬州市	0.033613	16	0.94	0.153821	48	0.812	0.012971	79	0.688	2.44
阳泉市	0.012065	113	0.552	0.143335	55	0.784	0.004212	270	-0.076	1.26

4. 城市外部发展效应子系统

二级指标	城市外部发展效应子系统									城市发展外部效应子系统							
三级指标	工业废水排放达标率			工业二氧化硫去除率			工业烟尘去除率			三废综合利用产品产值（万元）	三废综合利用产品产值比重				产出污染处理率			分值小计
城市	数值	排名	分值	数值	排名	分值	数值	排名	分值		地方生产总值（万元）	数值	排名	分值	数值	排名	分值	
杭州市	0.968795	139	0.448	0.509605	157	0.376	0.971741	178	0.292	1799985	59491687	0.030256	4	0.988	0.000137	276	-0.1	2.004
无锡市	0.992691	58	0.772	0.652115	75	0.704	0.989026	82	0.676	161814	57933000	0.00293	141	0.440	0.000152	273	-0.088	2.504
常州市	0.999814	21	0.92	0.554359	134	0.468	0.985796	116	0.54	464245	30448900	0.015247	15	0.944	0.000278	252	-0.004	2.868
苏州市	0.995067	41	0.84	0.265465	225	0.104	0.988289	101	0.6	639327	92289100	0.06927	56	0.780	0.000081	280	-0.116	2.208
珠海市	0.980405	105	0.584	0.634281	86	0.66	0.989535	76	0.7	12987	12085958	0.001075	219	0.128	0.000718	178	0.292	2.364
绍兴市	0.983923	87	0.656	0.422428	184	0.268	0.945105	214	0.148	193442	27952029	0.006920	57	0.776	0.000280	251	0	1.848
大连市	0.952737	184	0.268	0.777582	26	0.9	0.988964	85	0.664	39367	51581621	0.00763	242	0.036	0.000176	268	-0.068	1.8
北京市	0.987558	76	0.7	0.695585	53	0.792	0.988975	84	0.668	34366	141135800	0.00243	271	-0.080	0.000063	281	-0.12	1.96
上海市	0.980189	109	0.568	0.612247	99	0.608	0.991229	65	0.744	170379	171659800	0.000993	226	0.100	0.000050	282	-0.124	1.896
宁波市	0.954718	179	0.288	0.867882	12	0.956	0.995111	16	0.94	230911	51630017	0.004472	96	0.620	0.000182	266	-0.06	2.744
嘉兴市	0.985918	84	0.668	0.576164	123	0.512	0.983426	129	0.488	158982	23002027	0.006912	58	0.772	0.000369	237	0.056	2.496
东营市	1	1	1	0.787934	23	0.912	0.995019	18	0.932	135256	23599400	0.005731	73	0.712	0.000393	230	0.084	3.64
威海市	1	1	1	0.43802	179	0.288	0.98358	128	0.492	7224	19447000	0.000371	261	-0.040	0.000415	226	0.1	1.84
沈阳市	0.962866	153	0.392	0.531452	147	0.416	0.974885	168	0.332	15373	50175427	0.000306	266	-0.060	0.000164	269	-0.072	1.008

二级指标																	
							城市发展外部效应子系统										
三级指标	工业废水排放达标率			工业二氧化硫去除率			工业烟尘去除率			三废综合利用产品产值（万元）	地方生产总值（万元）	三废综合利用产品产值比重			产出污染处理率			分值小计
城市	数值	排名	分值	数值	排名	分值	数值	排名	分值			数值	排名	分值	数值	排名	分值	
天津市	0.999543	25	0.904	0.632171	89	0.648	0.98901	83	0.672	192650	92244600	0.02088	177	0.296	0.000095	278	-0.108	2.412
深圳市	0.963893	150	0.404	0.541527	143	0.432	0.997775	1	1	30022	95815101	0.000313	265	-0.056	0.000087	279	-0.112	1.668
厦门市	0.999776	23	0.912	0.355795	205	0.184	0.996364	8	0.972	4521	20600737	0.000219	273	-0.088	0.000381	234	0.068	2.048
烟台市	1	1	1	0.682677	57	0.776	0.992026	54	0.788	61295	43584600	0.001406	199	0.208	0.000205	262	-0.044	2.728
青岛市	0.980648	103	0.592	0.701314	52	0.796	0.994371	25	0.904	143532	56661900	0.002533	157	0.376	0.000157	271	-0.08	2.588
武汉市	0.992032	59	0.768	0.638214	84	0.668	0.994957	19	0.928	251718	55659300	0.004522	91	0.640	0.000157	272	-0.084	2.92
长沙市	0.912131	238	0.052	0.469202	169	0.328	0.806543	260	-0.036	68363	45470573	0.001503	196	0.220	0.000160	270	-0.076	0.488
舟山市	0.96651	143	0.432	0.346631	210	0.164	0.939594	220	0.124	13567	6443170	0.002106	175	0.304	0.001165	95	0.624	1.648
马鞍山市	0.983282	91	0.64	0.488946	163	0.352	0.994853	22	0.916	48227	8110148	0.005947	71	0.720	0.001014	114	0.548	3.176
鄂尔多斯市	0.953509	181	0.28	0.612517	98	0.612	0.978997	156	0.38	32754	26432300	0.001239	208	0.172	0.000321	245	0.024	1.468
淄博市	1	1	1	0.722223	48	0.812	0.988328	100	0.604	391380	28667500	0.013652	18	0.932	0.000315	246	0.02	3.368
太原市	0.973797	123	0.512	0.730147	42	0.836	0.989388	78	0.692	134333	17780539	0.007555	47	0.816	0.000505	214	0.148	3.004
镇江市	0.985098	85	0.664	0.755658	31	0.88	0.99134	64	0.748	65601	19876400	0.003300	129	0.488	0.000458	219	0.128	2.908
昆明市	0.99549	39	0.848	0.871543	10	0.964	0.993731	36	0.86	211834	21203700	0.000990	31	0.880	0.000450	220	0.124	3.676
南京市	0.952048	186	0.26	0.840049	16	0.94	0.988895	86	0.66	210436	51306500	0.004102	105	0.584	0.000181	267	-0.064	2.38
福州市	0.952033	187	0.256	0.545114	140	0.444	0.993784	34	0.868	29666	31234092	0.000950	228	0.092	0.000266	254	-0.012	1.648
济南市	0.996782	33	0.872	0.680068	60	0.764	0.991066	66	0.74	146485	39105271	0.003746	120	0.524	0.000227	260	-0.036	2.864

二级指标	城市发展外部效应子系统																		
三级指标	工业废水排放达标率			工业二氧化硫去除率			工业烟尘去除率			三废综合利用产品产值比重					产出污染处理率			分值小计
城市	数值	排名	分值	数值	排名	分值	数值	排名	分值	三废综合利用产品产值（万元）	地方生产总值（万元）	数值	排名	分值	数值	排名	分值	
中山市	0.970214	133	0.472	0.028891	276	-0.1	0.940741	218	0.132	30173	18506521	0.001630	190	0.244	0.000349	241	0.04	0.788
广州市	0.965146	148	0.412	/	283	-0.128	/	284	-0.132	44437	107482828	/	281	-0.120	/	283	-0.128	-0.096
晋城市	1	1	1	0.445283	174	0.308	0.960169	196	0.22		7305428	0.06083	67	0.736	0.001098	103	0.592	2.856
南通市	0.993506	51	0.8	0.706151	51	0.8	0.977033	162	0.356	87654	34656700	0.002529	158	0.372	0.000257	255	-0.016	2.312
金华市	0.955561	174	0.308	0.643075	81	0.68	0.981418	143	0.432	126754	21100441	0.06007	70	0.724	0.000408	228	0.092	2.236
芜湖市	0.993264	53	0.792	0.478535	165	0.344	0.951503	208	0.172	78214	11085924	0.007055	53	0.792	0.000729	175	0.304	2.404
湖州市	0.960599	161	0.36	0.422813	183	0.272	0.986689	111	0.56	87423	13017294	0.006716	60	0.764	0.000607	196	0.22	2.176
铜陵市	0.995567	38	0.852	0.964768	2	0.996	0.99229	50	0.804	81779	4667000	0.017523	12	0.956	0.002109	33	0.872	4.48
呼和浩特市	1	1	1	0.9	4	0.988	0.900003	245	0.024	/	18657116	/	281	-0.120	0.000500	215	0.144	2.036
包头市	0.982619	92	0.636	0.610948	102	0.596	0.991774	56	0.78	36802	24608100	0.001496	197	0.216	0.000350	240	0.044	2.272
乌海市	0.994485	44	0.828	0.115506	257	-0.024	0.988551	91	0.64	45562	3911235	0.011649	24	0.908	0.001788	45	0.824	3.176
唐山市	0.982499	93	0.632	0.632702	88	0.652	0.989233	80	0.684	435115	44691588	0.009736	33	0.872	0.000194	264	-0.052	2.788
廊坊市	0.997448	29	0.888	0.448442	173	0.312	0.975684	166	0.34	19370	13510982	0.001434	198	0.212	0.000597	198	0.212	1.964
佛山市	0.95454	180	0.284	0.502173	160	0.364	0.967582	184	0.268	59097	56515223	0.001046	220	0.124	0.000143	275	-0.096	0.944
辽阳市	0.997961	28	0.892	0.690085	54	0.788	0.926618	229	0.088	18684	7354295	0.002541	155	0.384	0.001185	93	0.632	2.784
龙岩市	0.984159	86	0.66	0.320929	214	0.148	0.99156	59	0.768	194348	9908973	0.019613	8	0.972	0.000773	167	0.336	2.884
克拉玛依市	1	1	1	0.345546	211	0.16	0.584371	273	-0.088	3643	7113531	0.000512	251	0.000	0.000904	141	0.44	1.512
扬州市	0.983331	89	0.648	0.681989	58	0.772	0.921048	236	0.06	26693	22294884	0.001197	210	0.164	0.000387	231	0.08	1.724
阳泉市	1	1	1	0.639648	82	0.676	0.977606	159	0.368	16580	4293774	0.003861	113	0.552	0.002032	36	0.86	3.456

2012 中国城市科学发展综合评价报告

5. 城市经济发展水平母系统

一级指标	城市经济发展水平系统												
二级指标	城市发展总水平子系统			发展要素利用效率水平子系统			科技先进性水平子系统			发展外部效应子系统			分值合计
城市	数值	排序	分值	数值	排序	分值	数值	排序	分值	数值	排序	分值	
杭州市	1.896	1	1.000	2.856	111	0.560	2.904	2	0.996	2.004	162	0.356	2.912
无锡市	1.460	40	0.844	3.980	38	0.852	2.260	29	0.888	2.504	105	0.584	3.168
常州市	1.372	49	0.808	3.324	81	0.680	2.188	34	0.868	2.868	61	0.760	3.116
苏州市	1.632	14	0.948	4.788	8	0.972	2.064	40	0.844	2.208	144	0.428	3.192
珠海市	1.556	23	0.912	1.924	200	0.204	2.628	9	0.968	2.364	124	0.508	2.592
绍兴市	1.836	3	0.992	4.588	13	0.952	1.748	77	0.696	1.848	182	0.276	2.916
大连市	1.348	52	0.796	3.300	83	0.672	2.804	5	0.984	1.800	192	0.236	2.688
北京市	1.512	34	0.868	2.160	178	0.292	2.936	1	1.000	1.960	168	0.332	2.492
上海市	1.824	4	0.988	3.104	92	0.636	2.872	4	0.988	1.896	175	0.304	2.916
宁波市	1.532	26	0.900	3.520	66	0.740	1.972	48	0.812	2.744	75	0.704	3.156
嘉兴市	1.328	59	0.768	4.112	32	0.876	1.832	65	0.744	2.496	107	0.576	2.964
东营市	1.640	12	0.956	3.448	70	0.724	2.116	39	0.848	3.640	11	0.960	3.488
威海市	1.456	41	0.840	4.232	28	0.892	1.804	68	0.732	1.840	183	0.272	2.736
沈阳市	1.272	64	0.748	3.372	75	0.704	2.488	13	0.952	1.008	253	-0.008	2.396
天津市	1.268	65	0.744	2.880	109	0.568	2.176	35	0.864	2.412	116	0.540	2.716
深圳市	1.656	10	0.964	2.560	147	0.416	2.888	3	0.992	1.668	207	0.176	2.548

一级指标			城市经济发展水平母系统												分值合计
二级指标			城市发展总水平子系统			发展要素利用效率水平子系统			科技先进性水平子系统			发展外部效应子系统			
城市			数值	排序	分值	数值	排序	分值	数值	排序	分值	数值	排序	分值	
厦门市			1.248	72	0.716	1.892	205	0.184	2.492	12	0.956	2.048	158	0.372	2.228
烟台市			1.044	104	0.588	4.440	21	0.920	1.572	99	0.608	2.728	78	0.692	2.808
青岛市			1.636	13	0.952	4.140	31	0.880	1.672	87	0.656	2.588	97	0.616	3.104
武汉市			1.564	19	0.928	1.464	234	0.068	2.360	20	0.924	2.920	50	0.804	2.724
长沙市			1.384	47	0.816	3.780	50	0.804	2.500	10	0.964	0.488	280	-0.116	2.468
舟山市			1.320	61	0.760	3.024	99	0.608	2.500	10	0.964	1.648	210	0.164	2.496
马鞍山市			1.596	16	0.940	1.660	225	0.104	1.608	97	0.616	3.176	32	0.876	2.536
鄂尔多斯市			1.440	43	0.832	4.528	15	0.944	1.348	125	0.504	1.468	223	0.112	2.392
淄博市			1.700	6	0.980	2.024	189	0.248	1.564	101	0.600	3.368	19	0.928	2.756
太原市			1.656	9	0.968	0.612	273	-0.088	2.476	14	0.948	3.004	44	0.828	2.656
镇江市			1.236	78	0.692	3.368	77	0.696	1.768	73	0.712	2.908	54	0.788	2.888
昆明市			1.516	32	0.876	2.000	191	0.240	2.460	15	0.944	3.676	10	0.964	3.024
南京市			1.428	45	0.824	2.040	188	0.252	2.688	7	0.976	2.380	121	0.520	2.572
福州市			1.344	55	0.784	3.588	63	0.752	2.264	28	0.892	1.648	210	0.164	2.592
济南市			1.564	19	0.928	2.176	175	0.304	2.348	22	0.916	2.864	62	0.756	2.904
中山市			1.064	98	0.612	3.856	44	0.828	2.240	32	0.876	0.788	263	-0.048	2.268
广州市			1.516	32	0.876	2.300	164	0.348	2.768	6	0.980	-0.096	285	-0.136	2.068

一级指标	城市经济发展水平母系统												
二级指标	城市发展总水平子系统			发展要素利用效率水平子系统			科技先进性水平子系统			发展外部效应子系统			分值合计
城市	数值	排序	分值	数值	排序	分值	数值	排序	分值	数值	排序	分值	
晋城市	1.524	30	0.884	3.856	44	0.828	1.360	124	0.508	2.856	63	0.752	2.972
南通市	1.592	17	0.936	4.432	22	0.916	1.916	55	0.784	2.312	134	0.468	3.104
金华市	0.920	131	0.480	4.920	5	0.984	2.372	18	0.932	2.236	139	0.448	2.844
芜湖市	0.844	144	0.428	2.576	146	0.420	1.776	71	0.720	2.404	117	0.536	2.104
湖州市	1.252	71	0.720	3.432	73	0.712	1.904	57	0.776	2.176	149	0.408	2.616
铜陵市	0.956	123	0.512	1.648	226	0.100	1.704	82	0.676	4.480	2	0.996	2.284
呼和浩特市	1.772	5	0.984	1.676	223	0.112	2.056	41	0.840	2.036	160	0.364	2.300
包头市	1.244	75	0.704	1.604	228	0.092	2.044	43	0.832	2.272	136	0.460	2.088
乌海市	0.936	127	0.496	0.992	258	-0.028	2.048	42	0.836	3.176	32	0.876	2.180
唐山市	1.852	2	0.996	2.112	183	0.272	1.528	107	0.576	2.788	71	0.720	2.564
廊坊市	1.564	19	0.928	4.448	20	0.924	1.764	74	0.708	1.964	166	0.340	2.900
佛山市	1.264	66	0.740	2.928	105	0.584	2.680	8	0.972	0.944	258	-0.028	2.268
辽阳市	1.312	62	0.756	1.828	213	0.152	1.640	94	0.628	2.784	72	0.716	2.252
龙岩市	1.124	87	0.656	3.328	80	0.684	1.568	100	0.604	2.884	60	0.764	2.708
克拉玛依市	1.132	86	0.660	1.876	207	0.176	1.776	72	0.716	1.512	219	0.128	1.680
扬州市	1.624	15	0.944	4.516	16	0.940	2.440	16	0.940	1.724	201	0.200	3.024
阳泉市	1.552	24	0.908	0.800	266	-0.060	1.260	140	0.444	3.456	17	0.936	2.228

二、城市公共服务水平母系统

1．城市财政公共投入水平子系统

二级指标	城市财政公共投入水平子系统												
三级指标	人均社会保障性支出			人均医疗卫生支出			人均教育支出			人均公共服务财政支出			分值小计
城市	数值（元）	排名	分值	数值（元）	排名	分值	数值（元）	排序	分值	数值（元）	排序	分值	
杭州市	734.2906	39	0.848	479.1499	15	0.944	1216.34463	15	0.944	2536.046	13	0.952	3.688
无锡市	547.9925	92	0.636	359.9435	55	0.784	1291.155897	10	0.964	2216.989	30	0.884	3.268
常州市	543.2179	97	0.616	320.0523	86	0.66	884.3043762	54	0.788	1820.015	56	0.78	2.844
苏州市	608.1765	68	0.732	322.6669	80	0.684	1175.993887	17	0.936	2250.891	28	0.892	3.244
珠海市	834.1869	34	0.868	383.4827	42	0.836	1662.612036	6	0.98	3070.333	7	0.976	3.66
绍兴市	295.3389	233	0.072	310.401	97	0.616	917.0995319	42	0.836	1577.881	92	0.636	2.16
大连市	1379.821	7	0.976	401.3453	31	0.88	1126.240658	22	0.916	3054.178	9	0.968	3.74
北京市	1406.792	5	0.984	952.5801	3	0.992	2295.61238	2	0.996	5567.259	1	1	3.972
上海市	1574.5	2	0.996	697.8764	5	0.984	1812.122725	4	0.988	4656.467	3	0.992	3.96
宁波市	452.3716	141	0.44	480.7515	14	0.948	1172.957561	18	0.932	2237.212	29	0.888	3.208
嘉兴市	227.9689	258	-0.028	289.0122	126	0.5	952.9766926	37	0.856	1458.713	115	0.544	1.872
东营市	454.5901	137	0.456	334.3152	71	0.72	1232.061856	11	0.96	1959.21	44	0.828	2.964
威海市	1032.086	23	0.912	277.3619	146	0.42	1130.609626	21	0.92	2354.627	21	0.92	3.172

146

续表

二级指标	城市财政公共投入水平子系统												分值小计
三级指标	人均社会保障性支出			人均医疗卫生支出			人均教育支出			人均公共服务财政支出			
城市	数值（元）	排名	分值	数值（元）	排名	分值	数值（元）	排名	分值	数值（元）	排序	分值	
沈阳市	1169.504	13	0.952	330.1258	76	0.7	950.6612386	38	0.852	2507.702	16	0.94	3.444
天津市	1060.109	20	0.924	539.2904	11	0.96	1766.834449	5	0.984	3268.446	6	0.98	3.848
深圳市	597.7632	76	0.7	136.5214	269	-0.072	1200.872541	16	0.94	3014.165	11	0.96	2.528
厦门市	656.4713	55	0.784	410.3653	28	0.892	1228.603795	12	0.956	2406.964	20	0.924	3.556
烟台市	632.8932	61	0.76	321.3261	83	0.672	812.9061424	82	0.676	1735.996	63	0.752	2.86
青岛市	413.6942	164	0.348	226.8609	243	0.032	987.1120541	31	0.88	1578.656	91	0.64	1.9
武汉市	939.1926	28	0.892	391.722	37	0.856	769.479816	99	0.608	2130.049	35	0.864	3.22
长沙市	602.8973	74	0.708	244.4255	218	0.132	765.9934668	101	0.6	1705.945	67	0.736	2.176
舟山市	471.008	131	0.48	668.1534	6	0.98	1083.220339	23	0.912	2300.508	26	0.9	3.272
马鞍山市	492.3189	121	0.52	408.1931	29	0.888	881.8580834	55	0.784	1735.545	64	0.748	2.94
鄂尔多斯市	1514.359	4	0.988	844.1026	4	0.988	2248.892308	3	0.992	3882.528	4	0.988	3.956
淄博市	531.6567	100	0.604	277.741	145	0.424	890.6618134	52	0.796	1693.375	69	0.728	2.552
太原市	704.3995	43	0.832	240.6659	228	0.092	854.9131986	65	0.744	1740.331	61	0.76	2.428
镇江市	284.4302	239	0.048	249.4382	209	0.168	866.4494382	58	0.772	1419.99	129	0.488	1.476
昆明市	633.7941	60	0.764	287.7776	128	0.492	509.1768908	237	0.056	1590.704	88	0.652	1.964
南京市	573.6763	86	0.66	394.6054	34	0.868	955.2335165	36	0.86	1974.542	43	0.832	3.22
福州市	368.9389	191	0.24	255.376	199	0.208	786.8981026	92	0.636	1327.671	159	0.368	1.452
济南市	618.5098	65	0.744	309.1816	100	0.604	738.185685	111	0.56	1558.592	96	0.62	2.528

| 二级指标 | 城市财政公共投入水平子系统 | | | | | | | | | | | | |
| 三级指标 | 人均社会保障性支出 | | | 人均医疗卫生支出 | | | 人均教育支出 | | | 人均公共服务财政支出 | | | 分值小计 |
城市	数值(元)	排名	分值	数值(元)	排名	分值	数值(元)	排序	分值	数值(元)	排序	分值	
中山市	346.7819	204	0.188	152.4175	268	-0.068	1225.449888	13	0.952	1657.999	75	0.704	1.776
广州市	897.8757	31	0.88	404.3273	30	0.884	886.1864673	53	0.792	2421.462	19	0.928	3.484
晋城市	497.807	117	0.536	279.386	140	0.444	828.3947368	73	0.712	1548.855	99	0.608	2.3
南通市	387.2562	178	0.292	238.6707	230	0.084	893.081571	50	0.804	1456.826	116	0.54	1.72
金华市	291.4648	234	0.068	306.3735	103	0.592	901.3473723	46	0.82	1516.223	105	0.584	2.064
芜湖市	551.6784	90	0.644	443.0212	18	0.932	726.5989399	116	0.54	2035.437	38	0.852	2.968
湖州市	266.0677	246	0.02	286.4547	131	0.48	867.6814098	57	0.776	1422.616	128	0.492	1.768
铜陵市	1045.58	22	0.916	508.2873	13	0.952	901.3812155	45	0.824	2487.03	17	0.936	3.628
呼和浩特市	694.8504	45	0.824	341.3361	67	0.736	955.7167711	35	0.864	1875.129	49	0.808	3.232
包头市	1153.614	15	0.944	297.4398	117	0.536	1060.3125	25	0.904	2464.465	18	0.932	3.316
乌海市	1401.869	6	0.98	1009.346	2	0.996	1386.392523	8	0.972	3640.075	5	0.984	3.932
唐山市	591.5326	78	0.692	350.3034	60	0.764	794.4763915	88	0.652	1682.663	71	0.72	2.828
廊坊市	352.429	200	0.204	274.7479	154	0.388	791.7048579	91	0.64	1334.654	156	0.38	1.612
佛山市	346.0203	206	0.18	193.638	263	-0.048	959.9347132	33	0.872	1515.949	106	0.58	1.584
辽阳市	1219.473	10	0.964	334.0506	72	0.716	619.1500807	180	0.284	2150.855	33	0.872	2.836
龙岩市	440.625	152	0.396	339.8438	68	0.732	892.1601563	51	0.8	1665.395	74	0.708	2.636
克拉玛依市	705.8824	42	0.836	1442.455	1	1	2949.897698	1	1	4850.23	2	0.996	3.832
扬州市	355.7498	195	0.224	236.7182	232	0.076	814.7186729	81	0.68	1401.697	136	0.46	1.44
阳泉市	530.3141	101	0.6	279.0358	142	0.436	857.1292915	63	0.752	1627.904	80	0.684	2.472

2. 城市公共项目规模水平子系统（1）

二级指标	城市公共项目规模子系统（1）											
三级指标	每万人拥有医院、卫生院床位数			每万人拥有医生数			每万人在校高中以上学生数			人均城市道路面积		
城市	数值（元）	排名	分值	数值（人）	排名	分值	数值（人）	排序	分值	数值（m²）	排名	分值
杭州市	42.840	53	0.792	27.97	21	0.92	1012.40	25	0.904	10.93	110	0.564
无锡市	35.511	114	0.548	18.43	123	0.512	503.90	147	0.416	23.39	7	0.976
常州市	32.034	150	0.404	17.27	149	0.408	603.86	101	0.600	13.27	72	0.716
苏州市	35.189	119	0.528	17.43	143	0.432	401.23	203	0.192	24.45	6	0.98
珠海市	39.001	76	0.700	29.55	15	0.944	1123.91	16	0.940	32.32	3	0.992
绍兴市	31.773	153	0.392	19.53	106	0.58	627.82	85	0.664	18.56	21	0.92
大连市	45.152	30	0.884	23.73	50	0.804	861.30	35	0.864	13.59	69	0.728
北京市	43.818	41	0.840	33.63	12	0.956	755.32	50	0.804	7.91	171	0.32
上海市	44.922	31	0.880	18.54	119	0.528	535.32	132	0.476	7.24	187	0.256
宁波市	31.950	151	0.400	22.65	55	0.784	493.04	154	0.388	10.65	115	0.544
嘉兴市	31.216	158	0.372	17.46	142	0.436	601.04	105	0.584	11.63	98	0.612
东营市	47.757	20	0.924	21.81	62	0.756	967.75	27	0.896	22.29	9	0.968
威海市	58.399	4	0.988	26.09	33	0.872	734.06	56	0.780	27.77	4	0.988
沈阳市	52.828	11	0.960	25.73	36	0.86	948.01	29	0.888	11.07	106	0.58
天津市	33.926	127	0.496	21.92	61	0.76	745.13	51	0.800	11.35	99	0.608
深圳市	20.368	259	-0.032	21.22	72	0.716	263.35	237	0.056	34.41	2	0.996

城市公共项目规模子系统（1）

三级指标	每万人拥有医院、卫生院床位数			每万人拥有医生数			每万人在校高中以上学生数			人均城市道路面积		
城市	数值（元）	排名	分值	数值（人）	排名	分值	数值（人）	排序	分值	数值（m²）	排名	分值
厦门市	28.063	195	0.224	21.42	67	0.736	744.76	52	0.796	16.61	41	0.84
烟台市	42.556	55	0.784	22.14	60	0.764	672.13	76	0.700	16.96	39	0.848
青岛市	38.288	85	0.664	20.30	84	0.668	924.93	31	0.880	21.39	12	0.956
武汉市	46.123	25	0.904	25.62	38	0.852	1733.82	4	0.988	14.21	62	0.756
长沙市	56.786	7	0.976	25.93	34	0.868	1411.78	11	0.960	14.97	54	0.788
舟山市	36.209	103	0.592	22.52	56	0.78	504.52	146	0.420	7.46	184	0.268
马鞍山市	28.895	185	0.264	19.53	105	0.584	896.66	33	0.872	15.16	51	0.8
鄂尔多斯市	49.549	18	0.932	28.10	20	0.924	/	246	0.020	85.2	1	1
淄博市	46.047	26	0.900	17.28	148	0.412	824.84	39	0.848	9.02	150	0.404
太原市	61.232	3	0.992	38.21	6	0.98	1685.59	6	0.980	10	127	0.496
镇江市	27.868	199	0.208	17.58	139	0.448	673.04	75	0.704	17.61	28	0.892
昆明市	46.572	24	0.908	50.55	2	0.996	924.73	32	0.876	8.18	166	0.34
南京市	32.966	138	0.452	21.24	71	0.72	1522.68	9	0.968	17.46	31	0.88
福州市	32.499	143	0.432	19.97	93	0.632	1053.87	18	0.932	12.34	86	0.66
济南市	43.772	42	0.836	25.79	35	0.864	1702.78	5	0.984	16.97	38	0.852
中山市	32.386	146	0.420	17.24	151	0.4	394.41	205	0.184	12.15	87	0.656
广州市	44.696	34	0.868	26.42	29	0.888	1217.11	13	0.952	14.65	57	0.776

二级指标	城市公共项目规模子系统（1）									人均城市道路面积		
三级指标	每万人拥有医院、卫生院床位数			每万人拥有医生数			每万人在校高中以上学生数					
城市	数值（张）	排名	分值	数值（人）	排名	分值	数值（人）	排序	分值	数值（m²）	排名	分值
晋城市	33.697	130	0.484	25.28	40	0.844	373.83	212	0.156	10.87	111	0.56
南通市	35.191	118	0.532	18.50	121	0.52	449.44	180	0.284	8.84	152	0.396
金华市	29.102	183	0.272	20.10	87	0.656	595.42	109	0.568	14.92	55	0.784
芜湖市	44.143	39	0.848	22.19	59	0.768	971.36	26	0.900	23.16	8	0.972
湖州市	33.307	135	0.464	20.29	85	0.664	499.82	151	0.400	17.28	33	0.872
铜陵市	47.127	23	0.912	25.33	39	0.848	1015.77	24	0.908	10.62	117	0.536
呼和浩特市	39.729	67	0.736	24.30	47	0.816	1566.75	8	0.972	14.43	60	0.764
包头市	43.072	49	0.808	26.85	27	0.896	623.94	89	0.648	15.76	47	0.816
乌海市	54.150	9	0.968	23.83	49	0.808	417.36	198	0.212	14.04	65	0.744
唐山市	39.930	65	0.744	20.78	78	0.692	591.23	110	0.564	9.69	137	0.456
廊坊市	31.920	152	0.396	17.39	146	0.42	726.02	57	0.776	10.65	115	0.544
佛山市	30.038	169	0.328	16.43	157	0.376	371.26	214	0.148	6.08	213	0.152
辽阳市	52.910	10	0.964	21.07	76	0.7	319.03	231	0.080	13.29	71	0.72
龙岩市	40.512	63	0.752	17.39	144	0.428	700.28	70	0.724	6.71	198	0.212
克拉玛依市	44.246	37	0.856	26.39	30	0.884	/	246	0.020	21.94	10	0.964
扬州市	32.919	140	0.444	17.67	135	0.464	616.25	93	0.632	13.16	74	0.708
阳泉市	47.137	22	0.916	28.47	17	0.936	542.75	128	0.492	8.41	162	0.356

城市公共项目规模水平子系统（2）

二级指标	城市公共项目规模水平子系统（2）									
三级指标	每百万人剧场、影剧院数			每百人公共图书馆藏书数			每万人拥有公共汽车数			分值小计
城市	数值（座）	排名	分值	数值（册）	排名	分值	数值（辆）	排名	分值	
杭州市	4.824813	50	0.804	181.97	9	0.968	16.89	18	0.932	6.884
无锡市	7.528231	14	0.948	77.35	41	0.84	13.14	34	0.868	6.108
常州市	9.797518	5	0.984	67.16	50	0.804	11.06	53	0.792	5.708
苏州市	2.770083	111	0.56	125.88	19	0.928	13.21	32	0.876	5.496
珠海市	0.640205	250	0.004	82.68	35	0.864	13.15	33	0.872	6.316
绍兴市	6.30979	24	0.908	59.21	55	0.784	11.64	49	0.808	6.056
大连市	0.896861	235	0.064	178.23	10	0.964	15.43	24	0.908	6.216
北京市	9.280033	7	0.976	366.75	4	0.988	18.15	15	0.944	6.828
上海市	3.734746	68	0.732	482.09	2	0.996	12.99	35	0.864	5.732
宁波市	3.153331	94	0.628	127.86	17	0.936	15.47	23	0.912	5.592
嘉兴市	9.322974	6	0.98	123.28	21	0.92	12.01	45	0.824	5.728
东营市	8.836524	10	0.964	39.43	94	0.628	7.26	119	0.528	6.664
威海市	0.713012	247	0.016	46.53	76	0.7	14.19	28	0.892	6.236
沈阳市	5.674809	32	0.876	151.39	13	0.952	9.73	70	0.724	6.84
天津市	2.078042	144	0.428	127.77	18	0.932	8.87	86	0.66	5.684

续表

二级指标	城市公共项目规模子系统（2）									
三级指标	每百万人剧场、影剧院数			每百人公共图书馆藏书数			每万人拥有公共汽车数			分值小计
城市	数值（座）	排名	分值	数值（册）	排名	分值	数值（辆）	排名	分值	
深圳市	1. 542615	185	0. 264	883. 4	1	1	103. 11	1	1	5
厦门市	1. 416029	193	0. 232	185. 84	8	0. 972	18. 66	11	0. 96	5. 76
烟台市	3. 444317	82	0. 676	78. 75	39	0. 848	9. 73	70	0. 724	6. 344
青岛市	4. 587682	56	0. 78	58. 17	56	0. 78	16. 93	17	0. 936	6. 664
武汉市	6. 540623	19	0. 928	123. 9	20	0. 924	13. 45	31	0. 88	7. 232
长沙市	1. 136202	215	0. 144	97. 04	27	0. 896	14. 71	26	0. 9	6. 532
舟山市	5. 352364	39	0. 848	79. 26	38	0. 852	8. 91	85	0. 664	5. 424
马鞍山市	3. 657644	73	0. 712	43. 38	81	0. 68	7. 17	121	0. 52	5. 432
鄂尔多斯市	2. 564103	116	0. 54	42. 72	84	0. 668	12. 8	36	0. 86	5. 944
淄博市	1. 764836	165	0. 344	52. 89	61	0. 76	7. 26	119	0. 528	5. 196
太原市	2. 378121	126	0. 5	108. 89	24	0. 908	7. 76	110	0. 564	6. 42
镇江市	15. 40931	3	0. 992	73. 44	43	0. 832	9. 97	62	0. 756	5. 832
昆明市	5. 59093	36	0. 86	30. 57	122	0. 516	20. 63	5	0. 984	6. 48
南京市	3. 496503	79	0. 688	211. 77	7	0. 976	11. 27	52	0. 796	6. 48
福州市	3. 654252	74	0. 708	86. 56	33	0. 872	18. 91	10	0. 964	6. 2
济南市	1. 760047	166	0. 34	155. 81	12	0. 956	12. 18	44	0. 828	6. 66
中山市	6. 404099	21	0. 92	72. 13	45	0. 824	14. 24	27	0. 896	5. 3
广州市	1. 809599	162	0. 356	222. 67	6	0. 98	17. 31	16	0. 94	6. 76

| 二级指标 | 城市公共项目规模子系统（2） | | | | | | | | | |
| 三级指标 | 每百万人剧场、影剧院数 | | | 每百人公共图书馆藏书数 | | | 每万人拥有公共汽车数 | | | 分值小计 |
城市	数值（座）	排名	分值	数值（册）	排名	分值	数值（辆）	排名	分值	
晋城市	5.263158	40	0.844	12.76	254	-0.012	8.81	88	0.652	4.528
南通市	1.235924	209	0.168	37.62	99	0.608	3.41	221	0.12	3.628
金华市	3.727171	69	0.728	38.44	97	0.616	9.85	66	0.74	5.364
芜湖市	1.766784	164	0.348	27.1	143	0.432	12.79	37	0.856	6.124
湖州市	1.38217	197	0.216	81.16	36	0.86	6.14	143	0.432	4.908
铜陵市	4.143646	61	0.76	74.99	42	0.836	6.71	130	0.484	6.284
呼和浩特市	2.783577	110	0.564	120.67	23	0.912	15.78	20	0.924	6.688
包头市	6.400602	22	0.916	138.13	14	0.948	9.42	77	0.696	6.728
乌海市	3.738318	67	0.736	77.92	40	0.844	7.6	115	0.544	5.856
唐山市	1.97837	152	0.396	24.75	157	0.376	6.61	133	0.472	4.7
廊坊市	2.978918	102	0.596	33.65	110	0.564	6.11	145	0.424	4.72
佛山市	5.000695	45	0.824	80.59	37	0.856	9.94	64	0.748	4.432
辽阳市	1.075847	222	0.116	55.09	59	0.768	7.16	122	0.516	4.864
龙岩市	3.515625	77	0.696	24.88	155	0.384	4.84	176	0.3	4.496
克拉玛依市	5.11509	43	0.832	122.63	22	0.916	7.97	104	0.588	6.06
扬州市	1.34499	198	0.212	48.61	68	0.732	11.05	54	0.788	4.98
阳泉市	2.191381	134	0.468	45.8	80	0.684	8.85	87	0.656	5.508

153

3. 城市社保范围及水平子系统

二级指标	城市社保范围及水平子系统															分值小计
三级指标	养老保险参保覆盖率					医疗保险参保覆盖率					失业保险参保覆盖率					
	基本养老保险参保人数(人)	年末总人口(万人)	数值	排名	分值	基本医疗保险参保人数(人)	年末总人口(万人)	数值	排名	分值	失业保险参保人数(人)	年末总人口(万人)	数值	排名	分值	
杭州市	3839700	689.12	0.557189	13	0.952	3452400	689.12	0.500987	27	0.896	2439800	689.12	0.354046	12	0.956	2.804
无锡市	2038900	466.56	0.437007	21	0.92	2364600	466.56	0.506816	25	0.904	1562400	466.56	0.334877	13	0.952	2.776
常州市	1074000	360.8	0.297672	33	0.872	1333000	360.8	0.369457	65	0.744	795000	360.8	0.220344	22	0.916	2.532
苏州市	3510000	637.66	0.55045	14	0.948	3910000	637.66	0.613179	17	0.936	2568000	637.66	0.402722	9	0.968	2.852
珠海市	884600	104.74	0.844568	5	0.984	956400	104.74	0.913118	6	0.98	767600	104.74	0.732862	4	0.988	2.952
绍兴市	2705000	438.91	0.616299	10	0.964	1820700	438.91	0.414823	49	0.808	804300	438.91	0.183249	32	0.876	2.648
大连市	1643000	586.44	0.280165	35	0.864	4136000	586.44	0.705272	13	0.952	1239000	586.44	0.211275	24	0.908	2.724
北京市	9825000	1257.8	0.781126	6	0.98	10637000	1257.8	0.845683	7	0.976	7742000	1257.8	0.615519	6	0.98	2.936
上海市	8948900	1412.32	0.633631	9	0.968	9997400	1412.32	0.707871	12	0.956	5562000	1412.32	0.39382	10	0.964	2.888
宁波市	3835000	574.08	0.668025	8	0.972	2812800	574.08	0.489967	30	0.884	1862500	574.08	0.324432	14	0.948	2.804
嘉兴市	1591900	341.6	0.466013	19	0.928	1338100	341.6	0.391715	57	0.776	777500	341.6	0.227605	21	0.92	2.624
东营市	238000	184.87	0.128739	121	0.52	900000	184.87	0.486829	31	0.88	122100	184.87	0.066046	149	0.408	1.808
威海市	777000	253.61	0.306376	30	0.884	1226000	253.61	0.483419	32	0.876	416000	253.61	0.164031	41	0.84	2.6
沈阳市	2931000	719.6	0.40731	23	0.912	3240000	719.6	0.45025	38	0.852	1250000	719.6	0.173708	36	0.86	2.624
天津市	4699800	984.85	0.47721	18	0.932	4860000	984.85	0.493476	28	0.892	2461000	984.85	0.249886	18	0.932	2.756
深圳市	6913500	259.87	2.660369	1	1	4435100	259.87	1.706661	2	0.996	2586200	259.87	0.99519	2	0.996	2.992

二级指标	城市社保范围及水平子系统															分值小计
三级指标	养老保险参保覆盖率					医疗保险参保覆盖率					失业保险参保覆盖率					
	基本养老保险人数(人)	年末总人口(万人)	数值	排名	分值	基本医疗保险人数(人)	年末总人口(万人)	数值	排名	分值	失业保险参保人数(人)	年末总人口(万人)	数值	排名	分值	
厦门市	1586100	180.21	0.88014	4	0.988	2346900	180.21	1.302314	4	0.988	1256000	180.21	0.696965	5	0.984	2.96
烟台市	1623000	651.14	0.249255	46	0.82	2484000	651.14	0.381485	60	0.764	863000	651.14	0.132537	55	0.784	2.368
青岛市	2712000	763.64	0.355141	26	0.9	3243000	763.64	0.424677	44	0.828	1480600	763.64	0.193887	28	0.892	2.62
武汉市	3095800	836.73	0.369988	25	0.904	3396000	836.73	0.405866	51	0.8	1297100	836.73	0.15502	47	0.816	2.52
长沙市	1371900	652.4	0.210285	62	0.756	2625600	652.4	0.402452	53	0.792	692800	652.4	0.106193	77	0.696	2.244
舟山市	301200	96.77	0.311253	28	0.892	295900	96.77	0.305777	77	0.696	165300	96.77	0.170817	38	0.852	2.44
马鞍山市	452081	129.1	0.350179	27	0.896	745859	129.1	0.577737	19	0.928	190600	129.1	0.147637	52	0.796	2.62
鄂尔多斯市	174000	152.38	0.114188	145	0.424	259000	152.38	0.16997	182	0.276	142000	152.38	0.093188	91	0.64	1.34
淄博市	1112000	422.36	0.263283	41	0.84	1923000	422.36	0.455299	37	0.856	654000	422.36	0.154844	48	0.812	2.508
太原市	733000	365.5	0.200547	69	0.728	1968000	365.5	0.53844	23	0.912	757100	365.5	0.207141	25	0.904	2.544
镇江市	689100	270.71	0.254553	43	0.832	754500	270.71	0.278712	90	0.644	432700	270.71	0.159839	43	0.832	2.308
昆明市	947600	583.99	0.162263	87	0.656	3153000	583.99	0.539907	22	0.916	759900	583.99	0.130122	57	0.776	2.348
南京市	3315600	632.42	0.524272	15	0.944	2766600	632.42	0.437462	42	0.836	1975300	632.42	0.31234	15	0.944	2.724
福州市	1290600	645.9	0.199814	70	0.724	2440000	645.9	0.377767	62	0.756	824400	645.9	0.127636	59	0.768	2.248
济南市	1865000	604.08	0.308734	29	0.888	2545100	604.08	0.421318	47	0.816	915800	604.08	0.151602	49	0.808	2.512
中山市	1969300	149.18	1.320083	3	0.992	2334500	149.18	1.564888	3	0.992	1291000	149.18	0.865398	3	0.992	2.976

| 二级指标 | 城市社保范围及水平子系统 | | | | | | | | | | | | | | | 分值小计 |
| 三级指标 | 养老保险参保覆盖率 | | | | | 医疗保险参保覆盖率 | | | | | 失业保险参保覆盖率 | | | | | |
	基本养老保险人数(人)	年末总人口(万人)	数值	排名	分值	基本医疗参保人数(人)	年末总人口(万人)	数值	排名	分值	失业保险参保人数(人)	年末总人口(万人)	数值	排名	分值	
广州市	4845000	806.14	0.601012	11	0.96	6784000	806.14	0.841541	9	0.968	3360000	806.14	0.416801	8	0.972	2.9
晋城市	213900	216.23	0.098922	172	0.316	507000	216.23	0.234473	128	0.492	205000	216.23	0.094806	89	0.648	1.456
南通市	1113800	762.92	0.145992	101	0.6	1399000	762.92	0.183374	174	0.308	808300	762.92	0.105948	78	0.692	1.6
金华市	1039600	466.65	0.222779	53	0.792	886400	466.65	0.18995	167	0.336	544800	466.65	0.116747	68	0.732	1.86
芜湖市	526349	229.5	0.229346	52	0.796	1248600	229.5	0.544052	21	0.92	255200	229.5	0.111198	72	0.716	2.432
湖州市	1543000	259.98	0.593507	12	0.956	1017300	259.98	0.391299	58	0.772	408400	259.98	0.157089	45	0.824	2.552
铜陵市	205765	74.01	0.278023	36	0.86	445342	74.01	0.601732	18	0.932	141000	74.01	0.190515	29	0.888	2.68
呼和浩特市	373000	229.56	0.162485	86	0.66	433900	229.56	0.189014	168	0.332	395000	229.56	0.172068	37	0.856	1.848
包头市	552000	219.8	0.251137	45	0.824	742000	219.8	0.33758	67	0.736	418000	219.8	0.190173	30	0.884	2.444
乌海市	137167	53	0.258806	42	0.836	442282	53	0.834494	10	0.964	105013	53	0.198138	27	0.896	2.696
唐山市	1619200	735	0.220299	55	0.784	2067000	735	0.281224	89	0.648	753200	735	0.102476	80	0.684	2.116
廊坊市	423000	419.02	0.10095	167	0.336	833000	419.02	0.198797	157	0.376	235000	419.02	0.056083	173	0.312	1.024
佛山市	2785300	370.89	0.750977	7	0.976	4161100	370.89	1.121923	5	0.984	1552200	370.89	0.418507	7	0.976	2.936
辽阳市	515800	183.32	0.281366	34	0.868	783000	183.32	0.427122	43	0.832	209836	183.32	0.114464	69	0.728	2.428
龙岩市	380100	314.37	0.120908	136	0.46	912000	314.37	0.290295	87	0.656	186600	314.37	0.059357	163	0.352	1.468
克拉玛依市	159700	37.51	0.425753	22	0.916	259600	37.51	0.692082	14	0.948	139000	37.51	0.370568	11	0.96	2.824
扬州市	771000	459.12	0.16793	84	0.668	946700	459.12	0.206199	150	0.404	558500	459.12	0.121646	63	0.752	1.824
阳泉市	226200	130.78	0.172962	80	0.684	548500	130.78	0.419407	48	0.812	198200	130.78	0.151552	50	0.804	2.3

4. 城市公共服务水平母系统

一级指标	城市公共服务水平母系统									
二级指标	财政公共投入比重子系统			公共项目规模子系统			社保范围及水平子系统			分值合计
城市	数值	排序	分值	数值	排序	分值	数值	排序	分值	
杭州市	3.688	10	0.964	6.884	2	0.996	2.804	12	0.956	2.916
无锡市	3.268	26	0.9	6.108	31	0.88	2.776	14	0.948	2.728
常州市	2.844	53	0.792	5.708	45	0.824	2.532	34	0.868	2.484
苏州市	3.244	30	0.884	5.496	58	0.772	2.852	10	0.964	2.62
珠海市	3.66	12	0.956	6.316	21	0.92	2.952	5	0.984	2.86
绍兴市	2.16	103	0.592	6.056	34	0.868	2.648	23	0.912	2.372
大连市	3.74	9	0.968	6.216	24	0.908	2.724	16	0.94	2.816
北京市	3.972	1	1	6.828	5	0.984	2.936	6	0.98	2.964
上海市	3.96	2	0.996	5.732	42	0.836	2.888	9	0.968	2.8
宁波市	3.208	35	0.864	5.592	49	0.808	2.804	12	0.956	2.628
嘉兴市	1.872	126	0.5	5.728	43	0.832	2.624	26	0.9	2.232
东营市	2.964	49	0.808	6.664	10	0.964	1.808	88	0.652	2.424
威海市	3.172	37	0.856	6.236	23	0.912	2.6	31	0.88	2.648
沈阳市	3.444	20	0.924	6.84	4	0.988	2.624	26	0.9	2.812
天津市	3.848	5	0.984	5.684	46	0.82	2.756	15	0.944	2.748
深圳市	2.528	77	0.696	5	86	0.66	2.992	2	0.996	2.352

一级指标				城市公共服务水平母系统						
二级指标	财政公共投入比重子系统			公共项目规模子系统			社保范围及水平子系统			分值合计
城市	数值	排序	分值	数值	排序	分值	数值	排序	分值	
厦门市	3.556	15	0.944	5.76	41	0.84	2.96	4	0.988	2.772
烟台市	2.86	51	0.8	6.344	20	0.924	2.368	47	0.816	2.54
青岛市	1.9	123	0.512	6.664	10	0.964	2.62	28	0.892	2.368
武汉市	3.22	33	0.872	7.232	1	1	2.52	35	0.864	2.736
长沙市	2.176	101	0.6	6.532	14	0.948	2.244	57	0.776	2.324
舟山市	3.272	25	0.904	5.424	61	0.76	2.44	41	0.84	2.504
马鞍山市	2.94	50	0.804	5.432	59	0.768	2.62	28	0.892	2.464
鄂尔多斯市	3.956	3	0.992	5.944	35	0.864	1.34	131	0.48	2.336
淄博市	2.552	73	0.712	5.196	75	0.704	2.508	39	0.848	2.264
太原市	2.428	83	0.672	6.42	19	0.928	2.544	33	0.872	2.472
镇江市	1.476	165	0.344	5.832	40	0.844	2.308	51	0.8	1.988
昆明市	1.964	118	0.532	6.48	16	0.94	2.348	49	0.808	2.28
南京市	3.22	33	0.872	6.48	16	0.94	2.724	16	0.94	2.752
福州市	1.452	169	0.328	6.2	25	0.904	2.248	56	0.78	2.012
济南市	2.528	76	0.7	6.66	12	0.956	2.512	37	0.856	2.512
中山市	1.776	135	0.464	5.3	70	0.724	2.976	3	0.992	2.18
广州市	3.484	18	0.932	6.76	6	0.98	2.9	8	0.972	2.884

一级指标	城市公共服务水平母系统									分值合计
二级指标	财政公共投入比重子系统			公共项目规模子系统			社保范围及水平子系统			
城市	数值	排序	分值	数值	排序	分值	数值	排序	分值	
晋城市	2.3	93	0.632	4.528	111	0.56	1.456	118	0.532	1.724
南通市	1.72	142	0.436	3.628	167	0.336	1.6	107	0.576	1.348
金华市	2.064	110	0.564	5.364	67	0.736	1.86	81	0.68	1.98
芜湖市	2.968	48	0.812	6.124	29	0.888	2.432	42	0.836	2.536
湖州市	1.768	136	0.46	4.908	91	0.64	2.552	32	0.876	1.976
铜陵市	3.628	13	0.952	6.284	22	0.916	2.68	20	0.924	2.792
呼和浩特市	3.232	32	0.876	6.688	9	0.968	1.848	83	0.672	2.516
包头市	3.316	24	0.908	6.728	7	0.976	2.444	40	0.844	2.728
乌海市	3.932	4	0.988	5.856	37	0.856	2.696	19	0.928	2.772
唐山市	2.828	59	0.768	4.7	102	0.596	2.116	70	0.724	2.088
廊坊市	1.612	155	0.384	4.72	101	0.6	1.024	168	0.332	1.316
佛山市	1.584	158	0.372	4.432	117	0.536	2.936	6	0.98	1.888
辽阳市	2.836	55	0.784	4.864	93	0.632	2.428	43	0.832	2.248
龙岩市	2.636	69	0.728	4.496	114	0.548	1.468	116	0.54	1.816
克拉玛依市	3.832	6	0.98	6.06	33	0.872	2.824	11	0.96	2.812
扬州市	1.44	171	0.32	4.98	88	0.652	1.824	85	0.664	1.636
阳泉市	2.472	80	0.684	5.508	57	0.776	2.3	52	0.796	2.256

2012中国城市科学发展综合评价报告

三、城市居民实际享有水平母系统

1. 城市居民收入水平子系统

二级指标	城市居民收入水平子系统												
三级指标	城镇居民人均可支配收入			农村居民人均纯收入			城乡居民收入比			城镇化对居民收入的影响			分值小计
城市	数值（元）	排序	分值	数值（元）	排序	分值	数值	排序	分值	数值	排名	分值	
杭州市	30035	8	0.972	13186	13	0.952	0.439021	73	0.712	1.195884	30	0.884	3.52
无锡市	27750	11	0.96	14002	8	0.972	0.504577	21	0.92	/	240	0.044	2.896
常州市	25875	18	0.932	12637	15	0.944	0.488386	28	0.892	1.141528	103	0.592	3.36
苏州市	30366	5	0.984	14657	4	0.988	0.482678	34	0.868	/	240	0.044	2.884
珠海市	25382	21	0.92	10187	28	0.892	0.401347	114	0.548	1.146501	87	0.656	3.016
绍兴市	30164	7	0.976	13651	10	0.964	0.452559	60	0.764	1.151685	81	0.68	3.384
大连市	21293	42	0.836	12317	16	0.94	0.578453	8	0.972	1.150127	85	0.664	3.412
北京市	29073	10	0.964	13262	12	0.956	0.456162	56	0.78	1.112629	192	0.236	2.936
上海市	31838	3	0.992	13746	9	0.968	0.431748	79	0.688	1.122743	162	0.356	3.004
宁波市	30166	6	0.98	14261	7	0.976	0.472751	42	0.836	1.131402	130	0.484	3.276
嘉兴市	27487	12	0.956	14365	5	0.984	0.522611	16	0.94	1.176609	48	0.812	3.692
东营市	23796	30	0.884	8427	53	0.792	0.354135	189	0.248	/	240	0.044	1.968
威海市	22235	38	0.852	10517	25	0.904	0.472993	41	0.84	/	240	0.044	2.64
沈阳市	20541	49	0.808	10022	30	0.884	0.487902	30	0.884	1.119475	174	0.308	2.884

二级指标	城市居民收入水平系统												分值小计
三级指标	城镇居民人均可支配收入			农村居民人均纯收入			城乡居民收入比			城镇化对居民收入的影响			
城市	数值（元）	排序	分值	数值（元）	排序	分值	数值	排序	分值	数值	排名	分值	
天津市	24293	29	0.888	11801	18	0.932	0.485778	32	0.876	1.153162	79	0.688	3.384
深圳市	32381	2	0.996	32381	1	1	1	1	1	1.180954	45	0.824	3.82
厦门市	29253	9	0.968	10033	29	0.888	0.342973	203	0.192	1.205582	25	0.904	2.952
烟台市	23288	32	0.876	9916	31	0.88	0.425799	84	0.668	/	240	0.044	2.468
青岛市	24998	28	0.892	10550	24	0.908	0.422034	90	0.644	/	240	0.044	2.488
武汉市	20806	48	0.812	8295	57	0.776	0.398683	119	0.528	1.146974	86	0.66	2.776
长沙市	22814	35	0.864	11206	21	0.92	0.49119	25	0.904	1.141869	101	0.6	3.288
舟山市	26242	17	0.936	14265	6	0.98	0.543594	14	0.948	1.09895	212	0.156	3.02
马鞍山市	23159	34	0.868	9331	36	0.86	0.40291	109	0.568	1.159517	68	0.732	3.028
鄂尔多斯市	25205	24	0.908	8756	48	0.812	0.347391	199	0.208	1.166748	60	0.764	2.692
淄博市	21784	41	0.84	9195	42	0.836	0.422099	89	0.648	/	240	0.044	2.368
太原市	17258	108	0.572	7611	76	0.7	0.441013	70	0.724	1.13898	115	0.544	2.54
镇江市	23224	33	0.872	10874	23	0.912	0.468223	46	0.82	1.119401	175	0.304	2.908
昆明市	18876	67	0.736	5810	174	0.308	0.307798	233	0.072	1.201891	27	0.896	2.012
南京市	27383	13	0.952	11128	22	0.916	0.406384	101	0.6	/	240	0.044	2.512
福州市	22723	36	0.86	8543	52	0.796	0.375963	155	0.384	1.493289	2	0.996	3.036
济南市	25321	23	0.912	8903	44	0.828	0.351605	190	0.244	/	240	0.044	2.028
中山市	25357	22	0.916	14928	3	0.992	0.588713	5	0.984	1.119935	168	0.332	3.224

二级指标							城市居民收入水平子系统						
三级指标	城镇居民人均可支配收入			农村居民人均纯收入			城乡居民收入比			城镇化对居民收入的影响			分值小计
城市	数值（元）	排序	分值	数值（元）	排序	分值	数值	排序	分值	数值	排名	分值	
广州市	30658	4	0.988	12676	14	0.948	0.413465	96	0.62	1.207645	23	0.912	3.468
晋城市	17353	103	0.592	5899	170	0.324	0.339941	206	0.18	1.186193	41	0.84	1.936
南通市	21825	39	0.848	9914	32	0.876	0.45425	58	0.772	1.218545	22	0.916	3.412
金华市	25029	27	0.896	10201	27	0.896	0.407567	100	0.604	1.11225	193	0.232	2.628
芜湖市	18727	68	0.732	7834	68	0.732	0.418326	94	0.628	1.122901	161	0.36	2.452
湖州市	25572	20	0.924	13288	11	0.96	0.519631	17	0.936	1.113799	187	0.256	3.076
铜陵市	18690	69	0.728	7266	86	0.66	0.388764	137	0.456	1.123843	157	0.376	2.22
呼和浩特市	25174	25	0.904	8746	50	0.804	0.347422	198	0.212	1.151359	82	0.676	2.596
包头市	25862	19	0.928	8766	47	0.816	0.338953	209	0.168	1.126357	147	0.416	2.328
乌海市	19741	55	0.784	9245	40	0.844	0.468315	45	0.824	1.140913	107	0.576	3.028
唐山市	19556	60	0.764	8310	56	0.78	0.424934	86	0.66	1.496232	1	1	3.204
廊坊市	19576	59	0.768	7589	78	0.692	0.387669	139	0.448	1.480901	3	0.992	2.9
佛山市	27245	15	0.944	12202	17	0.936	0.447862	66	0.74	1.11813	178	0.292	2.912
辽阳市	16570	128	0.492	8095	61	0.76	0.488533	27	0.896	1.139984	110	0.564	2.712
龙岩市	18406	72	0.716	6931	105	0.584	0.376562	154	0.388	1.329205	11	0.96	2.648
克拉玛依市	17295	107	0.576	10296	26	0.9	0.595317	4	0.988	1.057423	231	0.08	2.544
扬州市	19537	61	0.76	9462	34	0.868	0.484312	33	0.872	/	240	0.044	2.544
阳泉市	17084	111	0.56	6560	124	0.508	0.383985	145	0.424	1.277876	14	0.948	2.44

2. 城市居民生活环境水平子系统

二级指标	城市居民生活环境水平子系统															
三级指标	人均绿地面积			生活垃圾无害化处理率			生活污水处理率			人均生活用电量			人均生活用水量			分值小计
城市	数值(m²)	排序	分值	数值	排序	分值	数值	排序	分值	数值(千瓦*时)	排序	分值	数值(吨)	排序	分值	
杭州市	35	107	0.576	100	1	1	93.22	23	0.912	1166.869	19	0.928	50.24378	47	0.816	4.232
无锡市	72	22	0.916	100	1	1	84.1	98	0.612	1062.516	25	0.904	58.22053	32	0.876	4.308
常州市	32	131	0.48	100	1	1	74.5	155	0.384	921.4402	33	0.872	50.53348	46	0.82	3.556
苏州市	58	32	0.876	100	1	1	71.24	167	0.336	1265.931	16	0.94	70.44292	17	0.936	4.088
珠海市	55	39	0.848	92.34	136	0.46	78.81	142	0.436	1300.306	13	0.952	85.55471	6	0.98	3.676
绍兴市	53	45	0.824	100	1	1	79.9	137	0.456	797.5092	44	0.828	35.00923	91	0.64	3.748
大连市	60	29	0.888	86	161	0.36	94.2	18	0.932	772.2901	51	0.8	24.07152	147	0.416	3.396
北京市	53	45	0.824	96.95	105	0.584	80.98	129	0.488	1143.624	20	0.924	52.27401	43	0.832	3.652
上海市	89	16	0.94	84.9	173	0.312	81	127	0.496	3490.848	1	1	72.94491	14	0.948	3.696
宁波市	44	71	0.72	100	1	1	70.44	175	0.304	1081.137	24	0.908	56.39579	34	0.868	3.8
嘉兴市	49	54	0.788	100	1	1	84.84	90	0.644	703.2716	64	0.748	21.82687	171	0.32	3.5
东营市	68	24	0.908	100	1	1	88.16	66	0.74	422.2196	178	0.292	22.13557	165	0.344	3.284
威海市	89	16	0.94	100	1	1	92.39	24	0.908	873.8628	37	0.856	22.54433	162	0.356	4.06
沈阳市	50	52	0.796	100	1	1	78	145	0.424	746.7851	56	0.78	33.23115	100	0.604	3.604
天津市	24	185	0.264	100	1	1	83	108	0.572	835.247	41	0.84	25.77012	137	0.456	3.132
深圳市	371	2	0.996	94.6	125	0.504	88.81	65	0.744	3181.999	3	0.992	193.0696	1	1	4.236

| 二级指标 | 城市居民生活环境水平子系统 | | | | | | | | | | | | | | | |
| 三级指标 | 人均绿地面积 | | | 生活垃圾无害化处理率 | | | 生活污水处理率 | | | 人均生活用电量 | | | 人均生活用水量 | | | 分值小计 |
城市	数值(m²)	排序	分值	数值	排序	分值	数值	排序	分值	数值(千瓦*时)	排序	分值	数值(吨)	排序	分值	
厦门市	91	15	0.944	96.93	106	0.58	90.96	40	0.844	1696.465	6	0.98	60.3962	29	0.888	4.236
烟台市	58	32	0.876	100	1	1	90.6	41	0.84	588.5634	98	0.612	21.38066	173	0.312	3.64
青岛市	60	29	0.888	100	1	1	85.29	84	0.668	988.461	30	0.884	45.45917	55	0.784	4.224
武汉市	30	141	0.44	85.01	166	0.34	94.96	15	0.944	1029.096	27	0.896	77.15932	11	0.96	3.58
长沙市	36	100	0.604	100	1	1	92.07	28	0.892	1424.453	10	0.964	110.0815	4	0.988	4.448
舟山市	26	168	0.332	100	1	1	57.31	220	0.124	667.9432	74	0.708	22.9346	158	0.372	2.536
马鞍山市	78	20	0.924	82.07	178	0.292	85.76	83	0.672	569.1091	105	0.584	57.58572	33	0.872	3.344
鄂尔多斯市	291	3	0.992	85.08	164	0.348	84.44	97	0.616	1207.84	18	0.932	32.39816	105	0.584	3.472
淄博市	54	42	0.836	100	1	1	92.26	25	0.904	530.5901	120	0.524	18.43705	201	0.2	3.464
太原市	29	150	0.404	94.8	123	0.512	66.1	192	0.236	673.6816	72	0.716	34.18126	97	0.616	2.484
镇江市	63	28	0.892	100	1	1	65.99	194	0.228	724.8624	58	0.772	39.29296	76	0.7	3.592
昆明市	34	114	0.548	85	167	0.336	83.56	103	0.592	1285.859	15	0.944	42.22256	65	0.744	3.164
南京市	141	11	0.96	80	188	0.252	59.16	214	0.148	909.3842	34	0.868	54.89542	36	0.86	3.088
福州市	43	75	0.704	98.25	98	0.612	83.41	105	0.584	1615.674	8	0.972	52.91373	41	0.84	3.712
济南市	34	114	0.548	84.61	174	0.308	89.6	54	0.788	859.8069	40	0.844	33.03833	101	0.6	3.088
中山市	10	265	-0.056	100	1	1	90.05	44	0.828	1782.209	5	0.984	40.99745	70	0.724	3.48

二级指标	城市居民生活环境水平子系统															分值小计
三级指标	人均绿地面积			生活垃圾无害化处理率			生活污水处理率			人均生活用电量			人均生活用水量			
城市	数值（m²）	排序	分值	数值	排序	分值	数值	排序	分值	数值（千瓦*时）	排序	分值	数值（吨）	排序	分值	
广州市	187	7	0.976	/	268	-0.068	/	279	-0.112	1630.443	7	0.976	124.2921	3	0.992	2.764
晋城市	43	75	0.704	93.21	132	0.476	95.62	12	0.956	344.0046	211	0.16	28.34194	120	0.524	2.82
南通市	22	197	0.216	100	1	1	83	108	0.572	602.5858	93	0.632	39.47244	75	0.704	3.124
金华市	29	150	0.404	99.31	92	0.636	70.23	176	0.3	645.5628	80	0.684	24.21934	146	0.42	2.444
芜湖市	46	63	0.752	100	1	1	70.84	169	0.328	571.2454	103	0.592	43.25294	60	0.764	3.436
湖州市	34	114	0.548	100	1	1	84.77	91	0.64	654.3526	77	0.696	31.92837	107	0.576	3.46
铜陵市	104	13	0.952	95.82	113	0.552	68.75	183	0.272	492.215	141	0.44	25.40709	140	0.444	2.66
呼和浩特市	22	197	0.216	97.88	100	0.604	95.99	8	0.972	788.4373	47	0.816	24.46914	143	0.432	3.04
包头市	55	39	0.848	92.4	135	0.464	83.88	100	0.604	909.0877	35	0.864	22.93333	159	0.368	3.148
乌海市	40	86	0.66	81.53	180	0.284	89.75	51	0.8	376.3396	201	0.2	67.92453	20	0.924	2.868
唐山市	30	141	0.44	100	1	1	94.11	19	0.928	231.714	260	-0.036	27.61031	125	0.504	2.836
廊坊市	53	45	0.824	95.1	117	0.536	86.11	78	0.692	516.8823	125	0.504	22.13237	166	0.34	2.896
佛山市	14	250	0.004	95.59	115	0.544	79	140	0.444	1258.327	17	0.936	42.22546	64	0.748	2.676
辽阳市	47	61	0.76	67.16	209	0.168	78.45	144	0.428	443.7034	161	0.36	21.99148	168	0.332	2.048
龙岩市	26	168	0.332	97.27	103	0.592	82.02	118	0.532	969.6256	31	0.88	14.02677	236	0.06	2.396
克拉玛依市	59	31	0.88	94.87	121	0.52	92.12	26	0.9	538.4964	116	0.54	33.37777	99	0.608	3.448
扬州市	28	156	0.38	87.5	147	0.416	68.94	182	0.276	736.8795	57	0.776	25.82462	136	0.46	2.308
阳泉市	27	162	0.356	100	1	1	82.99	112	0.556	318.287	227	0.096	28.125	121	0.52	2.528

3. 城市居民就业水平子系统

二级指标	城市居民就业水平子系统						
三级指标	城镇化对就业的影响			城镇登记失业率			分值小计
城市	数值	排名	分值	数值	排名	分值	
杭州市	0.823567	36	0.86	0.022	22	0.916	1.776
无锡市	/	240	0.044	0.026	41	0.84	0.884
常州市	0.989228	152	0.396	0.026	41	0.84	1.236
苏州市	/	240	0.044	0.028	60	0.764	0.808
珠海市	0.938314	92	0.636	0.027	49	0.808	1.444
绍兴市	0.921006	75	0.704	0.03	77	0.696	1.4
大连市	1.030954	194	0.228	0.027	49	0.808	1.036
北京市	0.925791	79	0.688	0.014	4	0.988	1.676
上海市	0.978393	140	0.444	0.042	252	-0.004	0.44
宁波市	0.936879	90	0.644	0.057	287	-0.144	0.5
嘉兴市	0.946977	97	0.616	0.034	128	0.492	1.108
东营市	/	240	0.044	0.019	12	0.956	1
威海市	/	240	0.044	0.015	5	0.984	1.028
沈阳市	0.9894	153	0.392	0.031	89	0.648	1.04
天津市	1.056392	207	0.176	0.036	151	0.4	0.576
深圳市	0.973821	132	0.476	0.025	34	0.868	1.344

二级指标	城市居民就业水平子系统							
三级指标	城镇化对就业的影响			城镇登记失业率			分值小计	
城市	数值	排名	分值	数值	排名	分值		
厦门市	0.82906	37	0.856	0.033	112	0.556	1.412	
烟台市	/	240	0.044	0.033	112	0.556	0.6	
青岛市	/	240	0.044	0.029	67	0.736	0.78	
武汉市	0.971274	129	0.488	0.041	233	0.072	0.56	
长沙市	0.88582	51	0.8	0.03	77	0.696	1.496	
舟山市	0.81318	34	0.868	0.029	67	0.736	1.604	
马鞍山市	0.953093	104	0.588	0.031	89	0.648	1.236	
鄂尔多斯市	0.860813	44	0.828	0.022	22	0.916	1.744	
淄博市	/	240	0.044	0.027	49	0.808	0.852	
太原市	0.932638	85	0.664	0.034	128	0.492	1.156	
镇江市	1.035137	197	0.216	0.023	25	0.904	1.12	
昆明市	0.924627	78	0.692	0.021	20	0.924	1.616	
南京市	/	240	0.044	0.026	41	0.84	0.884	
福州市	0.816579	35	0.864	0.031	89	0.648	1.512	
济南市	/	240	0.044	0.038	182	0.276	0.32	
中山市	0.729612	18	0.932	0.021	20	0.924	1.856	

二级指标	城市居民就业水平子系统						分值小计
三级指标	城镇化对就业的影响			城镇登记失业率			
城市	数值	排名	分值	数值	排名	分值	
广州市	1.011995	173	0.312	0.023	25	0.904	1.216
晋城市	0.930172	82	0.676	0.024	31	0.88	1.556
南通市	0.952958	102	0.596	0.027	49	0.808	1.404
金华市	1.022404	183	0.272	0.03	77	0.696	0.968
芜湖市	0.68534	14	0.948	0.03	77	0.696	1.644
湖州市	1.102751	215	0.144	0.032	100	0.604	0.748
铜陵市	0.886944	52	0.796	0.039	193	0.232	1.028
呼和浩特市	1.080225	211	0.16	0.039	193	0.232	0.392
包头市	0.929903	81	0.68	0.038	182	0.276	0.956
乌海市	0.983622	147	0.416	0.043	270	-0.076	0.34
唐山市	0.973743	131	0.48	0.041	233	0.072	0.552
廊坊市	0.975782	138	0.452	0.02	16	0.94	1.392
佛山市	1.034071	195	0.224	0.019	12	0.956	1.18
辽阳市	0.780822	21	0.92	0.027	49	0.808	1.728
龙岩市	1.056742	208	0.172	0.029	67	0.736	0.908
克拉玛依市	1.06241	209	0.168	0.015	5	0.984	1.152
扬州市	/	240	0.044	0.027	49	0.808	0.852
阳泉市	0.953657	105	0.584	0.038	182	0.276	0.86

4. 城市居民消费水平子系统

城市居民消费水平子系统

一级指标	城市居民消费水平子系统															
二级指标	城镇居民恩格尔系数			人均年末储蓄余额			人均住宅建筑面积 (m²)			居住支出占消费支出比重 (%)			人均社会消费品零售额 (元)			分值小计
城市	数值	排序	分值	数值	排序	分值	数值	排名	分值	数值	排序	分值	数值	排序	分值	
杭州市	0.385281	183	0.272	57334.57	7	0.976	30.86	109	0.568	10.16382	118	0.532	24653.41	14	0.948	3.296
无锡市	0.372451	157	0.376	48310.31	11	0.96	35.8	35	0.864	10.89106	227	0.096	28635.32	5	0.984	3.28
常州市	0.325777	59	0.768	43745.95	15	0.944	36.7	30	0.884	10.4169	151	0.4	22956.55	18	0.932	3.928
苏州市	0.350746	105	0.584	44469.98	13	0.952	34.8	51	0.8	10.19244	122	0.516	22944.12	19	0.928	3.78
珠海市	0.34973	103	0.592	62906.26	5	0.984	28.59	156	0.38	10.38444	146	0.42	31115.69	3	0.992	3.368
绍兴市	0.345815	94	0.628	39603.45	22	0.916	36.62	31	0.88	10.99006	238	0.052	17359.79	40	0.844	3.32
大连市	0.370627	147	0.416	50445.67	9	0.968	25.67	189	0.248	9.68346	59	0.768	24510.54	15	0.944	3.344
北京市	0.320708	50	0.804	86040.61	1	1	/	219	0.128	11.0783	247	0.016	31762.69	2	0.996	2.944
上海市	0.335216	72	0.716	70566.25	3	0.992	34.6	54	0.788	10.92462	231	0.08	26362.55	10	0.964	3.54
宁波市	0.355252	116	0.54	43518.25	16	0.94	30.22	123	0.512	10.94548	234	0.068	22394.61	22	0.916	2.976
嘉兴市	0.328764	65	0.744	36175.53	31	0.88	35.23	44	0.828	10.92288	230	0.084	17743.89	38	0.852	3.388
东营市	0.283709	9	0.968	34514.32	37	0.856	33.24	72	0.716	10.44066	155	0.384	19084.03	33	0.872	3.796
威海市	0.287828	14	0.948	33838.39	38	0.852	21.79	213	0.152	10.70646	208	0.172	24384.55	16	0.94	3.064
沈阳市	0.317493	45	0.824	41182.22	19	0.928	30.16	124	0.508	10.24462	126	0.5	25485.65	13	0.952	3.712
天津市	0.358652	125	0.504	43364.43	18	0.932	31.28	102	0.596	9.82812	73	0.712	22339.34	23	0.912	3.656
深圳市	0.355373	117	0.536	64761.38	4	0.988	/	219	0.128	9.47408	39	0.848	28931.38	4	0.988	3.488

续表

一级指标																
二级指标	城市居民消费水平子系统															
城市	城镇居民恩格尔系数			人均年末储蓄余额			人均住宅建筑面积			居住支出占消费支出比重			人均社会消费品零售额			分值小计
	数值	排序	分值	数值	排序	分值	数值(m²)	排名	分值	数值(%)	排序	分值	数值(元)	排序	分值	
厦门市	0.364461	134	0.468	39214.56	23	0.912	32.17	89	0.648	10.03834	102	0.596	19400.31	30	0.884	3.508
烟台市	0.323961	57	0.776	30285.48	52	0.796	29.38	142	0.436	10.034	100	0.604	20273.9	27	0.896	3.508
青岛市	0.373795	159	0.368	33402.06	41	0.84	27.42	173	0.312	10.45702	158	0.372	22492.64	21	0.92	2.812
武汉市	0.370393	146	0.42	36694.52	28	0.892	31.85	97	0.616	10.36154	142	0.436	26268.82	12	0.956	3.32
长沙市	0.336295	76	0.7	30848.99	50	0.804	30.88	108	0.572	10.3809	144	0.428	26481.06	8	0.972	3.476
舟山市	0.357241	119	0.528	36646.08	29	0.888	31.72	98	0.612	10.2463	127	0.496	18960.12	34	0.868	3.392
马鞍山市	0.371757	153	0.392	25831.49	73	0.712	34.07	61	0.76	9.8313	74	0.708	10812.05	100	0.604	3.176
鄂尔多斯市	0.260392	3	0.992	30066.67	54	0.788	39.61	13	0.952	10.33812	137	0.456	19487.18	29	0.888	4.076
淄博市	0.285485	10	0.964	28925.46	58	0.772	32.66	82	0.676	9.27566	28	0.892	22185.64	24	0.908	4.212
太原市	0.30646	28	0.892	56760.67	8	0.972	19.58	217	0.136	9.73656	65	0.744	19639.61	28	0.892	3.636
镇江市	0.399129	218	0.132	31896.42	48	0.812	39.1	16	0.94	10.48572	164	0.348	18127.79	35	0.864	3.096
昆明市	0.395651	210	0.164	36364.96	30	0.884	/	219	0.128	10.99494	239	0.048	14853.74	56	0.78	2.004
南京市	0.351542	107	0.576	43854.27	14	0.948	30.1	127	0.496	11.10068	249	0.008	28580.68	6	0.98	3.008
福州市	0.389466	194	0.228	32734.93	44	0.828	/	219	0.128	10.3559	138	0.452	22828.96	20	0.924	2.56
济南市	0.316221	41	0.84	32086.77	47	0.816	29.7	133	0.472	10.1099	115	0.544	26436.8	9	0.968	3.64
中山市	0.391759	200	0.204	46229.34	12	0.956	41.8	9	0.968	10.68634	203	0.192	20752.76	25	0.904	3.224

| 一级指标 | | | | | | | | | 城市居民消费水平子系统 | | | | | | | | |
| 二级指标 | 城镇居民恩格尔系数 | | | 人均年末储蓄余额 | | | 人均住宅建筑面积 | | | 居住支出占消费支出比重 | | | 人均社会消费品零售额 | | | 分值小计 |
城市	数值	排序	分值	数值	排序	分值	数值（m²）	排名	分值	数值（%）	排序	分值	数值（元）	排序	分值	
广州市	0.33284	69	0.728	73189.06	2	0.996	/	219	0.128	10.49268	166	0.34	35219.34	1	1	3.192
晋城市	0.275364	6	0.98	26954.46	66	0.74	30.4	119	0.528	8.99268	16	0.94	8382.294	144	0.428	3.616
南通市	0.35562	118	0.532	36783.14	27	0.896	38.3	22	0.916	10.55464	177	0.296	17537.33	39	0.848	3.488
金华市	0.32624	60	0.764	37786.42	24	0.908	34.38	55	0.784	10.94024	233	0.072	17074.68	42	0.836	3.364
芜湖市	0.386133	186	0.26	21368.45	92	0.636	28.06	167	0.336	9.64128	55	0.784	12696.4	72	0.716	2.732
湖州市	0.368359	139	0.448	28392.61	62	0.756	31.96	95	0.624	10.08584	109	0.568	17833.17	37	0.856	3.252
铜陵市	0.352644	112	0.556	26641.96	70	0.724	26.7	176	0.3	11.15726	257	-0.024	13695.25	63	0.752	2.308
呼和浩特市	0.299747	23	0.912	32352.47	46	0.82	30.16	124	0.508	10.5692	181	0.28	26326.5	11	0.96	3.48
包头市	0.316233	42	0.836	28266.04	63	0.752	30.44	116	0.54	11.07912	248	0.012	27515.31	7	0.976	3.116
乌海市	0.289748	16	0.94	35939.89	33	0.872	30.68	112	0.556	11.15092	256	-0.02	13399.87	67	0.736	3.084
唐山市	0.323251	55	0.784	33172.62	42	0.836	22.9	208	0.172	10.59418	188	0.252	14963.59	55	0.784	2.828
廊坊市	0.297877	22	0.916	26693.45	69	0.728	/	219	0.128	9.48082	41	0.84	9604.319	119	0.528	3.14
佛山市	0.337213	79	0.688	61964.42	6	0.98	38.7	20	0.924	10.50828	168	0.332	23435.59	17	0.936	3.86
辽阳市	0.37955	173	0.312	28429.16	61	0.76	22.74	209	0.168	10.00092	93	0.632	11221.57	94	0.628	2.5
龙岩市	0.376718	167	0.336	15484.45	147	0.416	35	46	0.82	9.41408	38	0.852	12194	79	0.688	3.112
克拉玛依市	0.303942	27	0.896	50024.55	10	0.964	35.63	39	0.848	11.48372	277	-0.104	8896.982	135	0.464	3.068
扬州市	0.372372	156	0.38	28074.26	64	0.748	35	46	0.82	11.2156	259	-0.032	16277.18	46	0.82	2.736
阳泉市	0.337656	82	0.676	33526.25	40	0.844	24	205	0.184	9.51456	43	0.832	11721.34	83	0.672	3.208

5. 城市居民实际享有水平母系统

| 一级指标 | 城市居民实际享有水平母系统 | | | | | | | | | | | | |
| 二级指标 | 居民收入水平子系统 | | | 居民生活环境水平子系统 | | | 居民就业水平子系统 | | | 居民消费水平子系统 | | | 分值合计 |
城市	数值	排序	分值	数值	排序	分值	数值	排序	分值	数值	排序	分值	分值合计
杭州市	3.52	3	0.992	4.232	8	0.972	1.776	9	0.968	3.296	39	0.848	3.78
无锡市	2.896	38	0.852	4.308	5	0.984	0.884	138	0.452	3.28	40	0.844	3.132
常州市	3.36	11	0.96	3.556	40	0.844	1.236	75	0.704	3.928	3	0.992	3.5
苏州市	2.884	39	0.848	4.088	13	0.952	0.808	150	0.404	3.78	9	0.968	3.172
珠海市	3.016	26	0.9	3.676	27	0.896	1.444	40	0.844	3.368	30	0.884	3.524
绍兴市	3.384	9	0.968	3.748	21	0.92	1.4	47	0.816	3.32	37	0.856	3.56
大连市	3.412	6	0.98	3.396	52	0.796	1.036	108	0.572	3.344	33	0.872	3.22
北京市	2.936	33	0.872	3.652	30	0.884	1.676	17	0.936	2.944	79	0.688	3.38
上海市	3.004	27	0.896	3.696	25	0.904	0.44	239	0.048	3.54	17	0.936	2.784
宁波市	3.276	13	0.952	3.8	20	0.924	0.5	223	0.112	2.976	75	0.704	2.692
嘉兴市	3.692	2	0.996	3.5	42	0.836	1.108	93	0.632	3.388	28	0.892	3.356
东营市	1.968	106	0.58	3.284	59	0.768	1	115	0.544	3.796	7	0.976	2.868
威海市	2.64	53	0.792	4.06	15	0.944	1.028	109	0.568	3.064	67	0.736	3.04
沈阳市	2.884	39	0.848	3.604	35	0.864	1.04	107	0.576	3.712	10	0.964	3.252
天津市	3.384	9	0.968	3.132	71	0.72	0.576	204	0.188	3.656	11	0.96	2.836
深圳市	3.82	1	1	4.236	6	0.98	1.344	57	0.776	3.488	22	0.916	3.672

城市居民实际掌有水平母系统

二级指标 城市	居民收入水平子系统			居民生活环境水平子系统			居民就业水平子系统			居民消费水平子系统			分值合计
	数值	排序	分值	数值	排序	分值	数值	排序	分值	数值	排序	分值	
厦门市	2.952	31	0.88	4.236	6	0.98	1.412	44	0.828	3.508	19	0.928	3.616
烟台市	2.468	69	0.728	3.64	33	0.872	0.6	197	0.216	3.508	19	0.928	2.744
青岛市	2.488	66	0.74	4.224	9	0.968	0.78	157	0.376	2.812	88	0.652	2.736
武汉市	2.776	42	0.836	3.58	37	0.856	0.56	207	0.176	3.32	37	0.856	2.724
长沙市	3.288	12	0.956	4.448	4	0.988	1.496	36	0.86	3.476	25	0.904	3.708
舟山市	3.02	25	0.904	2.536	119	0.528	1.604	25	0.904	3.392	27	0.896	3.232
马鞍山市	3.028	23	0.912	3.344	55	0.784	1.236	75	0.704	3.176	50	0.804	3.204
鄂尔多斯市	2.692	47	0.816	3.472	44	0.828	1.744	12	0.956	4.076	2	0.996	3.596
淄博市	2.368	75	0.704	2.484	125	0.504	0.852	143	0.432	4.212	1	1	2.956
太原市	2.54	61	0.76	3.592	36	0.86	1.156	87	0.656	3.636	13	0.952	2.872
镇江市	2.908	35	0.864	3.164	66	0.74	1.12	90	0.644	3.096	61	0.76	3.128
昆明市	2.012	100	0.604	3.088	75	0.704	1.616	24	0.908	2.004	163	0.352	2.604
南京市	2.512	62	0.756	3.712	24	0.908	0.884	138	0.452	3.008	74	0.708	2.62
福州市	3.036	22	0.916	3.088	74	0.708	1.512	34	0.868	2.56	113	0.552	3.244
济南市	2.028	99	0.608	3.48	43	0.832	0.32	258	-0.028	3.64	12	0.956	2.244
中山市	3.224	14	0.948	3.48	43	0.832	1.856	5	0.984	3.224	45	0.824	3.588
广州市	3.468	4	0.988	2.764	100	0.604	1.216	81	0.68	3.192	49	0.808	3.08

续表

一级指标	城市居民实际享有水平母系统												分值合计
二级指标	居民收入水平子系统			居民生活环境水平子系统			居民就业水平子系统			居民消费水平子系统			
城市	数值	排序	分值	数值	排序	分值	数值	排序	分值	数值	排序	分值	
晋城市	1.936	113	0.552	2.82	97	0.616	1.556	28	0.892	3.616	14	0.948	3.008
南通市	3.412	6	0.98	3.124	73	0.712	1.404	45	0.824	3.488	23	0.912	3.428
金华市	2.628	54	0.788	2.444	128	0.492	0.968	121	0.52	3.364	31	0.88	2.68
芜湖市	2.452	71	0.72	3.436	49	0.808	1.644	20	0.924	2.732	98	0.612	3.064
湖州市	3.076	18	0.932	3.46	47	0.816	0.748	164	0.348	3.252	43	0.832	2.928
铜陵市	2.22	89	0.648	2.66	108	0.572	1.028	109	0.568	2.308	131	0.48	2.268
呼和浩特市	2.596	56	0.78	3.04	77	0.696	0.392	250	0.004	3.48	24	0.908	2.388
包头市	2.328	80	0.684	3.148	69	0.728	0.956	123	0.512	3.116	55	0.784	2.708
乌海市	3.028	24	0.908	2.868	91	0.64	0.34	256	-0.02	3.084	64	0.748	2.276
唐山市	3.204	15	0.944	2.836	95	0.624	0.552	210	0.164	2.828	86	0.66	2.392
廊坊市	2.9	36	0.86	2.896	89	0.648	1.392	50	0.804	3.14	53	0.792	3.104
佛山市	2.912	34	0.868	2.676	106	0.58	1.18	84	0.668	3.86	4	0.988	3.104
辽阳市	2.712	45	0.824	2.048	170	0.324	1.728	15	0.944	2.5	117	0.536	2.628
龙岩市	2.648	52	0.796	2.396	131	0.48	0.908	134	0.468	3.112	57	0.776	2.52
克拉玛依市	2.544	59	0.768	3.448	48	0.812	1.152	88	0.652	3.068	66	0.74	2.972
扬州市	2.544	59	0.768	2.308	137	0.456	0.852	143	0.432	2.736	95	0.624	2.28
阳泉市	2.44	72	0.716	2.528	120	0.524	0.86	141	0.44	3.208	46	0.82	2.5

四、E&G 综合体系

母系统 城市	定量分析系统									E&G 综合指数	
	城市经济发展水平系统			城市公共服务水平系统			城市居民实际享有水平系统				
	合计	排序	分值	合计	排序	分值	合计	排序	分值	分值总计	总排名
杭州市	2.912	19	0.928	2.916	2	0.996	3.78	2	0.996	2.92	1
无锡市	3.168	3	0.992	2.728	15	0.944	3.132	25	0.904	2.84	2
常州市	3.116	6	0.98	2.484	30	0.884	3.5	10	0.964	2.828	3
苏州市	3.192	2	0.996	2.62	21	0.92	3.172	24	0.908	2.824	4
珠海市	2.592	48	0.812	2.86	4	0.988	3.524	9	0.968	2.768	5
绍兴市	2.916	18	0.932	2.372	36	0.86	3.56	8	0.972	2.764	6
大连市	2.688	37	0.856	2.816	5	0.984	3.22	21	0.92	2.76	7
北京市	2.492	59	0.768	2.964	1	1	3.38	13	0.952	2.72	8
上海市	2.916	17	0.936	2.8	8	0.972	2.784	49	0.808	2.716	9
宁波市	3.156	4	0.988	2.628	18	0.932	2.692	56	0.78	2.7	10
嘉兴市	2.964	16	0.94	2.232	50	0.804	3.356	15	0.944	2.688	11
东营市	3.488	1	1	2.424	35	0.864	2.868	45	0.824	2.688	11
威海市	2.736	30	0.884	2.648	17	0.936	3.04	35	0.864	2.684	13
沈阳市	2.396	66	0.74	2.812	6	0.98	3.252	18	0.932	2.652	14
天津市	2.716	32	0.876	2.748	13	0.952	2.836	47	0.816	2.644	15
深圳市	2.548	52	0.796	2.352	38	0.852	3.672	4	0.988	2.636	16

| 母系统 | 城市经济发展水平系统 | | | 定量分析系统 | | | | | | E&G综合指数 | |
| 城市 | | | | 城市公共服务水平系统 | | | 城市居民实际享有水平系统 | | | | |
	合计	排序	分值	合计	排序	分值	合计	排序	分值	分值总计	总排名
厦门市	2.228	82	0.676	2.772	10	0.964	3.616	5	0.984	2.624	17
烟台市	2.808	25	0.904	2.54	22	0.916	2.744	52	0.796	2.616	18
青岛市	3.104	9	0.968	2.368	37	0.856	2.736	53	0.792	2.616	19
武汉市	2.724	31	0.88	2.736	14	0.948	2.724	54	0.788	2.616	19
长沙市	2.468	61	0.76	2.324	41	0.84	3.708	3	0.992	2.592	21
舟山市	2.496	57	0.776	2.504	29	0.888	3.232	20	0.924	2.588	22
马鞍山市	2.536	55	0.784	2.464	34	0.868	3.204	22	0.916	2.568	23
鄂尔多斯市	2.392	67	0.736	2.336	40	0.844	3.596	6	0.98	2.56	24
淄博市	2.756	29	0.888	2.264	45	0.824	2.956	39	0.848	2.56	24
太原市	2.656	40	0.844	2.472	33	0.872	2.872	43	0.832	2.548	26
镇江市	2.888	22	0.916	1.988	70	0.724	3.128	26	0.9	2.54	27
昆明市	3.024	11	0.96	2.28	43	0.832	2.604	65	0.744	2.536	28
南京市	2.572	50	0.804	2.752	12	0.956	2.62	64	0.748	2.508	29
福州市	2.592	48	0.812	2.012	66	0.74	3.244	19	0.928	2.48	30
济南市	2.904	20	0.924	2.512	27	0.896	2.244	87	0.656	2.476	31
中山市	2.268	76	0.7	2.18	53	0.792	3.588	7	0.976	2.468	32
广州市	2.068	108	0.572	2.884	3	0.992	3.08	31	0.88	2.444	33

母系统		定量分析系统									E&G 综合指数	
城市		城市经济发展水平系统			城市公共服务水平系统			城市居民实际享有水平系统				
		合计	排序	分值	合计	排序	分值	合计	排序	分值	分值总计	总排名
晋城市		2.972	15	0.944	1.724	96	0.62	3.008	36	0.86	2.424	34
南通市		3.104	8	0.972	1.348	132	0.476	3.428	12	0.956	2.404	35
金华市		2.844	23	0.912	1.98	71	0.72	2.68	58	0.772	2.404	35
芜湖市		2.104	101	0.6	2.536	23	0.912	3.064	32	0.876	2.388	37
湖州市		2.616	43	0.832	1.976	73	0.712	2.928	41	0.84	2.384	38
铜陵市		2.284	75	0.704	2.792	9	0.968	2.268	84	0.668	2.34	39
呼和浩特市		2.3	73	0.712	2.516	26	0.9	2.388	74	0.708	2.32	40
包头市		2.088	105	0.584	2.728	15	0.944	2.708	55	0.784	2.312	41
乌海市		2.18	89	0.648	2.772	10	0.964	2.276	83	0.672	2.284	42
唐山市		2.564	51	0.8	2.088	60	0.764	2.392	73	0.712	2.276	43
廊坊市		2.9	21	0.92	1.316	137	0.456	3.104	27	0.896	2.272	44
佛山市		2.268	76	0.7	1.888	83	0.672	3.104	29	0.888	2.26	45
辽阳市		2.252	80	0.684	2.248	48	0.812	2.628	63	0.752	2.248	46
龙岩市		2.708	35	0.864	1.816	90	0.644	2.52	67	0.736	2.244	47
克拉玛依市		1.68	149	0.408	2.812	6	0.98	2.972	37	0.856	2.244	47
扬州市		3.024	11	0.96	1.636	102	0.596	2.28	81	0.68	2.236	49
阳泉市		2.228	82	0.676	2.256	46	0.82	2.5	68	0.732	2.228	50

第五节 全部城市排名分布区域

一、西南地区城市排名分布表

重庆市

城市	总排名
重庆	163

四川省

城市	总排名
成都市	52
自贡市	244
攀枝花市	80
泸州市	265
德阳市	146
绵阳市	177
广元市	231
遂宁市	238
内江市	243
乐山市	194
南充市	275
眉山市	264
宜宾市	181
广安市	195
达州市	215
雅安市	167
巴中市	282
资阳市	252

贵州省

城市	总排名
贵阳市	103
六盘水市	256
遵义市	181
安顺市	268

西藏自治区

城市	总排名
拉萨市	287

云南省

城市	总排名
昆明市	28
曲靖市	212
玉溪市	104
保山市	277
昭通市	285
丽江市	237
普洱市	242
临沧市	253

二、西北地区城市排名分布表

陕西省

城市	总排名
西安市	71
铜川市	110
宝鸡市	108
咸阳市	128
渭南市	220
延安市	73
汉中市	175
榆林市	100
安康市	222
商洛市	232

甘肃省

城市	总排名
兰州市	117
嘉峪关市	60
金昌市	83
白银市	221
天水市	259
武威市	260
张掖市	192
平凉市	240
酒泉市	112
庆阳市	261
定西市	278
陇南市	257

青海省

城市	总排名
西宁市	171

宁夏回族自治区

城市	总排名
银川市	157
石嘴山市	217
吴忠市	283
固原市	279
中卫市	281

新疆维吾尔自治区

城市	总排名
乌鲁木齐市	99
克拉玛依市	47

180

三、华南地区城市排名分布表

福建省

城市	总排名
福州市	30
厦门市	17
莆田市	140
三明市	62
泉州市	67
漳州市	86
南平市	130
龙岩市	47
宁德市	142

广东省

城市	总排名
广州市	33
韶关市	73
深圳市	16
珠海市	5
汕头市	169
佛山市	45
江门市	88
湛江市	230
茂名市	254
肇庆市	132
惠州市	105
梅州市	102
汕尾市	269
河源市	183
阳江市	174
清远市	168
东莞市	72
中山市	32
潮州市	131
揭阳市	249
云浮市	155

广西壮族自治区

城市	总排名
南宁市	135
柳州市	151
桂林市	150
梧州市	250
北海市	179
防城港市	137
钦州市	275
贵港市	286
玉林市	273
百色市	217
贺州市	274
河池市	207
来宾市	245
崇左市	236

海南省

城市	总排名
海口市	134
三亚市	93

四、华北地区城市排名分布表

北京市

城市	总排名
北京市	8

天津市

城市	总排名
天津市	15

河北省

城市	总排名
石家庄市	57
唐山市	43
秦皇岛市	86
邯郸市	94
邢台市	211
保定市	148
张家口市	172
承德市	176
沧州市	111
廊坊市	44
衡水市	202

山西省

城市	总排名
太原市	26
大同市	190
阳泉市	50
长治市	65
晋城市	34
朔州市	70
晋中市	76
运城市	135
忻州市	139
临汾市	113
吕梁市	173

内蒙古自治区

城市	总排名
呼和浩特市	40
包头市	41
乌海市	42
赤峰市	200
通辽市	210
鄂尔多斯市	24
呼伦贝尔市	108
巴彦淖尔市	75
乌兰察布市	133

五、华中地区城市排名分布表

河南省

城市	总排名
郑州市	51
开封市	235
洛阳市	143
平顶山市	143
安阳市	147
鹤壁市	178
新乡市	162
焦作市	124
濮阳市	222
许昌市	97
漯河市	227
三门峡市	78
南阳市	198
商丘市	251
信阳市	238
周口市	233
驻马店市	258

湖北省

城市	总排名
武汉市	19
黄石市	165
十堰市	185
宜昌市	90
襄阳市	224
鄂州市	197
荆门市	164
孝感市	234
荆州市	262
黄冈市	203
咸宁市	201
随州市	199

湖南省

城市	总排名
长沙市	21
株洲市	89
湘潭市	127
衡阳市	206
邵阳市	280
岳阳市	158
常德市	188
张家界市	240
益阳市	248
郴州市	160
永州市	283
怀化市	247
娄底市	226

安徽省

城市	总排名
合肥市	59
芜湖市	37
蚌埠市	125
淮南市	196
马鞍山市	23
淮北市	225
铜陵市	39
安庆市	145
黄山市	81
滁州市	165
阜阳市	272
宿州市	270
巢湖市	190
六安市	266
亳州市	267
池州市	187
宣城市	107

江西省

城市	总排名
南昌市	154
景德镇市	208
萍乡市	215
九江市	219
新余市	122
鹰潭市	138
赣州市	263
吉安市	229
宜春市	204
抚州市	271
上饶市	193

六、华东地区城市排名分布表

上海市

城市	总排名
上海市	9

江苏省

城市	总排名
南京市	29
无锡市	2
徐州市	82
常州市	3
苏州市	4
南通市	35
连云港市	119
淮安市	117
盐城市	92
扬州市	49
镇江市	27
泰州市	64
宿迁市	188

浙江省

城市	总排名
杭州市	1
宁波市	10
温州市	54
嘉兴市	11
湖州市	38
绍兴市	6
金华市	35
衢州市	85
舟山市	22
台州市	53
丽水市	76

山东省

城市	总排名
济南市	31
青岛市	19
淄博市	24
枣庄市	129
东营市	11
烟台市	18
潍坊市	66
济宁市	105
泰安市	95
威海市	13
日照市	113
莱芜市	55
临沂市	153
德州市	115
聊城市	119
滨州市	57
菏泽市	214

七、东北地区城市排名分布表

辽宁省

城市	总排名
沈阳市	14
大连市	7
鞍山市	79
抚顺市	91
本溪市	96
丹东市	69
锦州市	101
营口市	55
阜新市	151
辽阳市	46
盘锦市	61
铁岭市	67
朝阳市	156
葫芦岛市	126

吉林省

城市	总排名
长春市	63
吉林市	122
四平市	170
辽源市	141
通化市	121
白山市	116
松原市	180
白城市	209

黑龙江省

城市	总排名
哈尔滨市	98
齐齐哈尔市	213
鸡西市	205
鹤岗市	184
双鸭山市	228
大庆市	84
伊春市	149
佳木斯市	186
七台河市	161
牡丹江市	158
黑河市	246
绥化市	255

第六部分　全国及七大区域图

华北地区城市综合排名位置图

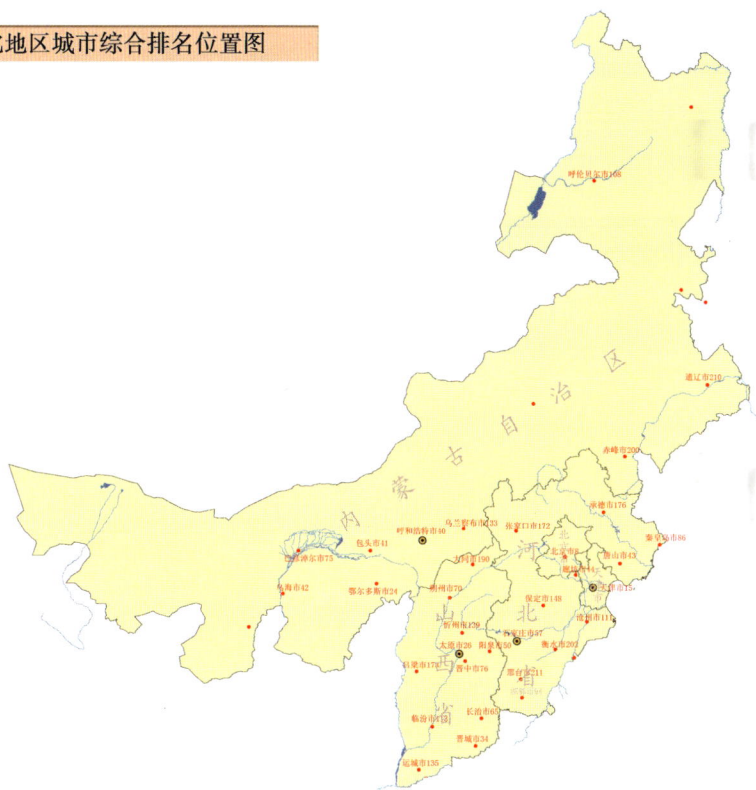

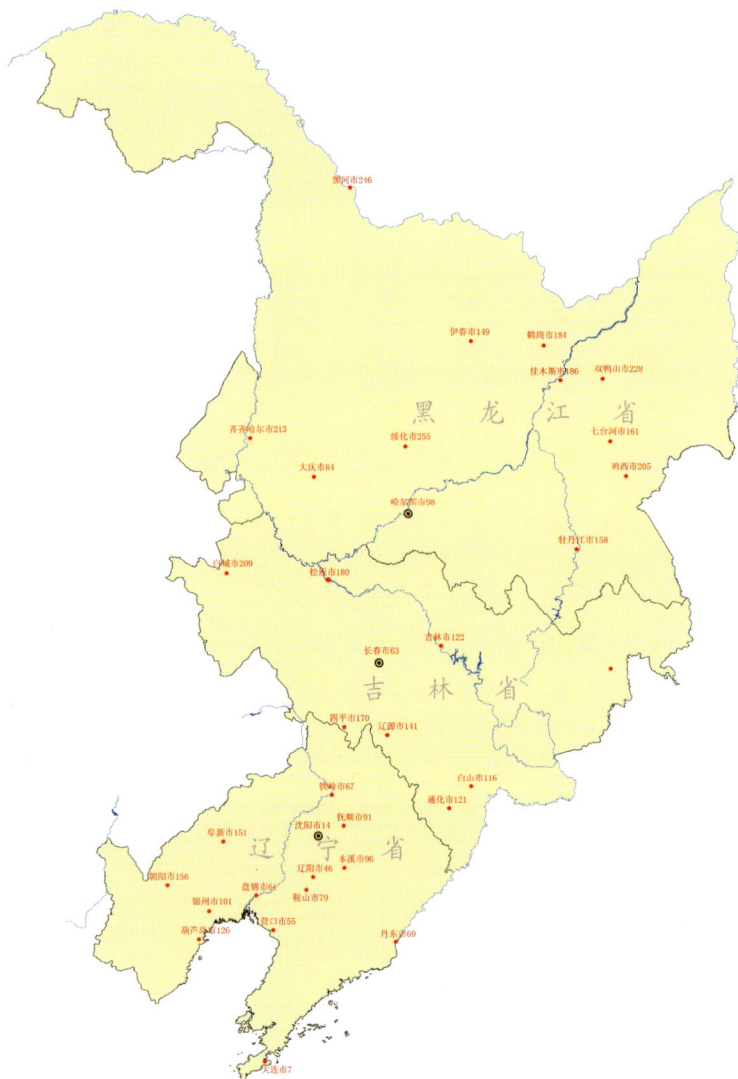

黑河市246

伊春市149　鹤岗市184

佳木斯市86　双鸭山市228

齐齐哈尔市213
绥化市255
大庆市84
哈尔滨市98
黑　龙　江　省
七台河市161
鸡西市205
牡丹江市158

白城市209
松原市180

吉林市122
长春市63
吉　林　省
四平市170　辽源市141

白山市116
铁岭市67
通化市121
抚顺市91
阜新市151
沈阳市14
本溪市96
朝阳市156
辽阳市46
盘锦市64
鞍山市79
锦州市101
营口市55
丹东市69
葫芦岛市126
辽　宁　省

大连市7

2012中国城市科学发展综合评价报告

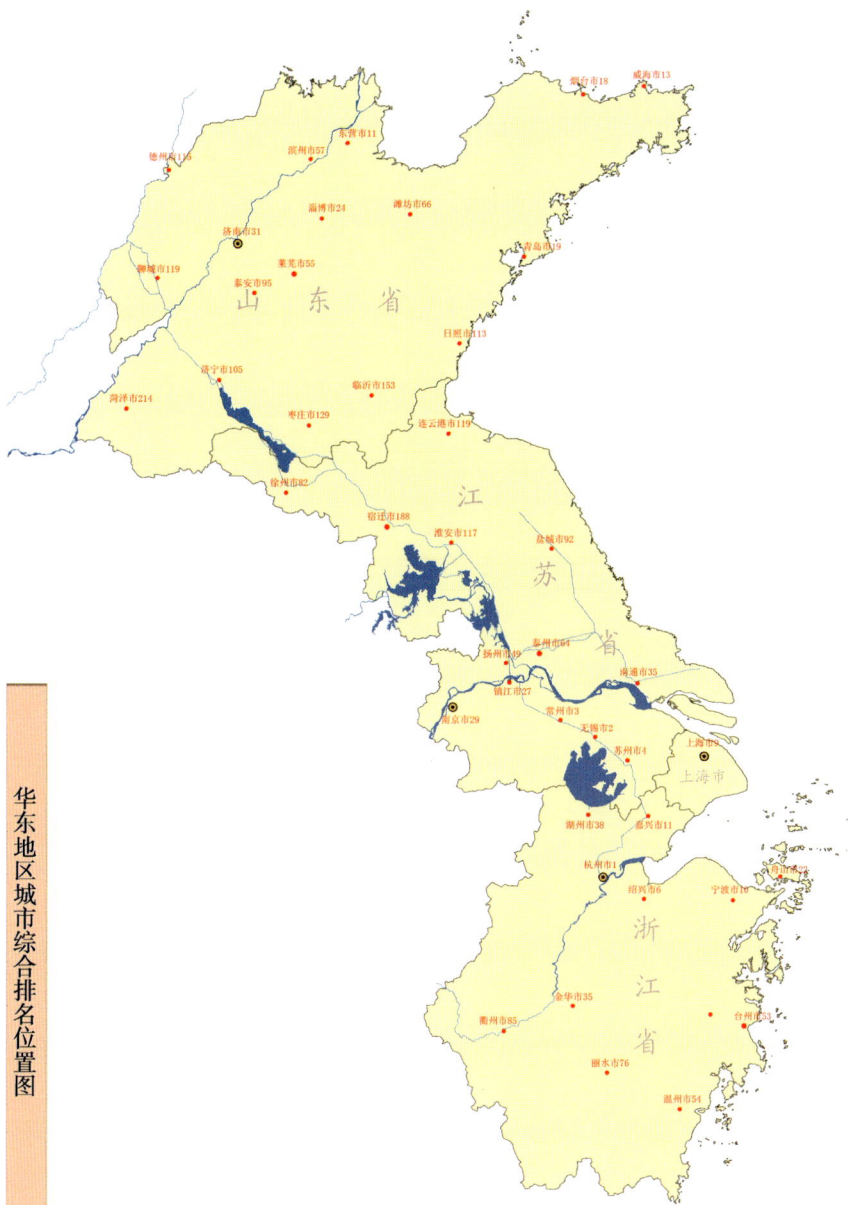

华东地区城市综合排名位置图

德州市115
滨州市57
东营市11
淄博市24
潍坊市66
济南市31
聊城市119
莱芜市55
泰安市95
青岛市19
山东省
济宁市105
日照市13
菏泽市214
临沂市153
枣庄市129
徐州市82
连云港市119
宿迁市188
淮安市117
盐城市92
江苏省
泰州市64
扬州市49
南通市35
镇江市27
常州市3
南京市29
无锡市72
苏州市4
上海市
湖州市38
嘉兴市11
杭州市1
绍兴市6
宁波市
浙江省
金华市35
台州市53
衢州市85
丽水市76
温州市54

2012中国城市科学发展综合评价报告

华南地区城市综合排名位置图

福建省

广东省

广西壮族自治区

海南省

华中地区城市综合排名位置图

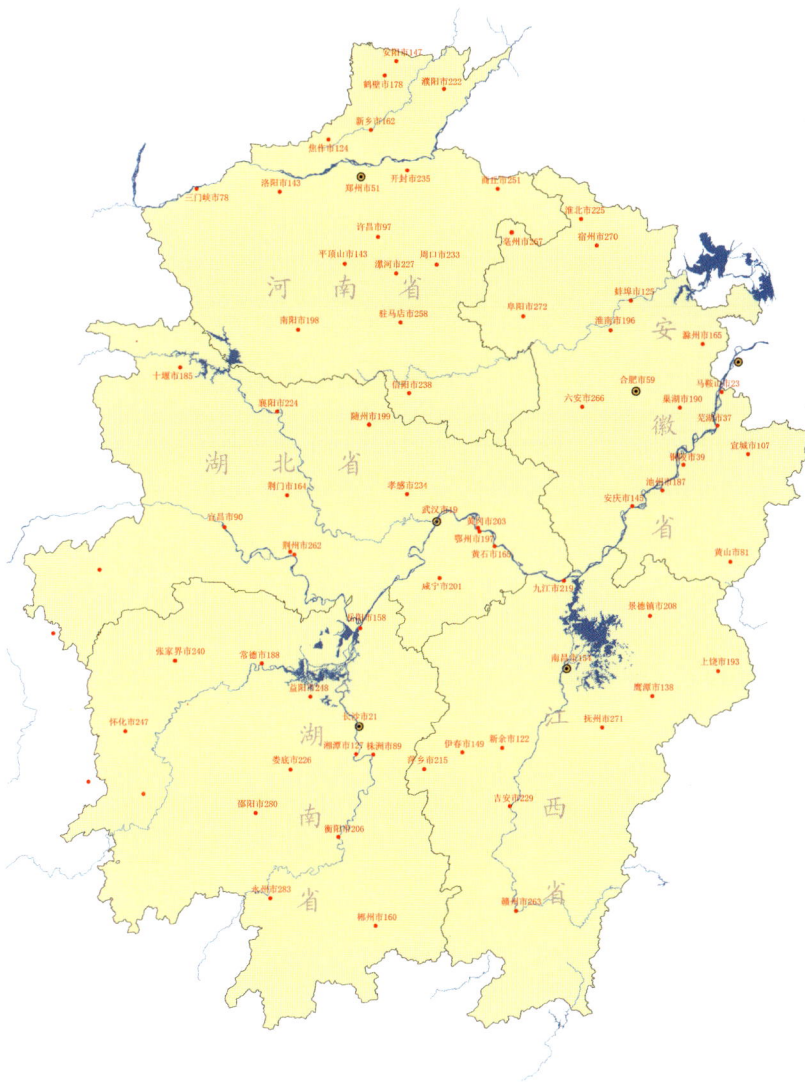

安阳市147
鹤壁市178   濮阳市222
新乡市162
焦作市124
三门峡市78   洛阳市143   郑州市51 开封市235   菏泽市251
许昌市97   淮北市225
平顶山市143   漯河市227   周口市233   亳州市207   宿州市270
河 南 省
南阳市198   驻马店市258   阜阳市272   蚌埠市129
滁州市165
信阳市238   潢川市196   安   马鞍山市123
十堰市185   合肥市59   巢湖市190   芜湖市37
黄冈市224   六安市266   徽   宣城市107
湖 北 省   随州市199   铜陵市39
荆门市164   孝感市231   安庆市145   池州市187
宜昌市90   武汉市19   鄂州市203   省   黄山市81
荆州市262   鄂州市197
黄石市163
咸宁市201   九江市210   景德镇市208
岳阳市158   南昌市45   上饶市193
张家界市240   常德市188   鹰潭市138
益阳市248   宜春市149   抚州市271
怀化市247   湘潭市125   醴陵市21   新余市122
株洲市89   萍乡市215   江
湖   娄底市226   吉安市229
邵阳市280   西
南   衡阳市206   省
永州市283   赣州市263
省   郴州市160

2012中国城市科学发展综合评价报告

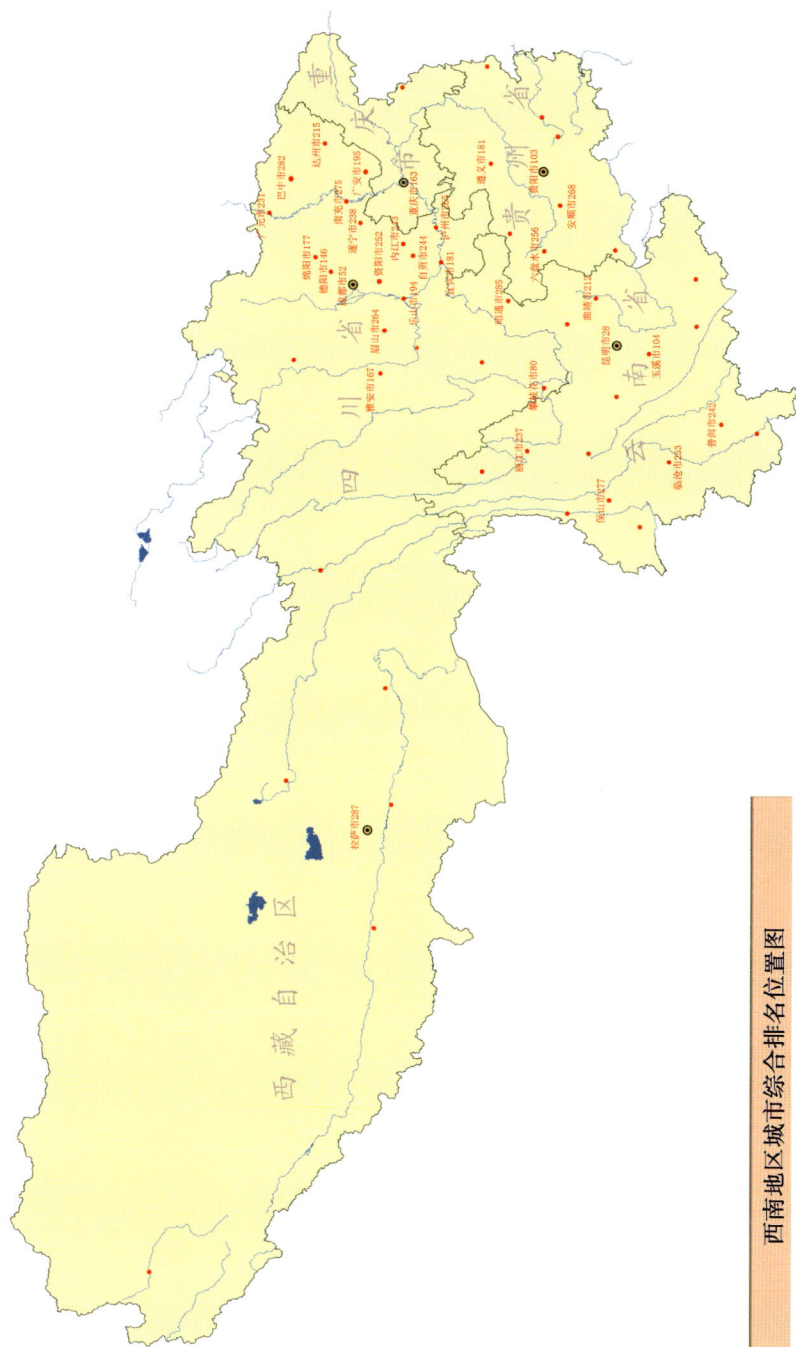

西南地区城市综合排名位置图

重庆市

贵州省

四川省

云南省

西藏自治区

巴中市282
达州市215
元江市237
南充市195
广安市196
绵阳市177
遂宁市288
德阳市252
内江市244
自贡市244
乐山市104
眉山市264
雅安市167
重庆市263
泸州市181
遵义市256
铜仁市181
贵阳市100
安顺市266
六盘水市...
昭通市295
曲靖市213
昆明市...
楚雄市80
玉溪市80
红河市237
文山市77
临沧市263
普洱市242
拉萨市267

第七部分　城市文化产业专题

开 篇 语

　　全球化大格局下，文化已然成为综合国力竞争的关键因素，经济社会的发展越来越借助于文化的参与和支持。世界上许多蜚声内外的城市，如啤酒之都慕尼黑、汽车之城底特律、美国雅典波士顿等等，都以特质文化为纽带成功集聚了众多资源，资本、技术、人才的汇聚最终推动城市形成一个规模庞大而体系健全的产业集群，城市也因此获得了持久发展的动力。

　　重视文化、崇尚文化是中华文明最显著的标志之一，也是中华文明从古至今得以延续不断的重要原因。极强的包容性使其经历数千年的积淀后，呈现出多元、庞杂而又自成系统的特有状态，不同的文化形式在不同时期所表现出的适应和演变能力各异，推动文化大发展大繁荣既具备许多有利条件，也面临一系列新情况和新问题。进入新的发展时期，文化日益成为社会和经济发展的重要战略资源，推动文化建设与经济建设、政治建设、社会建设的协调发展，已成为实现科学发展的必然要求。

　　作为文化与经济结合的产物，文化产业自然成为一座城市"软实力"的最直接表达。国家《文化产业振兴规划》提出要抓住机遇，大力振兴文化产业，于是各地纷纷出台发展文化产业的相关规划和政策，尤其近几年来，这一势头更是突飞猛进，一时间，各类文化产业及产业群如雨后春笋般在中华大地蓬勃兴起。

作为国家级的城市发展智库型研究机构，我们在本年度《报告》中特设文化产业专题。从面向全国各地级市征求所得的地方文化产业发展稿件中，整理出具有一定代表性的 12 篇，作为本专题的推荐交流稿件。为尽量保证研究的严谨性和公平性，选择的城市中包括了东部沿海城市和中西部内陆城市、历史文化名城和新兴的工业化城市。

我们期望通过本专题，一方面展示出我国在经济快速腾飞的同时，不断弘扬中华文明的辉煌和力量，传承历史、继往开来的坚定决心和伟大成就；另一方面，则是警示全球化趋势下，地方特色特别是民族特色的传统文化在强势文化的影响下快速式微，越来越多的地方在追求城市快速更新的过程中，逐渐忽略或者扭曲了对文化精神内涵的体悟。

我国文化产业发展模式及评述

一、引言

文化产业作为后工业时代经济再生的新动力，迅速成为席卷全球的一股浪潮。当前我国正处在全球化背景下的城市化及区域创新发展的进程中，城市发展面临着前所未有的机遇和挑战。要从根本上解决城市可持续发展问题，就必须彻底转变发展方式，由过去依靠廉价劳动力、大量原材料消耗的方式，转变为依靠知识、信息、技术、创意等新要素资源优势。文化产业不仅是满足人民群众日益增长的多样化、多层次、多方面文化需求的重要途径，也是推动我国 21 世纪经济转型和可持续发展的重要着力点和提升城市品质、增强城市凝聚力的重要依托。

自中国加入 WTO 以来，一方面，全球化的生产要素流动，有利于产生更大的集聚效应，降低我国文化产业生产成本，推动产业专业化、规模化，增强文化产品生产的及时性、创新性，形成品牌效应，提高产品品位；另一方面，我国文化产业面临着本土化与全球化的较量，文化产业的发展面临着巨大的挑战。本专题旨在我国文化产业发展的需求和宏观政策背景下，对不同类型的文化产业开发模式进行总结和梳理，并针对性的探讨我国文化产业发展遇到的问题。

二、文化产业发展背景

（一）需求拉动

近年来，我国文化产业增速明显，对国民经济增长的贡献不断上升，有望成为国民经济的支柱产业。2010 年，我国文化产业年均增速达到15%，高于美国（7%）和韩国（3.7%）等国家①。2008—2010 年，文

---

① 郑雄伟：《全球文化产业发展报告》，2012 年。

化产业法人单位增加值现价年均增长 24.2%，高于同期 GDP 的现价年均增长速度近 1 倍。2011 年，我国文化产业总产值预计超过 3.9 万亿元，占 GDP 比重将首次超过 3%①。

从结构上看，我国文化产业结构继续优化，服务行业比重有所上升。文化服务业增加值占文化产业法人单位增加值的 53.7%，比 2004 年增加 13.7 个百分点。2010 年，文化产品制造单位实现增加值 4391 亿元，文化产品销售单位实现增加值 638 亿元，文化服务提供单位实现增加值 5937 亿元。其中，文化产品制造单位、文化产品销售单位的增加值分别占文化产业法人单位增加值的 39.7% 和 5.8%，比 2004 年分别下降 8.0 和 4.8 个百分点。

从省域层面看，文化产业已经成为部分地区新的支柱性产业。2010 年，北京、上海、江苏、湖南、湖北、广东、云南等省市，文化产业增长速度年均超过 20%，占国内生产总值的比重均达到 5% 以上②。

表1   2010 年部分国家文化产业规模及增速

2010 年	文化产业总产值（亿美元）	占 GDP 比重	年增速
中国	1635	2.78%	年均 15%
美国	29240	20%	产业增加值年增长 7%（1977—2001 年）
韩国	650	6.2%	年均 3.7%
日本	11070	15%	—

资料来源：(国家统计局)《中国文化产业年度发展报告》，亚太总裁协会全球执行主席郑雄伟主持发布《全球文化产业发展报告》、《文化软实力蓝皮书：中国文化软实力研究报告 (2010)》。

我国"十二五"规划首次提出，未来 5—10 年将是我国现代化发展跨越"转型"难关的关键时期，宏观经济转向导致的文化需求空前释放、经济结构调整对现代服务业的扩张期待、数字化信息技术巨大进步推动新型业态的出现，都要求文化产业有一个超常的发展③。据预测，到 2015 年，文化产业有望成长为我国的支柱性产业。

（二）政策推动

近年来，我国各项政策体制与规划制度建设逐步完善，从政策层面上

---

① 叶郎：《中国文化产业年度发展报告》，北京大学出版社 2011 年版。

② 黄锡富：《推动文化产业成为国民经济支柱性产业》，《中国文化报新华网》。

③ 张晓明、胡惠林、章建刚：《中国文化产业发展报告》，社会科学文献出版社 2011 年版，第 1—12 页。

为文化产业的发展奠定了基础。党中央、国务院发布《国家"十二五"时期文化改革发展规划纲要》，首次提出"推动文化产业成为国民经济的支柱性产业"；文化部于 2012 年 2 月正式发布《文化部"十二五"时期文化产业倍增计划》，提出"十二五"期间，文化部门管理的文化产业增加值年平均现价增长速度高于 20%，2015 年比 2010 年至少翻一番，确立了实现倍增的奋斗目标。同时，明确了演艺、娱乐、动漫等 11 个重点行业的政策举措，具有很强的操作性[①]。此外，各地区文化产业规划政策的出台，对"十二五"期间各地区文化系统文化产业的发展都有重要的指导意义。

表 2   2015 年地区文化产业目标

地区	十二五目标	辽宁	文化产业增加值占 GDP 比重不低于 5%
北京	进一步强化文化创意产业的支柱地位，打造 3 大中心，整合提升 30 个市级文化产业集群区	黑龙江	文化产业增加值占 GDP 比重 5% 左右
上海	文化产业的增加值占 GDP 比重 12%	吉林	文化产业增加值占 GDP 比重 6% 左右
广东	文化产业增加值年均增长 12%，2015 年文化产业增加值超过 4500 亿元，占全省 GDP 比重 6.5%	河北	增加值年均增长 21% 以上，产业增加值达到 1500 亿元以上，占全省 GDP 比重达 5%
云南	文化产业增加值达 962.33 亿元，占全省 GDP 比重达 6.42%	天津	文化产业增加值年均增长 30%，成为城市支柱产业
湖南	实现年均增速 20%，2015 年全省文化产业总产出达到 4800 亿元，增加值达到 2000 亿元以上，占全省 GDP 比重达 7%	海南	文化产业增加值占 GDP 比重 4%，把国际旅游岛建设成为国家"十二五"文化产业示范区
江苏	把文化产业发展为国民经济支柱产业	陕西	文化产业增加值占 GDP 比重达 5% 以上
浙江	增加值超过 800 亿，占 GDP 比重达 5% 以上，文化服务业占比达 45% 以上	贵州	增加值达到 240 亿以上，年均增长率 20% 以上，在国民经济中比重接近全国平均水平
福建	文化产业增加值保持两位数增长，占 GDP 比重达 8% 以上	安徽	文化产业增加值超过 1200 亿，成为国民经济新支柱产业
山东	文化产业增加值翻两番，成为国民经济支柱产业	甘肃	文化产业增加值年均增长率 20% 以上，占全省 GDP 比重达 2%
江西	增加值年均增长 15%	重庆	文化产业增加值占 GDP 比重 5% 以上
山西	文化产业增加值占 GDP 比重 5% 以上	内蒙古	文化产业增加值占 GDP 比重 4% 左右

资料来源：各地十二五规划纲要和政府相关文件整理。

---

① 黄锡富：《推动文化产业成为国民经济支柱性产业》，《中国文化报新华网》。

三、文化产业发展模式及评述

根据国家统计局近日颁布的新修订《文化及相关产业分类（2012）》标准，文化产业从总体上可以划分为三类：一是生产与销售文化产品的行业；二是文化服务行业；三是具有较高文化附加值的行业。

本研究结合《文化及相关产业分类（2012）》和冯子标教授对文化产业所包含的产业内容的分类①，将文化产业划分为资源型、制造型和创意型，并对其发展模式进行总结和梳理。

（一）资源型文化产业

资源型文化产业是以文化资源为基础的产业，包括文化旅游业、博览业、民俗文化产业等。其特点是地域性强、特色明显，具有很强的垄断性和不可模仿创造性，因而具有明显的资源竞争优势。

1. 资源型文化产业发展特点

（1）资源丰富、有较强的比较优势，差异性大、文化消费具地方特色

我国长达5000年的文明历史，深沉隽永、大气内敛的东方文明，是其他任何国家都不可模仿和创造的独特文化，所拥有的文化资源和文化遗产，无论从数量还是质量上，相比其他国家都有明显的比较优势，为发展资源型文化产业提供了良好基础。

同时，文化是带有明显地方特色、个性化需求的精神自主性活动。我国的文化资源多样、差异性大，因此人们对文化产品和服务的消费具有非常强的本地文化特点。比如，地方戏曲作为文化产品推向市场，主要销售对象将是发源产生和推广该戏曲的地区②。

（2）依托文化资源发展旅游业，带动相关产业的发展

文化旅游业作为资源型文化产业的典型代表，直接依赖于文化资源，资源上的地域性与不可模仿性比较突出，旅游业的蓬勃发展有利于城市相关文化的推广，带来经济效益。

以云南为例，文化资源丰富，拥有众多动态符号文化资源，比如民族歌舞、民族服饰、大型节庆活动等，2007年云南国际旅游外汇收入为8.6亿美元，比2006年增长了30.5%。在文化旅游业的带动下，云南民族文化产品的复制、生产、服务与销售也形成规模，大力、深层次地开发传统

---

① 冯子标、焦斌龙：《大趋势文化产业解构传统产业》，社会科学文献出版社2005年版。

② 徐艳芳：《区域文化产业开发的比较优势研究》，《山东大学》2009年。

手工业产品，形成规模化生产格局，构建民族文化品牌。云南传统手工艺品产业的成功是旅游产业带动的结果，更是发挥了民族文化资源优势的结果。

（3）整合区域资源，推进城镇化和城乡统筹

随着生活条件的逐步改善，农村文化产业的发展相对于城镇文化产业而言，具有更大潜力，对于就近解决农村劳动人口就业，推进农村城镇化和城乡统筹具有极其重要的意义①。

以云南省为例，积极创新推出中国农村发展旅游业的第九种模式——"民族文化生态村"，依托省内旅游热点、自然生态景观、特色工艺品、特色文化村寨等资源，既注重文化的传承与保护，又注重文化的原生态存活态，按照《云南民族文化大省建设实施方案》和《云南民族文化大省建设"十五"规划》，把文化产业作为乡村建设的一个重要方面②。云南乡村文化产业已形成一定规模，全省形成滇中——滇西北——滇西——滇南几大市场为主要核心区域和发展重点的基本布局，带动了整个乡村文化业的发展③。

而在贵州，布依族主要聚居的黔南和黔西南两个苗族自治州，节日内容丰富、服饰独特、民族建筑风格独具地域特色、婚恋习惯古朴典雅。当地居民积极在交通条件较好、游客较多的旅游线路、景区和城市周边发展乡村旅游，积极引导农民参加旅游接待服务，既增加了农民就业岗位，又增加了农民的收入。近年在政府的倡导下，又大力发展民族风味餐饮和农家乐，吸引大量游客的同时带动了当地农产品的销售、农副产品的加工与开发。黔南50多个较成熟的乡村旅游村寨及1400个农家乐点，促进了近20万农民脱贫，为城乡待业人员提供了8700个就业岗位。2007年实现旅游总收入62.53亿元，其中乡村旅游人数占旅游总人数的30%左右④。

2. 发展中存在的问题

（1）资源型文化消费受时空限制

资源型文化产业相比其他两类（制造型、创意型）文化产业，受地

————————

① 谢名家：《文化产业的时代审视》，人民出版社2002年版。

② 冯子标、焦斌龙：《大趋势文化产业解构传统产业》，社会科学文献出版社2005年版。

③ 马翀炜、孙美璆、李德建：《乡村文化产业发展的路径及意义》，《西南边疆民族研究》2009年第6期。

④ 贵州省布依学会：《布依文化与乡村旅》，贵州民族出版社2008年版。

域、时间限制较多，对消费者的收入水平要求更高。资源型文化产品，比如旅游业，人们不能凭借一段视频或影像得到亲临其境般的体验，反观制造型或创意型文化产业，在运输业高速发展的今天，人们在居住地大都能消费得到。因此，同等收入水平下的居民，距离可消费地越远，相对的对资源型文化产业的消费需求会越小。

虽然我国整体进入小康社会，但大多数居民的收入仍然较低，收入的限制使得文化产品和服务成为少数人的选择，有限的文化消费中又主要集中在教育，有能力负担资源型文化消费的居民更是少之又少。关于我国文化产业需求规模，据《2004 年：中国文化产业发展报告》预计，"2020年达到人均 GDP 3000 美元，恩格尔系数 30%，文化需求占个人消费比重23%，总量为 42400 亿元。"但这只是一个构想，如果排除教育消费，我国文化消费需求将会减少，形势并不乐观。

（2）过度依赖资源，欠缺产品的深度市场开发

文化产业具有资源决定性，资源越丰富、差异性越大，文化产业越可能兴旺，同时发展方向也具有一定的多样性，并不是单一的生产。但要注意的是，文化资源的丰富并不一定意味着文化产业的兴旺，过于依赖文化资源的比较优势，就可能陷入"比较优势陷阱"①，丧失文化产业为我国带来的国际市场竞争力、国际分工体系上的优势。以广西宾阳炮龙节为例，每年农历正月十一晚上举行的炮龙节因其燃炮炸龙的刺激性和独特性、参与人群的广泛性、世代相传的民俗性，每年都会有百龙共舞、千炮齐鸣、万人同欢的场景。然而炮龙节主要采用"政府运作"模式，很难对市场需求做出及时准确的判断，使得产品的开发面临基础设施落后、服务接待能力差以及环境污染严重等问题。

（3）文化资源重复开发，产品同质化现象严重

文化旅游开发应有独特的层次感，根据当地明显的地方特色以及不可模仿复制的创造性，提升整体的品牌效应。湖南湘西山水风光资源丰富，是湖南省进入国家"西部大开发"的唯一地区，自然、原始的古朴历史文化吸引了众多游客。但现今很多开发是一拥而上，你方唱罢我登场，处处有看点，但都大同小异②，比如一个县搞摆手节，另一个县也赶紧跟上，一个景点把苗鼓作为重头戏，另一个景点也以此为卖点，同样的内容

---

① 比较优势陷阱：是指陷入或者陶醉于自己自然资源的、成本的，或者既有能力的比较优势而不能自拔。

② 中国城乡经济发展研究中心：《中国区县经济论坛上卷》，中国社会出版社2004 年版，第 1170—1171 页。

形成单调的格局，浪费了宝贵的文化资源，耗费了大量的人力物力，还对湘西文化旅游"大观园"品牌效应形成制约。

（4）缺少专项法规，不利于文化资源的保护

资源型文化产业的开发，在政府的宣传、包装以及媒体的关注下，逐渐走向商业化道路，但却缺少对文化资源的专项规划保护和规范化管理，使得部分原始、自然、朴实的文化特点被湮没。如凉山彝族火把节，作为彝族众多传统节日中规模最大、内容最丰富、场面最壮观、参与人数最多、民族特色最浓郁的节日，其民间性特点却日渐消失，某种程度上带有"官方化"印记，城市化和时尚化成为大型活动的主要追求①。

3. 资源型文化产业的开发策略

（1）面向国际市场，走外向型发展之路

加入 WTO 之后，随着改革开放的步伐加快，我国丰富的文化资源吸引了大量外资的涌入，为我国解决了发展中国家所面临的资本短缺问题；巨大的国际文化市场缓解了我国文化消费内需不足的问题。充分借助国际市场，将我国带有民族特色的文化产品对外推销，有利于确立我国文化产业全球化的发展战略。

（2）协调互补，合理划分市场，规避恶性竞争

城市资源型文化产业的发展，不仅要考虑到各城市自身资源条件，同时应周全考虑区域内其他相关城市类似资源产品的现有市场腹地和经营情况，合理选择适合本城市的创新产品，规避恶性竞争，做到区域内市场互为支持，协调互补。

（3）发展旅游新业态，开发旅游新产品

对资源型文化产业的发展，应在传统旅游业的基础上发展新业态，从种类结构、经营方式、组织形式、盈利模式等方面不断产生新的突破，以维持其可持续成长性。根据旅游者的需求和愿望，不断培育和创造新型旅游产品，或是注入新技术，或是融合新元素等，达到创造新产品或完成升级换代的任务，为旅游业发展增添新血液。

（4）兼顾各层级消费人群，多利益主体投资开发

在资源型文化产业的选择与开发过程中，不仅要满足高收入、高消费的少数阶层，更应兼顾中低收入消费水平的大众阶层。投资和开发主体可多样化，如公益为主、以基本国民休闲消费为主的政府主导投资型，公益与盈利相结合、满足中低端旅游消费的政府和企业联合开发，盈利为主、

---

① 李玉臻：《基于游客期望和感知的民族节庆旅游研究》，《北方民族大学学报》2009 年第 1 期。

满足各层次消费需求的企业自主开发等。

（5）加强基础设施和配套服务设施的建设

为提高资源所在地域如山区等的可达性，增强资源在市场中的竞争力，应多从人性化角度考虑，完善交通、通信、停车场等基础设施的建设，并加强住宿、餐饮、旅游指南等配套服务设施。

（6）关注生态友好和可持续发展原则

发展资源型文化产业，不可避免的要消耗地方上宝贵而有限的自然资源和土地资源，同时也会对生态环境造成不同程度的破坏。在开发选择上，应时刻考虑生态环境保护和可持续发展的原则，在创造客观市场和经济收入的前提下，尽量选择对珍贵的文化资源、土地资源消耗低，环境破坏少，具可持续性的产业类型。

（二）制造型文化产业

制造型文化产业，即以生产技术和产品制造为基础的产业，包括各类文化产品的制造及经营部门。随着我国制造业技术的飞速发展，以及消费者对文化产品需求总量的增加和类型的扩展，制造型文化产业在文化经济总产值中的比重急剧上升。在国内制造业发达地区，如广东、浙江、江苏等省市，当地政府推动文化产业与制造业耦合，各种文化用品、体育用品、工艺美术品等占据了文化产品中的较大比重。

1. 制造型文化产业发展特点

（1）通过产业集群进行错位发展，促进文化产业的区域协作

随着文化产业发展理念的不断深入，在"十二五"文化事业及文化产业整体安排和部署下，各省市纷纷提出了区域发展文化产业的战略部署和策略，强调区域竞合的作用。制造型产业作为区域竞争的市场主体，其发展更应注重互补协作、错位发展。

以长三角地区的文化产业集群模式为代表，江苏、浙江、上海的制造型产业发育具有明显的区域特点。

首先各有特色，一是依托于当地已有的生产要素和专业市场打造文化产业，如苏州镇湖的苏绣、浙江青田的石雕、上海的休闲娱乐等传统文化产业；二是由政府引导同类企业和产业资本从外部迁入，如苏州的手提电脑制造业、上海的创意产业、杭州的LOFT49和唐尚433等。其次，在区域层面，三者又存在一定差异：浙江以市场创造模式为主，往往以专业化市场为依托，以专业化分工为基础，生产性企业群落与商贸服务性企业群落并联耦合，根植性较强，如义乌依托于举世闻名的国际小商品城，已逐步形成文教体育用品、框画工艺品、年画挂历、印刷包装、制笔等五大优

势明显的文化产业集群；江苏以政府导向为主，政府致力于引进外资，发展外向型经济，如昆山为代表的 IT 产业、电子制造业集群等；而上海则是走从自发集聚到政府引导的发展之路，已经由制造型产业转向发展创意型产业。

目前，长三角地区等城市已经具有良好的经济基础和文化产业发展环境，形成了具有极化效应的核心圈层，并通过产业的关联和扩散效应，带动了周边地区的文化产业发展，形成长三角地区文化产业集群的块状分布格局。

（2）延伸产业链条完善产业园区，强化产业集聚效应和规模经济

工业、服务业等传统产业的升级通常要借助于文化要素的推动[1]，从简单的文化要素吸收与组合到文化要素的挖掘与创造，传统产业在其中不断提升，并加速了文化产业集群的形成，这一过程中，产业园区成为集群良好的成长环境。

我国的制造型文化产业目前正经历产业园的建设热潮，以浙江省为例，绍兴文化产业园、丽水文化工艺品园区、义乌文化产业园区、富阳体育用品制造块区、桐庐制笔工业区块等制造型文化产业集群都是产业链不断延伸、最终形成产业联合的结果。这些园区通过加工和利用文化资源，从事文化产品生产，各参与企业和诸多要素往往处于不同领域和阶段，着眼于自己的核心优势开展纵向合作，联手打造价值链，创造竞争优势。在关联企业集中化达到一定水平，也就是聚集规模基本形成后，各企业间的经济联系开始出现聚集效应。同时，和传统制造一样，随着生产规模的扩大和技术的不断提升，单位生产成本日趋下降，边际收益递减，产生规模经济。如我国最大的小商品集散地——义乌，凭借其小商品集群及强大的海外销售网络优势，已经成为动漫衍生产品的生产和销售中心[2]。

（3）借助技术提高产业附加值，推动文化产业的不断升级

与资源型文化产业相比，制造型文化产业往往意味着脱离了对文化资源的依赖，而转向运用现代生产技术从事文化产品生产制造活动。伴随着信息技术和虚拟技术的发展与运用，文化产业得以渗透到众多产业中，技术在产品和产值中占有的比重越来越大，进而成为这类文化产业的核心要素。

---

[1] 邹立清：《浙江省文化产业集群形成机理分析》，《关注政府》2008 年第 1 期。

[2] 朱旭光：《长三角文化产业集群模式的三维分析》，《经济论坛》2009 年第 2 期。

以长沙市的文化产业发展为例。长沙制造业力求把文化融入到工业、建筑、广告、园林、服装、家居等的设计当中，从"长沙制造"向"长沙创造"发展，使长沙品牌参与到国际文化市场的竞争中去。而作为长三角南翼先进制造业基地的宁波市，凭借先进的制造技术，已经在文具用品、印刷包装、八音琴以及工艺美术品制造等方面形成一定规模，具有一定发展优势，因此其产业发展更侧重于关注国内外同类企业的信息，加大对技术的改造升级，采取"生产技术—集约化经营—外向型"的发展模式。

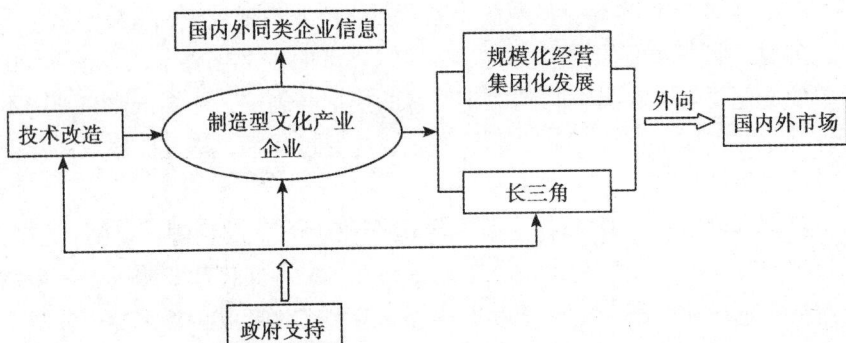

图1 宁波制造性文化产业发展模式图解[①]

另外，在一些本身制造型文化产业并不发达的地区，如广西，则选择采取"产业循环式发展模式"和"雁行形态发展模式"[②]，通过引进生产技术，面向国际和国内市场，开放资本合资进行生产，逐步培育自身技术进行国产化制造。

（4）引入市场竞争，制定文化政策，丰富投融资模式

资本是产业的血液，政策是产业的驱动，制造型文化产业要将文化转变为现实的产品和服务，尤其需要巨额资本支持和政策引导。现在很多城市已逐渐重视制定合理的文化政策，并改变以往单纯依靠国家与政府的投资模式，提供给中小企业更多发展壮大的机会。以浙江省为例，全省民营文化企业投资规模越来越大，经营领域越来越宽，目前已发展到4万多家，投资总规模达到230亿元以上，总收入300亿元以上，从业人员50

---

① 麻富游：《宁波市文化产业发展战略与模式选择研究》，《同济大学》2009年。

② 卢润德、张晓春、宁绍强：《广西文化创意产业发展模式探析》，《中国广告》2009年第1期。

余万人，其文化产业的形成与民营资本入注文化市场有着不可分割的联系。

2. 发展中存在的问题

（1）资源和能源消耗大，环境污染较为突出

虽然文化产品的生产制造和传统的制造业比起来能耗较少，但还是在不同程度上对环境造成了污染，如出版印刷业，老旧设备大量存在，技术落后、能耗高、污染高，环保方面前期投入不足，后期治理措施不到位，其电能等能源消耗对气候变化、环境酸化以及颗粒物的形成都将产生不可忽视的影响。

（2）产品高度外向，"两头在外"现象严重

在我国，制造型产业（包括文化产业制造业）的技术往往是外来的，只是利用当地廉价的土地、人力资源来进行加工，造成产品和市场两头在外，既不利于自主知识产权的发展，也使产业结构本身缺乏创新的动力。另一方面，存在高度外向、外贸依存度高的隐患，国际经济周期、经济循环等都会对产业的发展造成影响，产业抗风险能力较低。

（3）处于产业链和价值链的低端

经济学理论的"微笑曲线"（Smiling Curve）表明，在产业链中，附加值更多体现在两端（价值链上游的创意设计和价值链下游的市场销售），处于中间环节的加工、组装、制造附加值最低，形成了一个"U"字形曲线①。制造型文化产业则恰好处于"曲线"的中间部分，盈利较低。大量利润被来自国外的创意设计商和经销商攫取。因此，提升产业素质、优化产业内部结构成为很多地方文化产业战略转型的必然选择。

近20年以来，国际文化市场日益一体化，国际文化贸易蓬勃发展，国际文化产业分工体系正在迅速构建。目前，我国文化产业已通过"全球服务外包"的形式被纳入全球文化产业分工体系，但基本被限定在低端加工环节，成为国际文化产业制造大国和文化产业内容原创小国，在全球文化产业分工中的战略劣势局面已经形成。为此，必须重新全面地研究与部署中国文化产业发展总体战略。

（4）市场准入门槛仍然较高

在文化产业集群的形成过程中，大企业是重要客户，是新产品的需求者，是小企业进入市场的途径，也是小企业的孵化器。大量中小企业联合在大企业的周围，共同构成了灵活的生产网络，大公司的主要任务则是为

---

① 王亚川：《论文化产业内部结构的划分与演进——基于核心要素的视角》，《北京社会科学》2003年第3期。

那些分离出去的、在其周围形成网络的小公司提供中心服务。

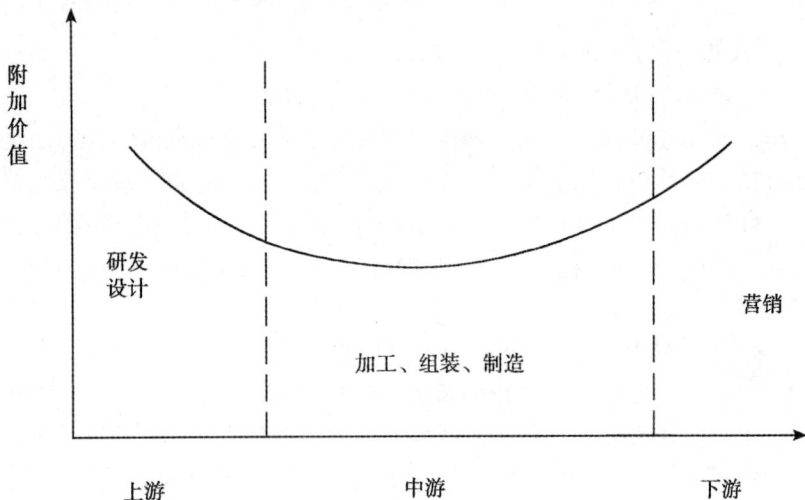

图 2   微笑曲线①

但目前，我国制造性文化产业的市场准入门槛依然较高，应适度降低门槛，鼓励社会资本对文化产业进行投资经营，实行投资主体的多元化、社会化。以江苏拥有的众多大型文化企业集团为例，这些由政府投资打造的文化产业集团属于垂直一体化的生产方式②，集团集创意起源、文化产品制造、发行和分销于一体，不利于分工的形成，无法担当起文化产业集群"种子"的重任。因此，应打破国有企业在某些文化产业中的垄断地位，引入竞争机制。只有当大型文化企业面临竞争压力时，才可能考虑与其他企业分工协作以降低成本或减小风险。

3. 制造型文化产业的开发策略

制造型文化产业适于在文化资源富集程度较低、经济水平较低的地区发展。在这类地区，必然面临社会经济基础薄弱、资源价值不高、资源总量偏少等多重困境，且易受政府部门落后观念的制约，但这往往意味着制造业必然成为发展文化产业的首选。在如今市场经济覆盖面不断扩大的形势下，产业分工越来越明显和细化，发展产业时，应将着力点放在积极融

---

① 陈鹏、郑翼村：《"微笑曲线"理论对我国产业结构高度化的启示》，《市场论坛》2006 年第 11 期。

② 何娣、朱喆：《江苏文化产业集群发展对策研究》，《江苏社会科学》2009 年第 5 期。

入其他文化产业发展类型的地区，在产业分工中寻找自身定位，在制度、政策上不断创新，优化投资环境，主动承接其他地区文化产品制造的转移，建立、拉长制造型文化产业链条，赢得市场的主动权。同时，文化资源富集程度较低，也不代表其区域文化资源处于绝对空白状态，不排除区域内依然有一定数量的、开发价值较高的特色文化资源，由于数量上的劣势，无法进行大规模综合开发，只能进行适度或单项开发。因此，应尽可能挖掘本地区潜在的、特色的文化资源，如对散于民间的传统工艺品制造进行市场化包装、规模化开发。

在具体制定产业开发策略时，应注意以下几点：

（1）改变思维方式

制造业不只是产品的生产工厂和单纯的生产关系，在制造过程中可以传播很多文化因子，对设计和质量的追求可以形成一种更新颖、更具特色的文化传播形式。比如丰田公司，传播的就是日本的质量文化。制造型文化产业应把文化融入到当地工业、建筑、广告、园林、服装、家居等产业的设计、宣传以及经营等环节中，从"制造"向"创造"发展，使得品牌形象和品牌效应能够得到最大的体现，从而提升国际竞争力。

（2）面向两个市场

以制造型文化企业和文化营销公司的互动合作为主体，面向国内、国际两个市场，通过精心整理包装出一批有基础、有潜质的项目，面向海内外招商，引进高水平的大企业集团进行品牌开发。同时衡量综合实力，瞄准顶尖水平进行大策划、大制作、大包装、大营销，以品牌开拓市场。

（3）提升产业优势

制造型文化产业要加快从单纯依赖数量、规模扩张的粗放型增长方式向大力提高质量、效益的集约型发展方式转变，进一步优化产业结构，推动产业集聚，形成规模经济效益，提高集约化经营的能力和水平。围绕增强企业核心竞争力，加快文化产业结构调整和资产重组，通过跨地区跨行业的联合、兼并、重组，重点培育和发展一批实力雄厚、具有较强竞争力和影响力的大型文化企业和企业集团，提高产业集中度和集约化经营水平。

（4）依托先进技术

文化产业需要有原创内容的创新，而高新技术的发展则为制造型文化产业加速发展提供了条件，随之而来的信息化、数字化、网络化、智能化趋势，甚至主导着未来文化产业的发展。制造型文化产业必须和现代科技发展有效地结合在一起，积极运用高科技改造各种制造产品具有巨大的经济意义，可以成为一种新的经济资源，最终产生关联度极高的拉动效应。

三、创意型文化产业

创意型文化产业，即以知识创造为基础的产业，包括演艺业、音像业、游戏业、广播电视业、报业、广告业等。创意型文化产业具有"三高两低"的特征，即"高附加值、高技术含量、高关联度"和"低能耗、低污染"。产业经济力的创造来自于人脑的创意，如广播、电影、电视等产品的创作是通过创意与光电技术、计算机仿真技术、传媒等相结合而完成的，对能源无过多的需求，也不会对环境造成太大影响。因此，创意型文化产业作为一种顺应转型要求的产业，将成为我国未来文化产业的发展重点。

1. 创意型文化产业发展特点

目前，我国的创意性文化产业一般有两种模式①。一是由政府对已经自发集聚了创意产业的地方进行总体规划，并提供优惠政策支持其发展成为创意产业园区。二是由政府积极主动规划，并通过政策性的支持发展创意产业园区。第一种模式发展的较为成熟，尤其是我国北京、上海、广州、深圳等正走向国际化的中心城市，处于产业升级、全面调整产业结构的重要历史时刻，创意型文化产业的发展因此也具有鲜明的特点。

（1）政府注重创意产业的发展

受转型压力和国际趋势的影响，地方政府大多把发展创意产业作为城市发展的重要抓手。如上海把推动创意产业作为实施"科教兴市"战略的重要内容。政府在建立创意产业园实行"三个不变"政策，即创意产业园区的房屋产权关系不变、房屋建筑结构不变、土地性质不变，这些政策给创意企业以优惠的入驻前提。

（2）政府引导与市场配置相结合

政府积极搭建文化公共服务平台，通过组建创意产业中心、设计中心等，引导和支持有积极性、有能力的地区、企业和社会其他组织参与文化创意产业园区建设；鼓励和引导高校、企业及各类协会等社会资源，发挥专业优势参与其中；采取各项措施加强对文化创意产品的知识产权保护。

（3）龙头企业带动产业发展

积极培育、扶持龙头企业带动产业发展，如中央电视台、北京电视台等电视传媒龙头，带动了节目制作、广告经营、技术服务、演艺传播等相

---

① 王三银：《南京文化创意产业发展模式研究》，《南京航空航天大学》2009年。

关行业的发展。资料显示，北京市与电视直接相关联的节目策划、后期制作等公司有 1000 多家，间接相关联的公司有 3800 多家。

（4）多元支撑形成产业新格局

在龙头企业的带动下，创意型文化产业的发展渗透到各个领域。以北京为例，软件、网络及计算机服务，新闻出版，设计服务和广播、电视、电影等四大优势行业已经成为文化创意产业发展的主体力量。

（5）集群化发展态势明显

我国创意产业明显形成了珠三角、环渤海和长三角等"三极"分布格局，中部地区的湖南、湖北，西部地区的四川、陕西也具备了良好的产业基础。截至 2011 年 4 月，国家已命名的文化创意产业各类相关基地、园区已达 350 个，其中文化产业示范园区和基地在全国 32 个省（自治区、直辖市）都有分布，软件和动漫产业基地集中分布于中东部地区中心城市，以及成都、西安等西部区域中心城市。在全国 204 家文化产业基地中，东部沿海地区 84 家，占基地总数的 41.17%；东北地区 21 家，占10.29%；中部 44 家，占 21.56%；西部 55 家，占 26.96%。11 家国家级软件产业基地主要分布在北京、上海、西安、南京、济南、成都、广州、杭州、长沙、大连、珠海等东部经济发达城市及中西部区域中心城市。8个国家数字出版基地主要分布在上海、重庆、杭州、长沙、武汉、天津、广州、北京等科技和文化融合能力强的城市。

东部城市文化创意产业发展特色明显。北京作为全国领先的科技创意中心，特色集群发展的态势明显，动漫游戏的研发与电信、IT 软件和硬件、出版和传媒等行业的关联度较大，中关村软件产业先导基地、798 艺术区、石景山数字娱乐产业基地等一批特色鲜明的集聚区逐步形成，成为北京文化创意产业的重要空间载体。上海创意产业的发展则充分发挥了集聚区的群体竞争优势和规模效益，以保护上海老工业历史建筑和老工厂为载体的创意产业集聚兴起，形成了各具特色的主体产业和配套价值链，目前已授牌 18 家集聚区。深圳是中国现代平面设计的发源地，逐渐发展成为南方著名的创意设计之都，以腾讯、A8 音乐、华强文化、华视传媒等为代表的高成长型文化科技型企业，依托高新技术，以数字内容为主体、以自主知识产权为核心迅速发展。

2. 发展中存在的问题

（1）投资文化产业收益不稳定

创意型文化产业的潜力巨大，但对于资本的运作则有较高的要求，需要保障投资收益的可预期性和稳定性。例如，2009—2010 年，仅北京地区就通过供应链融资、项目打包贷款等方式向 11 部电影发放贷款金额 2.45 亿，但是成功者凤毛麟角。文化创意产业是没有抵押的轻资产模式，因此，创意型文化产业目前缺乏金融投资的稳定性和透明性，也缺少一整套有利于促进文化创意产业发展的引导机制、激励机制、保护机制和风险分担机制。

（2）创意产业链条尚未形成

产业和项目载体以及公共技术服务设施不足，不能满足企业发展需要。"大而不全，小却不专"是文化创意产业发展的现实写照。目前不少城市都建有动漫园区，许多高校都开设动漫游戏专业，不少地区都举办各类动漫游戏比赛，动漫游戏展。尽管如此，但就动漫游戏产业总体来看，企业规模小，原创能力不足，核心竞争力弱，经营模式亟须创新，完整的产业链尚未形成。

（3）创意产业发展环境欠佳

企业发展普遍面临资金缺乏、融资困难、高水平人才不足、市场拓展乏力的局面，有效的赢利模式尚未确立。政策环境不够完善，融资环境不够理想，创意企业的价值评估存在许多不确定性，导致企业尤其是一些中小企业从银行获取贷款的门槛比较高，而风险投资机构和民间资本对文化创意产业发展前景缺乏深入的研究和足够的了解，往往不愿轻易下单。同时市场环境不够成熟，企业发展初期多以模仿创新和技术跟踪为主，普遍存在知识产权保护的相关政策法规不健全、保护不力和保护意识不强等现象。

3. 创意型文化产业的开发策略

创意型文化产业适于在文化资源富集程度较低、经济水平较高的地区发展。此类地区发展文化产业将面临资源"瓶颈"，但其拥有较为发达的市场经济环境，具备了发展产业所需的技术、资本、人才和市场优势，大可走出一条不同于一般文化产业发展的道路。

譬如深圳，缺乏悠久的历史，文化资源富集程度较低，甚至一度被称为"文化沙漠"，但特区的建立为其带来巨大的经济优势，在雄厚的经济基础和先进的科技支撑下，深圳日益形成独具特色的"市场拉动型"产业发展模式，通过建立文化创意基地和园区，走专业化、集约化、规模化道路，着力推进文化创意产业的集群发展。在《深圳市文化产业发展规划纲要》中，深圳市政府已经制定各行业规划，重点发展创意设计业、动漫游戏业、数字视听业、新媒体产业、演艺娱乐业、高端工艺美术业等包括新兴文化产业在内的创意型文化产业，积极推动文化产业成为深圳市继信息制造业、物流业、金融业之后的第四大支柱产业，着力打造"设计之都"。

在进行创意型文化产业开发时，可采取以下几种策略。

（1）给予开放、优惠的扶持政策，注重维护知识产权

目前我国对创意型文化产业已经空前重视，在此基础上，通过政策手段，鼓励多元投资机制和多种经营方式，鼓励非文化产业对文化机构的投入，促使产业和文化的自然融合，已经形成一种社会共识。参看国际经验，仅纽约市就有500多家私人所有的艺术团体和公立的艺术团体享有同等的待遇。另外，纽约文化机构被分为盈利性和非盈利性两种类型，各自的比例大约都是50%。

同时，要注重对知识产权的保护。创意型产业的内容是具有自主知识产权的产品和服务。保障创意是创造创意之源，从某种意义上说，知识产权保护是文化产业崛起、发展的重要基础。

（2）健全产业发展所需的社会环境机制

创意型文化产业的发展，还要尽快融入规范的文化市场。通过机制化的法律、法规等手段来调控文化市场，可逐步建立起完备和成熟的创意产业发展环境。例如美国的《联邦税收法》就明文规定，对非营利文化团体和公共电视台、广播台免征所得税，并减免资助者的税额，这保证了文化发展所需要的充足的资金来源；而《版权法》、《电子盗版禁止法》等一系列版权保护法规，也为文化创意产业的健康发展提供了完备的发展环境①。

（3）为产业发展培养创意人才和服务机构

创意型文化产业注重对人和知识的依赖。创意性人才是创意型文化产业的核心；文化创意产品是人的知识、智慧与灵感在特定行业中的物化表现。因此，培养创意型人才是产业发展的重要生产力。以纽约市为例，政府设立了大量非营利的创意产业教育和培训机构，如朱丽亚特学校、帝舍艺术学校和帕洛特研究中心等；政府还在市立中小学开设了大量的艺术课程，不仅为城市未来发展培养创意人才，还培养了创意产品的潜在消费者。同时，纽约有很多为创意者或创意企业提供服务的机构，如美国图文艺术研究会、美国广告经销协会、国家视觉艺术互助协会等等，范围非常广泛，从新科技和商业技巧的培训到产业宣传和交流活动。此外，纽约还是大量艺术服务组织的基地，他们提供着大量的服务，如特殊技能的培

---

① 郑洪涛：《基于区域视角的文化创意产业发展研究》，《河南大学》2008年。

训、发展艺术团体等，最大限度地满足了创意者和艺术组织的需要。

四、思考与讨论

（一）文化产业的区域开发策略

我国地域广阔，文化资源富集程度和经济发展水平差异巨大。针对不同的区域特征，因地制宜的发展文化产业才能顺应经济发展规律，并发扬当地文化特质。根据经济发展水平和资源富集程度，可以划分出四类地区，并对应四种不同的文化产业开发策略。

表3　　　　　　　　　　　经济水平与文化资源富集程度建构表

	经济水平较高	经济水平较低
文化资源富集程度较高	C 类地区（复合型开发策略）	B 类地区（资源型开发策略）
文化资源富集程度较低	D 类地区（创意型开发策略）	A 类地区（制造型开发策略）

文化资源富集程度较低、经济水平较低的 A 类地区，发展文化产业将面临着社会经济基础薄弱、资源价值不高、资源总量偏少等多种困境，且易受政府部门落后观念的制约。如前文说述，此条件下，A 类地区发展文化产业首选的开发策略应为制造型，在文化资源开发方面，对本地区潜在的、特色的文化资源进行适度或单项开发，加大宣传、完善包装，挖掘文化产品价值。

对文化资源富集程度较高、经济水平较低的 B 类地区，发展文化产业应首选资源型开发策略，将资源优势转换为产业优势。地方政府应着力于对文化载体的保护和监管、专项文化产业开发、文化事项的整合、文化形象的塑造和宣传。避免过度开发文化资源，造成文化生态环境恶化、文化资源流失、破坏甚至毁灭；避免在未进行较为系统全面的文化资源普查和市场风险评估的情况下，就盲目上马一系列文化景观，造成预期的经济效益和社会效益破产、资源浪费闲置。

文化资源富集程度较高、经济水平较高的 C 类地区，能够有效整合资源，并具有人才、资本、技术、市场等多项优势。因此，合理的开发策略为复合型，即资源型文化产业和创意型文化产业全面推进。

文化资源富集程度较低、经济水平较高的 D 类地区，发展文化产业应选取的开发策略为创意型。通过强大的经济极化效应，吸引人才等外部要素的集聚，形成创意型文化产业集群开发的格局。

（二）投融资机制的创新

我国文化产业在投资机制上的不平衡，主要表现为投资结构不合理，国家的投资比重过大，社会资本和利用外资的比重则相对偏少。甚至在法规上对外资和民资进入一些基础性的文化产业领域都设置了较多限制，从而影响了文化产业的全面发展。

文化产业是巨大的产业群体，是跨行业、跨地区关联度高的产业系统。而我国文化管理仍然实行高度集中的统一管理，省市政府权限较弱。这种自上而下的管理方式，一方面造成了不够灵活的文化调控体系，导致政府难以针对产业特点，及时做出符合产业规律、有利于文化产业建设的规划、政策和措施[①]。另一方面，政府过多干预，层层审批，影响了省市政府推动文化产业发展和实施有效监督的积极性，并造成管理弱化，导致消费需求的不足和文化商品的短缺。

（三）文化产业发展向文化事业建设的延伸

文化产业是一个城市乃至一个国家"软实力"的最好体现。但事实上，文化产业或者说狭义上的文化产业并不是文化发展的全部。随着我国市场经济体制的逐渐形成，一些文化管理部门以行政手段将文化事业单位推向市场，采取减少经费或不给经费的措施，不管其文化产品是否有市场上的经济效益，统统让其自谋生路，导致许多文化单位被迫改行或压缩，那些难以直接获得市场效益的社会科学、教育事业、文物单位等陷入了极其困难的境地。

作为产业发展的基础，完善、扎实的文化事业建设也十分重要。片面侧重经济增长，将物质文明建设作为重点，忽视了文化精神建设的重要性，把文化发展片面归为文化产业的繁荣创新，忽视了文化事业在推动文化精神层面上的重要作用。这都将导致文化和文化产业的脱节，丧失文化产业区别于其他产业的最大特色。

因此，推动文化产业发展向文化事业建设的延伸应当也必须成为未来努力的方向。城市文化产业发展与建设，应坚持以文化惠民工程为载体，以文化产业项目为抓手，狠抓公共文化服务体系建设，使城市居民成为文化发展的直接受益者。

（本报告参与人员：指导：杨旭、袁崇法；写作：郑樱、李燕、李天娇、汤丹阳、王璐；材料收集：郑樱、张文宁；城市稿件汇编：张文宁、汤丹阳）

[①] 陈鹏、郑翼村：《"微笑曲线"理论对我国产业结构高度化的启示》，《市场论坛》2006 年第 11 期。

常州市文化产业发展特色及主要措施

2012中国城市科学发展综合评价报告

常州是一座有着深厚人文底蕴的历史文化古城，改革开放以来，在经济快速发展的同时，文化建设也都取得了显著的成果。连续三年被评为江苏省文化发展水平先进地区，连续两年获得"全国文化体制改革工作先进地区"荣誉称号。拥有常州创意产业基地、常州恐龙园股份有限公司、常州广告产业园区、国家级文化和科技融合示范基地的4家国家级文化产业园区（基地）。近年来，在政府的有效推动下，5000多家文化企业正在日新月异地发展，近百个文化产业项目正在紧锣密鼓地实施，9大文化行业正显示出蓬勃与生机，全市文化产业呈现出强势发展、顺势上扬的良好局面。

一、主要特色

确定以动漫游戏业、影视传媒业、文化旅游业、工艺美术业、印刷复制业、广告会展业等6大行业为主，演艺娱乐业、创意设计业、出版发行业等3大行业为辅的文化产业发展方向。重点做好4大行业，打造4大品牌：

1. 动漫游戏品牌

全市有动漫游戏企业100多家，拥有两家国家重点动漫企业，3个产品成为国家重点动漫产品，20家国家认定的动漫企业；5家企业和5个项目成为"国家文化出口重点企业和重点项目"。中国（常州）国际动漫艺术周已连续举办8年，动漫已成为常州的一张城市名片，亦为常州文化产业的核心品牌。

2. 文化旅游品牌

"无中生有"的中华恐龙园、"借题发挥"的春秋淹城、"化虚为实"的嬉戏谷，以佛教文化为特色的天宁寺和天宁宝塔，以道教文化和养生文化为特色的茅山风景区，以湖光山色为特色的天目湖旅游度假区等文化旅游品牌在国内外享誉盛名。

3. 文化制造品牌

全市拥有印刷企业1000多家，2011年年产值已近70亿。包装装潢、邮票、明信片等高附加值印务，高仿真古籍印刷、绿色环保印刷、高新技术印刷等创意印刷成为常州市印刷企业的品牌特色。

4. 影视传媒品牌

以广播电视为主体，集聚互联网站、移动电视、网络电视等多种现代媒体，动漫、出版、影视剧等多种文化创意产业形态的大型传媒中心——常州现代传媒中心将于2012年建成。

二、主要措施

常州市以满足人民日益增长的精神文化需求作为出发点和落脚点，充分发挥党委政府的引导、协调和服务功能，在产业规划、政策扶持、资金投入、公共服务、人才培养上引导和促进文化产业快速发展。

1. 在规划方面，注重前瞻性

成立文化体制改革领导小组、创意产业领导小组，研究制定文化产业发展战略、规划和政策，指导和协调解决产业发展中的重大问题。制定《深化文化体制改革，加快文化常州建设三年行动计划》（常发〔2009〕20号）、《关于贯彻落实党的十七届六中全会精神　大力推进文化名城建设的意见》（常发〔2011〕36号）等文件，对近期几年文化产业发展形成全市层面的整体规划。

2. 在政策方面，注重引导性

先后出台《关于加快建设文化常州的意见》（常发〔2007〕18号）、《关于加快文化事业和文化产业发展若干经济政策的意见》（常政发〔2007〕75号）、《关于鼓励和扶持动漫产业发展的若干规定》（常政发〔2007〕115号）、《关于鼓励和扶持创意产业发展的若干意见（常政发）〔2008〕184号》等多个文件，在组织、人员、资金、政策等方面为产业发展提供保障。

3. 在资金方面，注重针对性

2006年至2008年，市财政每年安排2000万元扶持动漫产业发展专项资金。2009年起，市区两级财政安排5000万元，连续5年，将共投入2.5亿元专项扶持创意产业。2010、2011年分别设立文化产业引导资金640万、700万元，对重点文化产业项目进行扶持。2012年起，设立文化产业信贷风险补偿专项资金，主要用于政府推动银行加大对常州文化企业的放贷力度。

4. 在服务方面，注重公共性

以创意产业为例，常州市搭建了国家级二维无纸动漫技术公共服务平台、省级创意人才培训中心、动漫衍生产品研发中心、国际交流合作中心、产权交易平台等公共服务平台，形成了从注册办照到装修入住、从研发到制作生产、从衍生开发到市场打造、从人才培养引进到企业扶持培育、从融资到销售的一条龙服务体系。

5. 在人才方面，注重长效性

常州市制定《常州市宣传文化系统"六个一批"人才建设工作实施意见》，加快对文化产业人才的引进和培养。建立"江苏省服务外包人才培训基地"——常州创意人才培训中心，江苏省首家动漫高技能人才专项实训基地——苏常动漫技能培训中心。常州市与韩国文化产业振兴院签署了《中韩游戏产业人才培训合作备忘录》，全方位加强文化人才的培养。

6. 在宣传方面，注重实效性

编印《常州文化产业招商手册》，开通"常州文化产业网"，创办《常州文化产业》杂志，编撰《常州市文化产业发展报告》，线上线下共同推介常州文化产业。打造"文化产品出口运营一体化电子商务平台"等网络营销推广平台，加快文化产品走出去的步伐。

（稿件由常州市文化主管部门提供）

成都：发掘文化遗产资源
发展文博旅游产业

近年来，成都市通过改革文化体制，创新融资机制，完善产业政策，提高服务水平等举措，以重大产业项目为带动，以骨干企业为支撑，着力发展文博旅游、传媒、创意设计、演艺娱乐、文学与艺术品原创、动漫游戏和出版发行等重点行业，2010 年全市文化创意产业法人单位有 6656 家，从业人员 63.26 万人，主营业务收入 1717.76 亿元，与 15 个副省级城市比较，2010 年文化产业增加值在副省级城市居中上水平。

成都市是国务院 1982 年公布的第一批历史文化名城，具有丰富的历史文化资源。发掘文化遗产资源，发展文博旅游产业，既是成都市文化产业的显著特色，也是文化产业的重要支柱，截至 2010 年底，成都市文博旅游业法人单位 1142 家，从业人员 2.01 万人。

一、措施及经验

（一）通过持续举办"非遗节"，打造国际化的"非遗之都"，拉动产业发展

2007、2009、2011 年，成都市连续成功举办了三届中国成都国际非物质文化遗产节，每一届"非遗节"参与的国内外游客和市民均在 500 万人左右。第二届"非遗节"后，文化部批准"非遗节"定点成都，持续举办，为此，成都市在青羊区规划建设了占地 1700 多亩的国际非物质文化遗产博览园，该园区已经完成了一期工程，并作为主会场，成功举办了第三届"非遗节"。

（二）打造"三国文化"、"金沙文化"、"诗歌文化"三大文博品牌

1. 打造"三国文化"品牌

成都武侯祠博物馆是全世界影响最大的三国遗迹博物馆，2011 年产业收入 8580 万元，接待游客 365.5 万人。

2. 打造"金沙文化"品牌

成都金沙遗址博物馆是在古蜀文明重大考古发现——金沙遗址原址兴建的专题博物馆，抓住"太阳神鸟"金箔图案成为中国文化遗产标志的契机，努力打造金沙文化品牌。

3. 打造"诗歌文化"品牌

杜甫草堂博物馆是现存杜甫行踪遗迹中规模最大、保存最完好的博物馆。

（三）出台支持政策，聚集民间藏品，创建全国民办博物馆发展示范城市

为聚集民间藏品，进一步丰富城市文博旅游资源，2010年，成都市委、市政府出台了《关于促进民办博物馆加快发展的意见》，市政府印发了《成都市民办博物馆管理办法》，截至2011年12月，成都市民办博物馆数量已达到62座。

（四）发挥国企优势，打造城市历史文化街区和"天府古镇"

成都宽窄巷子在全国首创运用"修旧如旧"、"落架重修"的保护手法，是中国唯一的以老成都历史遗存的原真文化和建筑格局为本底，展现老成都典型生活样态的"文化标本"，自2008年对外开放以来共接待中外游客累计4000万人次，街区年经营产值超过3亿元，已成为展示成都文化的亮丽名片。

二、"十二五"发展目标

"十二五"时期，成都市将继续深入挖掘历史文化遗产的文化魅力，推动文博旅游业加快发展，力争实现年均增加值20%以上，进一步提高文博旅游对文化产业的支撑作用。

（一）打造国际非物质文化遗产博览园

2009年8月，国家文化部正式确定成都成为国际非物质文化遗产节的永久会址。成都市委市政府以此为契机，按照国际化标准建设了国际非物质文化遗产博览园。"十二五"期间将进一步将其打造成国际非物质文化遗产节永久载体，非遗生产性保护的永久平台，建成集非遗文化保护传承、非遗产品生产性开发、科普教育、会议会展、休闲娱乐等功能于一体的文化旅游胜地。

（二）建设民办博物馆"一中心三聚落"

根据《成都市民办博物馆发展规划（2010—2015）》，实施民办博物馆"一中心、三聚落"建设，即完成东部新城文化创意产业综合功能区成都民办博物馆聚集中心的打造，完成大邑安仁中国博物馆小镇、龙泉驿区洛带古镇博物馆聚落、都江堰市青城山镇博物馆村落的打造。

（三）实施文博旅游业"三区两片"重点项目

为推进成都市文博旅游业的进一步发展，成都市将实施大慈寺历史文化保护街区、水井坊历史文化保护街区、宽窄巷子历史文化保护街区二期、安仁中国博物馆小镇、浣花文博旅游产业片区的三区两片重点项目。

（四）重点培育"天府古镇"品牌

发挥成都企业优势，依托街子古镇、黄龙溪古镇、平乐古镇、五凤古镇、西来古镇、龙池小镇等项目，培育"天府古镇"品牌。按照"区域统筹、资源整合"的开发理念，突出产品的特色和创意。以古镇开发为核心带动周边旅游资源的开发，形成完善的区域文化旅游产业链，进一步提升"天府古镇"的品牌影响力，发挥旅游对文化产业的带动作用。

（五）提升市属博物馆现代化水平

以武侯祠博物馆、杜甫草堂博物馆、金沙遗址博物馆为重点，在继续深挖深厚历史资源条件下，充分运用视听、影像、信息、多媒体、互联网等技术手段，提高展陈技术的数字化、信息化水平，延伸文博旅游产业链，提升文博旅游品牌影响力。

（稿件由成都市文化主管部门提供）

杭州市文化创意产业发展情况

近年来，杭州市紧紧围绕建设文化名城、文化强市和打造"全国文化创意中心"的目标，以科学发展观为指导，注重文化创新，大力发展文化创意产业，助推经济转型升级，取得了良好的社会效益和经济效益。

一、杭州市发展文化创意产业的主要举措

1. 确立发展目标。在市第十次党代会上，杭州首次提出了打造全国文化创意产业中心的目标。2011 年底下发的《杭州市"十二五"文化创意产业发展规划》进一步提出，到"十二五"末，把杭州打造成为文化、环境、生活、创业高度融合为特色的全国文化创意中心。

2. 突出发展重点。坚持"有所为有所不为"，立足杭州市比较优势，重点发展信息服务业、动漫游戏业、设计服务业等八大重点行业，着力打造西湖创意谷、之江文化创意园、西湖数字娱乐产业园等市级文化创意产业园区，引领全市产业发展。

3. 健全组织机构。建立了市文化创意产业指导委员会，统一协调指导全市文创产业发展。成立市、区县（市）两级文创办工作机构，切实加强了全市文创产业协调指导工作。

4. 完善规划政策。先后制定出台了《关于打造全国文化创意产业中心的若干意见》、《杭州市"十二五"文化创意产业发展规划》、《关于统筹财税政策扶持文化创意产业发展的意见》等 30 多项政策文件，涉及财政税收、园区建设、人才培养、投融资等各个方面。同时专门设立了市文化创意产业专项资金，2011 年达 4.11 亿元。

二、杭州市发展文化创意产业取得的主要成效

经过近年来的培育发展，杭州市的文化创意产业取得了明显成效，主要表现在以下几个方面。

1. "申都"工作取得成功。2012 年 5 月 15 日，联合国教科文组织正式批准杭州加入联合国教科文组织全球创意城市网络，成为"工艺和民间艺术之都"。由此，杭州成为了全球创意城市网络第 31 个成员城市，也是国内第一个以此为主题加入该网络的城市。

2. 产业实力不断提升。自 2007 年以来，全市文化创意产业增加值年均增速高于全市 GDP 增速 5.7 个百分点。2011 年，全市文化创意产业实现增加值 843.30 亿元，占全市 GDP 比重 12.03%。在亚太文化创意产业协会发布的《2011 两岸城市文化创意产业竞争力调研报告》中，杭州文创竞争力在两岸 36 个重点城市中排名第三，位居上海、北京之后，深圳、台北之前。

3. 新兴业态日益兴起。动漫产业异军突起，2011 年，全市原创动画作品共计 34606 分钟获得动画片发行许可证，连续三年位居全国各城市之首。获得国家广电总局推荐的优秀动画片共 12 部，推荐数量连续两年位居全国各城市第一。

4. 园区建设扎实推进。目前，杭州市拥有 5 家国家动画产业（教育）基地，5 家国家文化产业示范基地。

5. 人才队伍持续壮大。引进了一大批文化名人，认定了 10 家大学生创业孵化基地和 14 家大学生实训基地，实训大学生数量超过 1 万人。

6. 品牌建设成效明显。中国国际动漫节已成功举办八届，被誉为目前国内规模最大、人气最旺的动漫盛会；中国杭州文化创意产业博览会办展质量明显提高。在第六届"创意中国·和谐世界"文化产业国际论坛上，杭州市被授予全球文化产业领军城市"创意示范奖"，成为中国唯一获此殊荣的城市。

7. 文化科技加速融合。2012 年 5 月 18 日，杭州市被中宣部、科技部等国家五部委联合命名为全国第一批"国家级文化和科技融合示范基地"。同时，杭州还先后被国家有关部委（局）授予"国家第一批三网融合试点城市"和"国家数字出版基地"等荣誉称号。

三、杭州市发展文化创意产业未来工作规划

"十二五"时期，是杭州市加快文化创意产业发展的重要机遇期。下一步，杭州将深入贯彻落实第十一次党代会精神，积极推动文创产业又好又快发展，全力打造全国文化创意中心，把"打造东方品质之城、建设幸福和谐杭州"作为新的贡献目标。

1. 全面启动文创人才梯队工程。继续实施"青年文艺家发现计划"

221

等一批重点项目，每年投入 4500 万元，用于培养文创产业人才队伍，把杭州打造成为名副其实的"文化人天堂"。

2. 持续推进产业园区示范工程。加快国家数字出版基地和市级文创产业园区（楼宇）建设，进一步优化园区布局，加快提升文创园区竞争力，力争到 2015 年全市市级文创园区达到 20 个，国家级示范园区（基地）达到 15 个。

3. 着力实施大企业培育工程。用好市文创产业专项资金，加大扶优扶强力度，推动符合条件的文创企业加快上市，培育一批行业龙头文创企业（集团），形成资本市场的"杭州文创板块"。

4. 深入推进文创品牌创建工程。继续办好中国国际动漫节、中国杭州文化创意产业博览会等重点会展活动。以成功创建联合国教科文组织全球创意城市网络"工艺和民间艺术之都"为契机，最大限度地吸引和集聚全球创意资源，进一步提高杭州文化创意产业在国内外的影响力。

5. 大力实施文化科技融合工程。以获得"国家级文化和科技融合示范基地"荣誉称号为契机，制定《杭州国家级"文化和科技融合示范基地"建设规划》，成立专门机构，深入推动文化与科技融合，加快培育一批创新能力强的文化科技企业。

6. 加快推进文创产业西进工程。充分挖掘五县市的特色地方文化资源，出台专项政策，排出一批项目，积极发展一批特色文创产业，加快建设一批特色乡镇、街道，推动五县（市）文创产业跨越式发展，进一步加快城乡区域统筹发展。

（稿件由杭州市文化创意产业办公室提供）

开封文化旅游产业发展现状

开封作为中原经济区的核心区，在文化产业方面，充分发挥自身的资源优势，认真贯彻落实党的十七届六中全会和省委九届三次会议精神，紧紧围绕宋文化集中展示区、华夏历史文明传承创新先行示范区、建设国际文化旅游名城目标定位、以大宋文化为特色、以全城一景为亮点、以文商旅融合发展为模式、以项目建设为载体、以八大产业为支撑、以改革创新为动力，不断探索文化产业发展新模式。

一、挖掘文化资源，助推文化产业发展

开封市文化资源丰富、城市格局悠久、古城风貌浓郁、北方水城独特，具有诸多特色鲜明的文化要素。发展文化产业具有良好的基础优势：

1. 历史文物遗存众多

开封市现有 13 处文物遗存、遗址被列为国家级文物保护单位，38 处被列为省级文物保护单位。

2. 基础性文化资源广泛丰富

开封是著名的书画之乡、戏曲之乡、木版年画艺术之乡、盘鼓艺术之乡和菊花之乡，名人文化、宋词文化、饮食文化、黄河文化等都极具开发价值。

3. 非物质文化遗产形态完整

开封市有许多已传承千年的非物质文化遗产，现已有 7 个被确定为国家级非物质文化遗产，13 个被列入省级非物质文化遗产名录。

基于以上良好的基础优势，开封市将发展文化旅游业列入振兴开封的"六大战略"和"三个跨越"之一，将文化与旅游的高度融合，以文化为魂，旅游为体，商业为力，着力打造文化旅游品牌，实现了文化旅游业的快速发展。2011 年，文化产业增加值 53 亿元，同比增长 27%；全市接待游客 3900 万人次，同比增长 12%，旅游综合收入 155 亿元，同比增

长 21%。

文化产业已经成为开封的支柱产业，初步形成了文化旅游业、文艺演出业、书画工艺美术业、饮食文化业、休闲娱乐业、会展收藏文化业、传媒出版业、文化培训业八大产业，全方位发展文化产业的新格局已初步形成。

2008 年，开封宋都古城文化产业园区被省文化厅命名为省级文化产业示范园区，2011 年初，被国家文化部命名为国家级文化产业示范园区，是河南省唯一一家，也是中部六省唯一一家国家级文化产业示范园区。

二、以文化产业园区为载体，文化产业集聚发展

以开封宋都古城文化产业示范园区为载体，重点抓好文化产业集聚区建设。针对开封特色文化产品，力争建成开封汴绣产业集聚区、木版年画集聚区等文化产品集聚区，打造刺绣产品、木版年画产品等全国文化产品集散地。

三、规划引领，一张蓝图绘全城

为实现文化产业更好更快发展，开封市先后制定了一系列中长期规划，确立了文化旅游产业在经济社会发展中的战略地位。不断加大对文化旅游资源的开发和利用，深度挖掘开封得天独厚的文化资源优势，特别是通过了《中共开封市委、开封市人民政府关于加快推进宋都古城文化产业园区建设的实施意见》，为今后文化产业的发展提供了明确思路，形成了统一的规划蓝图，为建设全城一景、全城一园奠定了坚实的基础。

四、以项目建设为抓手，着力打造国际文化旅游名城

2009 年以来，相继启动了城墙修复工程、水系工程、繁塔—禹王台景区工程、书店街整修和文化提升工程、刘青霞故居改造修复工程、城摞城遗址博物馆工程、鼓楼复建等一批重大文化旅游项目。

开封东京梦华苑项目，以宋文化为核心，以《东京梦华录》为蓝本，以"二轴五区"为布局，集中建设以宋韵华章、北郊方坛、勾栏瓦肆、琼林食府、万姓交易等为主题的大型宋代风格建筑群，突出再现宋都古城繁华的街市、丰富的娱乐文化、多彩的民间习俗与奢华的皇家生活等，打造一个集观光旅游、休闲娱乐、餐饮购物等为一体的综合性文化产业园区，再现大宋千年繁华。

接下来要依托开封丰富的人文和自然资源，重点谋划储备一批文化旅游产业项目。以 20 平方公里面积的宋都古城文化产业园区为承载，让历史文化动起来、活起来，再现宋都古城风貌，使之成为全城一景、特色鲜明的宋文化主题公园。

五、新模式运作，探索文商旅融合发展

开封通过多种形式，学习借鉴先进经验，探索如何把自身的重要文物景点、旅游景点串联起来，以文化为魂，旅游为体，商业为力，形成特色突出，优势互补的"文商旅"一体产品链，推动文化旅游化、旅游文化化、文旅商业化，提升文化产业发展水平。

六、构建文化旅游产业政策扶持体系

为加快推进宋都古城文化产业园区建设，打造国际文化旅游名城、推动开封文化旅游产业大发展大繁荣，建立行之有效的奖励激励机制，从 2012 年起，设立了文化产业发展专项资金 3000 万元、旅游产业专项资金 5000 万元，用于重点文化旅游项目建设等方面的投入。同时在房租补贴、财政补贴、税收返还、金融、土地等方面出台了一系列优惠政策，形成了完善的文化产业扶持体系。

开封市将立足自己独特的资源优势，坚定不移地走打造特色城市之路，努力建设具有开封风格、开封特色、开封气派的中原经济区核心城市、中部地区休闲宜居城市、著名的国际文化旅游城市。

（稿件由开封市宋都古城古文化产业园区管委会提供）

洛阳：加快发展文化产业　努力建设
国际文化旅游名城

一、洛阳市文化历史资源优势

洛阳是我国"八大古都"之一，国务院首批公布的历史文化名城，历史上有 13 个王朝在洛阳建都，是中国历史上建都最早、朝代最多、历时最长的城市。

洛阳是华夏文明的发祥地，"丝绸之路"的东方起点之一，是中国70% 宗族大姓的起源地，全球 1 亿客家人的祖籍地，儒释道三教的滥觞地。在中华文明起源和发展过程中，河洛文化占有主体与核心地位，发挥着主流与主导作用，是中央文化、国家文化、国都文化、统治文化。以河洛文化核心内容为主干，逐步衍生出名人文化、牡丹文化、宗教文化、民俗文化、姓氏文化、园林文化等多元文化要素。

二、洛阳市文化产业发展成就

"十一五"期间，洛阳市文化产业呈现出全面发展的良好态势，产业规模和水平不断得到提升。

1. 产业构成趋向积极，集聚态势明显

新闻出版、广播影视、文化艺术等文化产业法人单位的核心文化层比重增大，网络文化、休闲文化等外围文化层发展迅速。

龙门、小浪底西霞院、汉魏故城和隋唐城遗址等文化旅游产业园区发展步伐加快。

2. 重点项目不断增加

开工建设了洛阳广电中心、洛阳市图书馆新馆、洛阳艺术学校新校区和洛阳市豫剧院、洛阳市曲剧团综合演艺中心等项目。

3. 示范带动作用增强

推出了 10 个文化产业示范村，重点开发牡丹花、唐三彩、青铜器等具有洛阳地域特色的文化产业。挖掘、扶持、推介了洛阳宫灯、竹编、剪纸、麦草画、梅花玉、观赏石等民间民俗工艺产业项目。全市各类文化专业村已发展到 25 个。

4. 品牌打造成效显著

"中国洛阳牡丹文化节"作为省部共办的国家级节会活动，至今已成功举办了 30 届，荣获中国节庆最高奖"十佳节庆奖"，现入选国家非物质文化遗产名录。

5. 产品市场空间扩大

2010 年，全市文化产业总产出 114.1 亿元，比"十五"末增长 128.2%；实现增加值 35.51 亿元，比"十五"末增长 108.5%；增加值占 GDP 的比重为 1.53%。相关从业人员 5.75 万人，文化产业从业人员人均实现增加值 3.44 万元，高于全市人均生产总值 3.2 万元的平均水平。

三、洛阳市特色文化产业介绍

（一）文化旅游产业

明确提出要在中原经济区建设中，传承弘扬河洛文化品牌，建设国际文化旅游名城，着力打造"千年帝都、牡丹花城、河洛之根、丝路起点"四张名片，把洛阳建成历史文化彰显、在国际上具有较高知名度和美誉度的国际文化旅游名城和世界级古都文化休闲目的地。

精心谋划实施重点项目：

一是以传统旅游景区改造提升为抓手，打造龙门石窟、白马寺、关林等一批精品文化旅游园区。

二是以国家大遗址保护工程为契机，建设隋唐洛阳城"一区一轴"保护性活化项目、汉魏故城国家考古遗址公园项目和偃师商城宫城遗址保护展示项目等一批国家级考古遗址公园。

三是以历史文化街区保护工程为契机，精心打造老城历史文化街区、涧西工业文化遗产街区等历史文化产业园区。

四是打造一批精品演艺项目和 3D 动漫电影。

（二）牡丹文化产业

自古以来就有"洛阳牡丹甲天下"之说，2011 年洛阳市又被中国花协命名为"中国牡丹花都"。牡丹文化产业经过多年来的持续发展，已经成为洛阳市的特色产业，从业人员达 3 万多人，年产值 10 多亿元。

一是以中国洛阳牡丹文化节为平台，举办国际高端文化、会展、商贸和旅游活动，实施牡丹文化旅游工程。

二是制定牡丹产业发展规划，扩大牡丹生产规模，提升生产水平，彰显"满城尽是牡丹花"的特色城市风貌。

三是扶持建设孟津平乐农民牡丹画创意产业园区，叫响"中国牡丹画第一村"品牌。把平乐打造成集"牡丹观赏、艺术创作，旅游观光，休闲娱乐，教育培训，产品交易"为一体的生态休闲旅游目的地。

四是大力实施牡丹系列衍生品研发生产，打造中国的牡丹产业总部。

四、洛阳市文化产业发展规划

今后几年，洛阳市将重点发展七大产业：

1. 广告传媒业。要做强传统传媒，开发新兴传媒。

2. 文化旅游业。深入推进国际文化旅游名城建设攻坚战，保护开发历史文化遗存，高水平规划、大手笔运作，市场化推进，突出"根文化"优势。

3. 艺术品及工艺美术业。提高艺术品创作水平，发展工艺美术品制作及批发零售业，发展古玩及收藏品市场，做大做强艺术品及工艺美术业。

4. 影视动漫业。要挖掘历史文化资源和现实题材，创作影视动漫作品，壮大洛阳影视动漫产业。

5. 演艺娱乐业。创作演艺精品，开发演艺娱乐项目，促进演艺娱乐业与旅游业融合，实现演艺娱乐与旅游观光相互促进，协调发展。

6. 会展业。优化会展环境，提高管理水平，积极承办高水平会议、展览、节庆、赛事等活动，拉动服务业发展。

7. 文化用品、设备生产制造业。引进市场前景较好的文化用品设备生产企业，走制造业与文化产业相融合的发展道路。

（稿件由洛阳市委宣传部文教科提供）

绍兴：寻找着力点，增强推动力

近年来，绍兴市着力推进文化产业发展，主要在营造发展环境、强化保障措施、出台扶持政策、加强政府引导、深化体制改革、建设产业园区、实施重大项目、促进文化消费等方面寻找着力点，采取新的发展措施，增强推动力，推动文化产业为绍兴的文化强市建设和经济转型升级服务，并取得了阶段性成果。

一、着力营造发展环境

1. 领导重视，提高对发展文化产业重要性的认识

2011 年绍兴市提出了重点实施包括文化产业跨越工程在内的"七大工程"，对文化强市和文化产业发展工作作了新的部署。

2. 健全组织，加强对发展文化产业的组织领导

市委市政府成立了绍兴市文化建设领导小组及其办公室，统一协调和研究解决文化建设和发展中的重大问题。

3. 出台政策，加大对发展文化产业的扶持力度

出台促进文化产业发展的新政策，进一步加大财政支持力度，强化要素保障，优化发展环境，加强统筹协调。鼓励发展新兴文化产业。加强传统工艺美术的保护、传承和发展。加快发展现代服务业，建立文化服务业推进组，推动文化服务业的发展。

二、着力加强政府引导

1. 制定实施文化产业的发展规划

根据《绍兴市十二五经济社会发展规划纲要》的总体部署，制定了《绍兴市十二五文化产业发展规划》，明确发展方向和重点，搞好总体布局。

2. 鼓励企业开拓文化产品市场

为企业开拓市场创造了一定的条件，调动了企业参展的积极性，打响

了绍兴文化产业品牌。

3. 积极引导民营资本投资文化产业

绍兴是民营经济大市，绍兴市政府加强对民营文化产业的扶持力度，降低准入门槛，引导民间投资，取得了成效。特别是在影视、动漫领域出现了一批民营文化企业。绍兴电影市场在竞争中快速扩张，产业规模持续扩大，发展前景良好。2010年全市电影票房收入达到4900万元，比2005年的1000万元增长了近5倍，2011年全市电影票房收入达7705亿元，比2010年增长57%。

三、着力深化体制改革

绍兴市积极推进全市文化体制改革，特别是针对经营性文化单位和准公益性文化单位，体制改革不断深入，以体制机制的转变来增强活力，增强竞争力，实现两个效益的最大化，促进文化产业的发展。文化市场管理体系也在综合执法改革中得到不断完善和加强。文化产业的市场主体不断增加，行业门类更加齐全。

四、着力推动产业集聚

在文化产业发展过程中，绍兴积极推动文化产业集聚区的形成和发展。如嵊州艺术村由老厂房改造而成，设立根雕、竹编、戏剧服装、古玩等大大小小的工作室40余个，成为当地民间工艺产业窗口展示、创作交流、产品交易和文化休闲的重要基地，并正在扩建为嵊州市文化创意产业园。

五、着力实施项目带动

政府有关部门树立"抓项目就是抓产业，抓产业必须抓项目"的理念，积极实施文化产业大项目带动战略，开展文化产业项目招商引资，做好项目落地的服务工作，有力地推动了文化产业的发展。这些重大文化产业项目的落地和投资建设，对绍兴文化服务业的发展、文化消费的带动和城市文化品位的提高具有较强的引领作用，建成后将为绍兴文化产业的嬗变作出积极贡献，也将为建设绍兴的文化休闲城市和经济的转型升级提供支撑和示范。

六、着力促进文化消费

绍兴城乡居民消费水平的不断提高，为文化产业发展提供了强劲的需求动力。电影、电视、文艺演出、图书、文化娱乐、网络游戏、旅游、艺术品收藏等文化消费十分活跃。这也得益于绍兴市促进文化消费的有效举措：

1. 扩大文化产品供给

近年来，绍兴市积极开展文化下乡、群众文化六进（进广场、进社区、进农村、进企业、进校园、进军营）活动，发展图书连锁经营、农家书屋、图书流动站，实施文化惠民措施，加大政府对公共文化产品的采购力度，扩大公益性文化产品供给，提升了人民群众的文化消费能力；同时，通过扩大市场化的文化产品供给，不断满足群众的文化需求，特别是这两年城市多厅电影城建设成为投资热点，增加了市场供给，也给消费者带来了实惠。

2. 实施全城旅游

绍兴古城全城旅游概念的推出和古城创建5A级旅游景区，使得文化旅游消费的群体在不断扩大，特别是外来游客的增加，文化旅游消费的量稳步增长，为绍兴文化产业的发展提供了巨大的需求动力，也为推动文化产业发展创造了良好的契机。同时实行博物馆、图书馆、文化馆和名人纪念馆等公益性文化场馆的免费开放，方便了群众的文化消费。

3. 鼓励发展文化服务业

文化服务业是发展现代服务业的重要组成部分，2011年，绍兴市政府出台了《关于进一步加快发展服务业的意见》，在市场准入、网点布局，政策优惠、要素保障等方面加以积极鼓励和推动，创造发展的条件，使文化服务业得到进一步发展，文化消费市场得到拓展，为满足人民群众日益增长的多元文化消费需求营造了良好的市场环境，市民文化消费的热情得到进一步激发。

（稿件由绍兴市文化广电新闻出版局提供）

深圳市文化产业发展基本情况

一、发展概况

近年来，深圳市积极推进文化体制改革，推动文化产业快速发展，文化产业已成为深圳第四大支柱产业，深圳已成为国内文化产业发展浪潮中的先锋城市之一。2011 年文化创意产业增加值占全市 GDP 的比重为 8%，成为带动经济快速健康发展的重要引擎。

二、产业发展主要特色

1. 行业发展全国领先

创意设计业优势地位明显，是中国现代平面设计的发源地，成为国内第一个被联合国教科文组织认定的"设计之都"。深圳还是中国最大的高端印刷及黄金珠宝生产基地。新闻出版、广播影视、文化会展等行业也都在全国具有重要的影响力。

2. 发展模式特色鲜明

深度挖掘、整合、联动相关产业资源，形成了"文化＋科技"、"文化＋金融"、"文化＋旅游"、"文化＋创意"、"文化＋休闲"等产业发展新模式。以高新技术创新文化生产方式的"文化＋科技"模式，为文化创意产业高端起步、跨越发展奠定了强大的技术保障。以文化产权交易所、文化产业投资基金为主导的"文化＋金融"模式，不断创新对文化企业的金融支持方式，构建了文化产权交易、文化产业投融资、文化企业孵化的重要平台。以主题公园、文化创意产业园区和基地为依托的"文化＋旅游"模式，有效延伸了文化创意产业链。

3. 集聚效应逐步显现

采用行业集聚、空间集中的发展策略，培育建设了一批文化创意产业重点项目，形成了区域发展特色，构建了较为合理的产业布局。

4. 要素市场加快建立

打造了全国唯一的国家级、国际化、综合性文化产业博览交易会。在国内较早建立了文化产权交易所，参与发起设立了首支国家级大型文化产业投资基金。

三、产业发展和投资环境

2005 年，把文化产业定位为深圳市第四大支柱产业，2011 年把文化创意产业定位为全市 6 个战略性新兴产业之一。

"十一五"期间，市区两级财政共安排文化产业发展专项资金 8.5 亿元，重点为一批原创研发、高速成长型的文化企业和项目提供了资助和扶持，有力地推动了深圳文化产业的快速发展。2011 年 10 月，《深圳文化创意产业振兴发展政策》实施，每年市财政安排 5 亿元扶持经费，为推动文化创意产业快速发展，将有效解决目前深圳文化创意产业发展中存在的资金投入不足、原创内容产业薄弱、关键技术研发能力不足、市场主体竞争力较弱和投融资"瓶颈"约束等问题。在深圳投资发展文化创意产业，可以在原创研发、贷款贴息、保险费资助、中小企业房租补贴等 20 多个方面享受到政府的资金资助、补贴或奖励，还可以在土地、税收、人才等方面享受相应的优惠政策。

四、发展目标

2011—2015 年，深圳市文化创意产业年均增长将达到 25% 左右，2015 年文化创意产业增加值将达到 2200 亿元，文化创意产业总产出将超过 5800 亿元。未来几年，瞄准文化创意和科技创新两大主攻方向，重点发展创意设计、文化软件、动漫游戏、新媒体及文化信息服务、数字出版、影视演艺、文化旅游、非物质文化遗产开发、高端印刷、高端工艺美术等十大产业，承继现有发展基础，努力形成新的特色优势领域，不断提高产业综合实力。

（一）努力方向

1. 促进产业结构不断优化

大力发展新兴文化业态，做大做强以创意内容为核心的文化服务业。努力将深圳打造成为我国乃至国际上重要的文化创意产业先锋城市、世界知名的"设计之都"和国际时尚创意中心。

2. 促进产业主体发展壮大

培育发展一批掌握核心技术、拥有原创品牌、具有较强市场竞争力的骨干文化企业和企业集团，加快规划建设一批文化创意产业重大项目，形成富有活力的优势企业群和具有特色的优势产业集群，使深圳成为具有世界水平的创意产业集聚区。

3. 促进创新能力显著提升

完善以企业为主体、市场为导向、产学研相结合的文化科技创新体系，提高文化企业的设备硬件水平和文化产品的科技含量，提升文化原创能力和研发能力，使深圳成为重要的文化创意产业创新中心和应用研发高地。

4. 促进市场体系日益完善

丰富文化产品市场，培育文化人才、信息、技术、资本等要素市场，开拓大众性文化消费市场，促进文化产品和服务的合理流动。推动文化产品和服务出口，拓展海外文化市场，使深圳成为中华文化"走出去"的重要基地。

（二）发展重点

1. 会展平台工程

坚持"专业化、国际化、市场化、精品化、规范化"的办展方针，突出文化产业核心层、文化创意度和"文化＋科技"特色，强化高端引领，增加科技含量，进一步提升文博会的国际知名度。

2. 技术支撑工程

在创意设计、动漫游戏、数字出版、影视制作、新媒体等领域加快建设一批技术水平先进、服务功能强大的文化创意产业公共技术平台，为文化创意企业提供仪器设备、科学数据、软件程序、检验检测等技术资源共享服务。

3. 产业集聚工程

建设一批创意设计产业园区基地，增强企业孵化和公共服务功能，完善创意设计产业链，为创意设计企业提供最佳的栖居、交流、发展环境，夯实创意设计业发展基础。

4. 文化金融工程

加强深圳文化产权交易所建设，打造立足深圳、对接港澳台、服务全国、面向世界的国家级文化产权交易、文化创意无形资产评估和投融资综合服务平台。

5. 传播推广工程

建立多形式、多渠道、广覆盖、高效率的文化传播平台，推广深圳文化精品、创意产品和文化服务。鼓励深圳文化企业在国内城市建设数字连锁影院、开展文化会展等活动，建立全国性的文化传播渠道。

（稿件由深圳市文体旅游局文化产业发展处提供）

温州市文化产业发展现状

近年来，温州市委、市政府高度重视文化产业发展，把发展文化产业作为文化大市建设的一项重点工作来抓。通过加大投入、优化环境、大力培育、调整布局等多项措施，文化产业发展取得了明显成效。2010年，温州市文化产业增加值100.58亿元，比上年增长22.70%，文化产业增加值占全市GDP总量的比重由上年的3.1%提升到3.47%。据初步统计，全市有文化产业单位15000家（其中法人单位近5000家），拥有资产210亿元，从业人员15万多人。其中，民营文化企业和个体文化工商户7600多家，从业人员12万余人，营业收入120亿元，投资千万元以上的民营文化企业56家。

1. 文化产业发展宏观环境不断改善

2006年1月，温州市委出台《温州市加快建设文化大市的决定》，全面实施包括文化产业在内的文化大市建设"六大工程"；2009年3月，出台《温州市推动文化大发展大繁荣纲要（2009—2012）》，把"促进文化产业发展"列为文化大发展大繁荣的"五大行动"之一；2011年3月，出台《关于促进文化产业发展的若干意见》，规定市财政每年安排2000万元作为文化产业发展专项资金，用于文化产业公共平台和重大项目的建设，并在税收、土地、投融资、人才引进等优惠措施方面作了"一揽子"规定。2012年4月，温州市政府下发《温州市文化产业发展"十二五"规划》，为今后一段时间的文化产业发展指明方向。

2. 国有文化单位实力稳中有升

温州市国有文化企业数量不多，但经过资源整合和内部改革后，经济效益和社会效益良好，特别是温州日报报业集团和温州广电传媒集团，已成为国有文化企业的领头羊。目前，温州日报报业集团下辖7个子公司，涉及户外媒体、广告创意、印刷发行等，2011年集团经营收入7.34亿元，同比增长10.5%，其中都市报2010年广告收入突破2亿元大关，

2011 年收入 2.2 亿元，同比增长 10%，居全国地市级前茅。

温州广电传媒集团积极拓宽产业发展领域，走多元化、集团化发展道路，现下辖 8 个文化产业子公司、市、县广播电视台 9 座，自办电视节目 12 套和广播节目 12 套，2011 年集团经营收入 6.01 亿元，同比增长 14%，其中广告收入 3.6 亿元，同比增长 10%，继续领跑温州文化产业发展。数字电视、移动电视等新传媒成为新的增长点，全市 1250 辆公交车安装了移动电视接收设备，年度广告收入 600 多万元；手机电视进入试播阶段；户外 LED 全彩显示屏项目进入开发阶段。

3. 民营文化产业方兴未艾

温州是民营经济的发祥地，民间资本活跃，民营企业众多，印刷、制笔、商务礼品、教玩具、工艺美术等民营文化产业在国民经济中占有较高比重。温州是"中国印刷城"，全市现有印刷企业 2794 家，从业人员 58000 多人，年产值 230 亿元，约占全市工业总产值的 4.3%。温州是"中国制笔之都"，全市现有制笔企业 200 余家，年产量 120 亿支笔，占全国的三分之一，居全国地级市首位。2011 年全市制笔业产值 35 亿元，出口交货值 17 亿元。温州是"中国教玩具之都"，全市现有教玩具企业 280 多家，2011 年实现工业产值近 30 亿元，其中游乐设备产值、市场份额占全国的 50% 以上。温州是"中国商务礼品市场基地"，平阳、苍南两县商务礼品加工、销售网络发达，建有龙港礼品城、瓯南礼品城、郑楼商务礼品城（街）等大型交易市场。两县共有商务礼品企业、个体工商户近 4400 家，年产值 87 亿元。温州是"百工之乡"，全市共有瓯塑、瓯绣、黄杨木雕、石雕、细纹刻纸等 32 个传统工艺美术品类、120 多个品种、300 多家企业，年产值 130 亿元。随着国家对文化产业领域的逐步放开，温州民间资本投资文化产业的积极性日益高涨，投资力度逐渐加大。耗资 1000 多万元的中国鞋文化博物馆、投资 4 亿元的温州文化商品市场、超大规模的商务礼品基地瓯南礼品城等都由民间资本投建而成。

4. 文化产业发展活力不断增强

2003 年起，温州市坚持区别对待、因地制宜、分类指导的原则，根据不同文化单位的性质和特点确定不同的改革路径，扎实平稳地推进文化体制改革，文化产业发展的活力进一步增强。以市场为导向的电影放映体制改革进一步激活电影市场。2010 年，全市电影票房突破 1 亿元大关，同比增长 40% 以上；2011 年票房收入 12767.5 万元，同比增长 30.3%，观众 280.5 万人次，同比增长 24.4%，再创温州电影票房纪录。公益性文化事业单位内部改革逐步深化，温州市图书馆、市体育俱乐部等单位积极创新和改进单位内部运行模式，推进人事、分配和社会保障制度改革，增强内部活力，提高工作效率、服务质量和服务水平。市级新闻媒体积极探索宣传和经营业务"两分开"的路子，新闻媒体的广告、印刷、发行、网络传输部分逐渐从事业体制中剥离，转制为企业，真正成为自负盈亏、自担风险的市场主体。

5. 文化创意产业崭露头角

温州文化创意产业起步较晚，但近几年通过旧厂房改造、与高校合作、民间资本参与等方式，取得了长足发展。浙江创意园对原温州冶金厂部分旧厂房进行改造，使原来的"制造工厂"变为"创意工厂"，入驻创意机构30余家。温州大学利用高校学科优势、人才资源优势，加强与温州轻工产业的衔接，在学校里创办文化创意园，积极服务传统产业转型升级、大学生创业创新。瓯江学院、城市学院、团委均创办创意园，入驻工作室百余个。

（稿件由温州市政府办公室文体涉外处提供）

徐州市文化发展现状

徐州自古为华夏九州之一，具有 5000 多年文明史和 2600 多年建城史，是国家历史文化名城。徐州是彭祖故国、刘邦故里、项羽故都，以"北雄南秀、楚风汉韵"为特质的徐州文化成为江苏重要的文化标志之一。近年来，市委、市政府充分发挥徐州历史底蕴深厚、文化资源丰厚、科教实力雄厚的比较优势，围绕建设区域性文化中心城市定位，深度挖掘文化内涵，着力塑造城市个性，全面打响文化品牌，全力构筑区域性文化高地，开创了文化发展繁荣的新局面。

一、文化体制改革激发新活力

对照省定"时间表"、"路线图"、"任务书"，全面完成了 6 家市直经营性文化事业单位、3 家文艺院团和各县（市）区的文化体制改革任务，特别是成功组建了徐州演艺集团和徐州文化产业集团，切实做到集团有资产、人员有待遇、企业有市场、创新有动力。

二、文化产业集聚呈现新亮点

坚持区域集中、产业集聚、企业集群，大力推动文化企业、文化项目入园进区，规划建设了创意 68 文化产业园、彭城壹号、南湖水街、滨湖新天地、老东门时尚街区等一批特色功能区，全市 20 多个文化产业园区集聚企业 2000 多家，有力地提升了文化产业的布局结构、产业规模和发展层次。

三、文化设施建设树立新形象

新建具有国内一流水准的徐州艺术馆、音乐厅、规划馆、档案馆、胡琴艺术博物馆等标志性文化工程，加快建设徐州广电大厦、徐州报业大厦、徐州奥体中心，对汉文化景区、窑湾古镇、钟鼓楼、汉画像石馆、徐州博物馆等文化设施进行提档升级，更好地展示和彰显了徐州地域文化特色。

四、文艺精品创作取得新成效

创作生产了电视连续剧《小小飞虎队》、柳琴戏《水远路长》、电影《此生此爱》、动漫片《如意岛上的小精灵》等文艺精品；全市有5个门类10部作品入选省第七届"五个一工程"奖，电视剧《老柿子树》获全国"五个一工程"奖。全市荣获全省广播电视十大名牌专栏3个、十大优秀专栏2个。

五、品牌文化活动展现新风采

李可染艺术节、马可艺术节、汉文化旅游节等文化节庆的影响日益广泛，"动感彭城"广场演出、"乐在农家"才艺展演等成为全省、全国特色文化活动。推进"书画徐州"建设，举办了四届"书画徐州"年展、"徐州百年百人书画展"、出版了《当代徐州百家中国画集》。

六、文化产业作为支柱产业培育发展

文化产业具有优结构、扩消费、增就业、促跨越、可持续的独特优势和特点，是推动经济转型升级的重要依托和支撑。今后一个时期，徐州市积极与发达地区展开同台竞争，加快构建业态布局合理、品牌特色鲜明、市场竞争力强的文化产业体系，力争到"十二五"末，全市文化产业增加值占GDP比重达7%左右。

1. 突出龙头企业带动

大力培育徐州报业传媒集团、徐州广电集团、徐州演艺集团、徐州文化产业集团、江苏大风乐器有限公司、邳州宝石玉器城等一大批大型骨干文化企业。积极培育一批富有徐州资源禀赋特点的字画、奇石、玉器、乐器、铁艺、印刷等龙头企业，打造实力强劲的徐州文化企业集群。坚持集团化、专业化、多元化并举，支持中小文化企业向"专、精、特、新"方向发展，形成一批富有活力、形态多样的文化企业"集团军"。

2. 突出重大项目建设

精心梳理编制全市文化产业重点项目计划书，科学认定，强化扶持，全力推动彭城欢乐世界、吕梁文化风景区、微山湖湿地公园、市民文化活动中心、龟山博物馆区等一批具有示范效应和产业拉动作用的重大项目，带动文化产业集群发展。加大招商引资力度，抓好项目筛选和包装推介，更多引进龙头型、航母式大项目，铆足徐州文化产业持续发展的后劲。

3. 突出园区集聚发展

像支持工业开发区一样扶持文化产业集聚区建设，全力打造老徐州历史文化片区、创意 68 文化产业园、徐州动漫产业园、九里山历史文化景区、窑湾古镇历史街区、江苏师大创意文化产业园、淮海经济区文化艺术品展示交易中心等文化功能集聚区，促进各种资源合理配置和产业分工，推动文化企业向园区集中，充分发挥文化产业集聚区的带动作用，打造一批影响力辐射力强的"文化航母"，提高文化产业规模化、集约化、专业化水平。

4. 突出科技支撑与业态融合

充分发挥现代科技对文化产业的巨大推动作用，瞄准文化科技发展前沿，推动文化与科技有效衔接，大力发展数字广播电视、数字出版、数字音乐、动漫影视、网络游戏等具有高成长性、高附加值的新兴文化业态。加快文化与科技、旅游、会展、动漫等关联产业的双向融合、深度融合、加速融合，形成一批高科技、多功能、多业态的数字化、信息化文化产业集群，推动文化产业跨越升级，使文化产业实现突破性增长。

（稿件由徐州市文化主管部门提供）

营口市文化产业发展现状

一、文化资源特色

营口历史悠久，文化灿烂，是一座有着 26 万年人类文明积淀的城市，为东三省第一个对外开放的港口城市，中国最早兴办近代工业的城市之一，是环渤海经济圈、辽宁沿海经济带和沈阳经济区唯一的交汇点。营口依河而建，因海而兴，具有丰富独特的文化资源。

目前，营口市有旅游景区（点）18 家、国家 3A 级旅游区 1 家、国家 4A 级旅游区 2 家；文物保护单位 96 家，其中国家级 4 家、省级 11 家、市级 32 家；非物质文化遗产项目 17 项，其中国家级 3 项、省级 5 项、市级 9 项。

营口市被誉为"中国乐器之都"，所属大石桥市、盖州市获得"中国书法之乡"的称号。营口的历史文化、河海文化、宗教文化、民俗文化和名人文化等文化资源蕴藏丰厚、特色鲜明，类型丰富，为文化产业发展奠定了坚实的基础。

二、文化产业发展情况

据统计测算，到"十一五"期末，营口市文化产业经营单位达到 3261 家，从业人员 21590 人，资产 73 亿元，营业收入 60.67 亿元，是"十五"期间的三倍，形成了门类比较齐全的文化产业体系，涵盖了印刷制造业、乐器制造业、广播电影电视服务业、歌舞娱乐业等多种形式的文化产业群体。其中，以印刷制造业、乐器产业、文化娱乐业、网络文化业、图书报刊业、文物和温泉海滨旅游业等文化产业群体在文化产业发展过程中发挥了引领作用。

三、重点特色文化产业情况

1. 音乐（乐器）产业集群

营口从 1952 年开始生产乐器，逐步形成了钢琴、风琴、手风琴、提琴、口琴及贝司、古筝（转调古筝国家专利）、吉他、古琴、键盘、外壳、音源、琴凳、谱架、乐器箱包等几十个系列产品。辽宁省乐器产品质量监督检验站暨国家轻工业乐器质量监督检测营口站，是我国三个国家级乐器检测站之一。营口乐器成为我国四大乐器生产基地之一，是辽宁省乃至东北三省、内蒙古自治区唯一的乐器特色文化产业。

营口市现有乐器生产企业、配件生产企业及专业手工企业百余家，琴凳产量国内最大。规划10平方公里的省级音乐（乐器）产业园区基地正在建设中，一期工程签约企业已全部入住。音乐（乐器）产业集群已被列入"辽宁省文化产业发展规划重点项目"。

目前，营口市在紧紧抓住国家加快发展文化产业，推进文化大发展大繁荣的有利时机，把营口放在全国乃至世界范围内的大坐标上考虑营口乐器产业的发展战略，以建设中国乐器之都为目标，以辽宁（营口）乐器产业园区为载体，依托营口原有技术、人才、市场、品牌等基础和优势，以"政府引导、市场化运作"的方式经营运作，走规模化、集群化、集约化道路，与科研院校联合科技研发、引进、培养、储备人才，打造中国最巨影响力的集乐器研发、制造、展示、贸易、信息、演艺、维修、教育、比赛、旅游、休闲及创意于一体的北方乐器研发制造中心、贸易展览中心、物流信息中心、售后服务中心、文化交流中心、教育培训中心、音乐艺术中心。

2. 温泉休闲娱乐产业集群

营口温泉位于我国著名的地热带，目前建成有熊岳和双台子两个温泉旅游度假核心集聚区。这两个温泉旅游区占地面积超过2平方公里，地下热水储量丰富，日出水量达8700吨，出水一般温度为80℃—90℃，甚至有100℃以上的沸腾水。

目前，营口市以打造中国北方最佳温泉城为目标，以可持续发展为开发建设根本理念，以温泉、海滨、冰雪、漂流等休闲旅游为特色，以大东北和环渤海为客源市场，以熊岳、双台两大温泉旅游核心区为支撑，高起点、科学规划整合营口地区温泉旅游资源，并以强有力的市场宣传推介活动为发展突破口，提高营口"中国北方最佳温泉城"的知名度和美誉度。

3. 印刷业产业集群

2010年在辽宁（营口）沿海产业基地，建设辽宁营口印刷高新技术产业园区（基地）。借"产业基地"这一平台，一方面继续做精做强做大大族冠华印刷装备制造产业，一方面以产业、技术、资金、设备、从业人员、配套服务设施等多方面的准入标准，通过政策、区位、资源、市场和技术五大导向，引导具有先进制造水平、经济规模和效益突出，有能力参与市场竞争，为印机制造商配套服务的相关企业、印刷耗材生产商和印刷厂进入产业基地，培育与市场需求相适应的"专、精、特、新"为特点的产业群，推动印刷业资源集中、提升综合竞争力，实现印刷产业专业化、规模化，带动地区经济发展，实现产业链集约化资源整合。

目前，按照"大项目——产业链——产业群"的发展思路，以辽宁营口印刷高新技术产业园区（基地）为依托，形成以龙头企业为核心的印刷出版产业集群，打造技术先进、规模集约、国际一流的集印刷设备制造、印刷耗材、印刷附属配套、出版包装为一体的大型文化企业集团。

4. 河海沿岸文化产业集群

营口西大街（辽河老街）坐落于辽宁省营口市辽河大街西段，核心区全长 1.3 公里，街区占地面积 20 余万平方米。西大街两侧较完整的百余年历史的近代优秀建筑 31 处，不仅形式、用途多样，更有中西合璧之美，更反映出中西文化的逐步融合，具有极高的历史价值。

河海沿岸文化产业集群的总体发展思路是，努力展现营口西大街的厚重人文历史，以西炮台和辽河入海口为依托，打造"海防公园"品牌，使其成为营口对外宣传名片；以西大街为依托，再现百年辽河老街风貌，建设成文化旅游观光商业一条街，打造（申报）具有营口河海特色的"中国历史文化名街"；引进战略投资者，发展动漫游戏产业，延伸产业链条，打造文化创意产业园区；大力发展庙会民俗文化，打造宗教民俗文化旅游产业。

（稿件由中共营口市委宣传部提供）

岳阳市文化产业发展概要

一、发展现状

岳阳是一座有着 2500 多年历史的文化名城，融名山、名水、名楼、名人、名文于一体，文化底蕴十分深厚。文化产业产值连续 6 年保持高速增长，预计 2012 年实现文化产业增加值 100 亿元，同比增长 21%，占 GDP 比重达到 5.0%。城乡居民恩格尔系数持续下降，文化消费支出比重不断上升。

二、发展思路

突出一个龙头，推进两翼联动，把握三个导向，挖掘四大品牌，壮大五大产业。"一个龙头"即以岳阳中心城区为文化产业发展的龙头；"两翼联动"即以环洞庭湖文化产业带与沿汨罗江文化产业带为两翼；"三个导向"即坚持目标导向、资源导向和问题导向不动摇；"四大品牌"即努力打造民俗文化、历史文化、工商文化和生态文化四大知名品牌；"五大产业"即推动文化旅游、演艺娱乐、文博会展、现代传媒和文化体育等五大文化产业强势发展。

三、发展重点

（一）文化旅游业

1. 打造核心景区。构建岳阳旅游的核心景区；打造岳阳旅游业的龙头，提升岳阳旅游的国际形象和核心竞争力。

2. 建设知名品牌。打造楼岛湖、龙舟文化、红色休闲、民俗文化、洞庭观鸟等文化品牌。

3. 延伸产业链条。构建观光、缅怀、度假、生态、探险、健身等多元旅游产品供给和多元旅游文化产品以及多元旅游商品；

4. 加强市场营销。重点打造一部宣传片、一首传唱歌曲、一套系列丛书、一台文化节目、一个著名节庆等"五个一"工程。

5. 推进项目建设：

（1）洞庭路历史文化街区文化遗产保护展示体系；

（2）国际龙舟文化节项目；

（3）南湖水上游乐休闲项目；

（4）三国水军操练场项目；

（5）爱情岛上爱情节项目；

（6）观岛节项目；

（7）岳阳楼旅游纪念品项目；

（8）屈子祠旅游纪念品项目。

（二）演艺娱乐业

1. 培育多元化的市场主体。加快事业单位转企进程，以市场运作型演艺公司为主体，公益型演艺公司为补充，同时保留重要艺术家和艺术团体的事业编制，强化市场竞争和优胜劣汰机制。

2. 推行专业化的经营管理。组建全市性文化演艺公司，整合和盘活全市演艺资源。

3. 打造特色化的知名品牌。集中力量打造一台体现巴陵特色的精品歌舞节目，将其与旅游结合起来，长期展演。

4. 实施精品化的重点项目。着力实施五大项目：一是恢复编排巴陵戏传统剧目项目；二是编排花鼓戏精品小戏剧团项目；三是《洞庭风情》大型实景综艺晚会项目；四是文化产业集团演艺大厦项目；五是保护与民掘汨罗长乐故事会项目。

（三）文博会展业

发挥岳阳文博传统优势，打造为国内独具特色的文博旗帜。

1. 推进市场化运作。发挥市场自我调节作用，规范和繁荣岳阳古玩市场。

2. 推进数字化管理。大力推动文博数字化改造工程；创新展览形式，用现代多媒体技术改进文博展示水平。

3. 推进集群化发展。打破行政和行业壁垒，以系统化、集群化思路推进文博产业整体快速发展，形成规模经济效应。

4. 推出特色化品牌。大举世界文化名人——屈原、世界文化名楼——岳阳楼两张国际名牌，大兴"走出去"战略。

5. 建设多元化项目：

（1）屈原文化产业园建设项目；

（2）文庙保护与展示体系项目；

（3）张谷英古建筑群保护与开发工程；

（4）岳阳市古玩市场项目；

（5）文化艺术会展中心开发工程；

（6）岳阳市博物馆改扩建项目；

（7）慈氏塔修缮与环境整治工程；

（8）临湘龙窖山瑶族千家峒遗址保护开发项目；

（9）岳阳近现代教育（岳阳教会学校）展示体系；

（10）杜甫文化园建设项目；

（11）罗子国城址保护展示体系；

（12）左宗棠纪念设施群；

（13）岳州窑遗址。

（四）现代传媒业

1. 集聚传媒企业。加快岳阳市广电集团的组建进程，强化报纸、电视媒体的平台优势和带动经济的影响力，形成以"声屏报刊网"为核心的全媒体产业群。

2. 打造媒体品牌。加强数字化内容产业开发，发展数码电影、数字电视、电子出版、数字艺术、视频点播、数字娱乐等新型文化传播方式。

3. 培育动漫企业。积极建设动漫产业园区，培育动漫品牌，积极带动职业培训、玩具文具、主题餐饮服务、主题公园旅游等多种产品的发展，形成新的业态形式。

4. 实施重点项目：

（1）岳阳广播电视集团建设项目；

（2）岳阳市影视文化创意基地项目；

（3）岳阳市印刷科技工业园项目；

（4）岳阳市青少年绿色网吧通道工程；

（5）兴建天伦城电影城；

（6）兴建动漫或动漫公园；

（7）岳阳市图书城。

（五）文化体育业

1. 加强科学管理。成立专门管理组织，引进专业团队管理运营大型体育赛事、大型体育场馆。

2. 组织重大活动。充分发挥甲 A、全国青年女篮、女排等竞赛项目以及市体育中心、水上娱乐训练基地等设施建设项目的带动作用。充分利用岳阳籍世界冠军的明星效应，推动岳阳与国内外体育界及知名体育公司的交流与合作。

3. 打造特色品牌。充分挖掘岳阳的水资源，积极发展水上运动项目、野外拓展训练等新兴体育产品。

4. 建设重点项目：

（1）岳阳市群众艺术馆兴建项目；

（2）岳阳市图书馆改扩建项目；

（3）岳阳市青少年文化活动中心兴建项目；

（4）体育中心建设项目；

（5）水上综合训练基地建设项目；

（6）全民健身广场建设项目。

（稿件由岳阳市文化产业开发中心提供）

上海市文化产业发展现状

自 1843 年开埠以来，上海就是中西、新旧文化的大熔炉，具有"海纳百川"的气势与胆识。而 2010 年上海世博会是 1851 年以来第一次以"城市"作为主题的世博会，这进一步提升了上海探索新型城市化道路，吸纳和包容人类多元文化的胸怀和能力。作为世博会的举办城市，上海在全国支持下，为办好一次"最成功、最圆满、最难忘"的世博会，做出了巨大努力，同时也从世博会的筹办和举办过程中，积累和获得了众多文化资源，依靠传统优势，突出文化创意，打造优势特色。

一、社会文化创意产业

1. 田子坊

田子坊原是上海市 20 世纪 50 年代典型的弄堂工厂，是典型的石库门建筑。2000 年进行改造，开发旧厂房 2 万平方米，吸引 18 个国家和地区的 70 余家企业，并形成了以室内设计、视觉艺术、工艺美术为主的产业特色。著名画家陈逸飞、尔冬强、王劼音、王家俊等艺术家的入驻，使小街渐渐吹起了艺术之风。如今，田子坊被誉为"上海的苏荷"。

2. 2577 创意大院

2577 创意大院是清朝洋务运动时期的枪炮局，解放后是解放军 7315 兵工厂。总占地面积 100 亩，建筑物 35 幢，其中 9 幢为历史保护建筑。大院融入了商务花园的规划理念，以创意大院颇具历史文化内涵的优秀建筑为班底，整旧如旧，创建全新生态理念的低密度、低容积、花园景观式商务办公区，并通过园内企业提供完善的物业服务及其他增值性服务。上海东方文化发展中心、上海美术家协会、德国 Fox Retail Group 设计展示等一批国内外知名创意企业先后入驻基地，目前入驻率达 100%。

二、优势特色创意产业

上海国际电影节、电视节，是扩大上海影视产业国际合作与文化交流的重要门户。借世博东风，第 13 届上海国际电影节具备了比以往历届电影节更大的吸引力和影响力，获得了更多的关注。由于 3D、IMAX 技术是上海世博会各展馆的热门展示手段，上海电影节专门组织论坛围绕 3D 电影的发展趋势展开讨论，还特意安排了"IMAX 影片展映单元"。作为一个年轻的国际电影节，上海国际电影节组织者有必要追问其"国际性"的外延何在，如何与"大"到柏林、戛纳、威尼斯国际电影节、"小"到釜山国际电影节、香港国际电影节展开"错位经营"，创造出属于自己的国际特色。

1. 准确的市场与文化定位是一个电影节得以成功的首要保障

依托中国强大的综合实力，依托上海在亚洲超级大都市群中的优势地位，上海国际电影节应当具有"Inter – Asia"（亚洲）的文化眼光以及整合亚洲电影市场的胸怀，力争在亚洲电影产业链中占据重要的一席。"Inter – Asia"价值链是通向"Inter-national"的必由之路。此外，上海国际电影节还应当与欧美等强势电影节保持良好的交流合作。

2. 建设和完善电影市场是检验一个国际性电影节是否成熟的重要指标之一

上海国际电影节逐渐打破"有奖无市"局面，单独设立"电影市场"，其中包括电影交易市场、影视基地推介、中国电影项目创投会等，试图包罗电影制作各环节，初步构建一个较为完整的电影市场框架。尽管电影市场的象征意义远远大于其市场效益，但此举标志着一直对海外电影采取严格"引进配额"制度的中国电影市场正在进一步开放门户。上海国际电影节正在从刻意营造影像嘉年华转向诚意而务实的市场经营理念。

3. 问题

影视产业的竞争，是技术革新的竞争，是市场模式的竞争，也是产业管理指导政策的竞争，但归根结底是核心文化理念的竞争。近一个世纪以来，上海之所以成为中国影视文化的重镇，取决于 20 世纪 20 年代以来蓬勃发展的都市电影传统，它使上海一度成为中国都市电影叙事的唯一"原型"。然而进入新世纪以后，这个原型的示范作用逐渐消隐。人们越来越发现，在上海出品的影视动漫作品中，其"海派"风格越来越稀薄，本土文化的自信心也在逐渐动摇，甚至丧失。在国际化语境下，围绕上海的叙事已经越来越难以承担"都市元叙事"的意义辐射功能。随着都市元叙事的消隐，上海已不再是当代都市叙事的发出者或终极对象，它既非中心，也非边缘，它只是全球化都市网络中的众多叙事节点之一。

在海外大片如《致命紫罗兰》中，上海浦东的金茂大厦、君悦大酒店与东方明珠广播电视塔构成了影片未来主义城市的典型地标;《碟中谍3》将上海西塘古镇、浦东陆家嘴群楼纳入动作景观的后景;《神奇四侠2》中 F4 将上海作为环游世界的一个站点;《变形金刚 2》曾经以在上海取景作为市场噱头。从积极的认同性角度来看,说明上海正在日益成为亚洲乃至全球瞩目的中心,或者说是中国电影票房市场的巨大潜力使然。但如果从都市电影叙事"原型"的研究思路来看,却证明所谓"海派"风格在全球都市化进程中不断遭逢的同质化经历。在此意义上,对当下上海影视题材的"海派"期待或许将封存于 20 世纪历史争论的风烟之中。而如何实现上海影像叙事乃至影视产业的在地化诉求,将是令业界感到困扰的话题。

4. 总结

上海应当以此次世博会为契机,在亚洲范围内致力于打造影视文化创意之都,只有这样,才能对外改变长期以来上海被世界影视文化所叙述、所展示的境遇,对内逐渐扭转上海影视文化产业与人才频繁"北上"与外流的被动局面,实现影视科技、文化、人才与产业的优化组合。

(稿件源于编委会自行搜集整理)

常州博物馆

常州嬉戏谷

成都国际非物质文化遗产节

成都平乐古镇

杭州白马湖生态创意城

杭州东方文化园

开封菊花花会主会场（龙亭公园）

开封宋都水系工程夜景

洛阳新区

洛阳龙门石窟

绍兴越剧明星版《梁山伯与祝英台》赴美巡演

绍兴第六届世界合唱比赛

深圳文化中心

深圳市第二届客家文化节

原温州冶金厂改造后的浙江创意园

温州大剧院

徐州欢乐文化产业园

徐州"创意 68 文化产业园"揭牌仪式

营口冰雪特色温泉

营口生产的手工小提琴

岳阳文化艺术汇展中心

岳阳楼

上海田子坊：城市老街区文化

上海大剧院

2012 中国城市
科学发展综合评价报告
——城市与人

2012 Comprehensive Evaluation and Grading
Report on China Urban Scientific Development

中国城市发展研究院
China City Development Academy
中国房地产研究会
China Real Estate Research Association
中国国际经济交流中心　联合编著
China Center for International Economic Exchanges
中国战略文化促进会
China Strategy Culture Promotion Associa

中国社会科学出版社

Copyright Statement of *Comprehensive Evaluation and Grading System (E&G) Design of China Urban Scientific Development*

2012 Comprehensive Evaluation and Grading Report of China Urban Scientific Development Editorial Organizations

Editorial Board

Preface

About Cities

(*Sun Jiazheng*, *vice chairman of the National Committee of the Eleventh Chinese People's Political Consultative Conference*)

With the development of economy and the progress of technology, the urbanization is obviously quickened. Currently the number and scale of cities are increased. The city population in the world is quickly rising after surpassing agricultural population. The global "city era" has approached.

The development of city civilization is the progress of history and influences people's lifestyle and social psychology extensively and profoundly. Urban development brings more comfort, convenience and opportunities for people as well as some new troubles and problems. Our city home on which we rely is faced with such problems as memory disappearance, convergent appearance, traffic jam and environmental degradation with different degrees. Urban development keeps meeting and stimulating people's physical demands but spiritual and psychological comfort and expectations are gradually lost.

City is the residence and spiritual home of urban dwellers. The principle of people-oriented should be adhered to while building the city. The planning, construction, management and services of the city should meet demands of the most extensive common people and meanwhile demands of different people groups should be satisfied. It is people's common with and requirement to create an ecological environment where people and Nature can live on friendly terms with each other. Faced with quick and convenient changes of modern life and the intense competition of market economy, people's physical demands have to be constantly satisfied but their psychological confusions and troubles should also be addressed. The process of the change and development of city cultural forms should be the process of people's spiritual demands being met, people's quality improved and all-round development of people. City construction and management call deep love and care of humanity. The spirit, environment and atmosphere of love and care of humanity should be an important yardstick for evaluating the city construction level and management quality.

People created tangible cities which in turn cultivate and shape people in an intangible way. Factors such as values, thinking, morality and social morals of urban dwellers are the comprehensive reflection of city cultural construction and the process in which city cultural construction plays its role. Both tangible city appearance and intangible city spirit are caused by certain culture. The building and evolution of cities due to culture have unconscious impact on the life and behaviors of city dwellers. The city is the container of culture. Streets, square, buildings, sculpture, equipment, afforestation and sketch in cities constitute cities' tangible and exterior physical system and influence our vision, listening, smell, touch and soul; meanwhile, they again carry human activities happening in cities. It is just these different, vivid and interesting activities that make cities popular and full of vitality.

Convergence should be refused and prevented while building cities; instead individuality and uniqueness should be protected and demonstrated. Modernization and internationalization is undoubtedly a double-edged sword. It is an indisputable fact that internationalization strikes traditions and modernization obliterates individuality. Only when cities' historical traditions, regional appearance and ethnic features are respected and cherished can the unique cultural charms of a city can be kept and demonstrated. A city is a history. We cannot sever the history. It is people's psychological needs and the responsibility that people should bear for ancestors and grandchildren to carefully protect historical and cultural heritage, maintain historical thread and keep historical memory.

In terms of urban construction, constant creation and upgrading should be made in order to be adapt to the development of era and lifestyle while traditions being inherited. A successful city must be a city with innovation while keeping its own cultural traditions. Historical traditions and cultural innovation in line with the era are the soul and vitality of urban development. It entails steadfast confidence and inclusive mind to make internal cultural innovation in city construction. It is China's basic state policy to open to the outside world. Harmony but not sameness is China's philosophical thinking. Pursuit of harmony is the value orientation of Chinese people.

City is never an isolated existence. It is found by hard and thorough research that it is village, agriculture and farmers that breed and nurse cities. This is especially true in China's urbanization process. It is the priority of urban development to repay the village, be kind to farmers and promote urban-rural harmonious development. It is a moral necessity as well as an essential condition for the city's own sustainable development.

Comprehensive evaluation and grading of China cities according to Scientific Outlook on Development is able to promote healthy development of society and economy of China cities. It is also a summary and confirmation of city culture. I sincerely hope that *Comprehensive Evaluation and Grading Report of China Urban Scientific Development* can be a success and make its unique contribution to China urban development.

Foreword

We have successively invited more than ten professional scholars and experts to hold about ten Seminars since March of 2011. We have fully discussed and studied such aspects as theme, framework, methodologies and module dividing. We changed the draft for several times and it took another four months to finish data analysis, questionnaire survey and commission authors to write on given topics, thus finally 2011 *Comprehensive Evaluation and Grading Report of China Urban Scientific Development* (*Report* for short)., What's different from before, is its basic framework. What's more, there is a specific theme—"city and people" for this year's *Report*. We re-regulated the perspective of evaluation. The focus is diverted to the clear and distinct point that cities should be developed for people, which is closely related to people's well-being.

Editorial Department

October 10, 2012

Report of China urban development in 2012

0　Introduction

China is in the process of rapid urbanization, which presents commonness with other cities in the world and individuality of itself. **The most significantly difference is urbanization is not synchronized with citizenization in China.** Due to the history and national conditions, a substantial part of long-time urban dwellers, especially dwellers living in large and medium-sized cities, don't have urban Hukou. Compared with the local residents, dwellers without urban Hukou can't enjoy equal opportunities in many aspects such as employment, residence, education, medical, social security, etc. On the other hand, dwellers without urban Hukou mark differences in income, city belonging and sense of identity with local residents. **All these characteristics have been presented by the survey of urban residents' living conditions and subjective evaluation, completed by China City Development Academy (CCDA) in 2011.** [1] Dwellers without urban Hukou are not completely in the full sense of citizens. They are limited in enjoying their public services, and have huge disparity with urban citizens in consciousness, mentality and behavior, such as city identity, self-discipline consciousness and behavior. The desynchrony of urbanization and citizenization has significant impacts on China's future urbanization and coordinated development of the economy and society. As a consequence, it's of great significance of promoting reform of the household registration system and equalization of social basic public service.

For these characteristics and facing problems in the process of China's urbanization, systematic research of urbanization is needed, which includes connotation and characteristic of urbanization, reference of urbanization theory and

---

[1]　Bai Nanfeng(2012) , Urban Residents'Living Condition& Assessment in China, *Compare*, 2, 192 – 247.

experience, analysis of China's urbanization tendency, coordination of urbanization and urban development elements, urbanization and public service, discussion of China's future urbanization path, etc.

1 Connotation and characteristic of urbanization

1. 1 Connotation of urbanization

Generally the connotation of urbanization mainly include four aspects: I . Urbanization of population refers to the process of rural population gathering into urban area, continuous increasing of urban population and urban population proportion; II. Regional urbanization refers to the process of gradually transfer rural region into urban region featured in high concentration of population; III. Urbanization of economic activity refers to the process of gathering economic relation and economic activity geographically and the tendency of production mode becoming urban economy; IV. urbanization of living style refers to that the behavior manner, idea, moral consciousness, social communication, education level, living habit, comprehensive quality and so on are transferred from rural style into urban style along with the changes on social identity, occupation and social role etc.

1. 2 Basic characteristics of urbanization

The core of urbanization is to improve the transferring of rural population into urban population, so as to achieve the coverage of infrastructure and public services to rural area, thus optimize the spatial layout of urbanization.

After 30 years of rapid development, the urbanization of China has already closed to the world average level. According to the sixth population census, it is indicated that the population in urban area of China in 2010 is 665, 580, 000; the urbanization rate reaches 49. 68% . Rural area and urban area make each half, the urbanization enters a new stage of transformation development. It can be seen from the development trace of world urbanization, China has an unprecedented urbanization scale and development speed . The urbanization rate is increased from 20% to 40% in only 20 years. [1]Substantively, in the statistic of

① YAO Shimou, LU Dadao, Wang Cong, etc (2011) Urbanization in China needs comprehensive scientific thinking: Exploration of the urbanization mode adapted to the special situation of China, *Geographical Research*, 10, 75 – 77.

current urbanization rate, the permanent resident population in urban area includes large amount of peasant-workers that the total amount closes to 1/3. It has not really realized"urbanization" on public service, social security and other aspects, therefore the quality of urbanization was not high.

During the period of China's urbanization entering new transformation development stage, its main characteristics can be summarized as follows:

1. 2. 1 Urbanization is transferred into development of quality from increasing of quantity

The essence of urbanization is the transferring of production mode and living style, rather than coarse expansion of city space and blind expansion of urban population. The influence of current international finance crisis has not been eliminated, international resource environment problem had an increased binding on macro-economy, the unbalance of domestic urbanization and social development has not only influenced the increasing of macro-economy, but also influenced the promotion of quality of urbanization. Under current system and planning system, the flowing population can not share same education and training with peer crowd, this firmly will impact the promotion of labor quality and city competitiveness. The domestic scholars believe that the urbanization process of our country will enter the transformation stage of stable development; the promotion of quality is the key point [1]During"Eleventh five year plan", the growth rate of GDP of China was up to 16. 56%, the average growth rate of urbanization level has reached 2. 93%. No matter promotion of urbanization speed, or promotion of urbanization quality, all of these have brought us with major challenges on our country's rural-urban planning and management, as well as public service equalization etc.

1. 2. 2 The claim of urbanization space has entered into infrastructure and basic public service equalization from industrial region.

It is indicated according to 2010 statistics that the social economic elements have appeared tremendous regional difference in eastern, middle and western region of our county. The urbanization population proportion in eastern region is 45%, it has absorbed nearly half urban population of China. Where, the population density in main urban concentration areas of Yangtze River delta, Pearl

---

① Zhou Yixing (2006), Thoughts on the speed of China's urbanization, *City Planning Review*, S1, 32 – 37.

river delta and Bohai sea ring are respectively up to 739 person/sq. km. , 608 person/sq. km. and 481 person/sq. km. ; however the population density of China in each sq. km. is 140 person in same period, the population density in western China is only 53 person. , Because the substantive difference of element, the eastern coastal area and regional center city represented by provincial capital would still have attraction of investment and population concentration, the unbalance of apace would be intensified gradually, more popular reflection on urban planning was the low configuration of rural infrastructure, low employment opportunity, education and medical planning etc. The economic transformation and new pattern of industrial zone transferring have exactly enhanced the absorption capability of urban area on surplus labor in rural area, but it also has in some extent caused the misinterpretation on urbanization, thus raising out the claim of infrastructure construction and basic public service equalization.

Table 1   Distribution of urban population in various regions in 2010

	GDP (billion Yuan)	Urban population (ten thousands)	Permanent resident population (ten thousands)	Urbanization rate (%)
Eastern area	232030.7	30293.7	50645.75	59.8
Middle area	86109.4	15822.36	36208.76	43.7
Western area	81408.5	14915.35	36056.29	41.4

Sources: 2011 Annual China Statistics.

1.2.3   The development mode of urbanization has entered market configuration source under the control of government from administrative mode.

In the past decades, it carried out resource configuration depending on administrative management system and administrative method, the higher the city administration level was, the more land index and special public fund for allocation would be, the stronger the public service capability was, the bigger the investment and consumption attraction would be, then the population would be more concentrated. The administration method will change the spatial layout of population flow, but under the influence of market law, the investment layout of enterprise will be influenced by the rising of land, labor and environment cost, the proportion of attracting peasant-workers in eastern area is continuously decreasing. In current stage, the processing of advanced and over-standard urban construction that violating the law of urbanization development based on slogan of attracting investment and promoting urbanization has caused too much external influence on economic development, it desires high quality urban planning construction and scientific urban management. It needs to satisfy the objective requirements of living of urban population and rural population during urbanization process and promote the level of urban public service according to the actual situation in certain region, it should use administration method and market-configuring-resource method to jointly guide the flow direction of urban population.

1.3 The outlook and research of China urbanization

In 2010, the urbanization rate of China has reached 49.68%, the urbanization population was about 666,000,000. According to the correction and development of Northam curve by relevant scholars, as well as the inference on urbanization saturation value[1][2], the urbanization speed of China has reached peak value in 2005, and the urbanization saturation value was about 80%, which was similar to current saturation value of US. Accordingly the urbanization level of China in current stage is roughly equal to the level of US in middle stage 1920, appearing development mode of"extensive, confusing". Therefore the urbanization rate of China in the future should be slowed gradually, it should be transferred from extensive mode into connotative development in the purpose of promoting urbanization quality, otherwise it will have risk to walk into"Excessive urbanization".

In spite of various"new type of urbanization"roads over the country, but no matter it is seen from foreign experience, historic development or recent overall national development tendency, the industrialization or commercializing are still key factors to improve urbanization, both have very high relevance. During the process of promoting urbanization through industrial transformation and structural upgrading, the slowing of future economic development speed is a very normal phenomenon, while it also will bring decreasing of urbanization rate.

Report of China urban development in 2012

---

① Chen Yanguang, Zhou Yixing (2005), Logistic progress of urbanization falls into four successive Phases: Revising Northam's curve with new spatial interpretation, *Economic Geography*, 6, 817 – 821.

② Chen Yanguang, Luo Jing (2006), Derivation of relations between urbanization level and velocity from logistic growth model, *Geographical Research*, 6, 1063 – 1072.

Today is a world with continuous deepening of globalization and informatization, important big cities or special big cities will bring relevant large development due to occupation of information network center, and they also may be upgraded into top central cities in China or world cities. But for some small cities, the economy of specialization is still the leading factor of city development, and it continuously improves the industrial structure transformation, and gradually transform into urban economy, so as to activate economy.

Whether Lewis dual economic structure theory is suitable for China, and whether Lewis turning point is coming, we still have dispute in the circle; it needs further experience research and complete theory. Meanwhile we should also carry out further study on whether the spatial difference is shrinking, whether it is dominated by polarization effect or diffusion effect.

2 Reference of urbanization theory and experience

2.1 Relevant theory of urbanization

2.1.1 Theory of urbanization stage

Northam curve is a theory mode often quoted in urbanization development study. The development of urbanization needs to experience startup period with low level and slow growth, then enter the rapid development period of urbanization, finally enter stable period at high level. According to the experience of developed country, the urbanization level should be preliminary stage below 30%, the means of livelihood provided by the 1st industry in such phase is not rich, the overall strength of national economy is weak, the social capital needed by the 2nd industry is deficient, so the urbanization rate is relevant slow ; 30% ~ 70% is middle stage, in this stage urbanization development enters acceleration period, the population and economic activities rapidly concentrate into the city, the urbanization level increases about one percent in each yea, the urban area has begun to develop to connotation while extending and expanding; over 70% are later stage, which is final stage of urbanization development, while the function of urban area is more complex and various, the urban area becomes the economic, scientific, culture, and trade center of that region. [1]

6

---

[1]   Wang Xiuling (2006), A developmental study of the overseas urbanizations, *Journal of Hebei Normal University*, 6, 42 – 45.

Northam curve has obtained good verification during the US urbanization development process. The urbanization level is only 5% when US carrying out the 1st population census in 1790, it is in primary stage. While in the middle of 19th century, along with the end of US civil war, the urbanization speed of US was developed rapidly, in 1920 the population of US has broken through 100 millions, in which over half of residents (51. 2%) living in urban area, now the urbanization level has reached middle stage. After 1920, the rising speed of population urbanization proportion is a little slowed. Since it enters 1970s, the proportion of urban population in the whole country basically kept stable, during the 30 year period from 1970s to the end of 20 century, the urbanization level was kept between 74% —77% [1].

2. 1. 2 Urbanization power theory

① Industrialization and urbanization

It can be seen from the experience of developed country, most scholars believe that the industrialization is the basic power of urbanization, both have significant relevance. Along with industrialization entering different stages, the level of urbanization is also gradually raised.

Britain is the earliest country to carry out industrialization and urbanization. Under the driving of industrial revolution, the urbanization process of Britain was very quick, Manchester, Birmingham, Liverpool and other industrial cities obtained rapid development and growth. Ruhr area of Germany, northern area of France, Atlantic coast area of US and other areas are with concentrated population formed along with the rapid concentration of capital, factory and population toward city area. On the development speed, the rapid development period of urbanization is generally in industrialization accelerating stage, i. e. the period of early stage of industrialization walking into middle stage of industrialization.

The urbanization of developed country is a gradually smooth process that population migration adapting economic structure, this is the classic Davis urbanization curve. It should be stressed that the 150-year gradual increasing urbanization process of western developed countries is mixed with their slow changes on urban-rural population structure. It can be seen from the urbanization process of

---

① Hunan Statistics Bureau (2002), Enlightenment of experience of urbanization development abroad for Hunan, *Bulletin of Hunan Statistics Bureau Census Center*, 4.

western developed countries such as Britain, US and so on, urbanization, gradual industrialization and economic changes were mixed together during the period. In this period, because the demand of urban labor force appears stable increasing, there should be stable migration flow from rural area to urban area. Meanwhile the progress of agriculture technology and the development of manufacturing industry has also absorbed surplus labor of agriculture sector, and it allows the agriculture labor to gradually transform into urban labor and resident.

The dual structure model theory of economic development has carried out better interpretation on the urbanization process of developing countries. In 1954, W· Arthur Lewis has created dual structure model theory of economic development, he has summarized the economic structures of developing countries into modern section and traditional section, he has set up dual section economic development model. He believes that in the society with dual economic structure, because traditional agriculture section has large amount of labor with low income, so the supply of labor force has complete elastic. The industrial sector can obtain unlimited labor force while it only needs to pay corresponding salary to survive in traditional agriculture section, this process will continue until the rural surplus labor is completed absorbed by city, the salary in rural area will be consistent with salary in urban area, the difference of rural-urban area is gradually eliminated, and the modernization of national economy . Based on which it has also developed Todaro model making significant influence in Rural-urban population migration and population urbanization research, this model has further explained the popular phenomenon in developing countries: coexistence of large scale migration of rural population to urban area and high unemployment rate of city .

② Globalization, informatization and urbanization

In recent years, the rapid development and deepening of globalization and informatization is one of the new economy factors to improve urbanization, urbanization continuously creates employment opportunities and changes spatial structure, population structure and social formation, such phenomenon is not only for developed countries, but also for developing countries.

"*Information industry, multinational company and urbanization of Asia Pacific country*" (1989) believes that"Technology, especially those technologies relate to communication and transportation, is an important factor of city transformation", because the third world accepts technical transformation, opens international trade and exchange, so its urbanization is also related to new technology. Specifically these new technologies have realized circulation within the world through multinational corporations-a kind of global production, taking the countries in Asian-Pacific region as examples, foreign investment and multinational corporations have improve the development of local information industry. Especially it has more and more obvious function on the development of big cities and megacities. Therefore, in the third world countries, foreign investment has made information technology becoming a kind of new driving force of urbanization through multinational corporation. If it can measure this kind of driving force form by using basic force-"pulling force"and"pushing force", obviously it is belonged to the scope of urban"pulling force", but it also has difference with traditional pulling force, because it is not from a city, but it is a product of foreign fund and technology functioning on a city.

③Industrial structure and urbanization

Urbanization level appears positive correlation relationship with 2nd and 3rd industry, this viewpoint has been stated in many documents[①]. The support of urbanization is the development of industry, gathering of industry and structure upgrading, therefore, besides leading industry, a city still should develop modern agriculture and 2nd and 3rd industry served to leading industry.

According to the diversity difference of industrial structure, Hoover(1937) is the earliest to divide gathering economy into localization economy (or specialization economy) and urbanization economy (or diversified economy). Localization economy refers to the promotion effect on production efficiency due to geographical concentration; urbanization economy refers to the promotion effect on production efficiency due to diversified industries of local economic system. [②]Comparing to urbanization economy, localization economy is a basic unit, it is a gathering economy of low level economic system, but urbanization econo-

9

① Zheng Jufen (2009), Literature review of theory study in urbanization, *Literature Review*, 11, 197 – 198.

② Wu Xuehua (2005), Study review of urbanization economy and localization economy in western countries, *Science and Management*, 6, 48 – 49.

my is a gathering economy of high level economic system. ①

It can make conclusion according to the empirical research of west counties: along with the expansion of city size and large increasing of economy, the production rate is improved, indicating that there is gathering economy. For manufacturing industry, especially heavy industry and industries with mature technology, the localization economy is more important than urbanization economy, comparing to big enterprise, small enterprise is easier to benefit from localization economy. Some small areas and small cities without diversified functions also should obtain bigger development force from specialization②.

In relevant domestic research, Feng Yunting(2005) has calculated the localization and urbanization elastic of industries in four cities including Zhejiang Yuyao, the conclusion indicates that in the four cities of Zhejiang with relevant mature manufacturing grouping, localization effect is more obvious than urbanization effect, gathering economy has greatly improved the process of urbanization.

2.1.3 Urbanization space increasing theory

Urbanization is a process of gathering labor force, capital and various economic elements on space, so it is a product of unbalanced development of space. Based on which it has developed many space increasing theories.

"Growth pole" theory③ is provided out by French economist F· Perrous. "Growth pole" originally refers to industries having pushing function on economic development, later it refers to the regions having such kind of industry on space sense. "Growth pole" theory points out that economic growth is not appeared at all places in same time, but it firstly appears on so'me"growth pole" under different strength. The key point of formation of growth pole is the existence of enterprise having innovation capability, these enterprises are always in dominant position, making the industrial sector where it is located become promoting section, under the function of its economic gathering effect, the promoting section and the enterprises having innovation capability generally gather and de-

---

① Feng Yunting (2004), Agglomeration economy effect and urbanization strategy in China, *Research on Financial and Economic Issues*, 9, 35 –41.

② Wu Xuehua (2005), Study review of urbanization economy and localization economy in western countries, *Science and Management*, 6, 48 – 49.

③ Liu Huihuang (2005), Dual structure analyzing framework of western urbanization theory: A document summary, *Journal of Shijiazhuang of University of Economics*, 1, 55 – 58.

velop in some regions and big cities, and making these regions and cities become the center of economic activities, thus having characteristics of domination and innovation, just like a"field pole"to produce attraction and radiation, so as to promote itself and the economic growth of other sections and regions.

In 1957 and 1958, K· G· Myrdal and A· O· Hirschman have respectively explained unbalanced regional economic development theory in their works "Economic theory and underdeveloped area"and" Economic development strategy". Firstly Hirschman provided out the theme"Development is a series of unbalanced chains", he pointed out"development is exactly processed by using leading section to motivate other sectors, by using one industry to trigger other industry's growth". In order to proof this viewpoint, he has provided out the concept of industry correlation effect, i. e. "forward correlation effect"and"backward correlation effect", to explain the functioning process that development of one industrial sector would lead development of other industrial sector in national economy. Secondly Myrdal and Hirschman have respectively provided out "Backwash Effects"—"Spread Effect", and "Polarized Effect"—"Trickling-down Effect" with basic same content.

"Core-edge theory" is officially provided out by J. R. Fridemna in this academic writing "Regional development policy" in 1966. In 1969, he has further incorporated the "core-edge" space polarization development thought as a kind of ordinary and adaptable theoretical model to explain the unbalanced development process between different regions or between rural area and urban area. He believes that any space economic system can be decomposed into core area and surrounding area with different attributes. This theory attempts to explain how one region is changed into the situation of having relation and unbalanced development from the situation of having no relation and isolated development, then changed into regional system having relation and balanced development from extremely unbalanced development.

Firstly, pre-industrialization stage: the productivity level is very low, the economic structure is mainly dominated by agriculture, the proportion of industrial production is smaller than 10%, the difference of economic development level in various regions are relevant small. The urban development speed is slow; they respectively appear independent center state. The economic relation between different regions is not tight, the production of city and the development speed are slow, the urban level system is not complete.

Secondly, the primary state of industrialization: the city begins to form, the proportion of industrial production in economy is between 10% —25%, the economic growth speed difference of core region and edge region begin to expand. The resource element inside or outside of region is flowed toward core region with relevant high gradient from edge region with relevant low economic gradient. The increasing of economic strength in core region firmly will lead to concentration of politic strength, make the unbalanced development of core region and edge region further expanding.

Thirdly, mature industrialization stage: rapid industrialization stage, the industrial production accounts for 25% —50% in the economy. The development of core region is very quick; there is unbalanced relation between edge regions. During the mature industrialization period, the resource element of core region begin to flow back to edge region, the industrial group of edge region begin to concentrate.

Fourthly, relevant balanced space stage: post-industrialization stage, the flowing of fund, technology, information and so on from core region to edge region is increased. The whole region becomes a city system having function relation; it forms a large scale urban region and starts balanced development having relation.

2.2 Classic urban model in foreign countries

2.2.1 Market-oriented model represented by Western Europe under the control of government

For well-developed market economy country represented by western Europe, the market system has played main role during urbanization process, the government has guided the health development of urbanization through legal, administrative and economic measures. Generally urbanization, marketization and industrialization has a relative coordinated and interactive relationship, it is a kind of synchronous type urbanization. It is featured in: firstly, industrialization and urbanization are promoted mutually. Generally tee urbanization is a product of modern industrialization. In recent years, along with the intensifying of competitiveness and global economic integration, the industrial structure of city continuously makes adjustment and new work division, the development pattern of city appears new status, the industrial development and city development are more inseparable. Secondly, government has played an irreplaceable function during the urbanization process. All countries have in some extent met land, house, traffic, environment, historic culture protection and other problems during the rapid development process of urbanization, the public policies of government involve wider range. After worldwar II, the rapid expansion of London has produced great pressure on agriculture land. In 1935, London has passed "Green belt development limiting act", the government of London has purchased land as "Greening isolation belt" to guide the urban construction and development, so as to reduce the damage on village environment and benefits. The central government has established rural and urban planning sector, planning has became the legal liability of local government.

During the urbanization process of western Europe and Japan, the population, land, capital and other economic elements related to urbanization can flow freely and configure freely, which firstly benefit from leading role of market system. Meanwhile, all countries stress to carry out necessary state interference on market competition and social security, they develop infrastructure in construction area, improve city environment, provide public service facilities, guide urbanization and marketization and mutual industrial development through completing legal system and preparing and implementing national urbanization strategy and public policy, they actively improve regional structure adjustment and correctly cope with rapid developing urbanization process. During this process, it uses administrative, tax and planning measures etc. to remedy the insufficiency of market system through continuous completion of system and timely adjusting government policy for problems appearing in various special stages.

2.2.2 Free style represented by US

US is the most well-developed capitalist country in the world, it is also a classic representative of market economy. During the process of its urbanization and city development, market has played an important role. Because the political system of US determines that the urban planning and management are belonged to local affair, the adjusting measure of federal government is weak, the government also has not timely carried out efficient guidance on capital-oriented urbanization development, leading to free urbanization development and paying high price for this. Its outstanding performance is excessive suburbanization, the city continuously extends to outside in low density, the urban construction is out-of-order, the space and social structure problems gradually stand out. Because the rapid development of US city in the first half of 20th century, traffic clogging in the center of city, environmental deterioration, house shortage, high crime rate and other problems gradually come out, rich families leave the high building at the center of city to live in suburban area, they begin to build up their own independent courtyard type low-storey house. Along with the development of economy and the popularization of automobile, many middle class families and ordinary residents also move to suburban area. On the space pattern of urban development, it is expressed as that the city is continuously extended to outside in low density along the highway, and developed to metropolitan areas including many continuous cities and towns. In 1970, the population in suburban area has not only exceeded the population in central city, but also has exceeded the population of none-city area.

However US also has paid heavy price for excessive suburbanization: severe land resource waste, continuously high economic costs, destroying of ecological environment, large amount of resource and energy consumption, intensifying of gap between the rich and the poor and other social problems. Since1970s of 20 century, the US government officers, scholars and ordinary people all begin to aware the disaster brought by excessive suburbanization, they have provided out the concept of " smart growth". Its main contents include emphasizing the compact model of land utilization, it encourages the development model dominated by public transportation and pedestrian traffic, utilizing land in mixing function, protecting open space, and creating comfortable environment, it encourages public participation, it intends to realize fairness of economy, environment and society through limitation, protection and coordination. This is a feedback for social and environmental problems brought by US city disorderly extending to suburban area in low density in long period under complete economic condition; it is a kind of operable management concept and management model taking sustainable development as value orientation, taking scientific management as measure.

2.2.3 Urbanization of developing countries constrained by colonial economy

Because the functioning of historic tradition and reality factor, the urbanization of most African countries, Latin America countries and Caribbean coun-

14

tries have direct relation with the situation that these counties are occupied by western powers as their colonies, so they have unique development model. It is expressed as the coexistence of industrialization dominated by foreign capitals and outdated traditional agricultural economy, the industrial development falls behind urbanization, the government has weak adjusting capability, urbanization changes radically. Its industrial development can not catch up with the process of urbanization; it is belonged to "excessive urbanization". Before World war II, Brazil, Mexico, Venezuela, Colombia and Peru, these five countries in half industrialized economic type have relevant equal urbanization rate and industrialization rate, they are all about 10% —15%. In 1960, the proportion of industrialization has no big change, it still maintain within 10% —15%, but the proportion of city with over 20000 people increases to 30% —50%. The urbanization roads in these area are very uneven, during the process of residents in rural area continuously flow into the urban area, its economy is gradually shrinking or stopping. The main problem is: Normal employment level is continuously decreasing; the poor population in the urban area is continuously increasing. There is serious shortage on necessary infrastructure in the city. The urban environment is worsening and the slum is increasing.

Urban development of Latin American and African countries is a typical excessive urbanization. The urbanization level closes to western countries, but the economic level is only 1/10—1/20 of western countries, so the urban development quality is very low. The main reasons of causing these phenomenon include the disjoining of urban development and economic development stage. Because the early industrialization development of Latin America countries is originated from the input of industrial capital of suzerain, the government fails to use foreign investment to develop its own national industry. Once the industrial capital of suzerain was withdrawn, it has no self-industry to support. Secondly it has ignored the transformation of traditional agriculture and the development of rural area, which had intensified the gap between rural area and urban area, leading large rural population pouring into urban area, which has further worsen the problem of insufficient urban employment, inhabitation, environment and education facilities. ①

---

① National Bureau of Statistics of China, (1983), Statistical yearbook of China, China Statistics Press.

3 Analysis of China's urbanization tendency

3. 1 Overall tendency of China's urbanization development

Since the establishment of new China, the urbanization of our country is accompanied by continuous system change, the overall tendency of development is not out of objective law, this is consistent with the urbanization stage theory"primary stage ——middle stage —— final stage", furthermore it appears obvious stage characteristic[1], in which reform and opening up have became an important turning point of our country's urbanization process. In the 30 years of reform and opening up, the urbanization rate of China population has increased from 17.9% in 1978 to 45.7% in 2008. Urbanization has not only brought us with large scale infrastructure and urban residence investment demand, but also has created tremendous consumption demand due to large scale rural population migration and living style transformation, all of above become the strong force for continuous and rapid increasing of China economy. During the practice process of over 30 year reform and opening up, the urbanization development of China has experienced a series of changes from supporting small cities to focusing on development of large cities, then the coordinated development of large, middle, small cities and small towns. Substantively such changes refer to that during the process of urbanization, the system of China is changed from limiting peasant entering city to allowing and guiding peasant entering city, finally encouraging peasant entering city. [2]

Specifically China urbanization process can be mainly divided into 7 stages.

3. 1. 1 Startup stage of urbanization development (1949—1957)

From 1949 to 1957, the working focus of China was changed from rural area to urban area, the urban economy has obtained health development, the number of city has increased to 176 from 132 in 1949; the proportion of urban population has increased to 10.95% from 4.7% in 1949 [3]; the proportion of urban

---

[1] Ma Xiaohe, Hu Yong - jun (2010), The process, problems and general layout of urbanization in China, *Reform*, 10, 30 - 45.

[2] Wang Yiming (2010), The development progress, challenge and transition of urbanization in China, *China Finance*, 04.

[3] Hu Jiquan (2005), Study on new urbanization development in China, Doctoral dissertation of Agricultural University of Southwest, 06.

population has increased to 15.4% from 10.6%. During this period, except for urbanization rate in 1955 is 0.2% lower than last year, urbanization rate in other years are all higher than last year [4].

3.1.2 Fluctuation stage of urbanization development (1958—1965)

From 1958 to 1961, the development of " Great Leap Forward "event has made national economy rapid expanding and urbanization population increasing blindly, the number of cities was increased to 208 in 1961 from 176 in 1957 [5]; the urban population was sharply increased from 99490000 in 1957 to 130730000 in 1960, the population has increased 31.4%, the annual increasing rate has reached 9.53% [4]. It has gradually canceled 52 cities after 1961, the total number of cities was 168 at the end of 1965, it has decreased 8 comparing the number in 1957.

3.1.3 Descending and stopping stage of urbanization development (1966—1978)

From 1966 to 1976, our country has entered 10 year "culture revolution" period, it has provided out the "Mountain, Scattering, Cave" policy on industrial pattern, the urban construction did not consider nature, transportation and other conditions, but emphasized scattering, therefore the social and economic development have suffered heavy impact and the urban development slowed down. In 1972, the urbanization level was slowed continuously until 17.1%, forming an obvious " valley bottom". After 1972, although the urbanization development was a little increased, but the speed was relevant slow. 6 During the six years from 1972 to 1978, the urbanization rate has totally increased 0.8%. Until the end of 1978, China's urbanization rate recovered to the level of 1966, i. e. 17.9% [4]. It can be seen from the number of cities, the total number of cities in China in 1977 is 190, which has only increased 22 [5] comparing with the number in 1965.

3.1.4 Recovery development stage of urbanization (1979—1983)

At the starting stage of reform and opening up during 1978 to 1983, the urbanization of our country has obtained a new opportunity. The rural reform has brought the development of urbanization with tremendous pushing force [5]; The commodity economy development, diversified investment channel, accelerated construction step of urban infrastructure, the expanding of urban employment channel absorbing large amount of peasant worker entering city, all of these can produce pulling force for urbanization development[4]. In February 1983, "Notice on several issues about reformation of party and government agencies at region, city and prefecture level "issued by State Council has provided out combination of region and city, implementing city-managing-county, so as to improve the rapid development of small towns. At the end of 1983, the number of cities in China has reached 289, which has increased 99 comparing to the number in 1977 [5]. From 1978 to 1983, the urbanization rate was raised from 17.9% to 23.5% [2].

3.1.5 Stable development stage of urbanization (1984—1992)

In October 1984, the Party Central Committee has officially provided out the concept of fully development of urban economic system reform and implementation of planned commodity economy system; in November the same year, the State Council has approved "Report of Ministry of Civil Affairs About Adjusting Organic Town Standard"; in 1986 the State Council has also approved "Report of Ministry of Civil Affairs About Adjusting City standard and City-managing-county Condition". Along with the decreasing of city and town standard, the number of cities was increased rapidly, and the urbanization level was promoted accordingly. From 1984 to 1992, the number of cities was increased from 300 to 517, organic towns was sharply increased from 6211 to 12,000, urbanization rate was raised from 23.0% in 1984 to 27.6% in 1992 ①.

3.1.6 Rapid development stage of urbanization (1993—2003)

Taking the South Tour Speech of Deng Xiaoping in the spring of 1992 and the opening of " The fourteenth NPC "as a symbol, our country has entered the stage of fully construction of socialist market economy system, the average economic growth rate was above 9%. Along with new round of economic development, urbanization has entered rapid development period [2]. During this stage, the urbanization rate of China has increased to 40.53% from 27.46%, the average number has increased 3.97%. In 2003, the organic city has reached 660, this number has increased 181 comparing to the number in 1991; the number of organic town has reached 20226 [3]. Taking modern city construction, small town development, establishment of economic development zone and industrial zone etc. as symbols, the urbanization of China was rapidly improved, the compre-

---

① Yang Feng, Tao Siwen (2010), The development process, characteristics and trends of China's urbanization, *Lanzhou Academic Journal*, 04.

hensive carrying capacity of city and the capacity of absorbing rural population have obtained obvious increasing . It can be seen after comparing to international number, the urbanization rate of China has been increased to 40% in 2003 from 20% in 1981, it has only spent 22 years to make double, however 120 years for Britain, 100 years for French, 80 years for Germany, 40 years for America, 30 years for Japan [①].

3. 1. 7 Coordinated development stage in rural and urban area (2004 to now)

Since 2003, the relation between rural area and urban area has entered new development stage, the urbanization development mode also has gradually changed from rapid urbanization to coordinating rural and urban area. On policy aspect, our country has strengthened the household reform to promote the coordinated development of rural and urban area. The 3rd plenary session of the 16th Party Congress pointed out that the agriculture population having stable occupation and house in a city can register household at employment location or residence place according to local regulation, enjoy rights of local residents according to the law, and bear corresponding liabilities. In 2010, " No. 1 document " of central government provided out policy to deepen household system reform, accelerate implementing and loosening policy of settlement condition in middle and small cities, small towns especially counties and central towns, improve agriculture population having condition to settle into urban area and enjoy same rights with local urban residents, improve the inhabitation condition of peasant workers through various channels, encourage the cities having condition to gradually incorporate the peasant workers having stable occupation and living in the city for certain years into urban housing security system, adopt targeted measures to solve the problem of new generation of peasant workers[3].

From 2004 to 2010, the urban population was increased from 542,830,000 to 669,780,000, annual growth rate was 3. 56%; the urbanization rate was increased from 41. 8% to 49. 68%, the average growth rate has reached 3. 03%. Until the end of 2010, the number of cities in/above prefecture-level has reached 287, our country has initially formed a national urban system scale structure pattern composed of 125 megacities that the total population in down-

Report of China urban development in 2012

---

① Wang Yiming (2010), The development progress, challenge and transition of urbanization in China, *China Finance*, 04.

town area was over 1 million, 109 large cities with 0. 5 million-1 million population, 49 middle cities with 0. 2 million- 0. 5 million population, and 4 small cities with population below 0. 2 million; it has formed a national urban system
scale structure pattern composed of pearl river delta metropolises area, Yangtze
river delta metropolises area, Beijing-Tianjin-Hebei (Bohai sea ring) metropolises area and coastal town development belt etc.

3. 2　Spatial difference pattern of our country's urbanization

In recent years, the urban population distribution and the general layout of
population urbanization level was not changed basically, the difference of population urbanization level at provincial level was gradually reduced year by year,
the difference mainly existed in regions with different policies, and its influence
was gradually enhanced[①].

This paper collected 2010 urbanization rate data of prefecture-level cities in
our country according to 2011 Annual City Statistics, and it has divided the urbanization rate of various prefecture-level cities into five groups(≤37. 56% 、
37. 59% —43. 00% 、43. 00% —51. 04% 、51. 12—62. 75% 、≥62. 80%) by u-
sing 5 division method, construct through space database. It makes conclusion
that the difference of China urbanization space pattern mainly exists following
two aspects.

3. 2. 1　The urbanization level exists distribution characteristic of high in east and low in west

Under the influence of rapid industrialization in eastern region of China
since reform and opening up, China's urbanization level has experienced the
transformation from "high in north and low in south" (the urbanization rate of
northern region is high, but the urbanization rate in southern region is low) to "
high in east and low in west" (the urbanization rate in eastern region in high,
but the urbanization rate in western region is low). In current stage, the regional
difference of China's urbanization level appears distribution characteristic of
"high in east and low in west". According to the urban population proportion in
east, middle, west and northeast regions in 2010, the urbanization rate in
China's east, middle, west and northeast regions are respectively 56. 7% 、
46. 3% 、44. 7% and 55. 3% . Shanghai, Beijing, Tianjin, the three traditional

---

① Lin Jian (2010), Provincial difference of urbanization level in terms of population since 2000: Based on emendation of statistical data, *City Planning Review*, 3, 48 – 56.

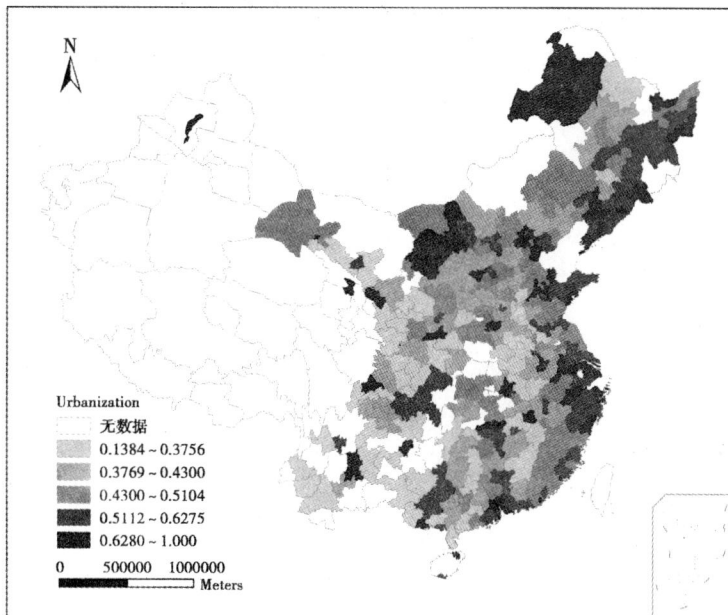

**Figure 1　2010 urbanization space pattern for prefecture-level
cities in China**

municipalities directly under the central government, Guandong, Jiangzhe and
some autonomous regions still rank the top of China ; however Tibet, Guizhou,
Yunnan, Gansu, Sichuan and other western provinces, as well as Henan, the
populous province, still rank the last six position.

Such kind of difference is obviously reflected in urbanization space pattern,
as shown in the figure, the urbanization rate in eastern coastal area is generally
relevant high, especially the cities in northeast old industrial base, Beijing-
Tianjin-Hebei metropolis circle, Shandong peninsula, Jiangsu coastal economic
zone, Yangtze river delta metropolis circle, Zhejiang coastal urban agglomeration, Haixi economic zone, Pearl river delta metropolis circle and Beibu gulf region are basically in group 4 and group 5 of urbanization grouping, they are belonged to high level urbanization, i. e. urbanization rate is over 50%, the
growth rate will slowed gradually, and it begins to focus on promotion of urbanization quality. However the cities in middle and west regions are mainly in
group 1, 2 and 3 of urbanization rate, they are belonged to middle and low urbanization level, i. e. less than 50%, they still will have a continuous and rapid
growth.

3.2.2 Some provinces with low urbanization level and weak economic foundation have appeared super-high speed development tendency

It was found in research that some provinces with low urbanization level and relevant weak economic foundation have appeared super-high speed urbanization development tendency[19]. Especially those middle urbanization regions between 30%—50%, e.g. Hebei, Henan, Shanxi, Jiangxi, Anhui, Hunan, Hubei, Chongqing and so on. Those high urbanization regions with above 50% urbanization rate, including Shanghai, Beijing, Tianjin, the three traditional municipalities directly under the central government (urbanization rate has exceeded 75%), three provinces in northeast region, as well as those low urbanization regions where the urbanization rate is lower than 30%, all appear the phenomenon of gradually raising of urbanization rate. The provincial level administrative region of China also observes the "Northam curve "law of urbanization development. For example, the provincial capital cities, deputy provincial cities in Midwest provinces of China, e.g. Shijiazhuang, Zhengzhou, Kaifeng, Xian, Nanchang, Hefei, Changsha, Wuhan etc. , have relevant high primacy ratio, the urbanization rate is relevant prominent, such kind of characteristic also can be seen from the figure.

4 Coordination analysis of China's urbanization and urban development elements

4.1 Coordination analysis of urban and social economic elements

4.1.1 The eastern region has obvious development advantages, the coordinating between regions needs to be enhanced.

In all 287 prefecture-level and above cities, there are 87 cities in the east, accounting for 30.3%, 81 in the middle, accounting for 28.2%; while 85 in the west, accounting for 29.6% and 34 in the northeast, accounting for 11.9%. The regional division situation is shown in table 4.1.

Table 2 Dividing of four major regional provinces in China

Region	City
East	Beijing, Tianjin, Hebei, Shanghai, Jiangsu, Zhejiang, Fujian, Shandong, Guangdong, Hainan
Middle area	Shanxi, Anhui, Jiangxi, Henan, Hubei, Hunan

Region	City
Western area	Inner Mongolia, Guangxi, Chongqing, Sichuan, Guizhou, Yunnan, Tibet, And Shaanxi, Gansu, Qinghai, Ningxia, Xinjiang
Northeast	Liaoning, Jilin, Heilongjiang

Ranking according to the comprehensive score of three systems (economic development level, public service level, actual enjoying level of residents), in the top 50 cities, there are 33 cities in east, accounting for 66%, and 8 in the middle, accounting for 16%; while 6in the west, accounting for 12%; and 3 in the northeast, accounting for 6%.

Ranking according to economic development indicators, in the top 50 cities, there are 39 in the east, accounting for 78%, and 6 in the middle, accounting for 12%, while 3 cities in the west, accounting for 6%; and 2 in the northeast, accounting for 4%;

Ranking according to the public service, in the top 50 cities, there are 22 in the east, accounting for 44%, and 7 in the middle, accounting for 14%; while 11 in the west, accounting for 22% and 10 in the northeast, accounting for 20%;

Ranking according to economic development indicators, in the top 50 cities, there are 33 in the east, account for 66% and 8 in the middle, accounting for 16%; while 4 in the west, accounting for 8% and 5 in the northeast, accounting for 10%;

Table 3   Statistic of number of top 50 cities in various indicators

Name of indicator	Eastern area	Middle area	Western area	Northeast
Comprehensive score of three systems	33	8	6	3
Economic development level system	39	6	3	2
Public service level system	22	7	11	10
Resident enjoying level system	33	8	4	5

It can be seen from comprehensive scores of urban development of top 50 cities and the rank of various indicators that comparing to last year, the number of cities in the east still is close to or even over half of the 50 cities and thedevelopment level of eastern area is obviously higher than other regions, in which the biggest difference is the economic development indicator and the public service input indicator difference is relevant small. However the development levels of cities in other regions have little difference, most of which are gradually deduced according to the sequence of middle, west, and northeast region. Such situation is related to our country's development policies, the globalization background of contemporary economy, and the regional division of our country's industries.

On one hand, the reform and opening up made the coastal area in the east of China improved significantlyin the development level and competitiveness, depending on its location advantage and development of export-oriented economy. But under the background of internationalization, the rapid economic growth of eastern region mainly depends on low-cost labor and extensive economy (benefit from land utilization), leading to its irrational industrial structure and lacking of self-innovation capability. But such economy is still at the end of industrial chain in international industrial labor division. Because the environment resource cost gradually increased along with economic development, such advantage is weakening; furthermore the international economic environment significantly impacts on the development, and the risk proof capability and stability of overall economic structure are weak.

On other hand, our country has still not formed relevant mature and interactive development pattern in east, middle, west and northeast. The northeast region and Midwest region of our country have rich labor force and land resource, but due to the economy is lacking of reasonable regional labor division, the resource elements can not be allocated reasonablely, the industrial transferring from eastern area to inland area can not be well connected. These have not only constrained rapid development process of Midwest area, but also have impacted the industrial transformation and upgrading in eastern coastal area.

4. 1. 2　The city internal economy and the coordination of social development level are still relevant low

In order to evaluate the coordination among three kinds of systems, we have divided the 287 cities into 6 ranking sections on the basis of ranking according to comprehensive score (taking 50 cities as one section). If all three kinds of system ranking of one city could enter the section with same comprehensive score, then the city would be regarded as relevant coordinated development city.

In the cities where comprehensive level entering top 50, those also can enter three kinds of systems include 14, accounting for 28%, and 5 in 51—100, accounting for 10%; while 4 in 101—150, accounting for 8%, and 2 in 151—200, accounting for 4%; there are 3 in 201—250, accounting for 6%, and 7 in 251—287, accounting for 14%, There are total 35 cities with relevant coordinated rank, only accounting for 12. 2% of all cities . The number has increased by 0. 7% comparing to year-on-year number of last year, but the overall coordination was still not high. Thereinto, the coordination level of first section is much higher than other sections, accounting for 40% of all coordinated cities.

In the 14 cities with better coordination in 1st section according to three kinds of systems, the middle area only include Taiyuan and the northeast area only include Dalian; there is no city in the west area entered, while others cities are all in the east. Except for Shanghai and Tianjin, there are(is) 3 in Jiangsu, 3 in Zhejiang, 3 in Shangdong, 1 in Guangdong, 1 in Liaoning, and 1 in Shanxi. These relevant coordinated cities are almost all concentrated in developed coastal area. Comparing to last year, the regional pattern does not show obvious transformation, and under the constraining of current urban system, the situation of economic development level has in large extent influenced the possibility of urban coordination development.

Table 4   Urban coordination rank situation

Ranking section	Relevant coordinated city
1 – 50	Hangzhou, Changzhou, Wuxi, Suzhou, Zhuhai, Shaoxing, Dalian, Shanghai, Jiaxing, Dongying, Weihai, Tianjin, Zibo, Taiyuan
51 – 100	Tangshan, Yingkou, Laiwu, Sanming, Huangshan
101 – 150	Jiaozuo, Bengbu, Huludao, Nanping
151 – 200	Luliang, Mianyang
201 – 250	Zigong, Laibin, Yiyang
251 – 287	Hezhou, Dingxi, Shaoyang, Bazhong, Zhaotong, Guigang, Lhasa

Note: the cities are listed in no particular order in the table.

4. 1. 3   The comprehensive advantage of municipalities directly under the central government, provincial capital city and municipalities with independent planning status still prominent

Taking rank based on comprehensive indicators as an example, there are 22 municipalities directly under the central government and provincial capital cities entering top 100, accounting for 71% of total 31 cities, in which 14 cities entering top 50, accounting for 45%; all 5 municipalities with independent planning status are listed into top 50.

According to economic development level, there are 15 municipalities directly under the central government and provincial capital cities entering top 100, accounting for 48.4% of total 31 cities, in which 10 listed into top 50, accounting for 32.3%; all 5 municipalities with independent planning status are listed into top 100, in which there are 3 listed into top 50.

In the aspect of public service input, there are 26 municipalities directly under the central government and provincial capital cities in top 100, accounting for 83.9% of total 31 cities, in which 16 listed into top 50, accounting for 51.6%; all 5 municipalities with independent planning status are listed into top 50.

In the aspect of resident enjoying level, there are 21 municipalities directly under the central government and provincial capital cities in top 100, accounting for 67.7% of total 31 cities, in which 13 listed into top 50, accounting for 41.9%; all 5 municipalities with independent planning status are listed into top 100, in which there are 3 listed into top 50.

Obviously under current government-dominated mode (from top to bottom) of China, the original advantage possessed by municipalities directly under the central government, provincial capital cities and municipalities with independent planning status is still prominent.

4.1.4 The effect of economic transformation is still not appeared

We continuously adopt the utilization efficiency of land, water, labor and energy in economic development indicator system, input level of scientific information and other technologies, external environment effects to evaluate the quality of development. In the cities that the economic development level entering top 50, there are 25 cities in which utilization efficiency of development element can enter top 50, accounting for 50%; there are 10 cities with relatively good external effects that can enter top 50, accounting for 20%; there are 22 cities according to their technology input level can enter top 50, accounting for 44%. There is a descending tendency comparing to last year, and none of cities can enter top 50 for all above three subsystems. The economic development transformation has not entered substantive stage, the cities show unobvious improvement on increasing element utilization level, consumption and pollution reduction, it could not achieve the expected objective only depending on increasing input, and the "inhibiting magic phrase" of energy on economic transformation is still tightening.

Further comparing the cities that economic growth efficiency entering top 10, among which the cities that development element utilization efficiency entering top 10 only include Suzhou and Yan'an, while none of the cities enter top 10 according to development external effects. The great pressure brought to resource and environment by high speed and low efficient extensive growth gradually come out, which reflects the unreasonable economic structure as well as outdated development concept and production technology level.

4.1.5 The public input increases, but the economic development and resident enjoying level are still not coordinated

Among the cities that the economic development level entering top 50, there are 15 cities that the public financial input entering top 50 at the same time, which increased by 114% comparing to the 7 cities of last year, but generally urban public input level was still not coordinated with economic development level.

Among the cities that the general economic development level entering top 50, there are 22 cities that the personnel benefit projects, resident social security coverage and level entering top 50, accounting for 44%; there are 20 cities that the resident living environment level entering top 50, accounting for 40%; and 11 cities that the resident employment level entering top 50, accounting for 22%; All the 3 items do not exceed half, and they slightly dropped comparing to last year.

Continuously comparing the synchronism extent of GDP per capita in urban area and the growth of per capita income, it is found that among the cities that the general economic development level entering top 50, there are 20 cities that the growth of per capita income entering top 50, accounting for 40%. Similarly in the cities that the general economic development level entering top 50, there are 22 cities that the scale of public service sharing projects entering top 50, accounting for 44%, including 11 municipalities directly under the central government and provincial capital cities.

It can be seen that the input of cities on public service is exactly increasing along with the economic development, but more investments are needed on service projects to benefit individual resident including both of local and non-local people, complete allocation route and assure the rights of residents.

4.2　Analysis of urbanization and urban economic development coordination

4.2.1　Urbanization and urban economic growth level

① Urbanization and GDP per capita

不同城镇化阶段的城市在人均 GDP 上存在显著差异。城镇化水平较低的城市,随着经济发展水平提高,城镇化水平提升的趋势较为明显;而城镇化水平较高的城市,其经济水平的差异则较大,如城镇化水平为 70% 的鄂尔多斯市,人均 GDP 达到 17.5 万元,而城镇化率 68.4% 的汕头市人均GDP 为 2.36 万元,城镇化率 71.3% 的武汉市为 5.90 万元。

The cities on different urbanization stage show obvious differences on GDP per capita. For cities with relatively low urbanization level, along with the increasing of economic development level, the tendency of urbanization level promotion is relatively obvious; but for cities with relatively high urbanization level, the difference of economic development level is relatively large, e. g. Ordos City with urbanization level of 70%, features GDP per capita of up to RMB 175000, but the GDP per capita of Shantou city with 68.4% urbanization rate is RMB 23600, while Wuhan city with 71.3% urbanization rate is RMB 59000 .

Comparing the general tendency of urbanization of China's cities with GDP per capita, the cities with GDP per capita obviously higher than average level include Ordos, Dongying, Daqing, Yulin and so on, most of which are resource type cities; the cities with the GDP per capita obviously lower than average level include Hegang, Fangcheng port, Chaozhou, Shantou and so on.

② Relation of urbanization and per capita income growth rate

For the whole country, the per capita income growth rate is not obvious related with urbanization level, the correlation coefficient is -0.0093. The per capita income growth rate in cities with relatively high and relatively low urbanization rate are rather consistent, and both growth rates keep about 1%; the per capita income growth rate in cities with middle level urbanization rate appears reletively large polarization tendency, e. g. the urbanization rate of Chengde city and Xingtai city are respectively 39.41% and 42.5%, while the per capita income growth rate are -1.6% and -1.4%, but the urbanization rate of Lang-

人均GDP（万元）

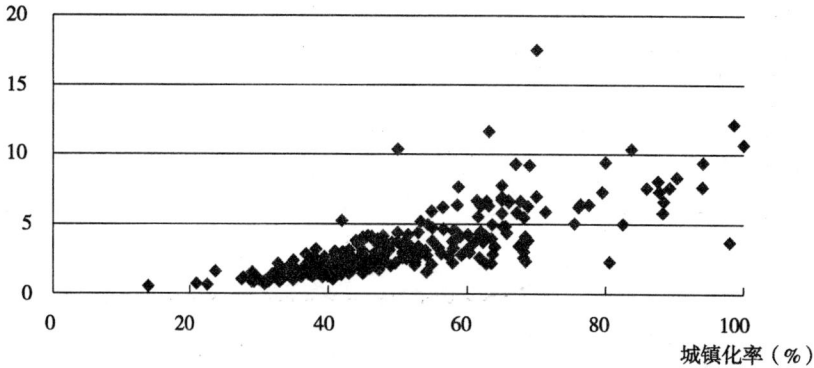

Figure 2   Urbanization and GDP per capita

fang city and Handan city are respectively 48. 8% and 46. 5%, while the per capita income growth rate are respectively up to 3. 6% and 2. 6%.

人均收入增长率

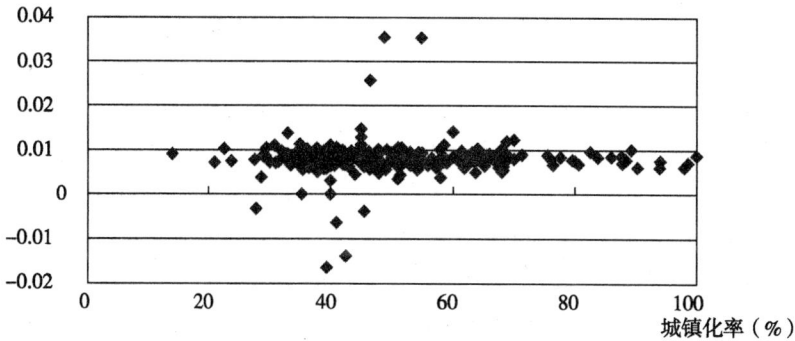

Figure 3   Urbanization and per capita income growth rate

③ Urbanization and salary growth rate

Urbanization level and salary basically have no relation since the correlation coefficient is 0. 0095, and the salary growth rate of all cities are basically between 0—0. 2%. It should be noted that the cities with low urbanization rate appear several high salary growth rates, e. g. the urbanization rate of Dingxi city is only 13. 83%, but its salary growth rate is up to 0. 4%; the urbanization rate of Guyuan city is 30. 85%, but the salary growth rate is up to 0. 5%. The salary growth rate in Shenzhen is especially outstanding, which is up to 1. 2%.

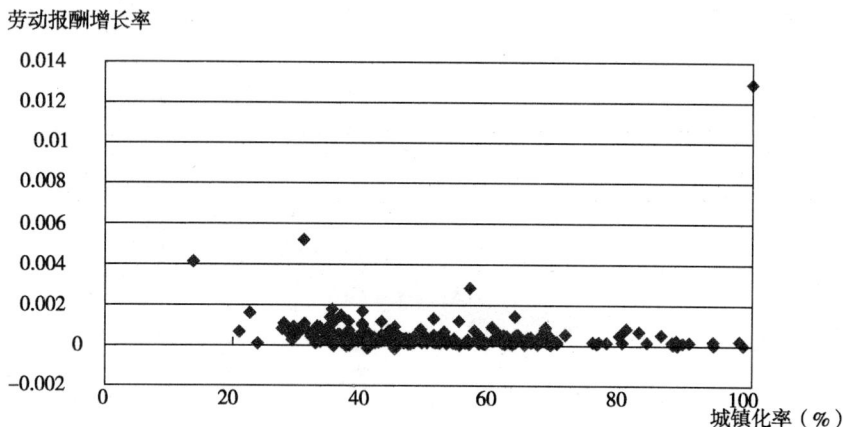

Figure 4   Urbanization and salary growth rate

4. 2. 2   Urbanization and urban economic management level

① Urbanization and production rate of unit land area(billion/km^2)

There is no linear relation between urbanization and the production rate of unit land area since the correlation coefficient is − 0. 0027, and the production rates of unit land area in most cities are below 2 billions/ km2. Generally the production rate of unit land area in cities with low urbanization rate is relatively low, but the production rate of unit land area in cities with middle and high urbanization rate have relatively large difference, for example in the case of 40% urbanization rate, the production rate of unit land area in Cangzhou is 4. 79 billion/ km^2 while the production rate of unit land area in Bengbu is 0. 61 billion / km^2; in the case of 90% urbanization rate the production rate of unit land area in Dongguan is 4. 615 billion/ km^2, while the production rate of unit land area in Jiayuguan is only 0. 37 billions/ km^2.

② Urbanization and output yield rate

The urbanization level and output yield rate have no obvious relation since correlation coefficient is − 0. 0274, and no matter the urbanization rate is in low, middle, or high stage, the output yield rates of most cities are between 0. 05—0. 1. Among them, cities with relatively high output yield rate include Sanya, Beijing, Shanghai, Xiamen, etc, indicating their economic output efficiencies are relatively high.

③ Urbanization and labour productivity(billion/10 thousand person)

The urbanization level and labor productivity do not have obvious linear relation. The cities with relatively low urbanization level shall have relatively small

单位土地面积产出率
（亿元/平方公里）

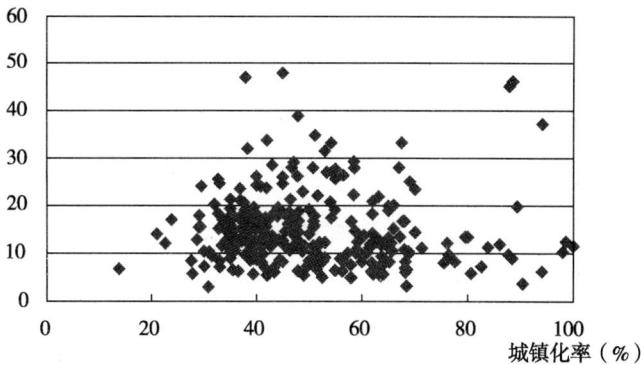

城镇化率（%）

Figure 5   Urbanization and production rate of
unit land area (billion/km2)

产出收益率

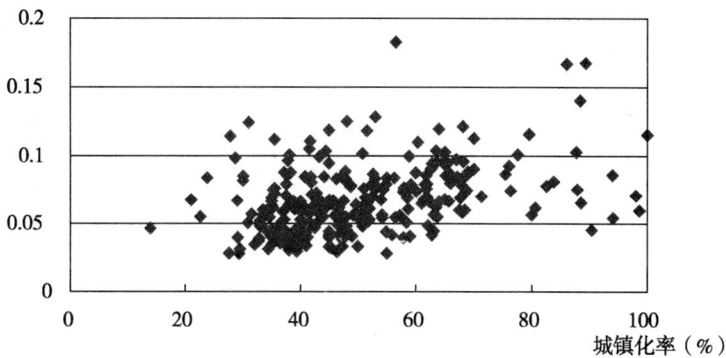

城镇化率（%）

Figure 6   Urbanization and output yield rate

labor productivity differences: for cities that the urbanization rate ais below 40%, the labor productivity are mostly distributed below 10 billion/ 10 thousand person; for partial cities that urbanization rate is a from 40% to 70%, the labor productivity are up to 20 billion/10 thousand person. The labor productivity difference between cities with relatively high urbanization level is relatively large, which is related to development characteristics of different cities.

Among the cities that the urbanization rate is up to 70%, the labour productivity of Dongguan is up to 35 billion/ 10 thousand person and Foshan is up to 26. 46 billion/ 10 thousand person, and these two cities are also cities with highest labour productivity.

劳动生产率
(亿元/万人)

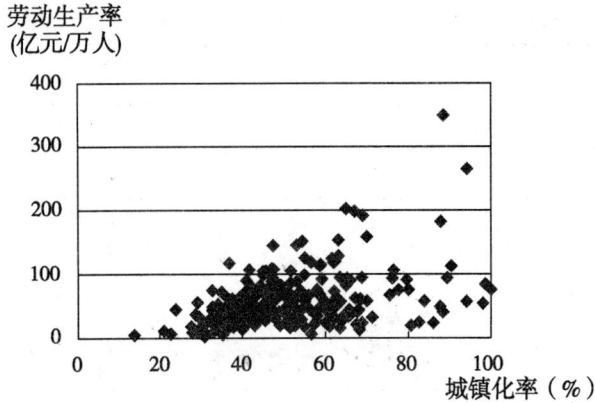

Figure 7　Urbanization and labour productivity (billion /10 thousand)

④ **Urbanization and water consumption of 10 thousand Yuan GDP (10 thousand ton)**

The water consumption of 10 thousand Yuan GDP of cities with low urbanization rate are all relatively low, but after entering 40%, the water consumption of average unit GDP slightly rises, furthermore the water consumption of unit GDP of all cities have appeared relatively large polarization. Cities with urbanization rate of about 60% stands out, since the highest water consumption of 10 thousand Yuan GDP was about 55 tons while the minimum value was 2. 8 tons.

每万元GDP水耗
（万吨）

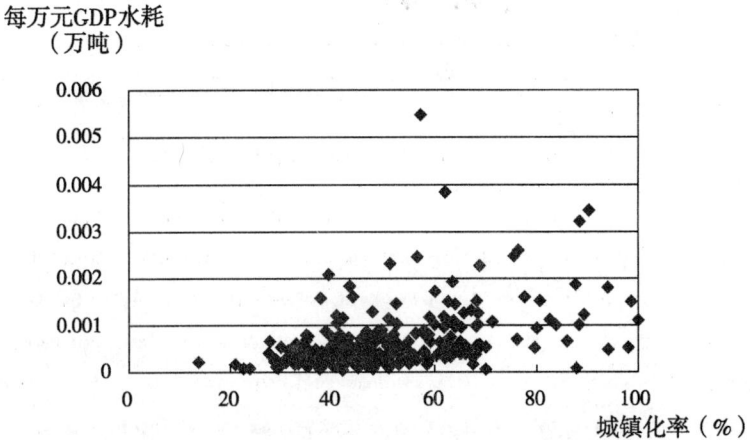

Figure 8　Urbanization and water consumption of 10
thousand Yuan GDP (10 thousand ton)

⑤ **Urbanization and electricity consumption of 10 thousand Yuan GDP(10 thousand kwh)**

The relation between electricity consumption of unit GDP and urbanization is similar to water consumption. The unit electricity consumption of cities with low urbanization rate is relatively small, but along with the increasing of urbanization rate, especially when it is up to 40% and after, the differences of unit electricity consumption between cities are obviously increased. Comparing to cities with similar urbanization rate, the cities with special high unit GDP electricity consumption include Baiyin, E'zhou, Shizuishan, Jiayuguan and Wuhai, and most of them are resource type heavy industrial cities.

每万元GDP电耗
(万千瓦时)

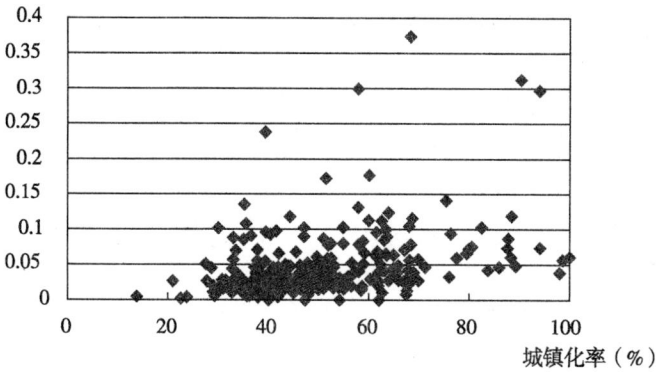

Figure 9   Urbanization and electricity consumption of
10 thousand GDP(10 thousand kwh)

⑥ **Urbanization and electricity consumption of 10 thousand gross output value(10 thousand kwh)**

The electricity consumption of 10 thousand gross output value of most cities are below 1000 kwh, and few cities with obviously high value include Hezhou, Laibin, Baiyin, Tongchuan, Shizuishan, and Wuhai.

4.2.3   Urbanization and urban scientific information level

① **Urbanization and science expense proportion**

The average science expense proportion of cities that the urbanization rate is 30% only accounts for 0.57; the average science expense proportion of cities that the urbanization rate is 50% accounts for 1.57%; the average science expense proportion of cities that the urbanization rate is 70% increases to 2.57%,

Report of China urban development in 2012

每万元工业总产值电耗
(万千瓦时)

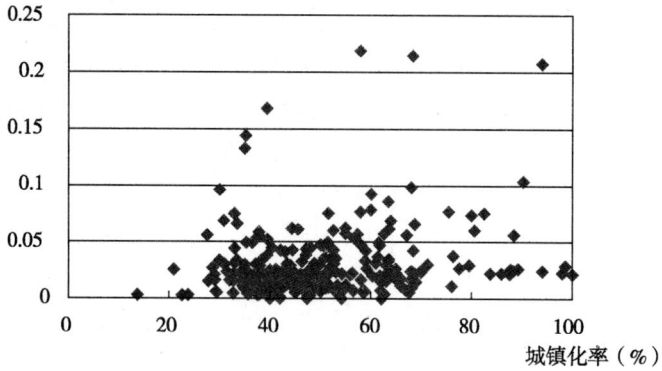

**Figure 10　Urbanization and electricity consumption of 10
thousand gross output value（10 thousand kwh）**

but for cities with urbanization rate of up to 80%, the average science expense
proportion increases to 3.07%.

科学支出比重

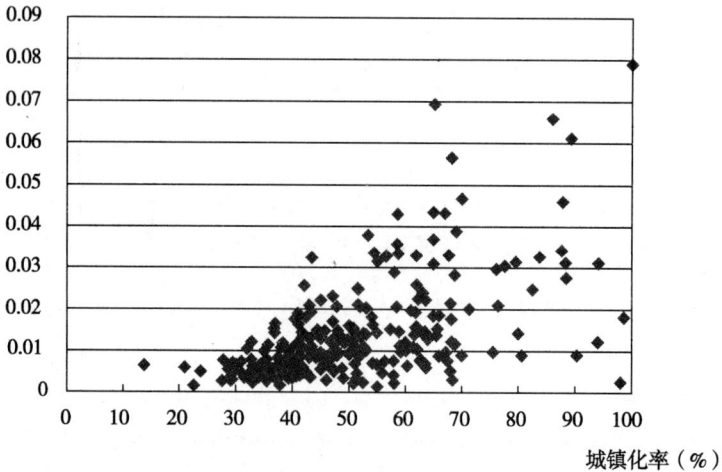

Figure 11　Urbanization and science expense proportion

34

②　**Urbanization and utilization rate of Internet(house/10 thousand
person)**

The urbanization and utilization rate of Internet have slight positive relation, the correlation coefficient is 0.0026. Especially for some cities that the urbanization rate is up to about 50%, the Internet utilization rates rise significant-

ly. The Internet utilization rate of the cities such as Ningde, Quanzhou, Fuzhou, Xiamen, Shanghai etc. is obviously higher than the cities with same level of urbanization. Except for Shanghai, all these cities are in Fijian province.

国际互联网使用率
（万户/万人）

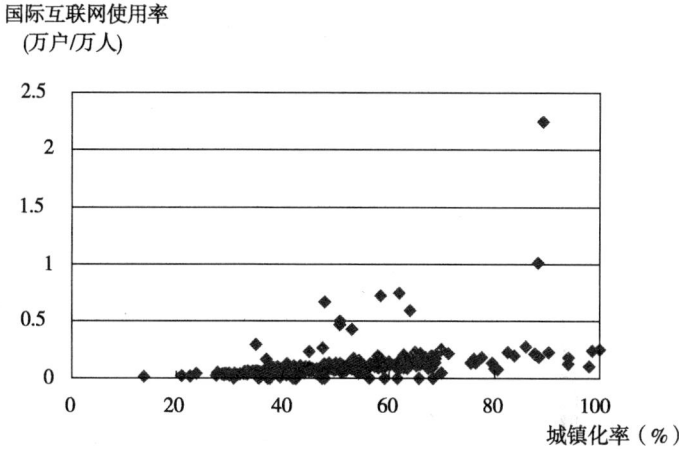

城镇化率（％）

Figure12　Urbanization and Internet utilization rate（house/10 thousand person）

③ Urbanization and the proportion of employee in information industry

Urbanization and the proportion of employee in information industry have little relation, and the correlation coefficient is 0. 0152. The proportions of population in information industry in most cities are between $0 \sim 2\%$. The cities with special high employee proportion in information industry include GuangYuan, Cangzhou and Beijingwith over 6% proportion, which is related to function and specialization level of city.

4. 2. 4　Urbanization and external effects of urban development

① Urbanization and the proportion of production value of three wastes comprehensive utilization product

Along with the promotion of urbanization, the proportion of production value of three wastes comprehensive utilization product appears tendency of firstly rising and lately reducing. For cities with low urbanization rate and high urbanization rate, the proportion of production value of three wastes comprehensive utilization product are all reletively low, but for some cities that the urbanization rate is between 40% and 60%, it is featured in relatively high proportion of production value of three wastes comprehensive utilization product, typical exam-

信息业从业人员比重

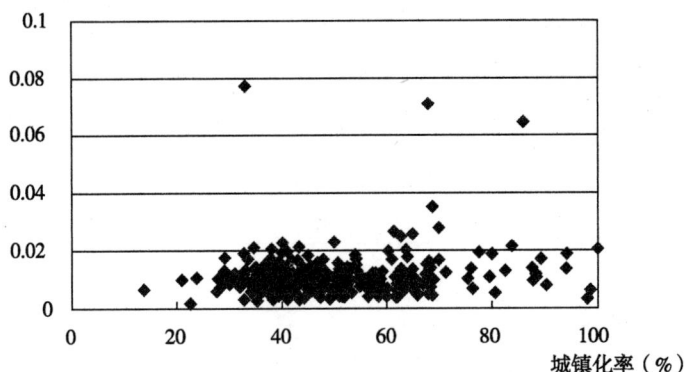

Figure 13　Urbanization and proportion of employee in information industry

ples are Yingtan, Jinchang, Guigang and so on.

三废综合利用产品
产值比重

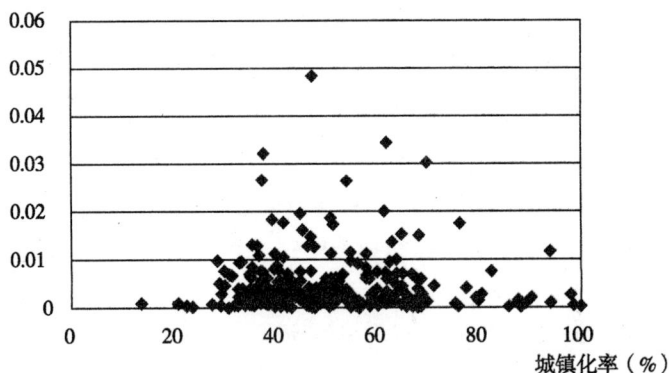

Figure 14　Urbanization and proportion of production value of three wastes comprehensive utilization product

② Urbanization and output pollution processing rate

Urbanization and output pollution processing rate appear weakly negative correlation tendency, the correlation coefficient is -0.0638. Generally, the higher the urbanization rate is, the lower the output pollution processing rate will be.

③ Urbanization and removal rate of industrial fume.

Along with the rising of urbanization rate, the removal rate of urban industrial fume should also correspondingly rise; furthermore the difference of indus-

产出污染处理率

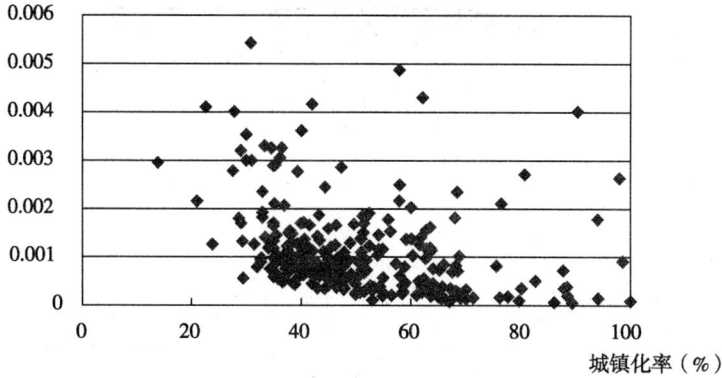

Figure 15   Urbanization and output pollution processing rate

trial fume removal rate a different cities appear convergent tendency. For cities that industrial fume removal rate are below 60%, the urbanization rate are mostly in middle and low level (below 50%).

工业烟尘去除率

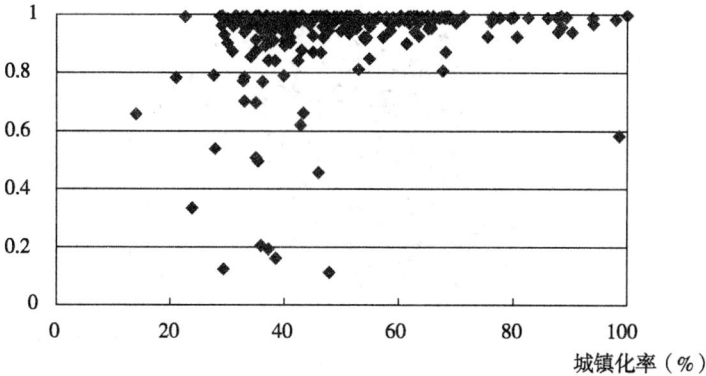

Figure 16   Urbanization and removal rate of industrial fume

④ Urbanization and target rate of industrial wastewater emission

The relation between urbanization and industrial wastewater emission is similar to the removal rate of industrial fume. Along with the rising of urbanization rate, the target rate of industrial wastewater emission also rised accordingly. In the cities that urbanization rate is up to or over 80%, the target rates of industrial wastewater emission are all controlled in 90% above.

⑤ Urbanization and removal rate of Industrial SO2.

Urbanization has no obvious relation with removal rate of Industrial SO2.

工业废水排放达标率

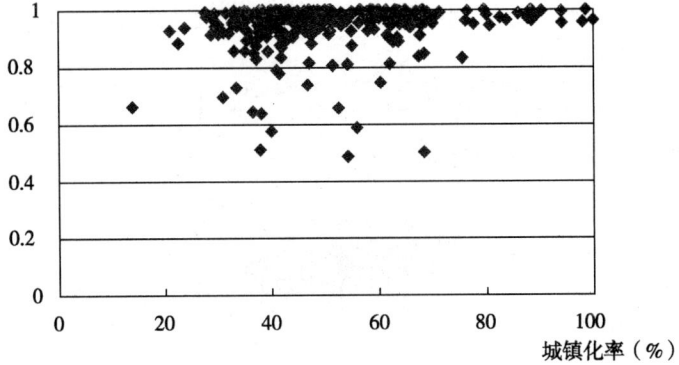

Figure 17   Urbanization and target rate of industrial
wastewater emission

The difference of removal rate of industrial SO2 between various cities is significant, with quite large amount of distribution between 0—1.

工业二氧化硫去除率

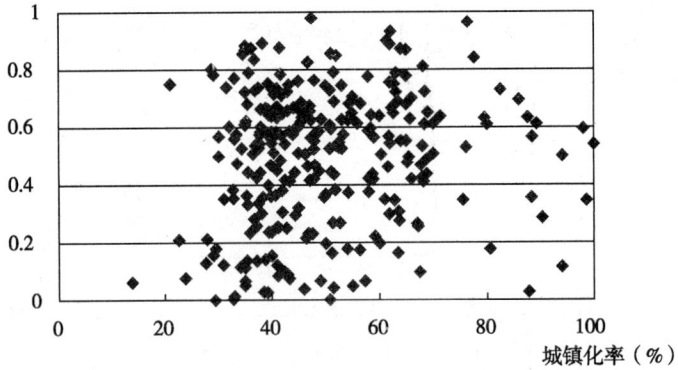

Figure 18   Urbanization and removal rate of Industrial SO2.

4.3   Analysis of urbanization and urban public service coordination

4.3.1   Urbanization and public finance input level

① **Urbanization and per capita social security expense (Yuan/ per-**
son)

The urbanization has no obvious relation with per capita social security expense, but for cities that urbanization rate is up to 70%, per capita social security expense is higher than the average level of other cities.

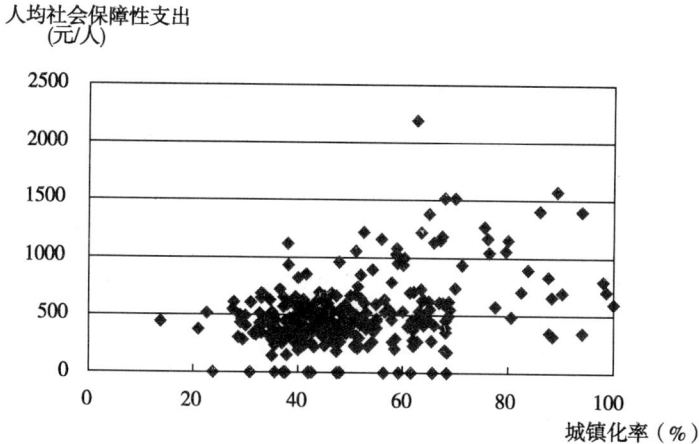

人均社会保障性支出
(元/人)

Figure 19 Urbanization and per capita social
security expense (Yuan/ person)

② **Urbanization and per capita public service financial expenditure (Yuan/ person)**

For cities that the urbanization rate is below 60%, the per capita public service financial expenditure are between 1000—2000, but for cities that urbanization rate is over 60%, the per capita public service financial expenditure are obviously high with also high variance. The highest per capita public service financial expenditure in Beijing is up to 5567 Yuan/person, while the lowest per capita public service financial expenditure in Dongguan is close to 640 Yuan/person, and difference between them is significant.

③ **Urbanization and per capita education expenditure (Yuan/person)**

For cities with middle and low urbanization rate, the difference of per capita education expenditure is not large, and they are basically about 500—1000 Yuan/ person. But the difference of per capita education expenditure in cities with relatively high urbanization rate is very large, e. g. the city with relatively high value includes Karamay city (2950 Yuan/person), and the city with relatively low value includes Jiayuguan (654 Yuan/person).

④ **Urbanization and per capita medical service expense (Yuan/person)**

It is similar to per capita education expense, taking urbanization rate 70% as a boundary, for cities with middle and low level of urbanization rate, the per capita medical service expenses are concentrated in 200—300 Yuan/person,

Report of China urban development in 2012

人均公共服务财政
支出(元/人)

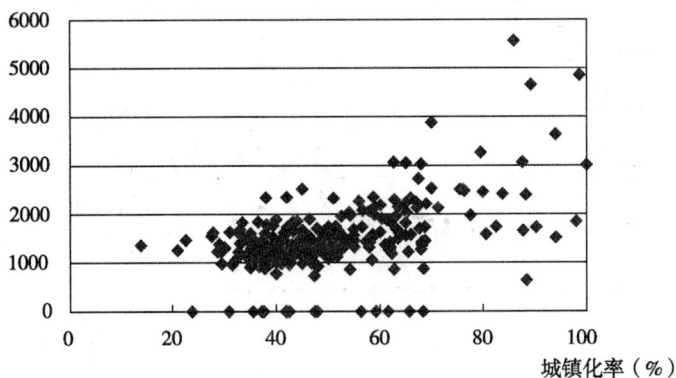

Figure 20   Urbanization and per capita public service financial
expenditure (Yuan/person)

人均教育支出
(元/人)

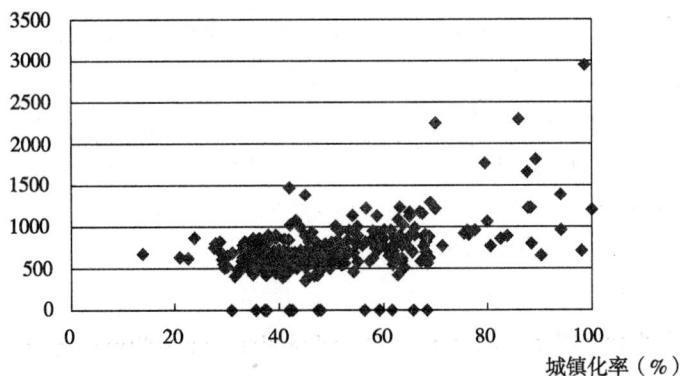

Figure 21   Urbanization and per capita education
expense (Yuan/person)

and the difference between various cities are relatively small; for cities with relatively high urbanization rate level, the difference of per capita medical service
expense is significant, e. g. the highest is for Karamay city with up to 1445
Yuan/person, while the lowest is for Dongguan city with only 65 Yuan/person.

4.3.2 Urbanization and the scale of urban public project

① **Urbanization and number of beds in hospital and health center per**
10 thousand people (set)

The relation between urbanization and number of beds in hospital and

人均医疗卫生支出
(元/人)

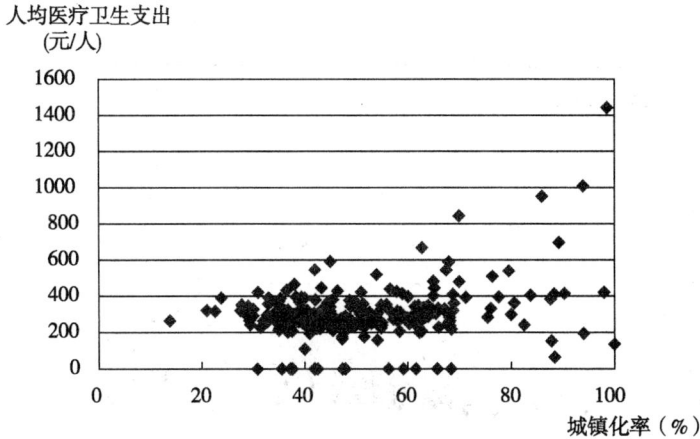

Figure 22   Urbanization and per capita medical service
expense (Yuan/person)

health center per 10 thousand people appears "Reversed U" type tendency; for cities that urban rate is lower than 60%, the number increases basically along with urbanization rate, regarding the number of beds in hospital and health center per 10 thousand people appears rising tendency; but for cities that urbanization rate is higher than 80%, along with the rising of urbanization level, the number of beds in hospital and health center per 10 thousand people appears descending tendency.

每万人拥有医院、卫生
院床位数(张)

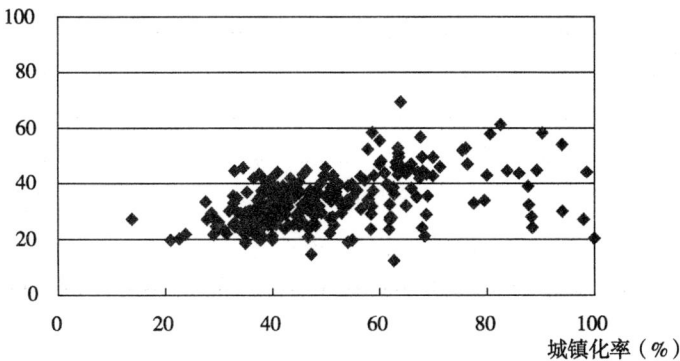

Figure 23   Urbanization and number of beds in hospital and
health center per 10 thousand people (set)

The number of doctors per 10 thousand people also appears same tendency, but there are some cities that the indicator value is obviously higher than av-

Report of China urban development in 2012

erage level, typically such as Daqing, Kunming, Qiqihar, Heihe, Wulancha-
bu, etc. , which are mainly cities with middle urbanization level.

每万人拥有医生数
（人）

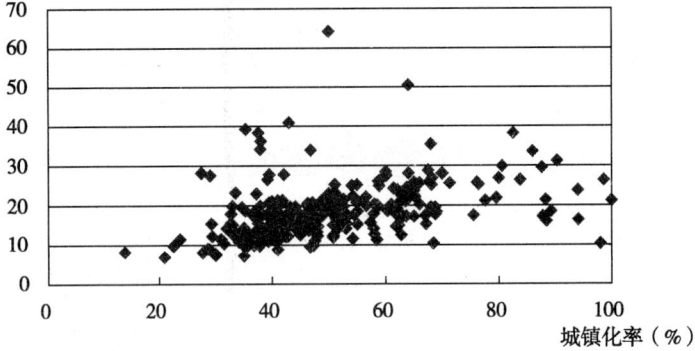

城镇化率（%）

**Figure 24   Urbanization and number of doctors per 10
thousand people(people)**

**② Urbanization and number of students in school above high school
level per 10 thousand people (people)**

The urbanization and education service scale also appear "reversed U" relation. The higher the urbanization rate is, the larger the number of students in
school above high school level per 10 thousand people (people) will be, especially in the section that urbanization rate is lower than 70%. But for cities that
urbanization rate are higher than 70%, there are many higher and lower values.

③ Urbanization and per capita urban road area(m²)

The higher the urbanization rate is, the larger the per capita urban road area will be, but most of them are within the indicator scope regulated by Ministry
of Construction. Ordos (85. 2 m²), SuiHua, Weihai have relatively high values
in groups with low and middle urbanization rate, while Zhuhai and Shenzhen
show relatively high values in the group with high urbanization rate.

**④ Urbanization and number of theaters and cinemas per million peo-
ple (sets)**

No matter the high or low urbanization rate, the numbers of theaters and
cinemas per million people (sets) are basically consistent, showing 0—10 sets,
except for Jiayuguan, Meizhou, Zhenjiang with obviously higher value.

⑤ Urbanization and number of buses per million people (set)

The urbanization degree and number of buses per million people (sets)

每万人在校高中以上
学生数（人）

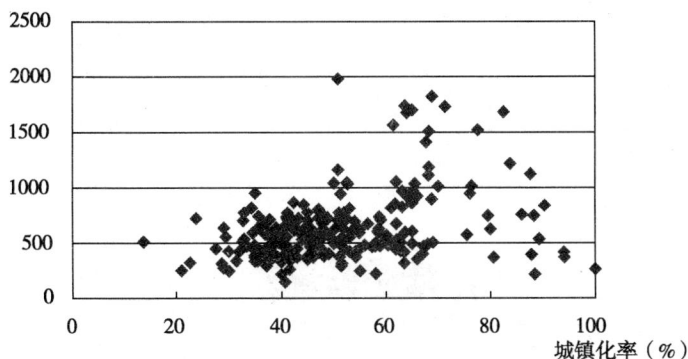

Figure 25　Urbanization and number of students in school above high school level per 10 thousand people（people）

人均城市道路面积
（平方米）

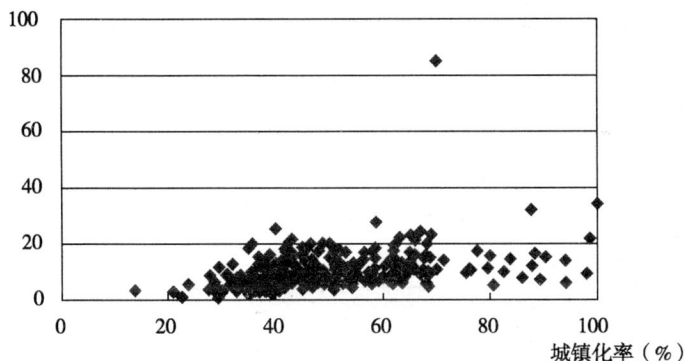

Figure 26　Urbanization and per capita urban road area（m²）

have weak positive relation; along with the rising of urbanization rate, the average tendency of number of buses per million people (sets) also appears rising state. Among them the urbanization rate of Xingtai city is 42. 5%, and the number of buses per million people is 12. 38; the urbanization rate of Shanwei city is 54. 18%, and the number of buses per million people is 44. 94; the urbanization rate of Shenzhen is 100%, and the number of buses per million people is 103. 11. These three cities are respectively top-ranked in different urbanization levels regarding public transportation ration.

每百万人剧场、影剧院
数（座）

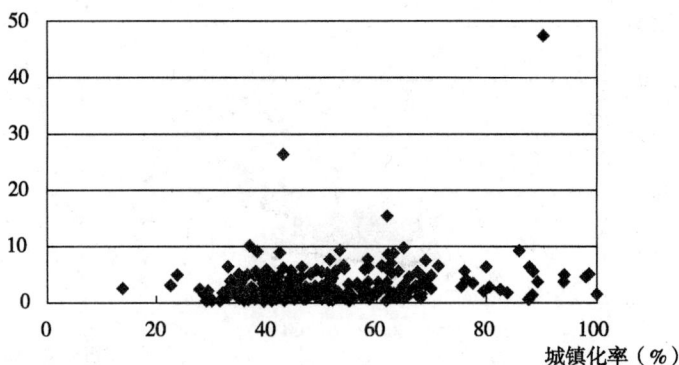

Figure 27   Urbanization and number of theaters and cinemas
per million people（sets）

每万人拥有公共汽车数
（辆）

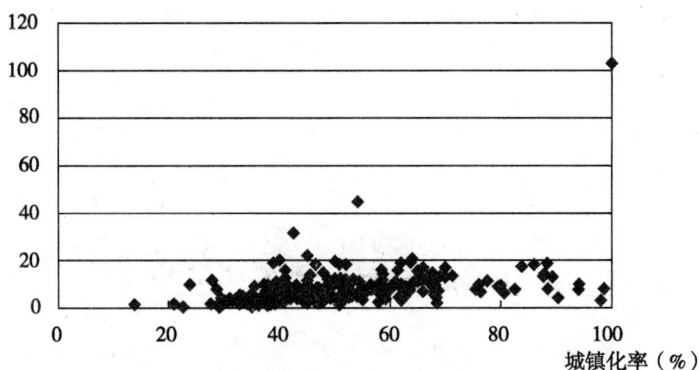

Figure28   Urbanization and number of buses
per million people（sets）

⑥ **Urbanization and number of books in public library per hundred people（volumes）**

The urbanization and number of books in public library per hundred people（volumes）appear positive relation, with correlation coefficient of 0. 0186. Generally along with the increase of urbanization rate, the number of books in public library per hundred people（volumes）increases; furthermore among districts that urbanization rate is greater than 70%, the indicator difference is also expanded accordingly.

每百人公共图书馆
藏书数（册）

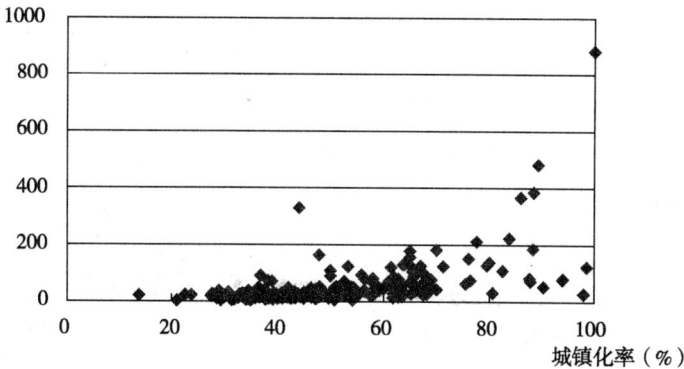

Figure29　Urbanization and number of books in public
library per hundred people (volumes)

4.3.3　Urbanization and urban social security level

The urbanization shows strong indicator type positive correlation with participating coverage rate of endowment insurance, coverage rate of medical insurance, and coverage rate of unemployment insurance. The higher the urbanization rate is, the higher the coverage rates of these three kinds of social security insurance will be; furthermore in high urbanization stage, for increase of each 1% urbanization rate, the increas extent of social security participating rate will also be larger comparing to low urbanization stage. In the three kinds of social security, the rising speed of coverage rate of medical insurance is the fastest. [1]

4.4　Coordination analysis of urbanization and urban residents enjoying public service

4.4.1　Urbanization and resident income level

The urbanization has quite strong positive relation with per capita disposable income of urban residents and per capita pure income of rural residents. The higher the urbanization rate is, the higher the urban resident income and rural resident income will be, indicating that urbanization has played certain role on improving the income of residents in both rural and urban areas. But comparing with the relation between urbanization and rural resident income, the relation between urbanization and urban resident income is stronger.

Report of China urban development in 2012

45

---

　① From chapter (3.2) to chapter 5, those adopted are data and conclusion obtained according to E&G assessment system analysis .

养老保险参保覆盖率

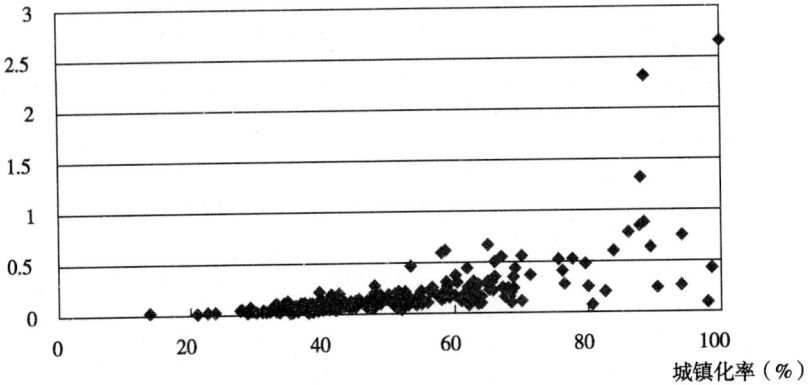

Figure 30   Urbanization and participating coverage rate of endowment insurance

医疗保险参保覆盖率

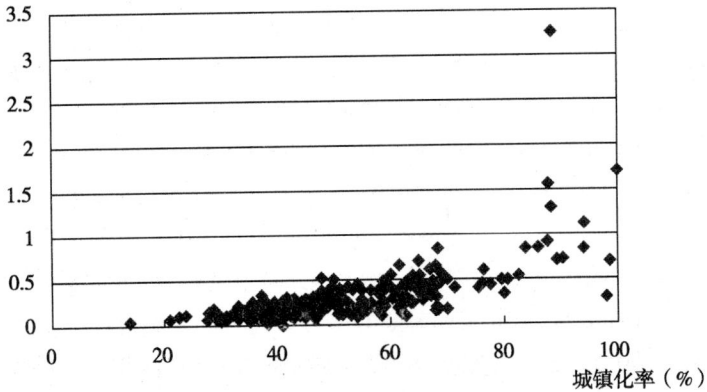

Figure 31   Urbanization and participating coverage rate of medical insurance

The urbanization and specific value of urban and rural resident incomes also have weak positive relation. The higher the urbanization level is, the bigger the specific value of rural and urban resident incomes will be, implying the increase of urban resident income is faster than rural resident income, which indicate that current urbanization stage is continually widening the gap between rural and urban area.

4.4.2   Urbanization and resident living environment level

The urbanization level has no obvious relation with per capita green land area, and the per capita green land areas of most cities are below 100 m^2. The cit-

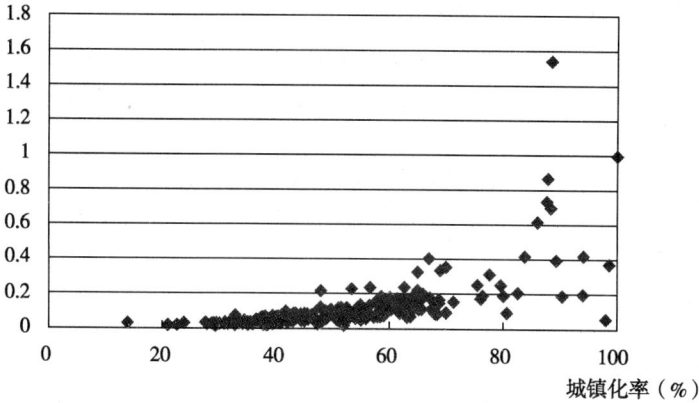

Figure 32　Urbanization and participating coverage rate
of unemployment insurance

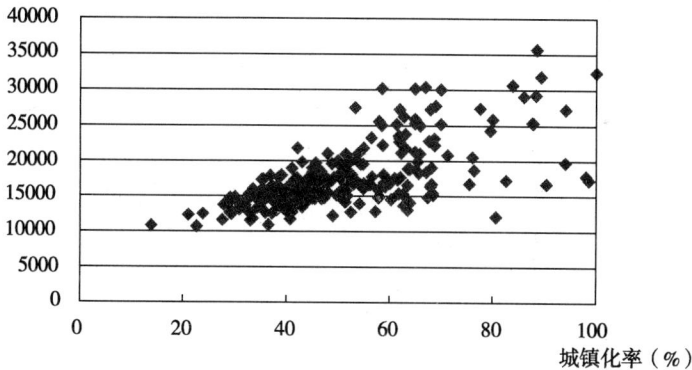

Figure 33　Urbanization and per capita disposable income
of urban residents (Yuan)

ies that per capita green land area exceeds 200 m^2 include few cities such as Xiamen, Shenzhen, Ordos, Huangshan, Shiyan etc.

For cities with relatively low urbanization level, the average living rubbish harmless treatment rate are relatively low. The the average living rubbish harmless treatment rates of cities such as Dazhou, Yibin and Fuzhou even can be lower than 20%, but for cities with over 80% urbanization rate, the living rubbish harmless processing rate are above 80%.

The relation between urbanization and living wastewater treatment rate is

城乡居民收入比

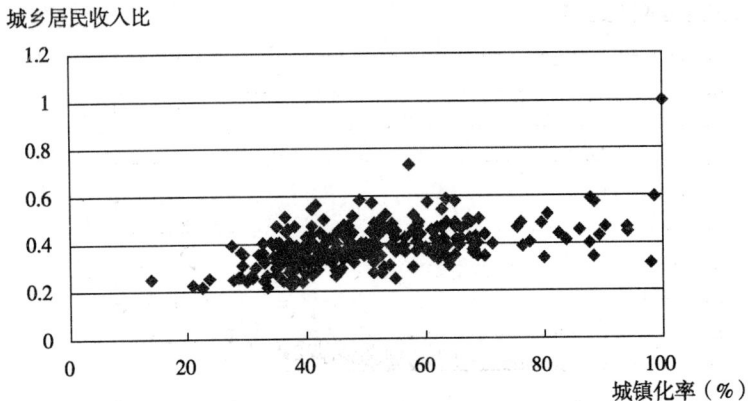

Figure 34　Urbanization and specific value of rural and
urban resident incomes

农村居民人均纯收入
（元）

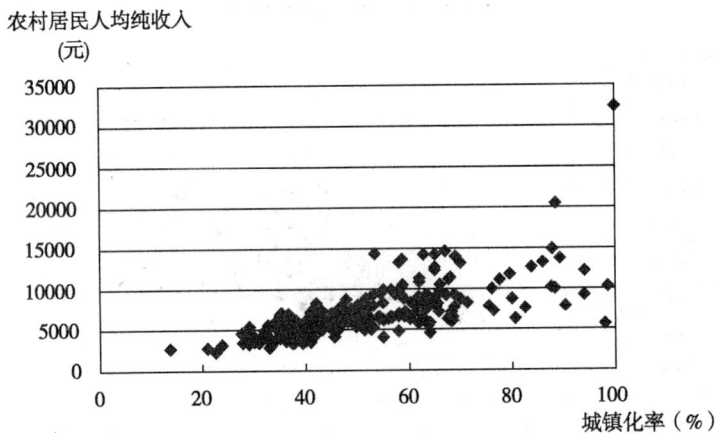

Figure 35　Urbanization and rural resident pure income（Yuan）

similar to rubbish harmless treatment rate, but shows lower relevance. Except for cities with low urbanization rate, the living wastewater treatment rate of many cities that urbanization rate are about 60% (such as Dandong, Qitaihe, Panzhi-hua, Chaozhou) are also below 40%.

The urbanization is positively related with per capita living water consumption; the correlation coefficient is up to 0.0194. The higher the urbanization rate is, the higher the per capita living water consumption will be, and the bigger the pressure on urban water supply system will be.

The urbanization is also positively related with per capita living electricity consumption, and the correlation coefficient is up to 0.0099. The higher the ur-

人均绿地面积（平方米）

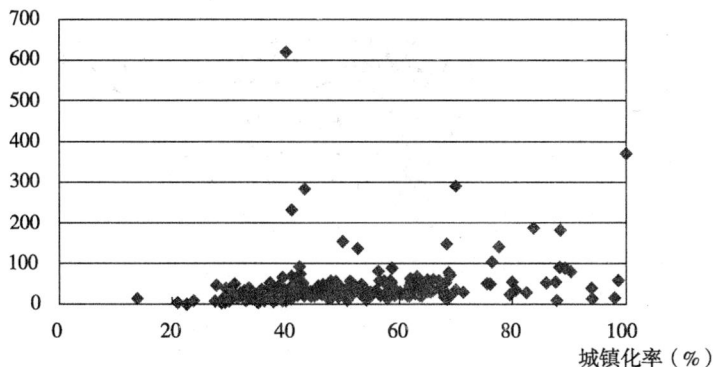

Figure 36 Urbanization and per capita green land area(m²)

生活垃圾无害化
处理率(%)

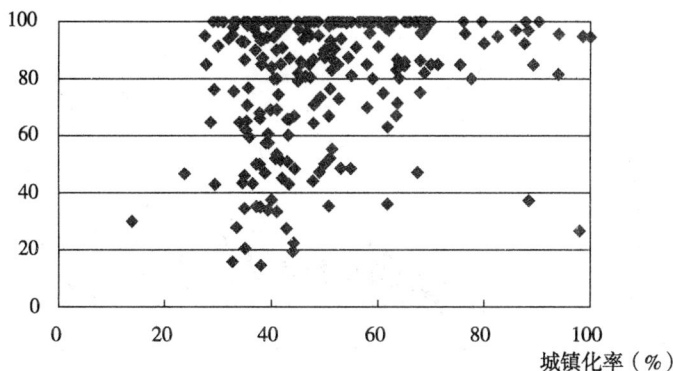

**Figure 37   Urbanization and living rubbish harmless
treatment rate (%)**

banization rate is, the higher the per capita living electricity consumption will be, and as the same the higher the power resource demand will be.

4. 4. 3 Urbanization and resident employment level

Urbanization rate has no obvious relation with registered unemployment rate in urban area. Generally the registered urban unemployment rate in low urbanization stage is relatively high, and there is an obvious process at about 40% urbanization rate, since for cities in middle and high stage of urbanization rate, the average level of their registered unemployment rates are all relatively low.

The specific value of urbanization and unemployment growth rate have no relation with the level of urbanization rate, since the value is basically stabilized

生活污水处理率(%)

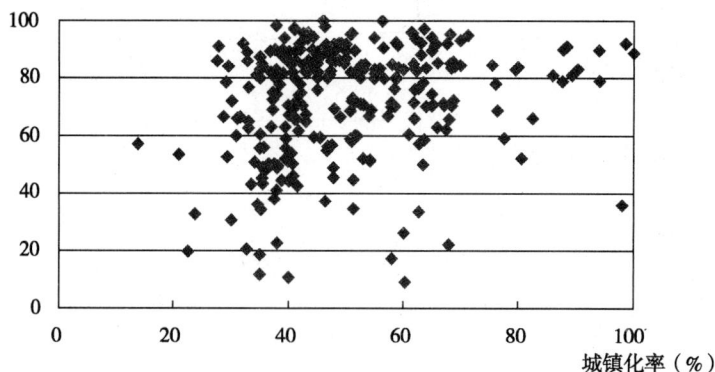

Figure 38 Urbanization and living wastewater treatment rate (%)

人均生活用电量
（千瓦/时）

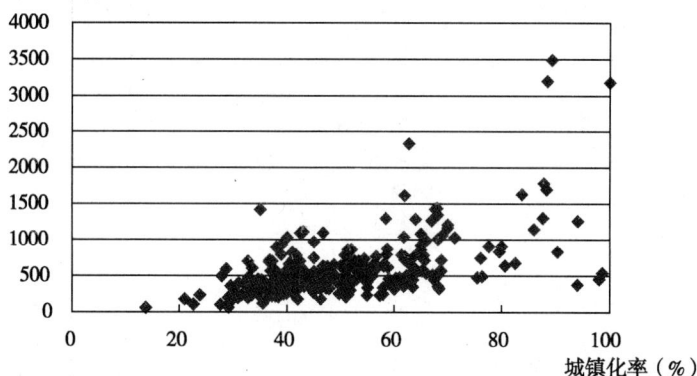

Figure 39 Urbanization and per capita living water consumption

at about 1, indicating that they keep growth tendency in same proportion. Some cities with slightly high value include Shangluo, Qujing, Pingliang, Datong and Haikou.

4.4.4 Urbanization and resident consumption level

Comparing with the districts in low urbanization level, Engel coefficients of the districts in high urbanization level are slightly low, and the average value is about 0.3. But such tendency is not very obvious. The urban resident Engel co-efficients in most cities are between 0.2—0.5, and the value of Fuzhou is the highest with up to 0.5226, while the value of Shuozhou is the lowest with 0.1181.

城镇登记失业率

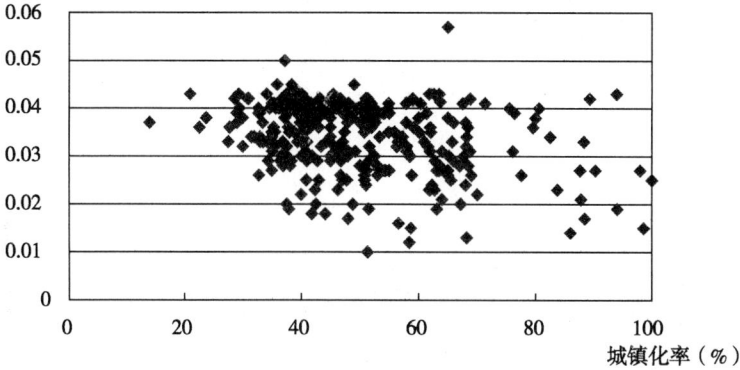

Figure 40   Urbanization and per capita living electricity
consumption (kwh)

城镇登记失业率

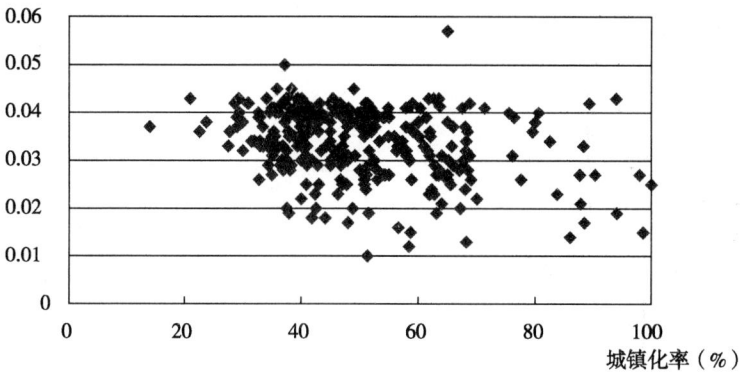

Figure 41   Urbanization and registered urban unemployment rate

The urbanization and per capita saving balance at the end of year appear positive relevance tendency, and the correlation coefficient is 0.0127. On one hand, the higher urbanization level of city is, the higher per capita saving balance at the end of year will be, which is consistent with the effect of resident income increase brought by urbanization. On the other hand, along with the increase of urbanization level, the differences of per capita saving balance among cities are also bigger.

As the same, the urbanization and per capita social consumption goods retail value also have relatively strong positive relevance, and the correlation coefficient is 0.0332. Along with the increase of urbanization level, the consump-

失业增长率与城镇化
增长率的比值

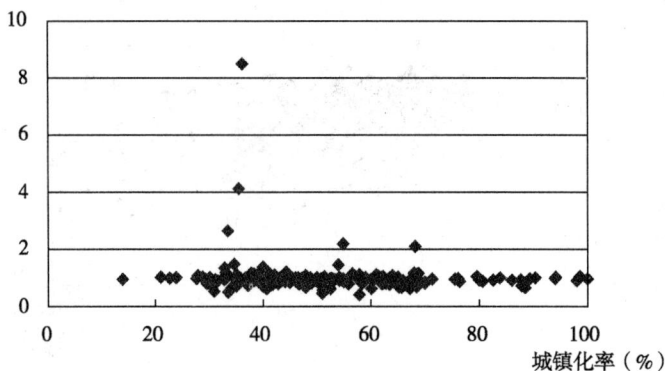

Figure 42　Specific value of urbanization and unemployment growth rate

城镇居民恩格尔系数

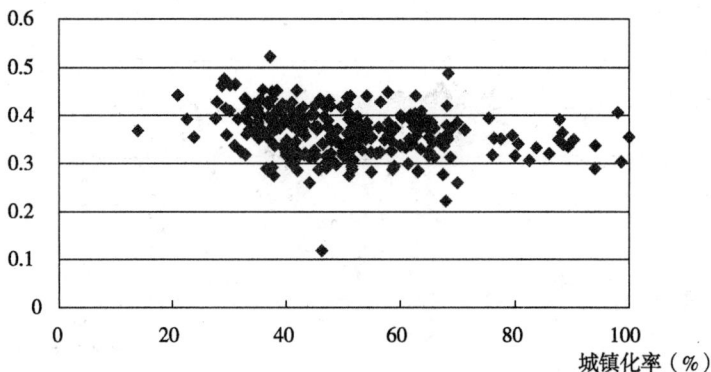

Figure 43　Urbanization and urban resident Engel coefficient

tion capability also becomes stronger, and per capita social consumption goods retail value also rises significantly.

The per capita house area has no obvious relation with urbanization level. The average value of per capita house area in various cities is about 30 square meters, and the highest value is in Dongguan city with 59. 58 square meters, while the lowest value is in Tianshui city with only 10. 29 square meters.

The urbanization also has no obvious relation with the proportion of inhabitation expense in consumption expense. The difference of proportions of inhabitation expense in consumption expense in various cities is not large, and the average value is about 10%, with the highest value 12. 64% for Xuancheng city

人均年末储蓄余额
（元/人）

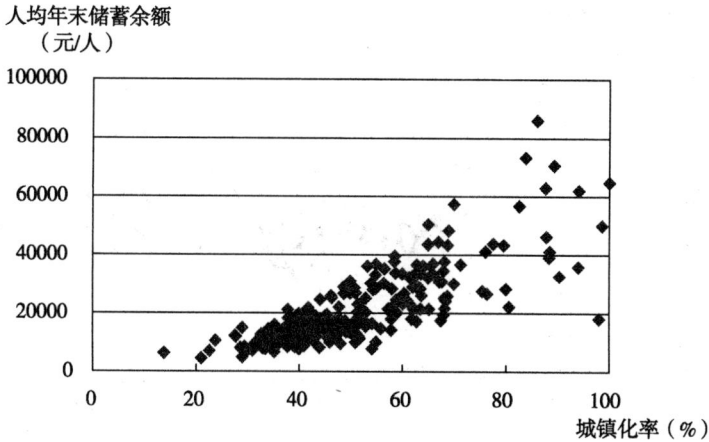

Figure 44   Urbanization and per capita saving balance
at the end of year(Yuan/person)

人均社会消费品零售额
（元/人）

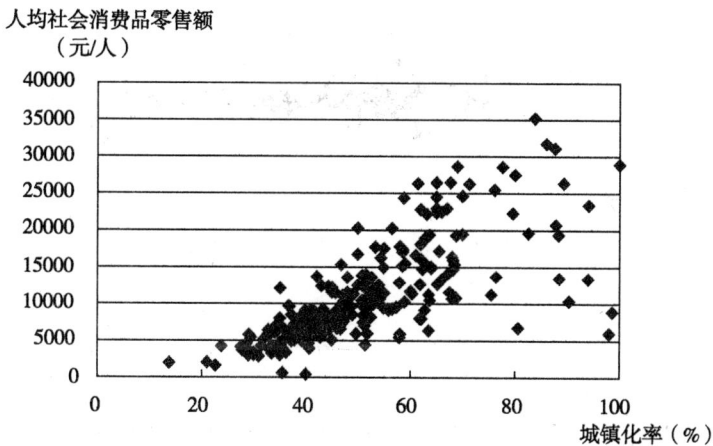

Figure 45   Urbanization and per capita social consumption
goods retail value(Yuan/ person)

and the lowest value 7. 80% for Baicheng city.

5   Analysis of urbanization and public service based on E&G assessment system

5. 1   Division of our country's urbanization stages

This study adopts five points division method to carry out grouping on the urbanization level of cities in prefecture-level so that the regional difference of different urbanization stage is obvious.

人均住宅建筑面积
（平方米）

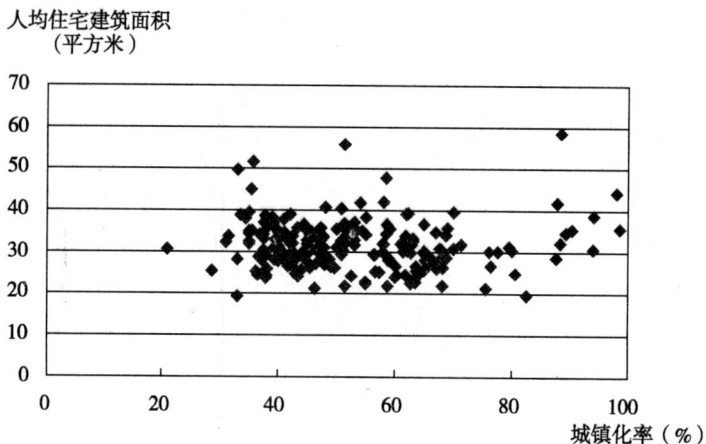

Figure 46　Urbanization and per capita house area(m²)

居住支出占消费支出比重

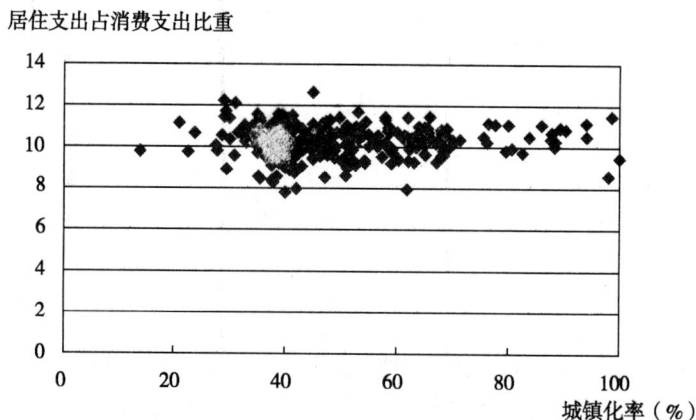

Figure 47　Urbanization and proportion of inhabitation
expense in consumption expense

5.1.1　Relatively low urbanization stage(≦ 37.56%)

The cities with relatively low urbanization level mainly concentrated in western area with the proportion up to 58.93%. Secondly, the cities in relatively low urbanization stage are mainly concentrated in middle area with 28.57% proportion.

Table 5   Regional distribution differences of prefecture-level cities in relatively low urbanization stage in 2010

	Eastern area	Northeast area	Middle area	Western area
Relatively low urbanization stage(≦ 37.56%)	8.93%	3.57%	28.57%	58.93%

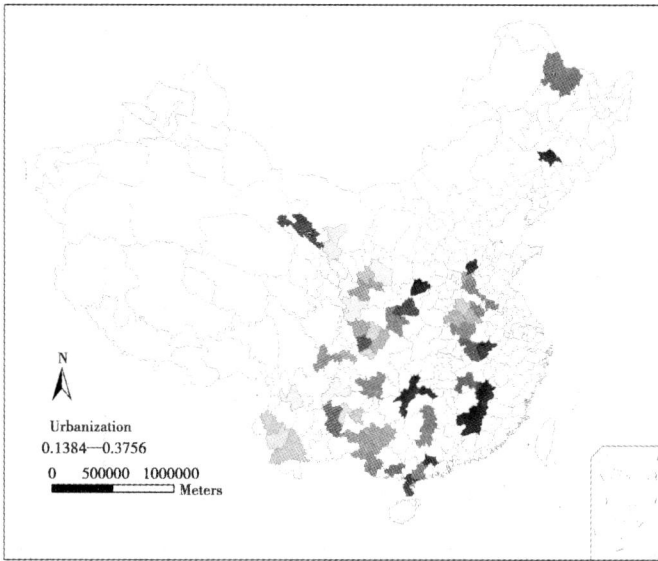

Figure 48   Distribution diagram of prefecture-level cities in relatively low urbanization stage

5.1.2   Middle and low urbanization stage(37.59%—43.00%)

The prefecture-level cities with middle and low urbanization stage in our country are mainly distributed in middle and west area with the proportion up to 75%. Specifically, the proportion of cities in middle area is higher than that of cities in west area.

Table 6   Regional distribution differences of prefecture-level cities in middle and low urbanization stage in 2010

	Eastern area	Northeast area	Middle area	Western area
Middle and low urbanization stage (37.59% —43.00%)	14.29%	10.71%	41.07%	33.93%

5.1.3   Middle urbanization stage(43.00%—51.04%)

The cities in middle urbanization level in China are mainly concentrated in

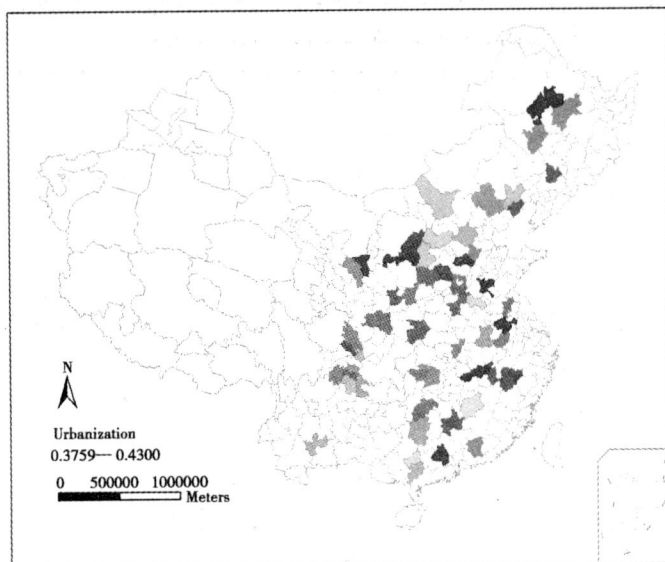

Figure 49 Distribution diagram of prefecture-level cities in
middle and low urbanization stage

eastern and middle regions accounting for 42. 86% and 35. 71% respectively.

Table 7 Regional distribution differences of prefecture-level cities in
middle urbanization stage in 2010

	Eastern area	Northeast area	Middle area	Western area
Middle urbanization stage(43. 00% – 51. 04%)	42. 86%	7. 14%	35. 71%	14. 29%

5. 1. 4 Middle and high urbanization stage(51. 12%—62. 75%)

In middle and high urbanization stage, the proportion of cities in east area is up to 46. 43%; Northeast area ranks second, and the proportion is up to 21. 43%.

Table 8 Regional distribution differences of prefecture-level cities
in middle and high urbanization stage in 2010

	Eastern area	Northeast area	Middle area	Western area
Middle and high urbanization stage (51. 12%—62. 75%)	46. 43%	21. 43%	17. 86%	14. 29%

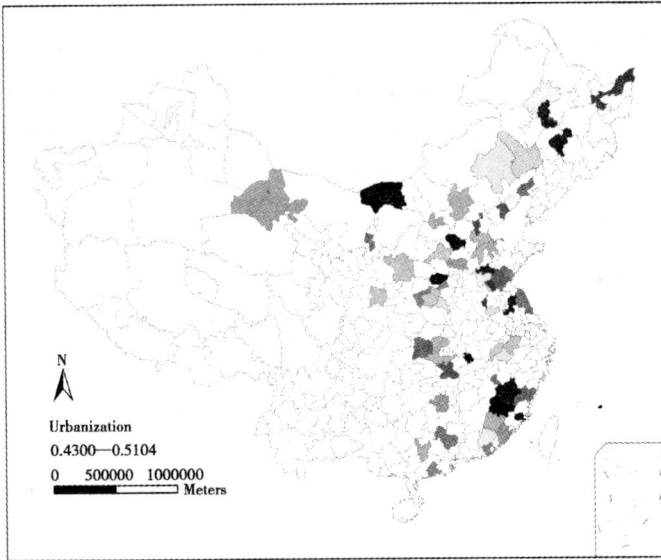

Figure 50　Distribution diagram of prefecture-level cities in middle urbanization stage

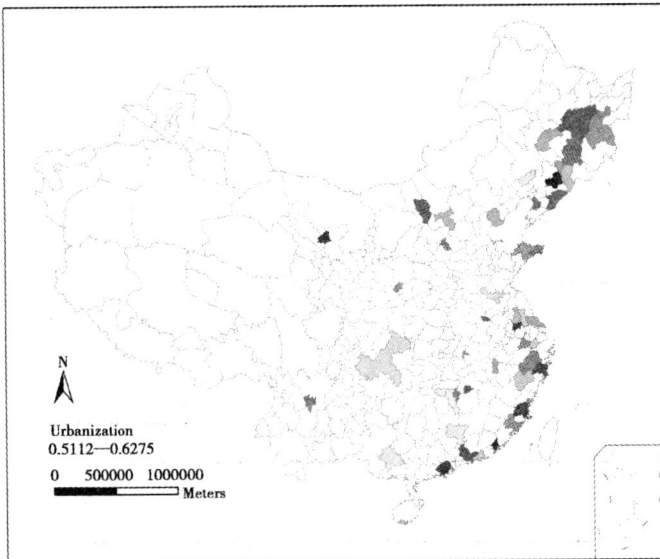

Figure 51　Distribution diagram of prefecture-level cities in middle and high urbanization stage

5.1.5 Relatively high urbanization stage(≧ 62.80%)

The cities with relatively high urbanization level in our country are mainly concentrated in eastern area with proportion up to 42.86%. Both middle area and northeast area have 9 prefecture-level cities respectively entered this stage. The western area has 14 cities reached high urbanization level, which are mainly provincial capitals or resource type cities.

Table 9   Regional distribution differences of prefecture-level cities in relatively high urbanization stage in 2010

	Eastern area	Northeast area	Middle area	Western area
Relatively high urbanization stage (≧ 62.80%)	42.86%	16.07%	16.07%	25.00%

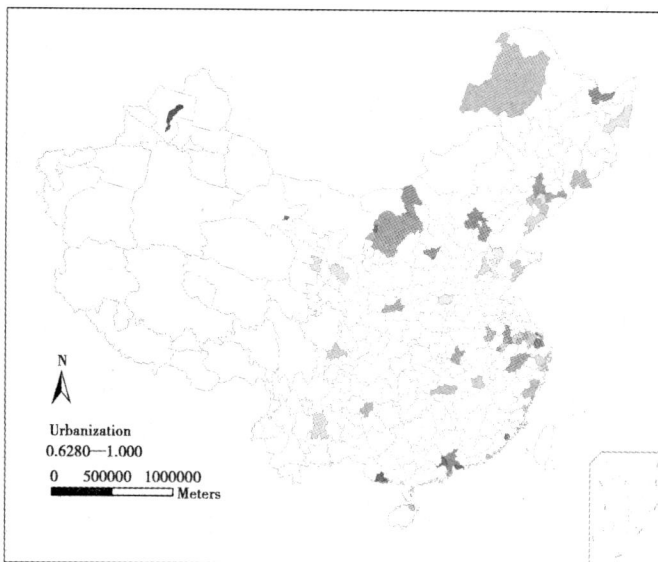

Urbanization
0.6280—1.000

0   500000   1000000
Meters

Figure 52   Distribution diagram of prefecture-level cities in relatively high urbanization stage

5.2   Analysis of difference of public service in different urbanization stages

5.2.1   Introduction of public service indicator system

In order to research the difference of type and input of public service in different urbanization stages, this study has divided public service into five subsystems including health care, education, transportation, culture and social security. In the health care subsystem, the number of beds in hospital and health center per 10 thousand people and the number of doctors per 10 thousand people are taken as evaluation indicators; In the education subsystem, number of teachers per 10 thousand students in middle school and number of teachers per 10 thousand students in primary school are taken as the evaluation indicators; In the transportation system, per capita urban road area and number of buses per 10 thousand people are taken as the evaluation indicators; In the culture subsystem, the number of theaters and cinemas per million people and number of books in public library per hundred people are taken as evaluation indicators; In the social security indicator, the participating coverage rate of endowment insurance, medical insurance and unemployment insurance as taken as evaluation indicators.

In subsequent analysis, in order to eliminate the difference caused by dimensional difference on indicator contribution, standardized processing on various indicators is carried out by using regulated method in this report. The standardized formula is as follow:

$$X_{STD} = \left(\frac{x_i - min(x_j)}{max(x_j) - min(x_j)} \right) \times 100$$

Thereafter assuming indicator weights are same, the indicators after dimensional processing are added to obtain the scores of different systems. In order to eliminate the influence on score due to different indicator number under different systems, the standardization processing is conducted again on the score of system with same processing measure. Finally the score threshold values of public service system obtained are distributed between 0—100.

5. 2. 2 Descriptive statistical analysis of public service in different urbanization stages

This section has carried out descriptive statistical analysis on five kinds of public service subsystems in different urbanization stages, and it has inspected the influence of various public services on urbanization rate by using one-way analysis of variance method. It is found according to F inspection result that all public services all have significant impacts on urbanization rate. In addition, the statistical analysis finds that our country's public service and urbanization have following 3 main characteristics in prefecture-level city scale:

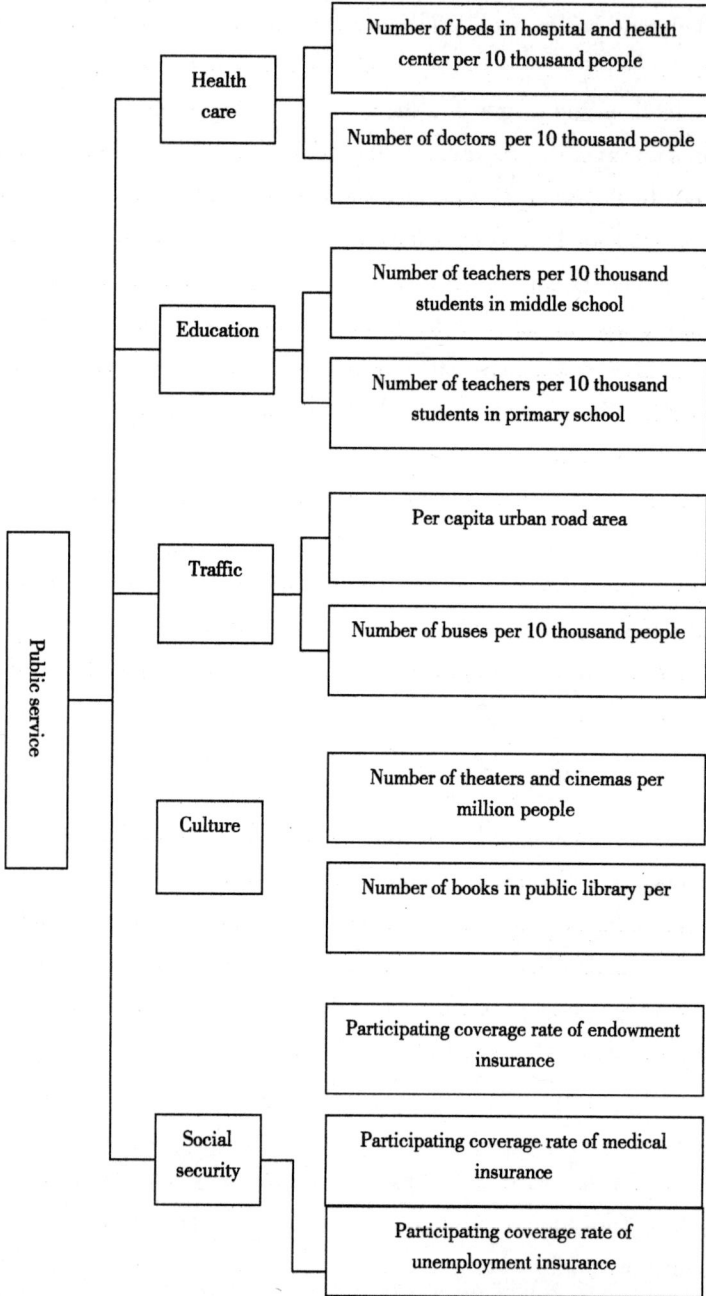

Figure 53   Public service indicator system

① The public service input categories in different urbanization stages have significant difference

In the relatively low urbanization level stage, the inputs in education and medical system in public service are the largest, while the emphasis extent of social security is seriously insufficient. Up to relatively high urbanization stage, the inputs of various public services all appear increasing tendency.

In the stage with relatively high urbanization level, the input of education system in public service begins to descend and the average input value of education system of cities in this stage is lower than cities in middle urbanization stage. In contrast, the inputs of cities with relatively high urbanization level in health care, traffic, culture and social security system show dramatic growth.

② The increase extents of public service input in different urbanization stage are different

Generally the input of our country's public service appears to experience a rapid increase period and a stable increase period, then another rapid increase period from relatively low urbanization stage to relatively high urbanization stage. This is because that it is related to the different purpose of public service input in different urbanization stages. In relatively low urbanization stage, public service more focus on satisfying the demand of citizens on basic public service during the rapid development process of urbanization. Along with the continuous promotion of urbanization level, the problem of insufficient public service is gradually relieved so that, high quality and humanized public service gradually become the focus of public service input instead. Thus the rapid increase of public service input of government is improved in relatively high urbanization development stage.

③ Along with the promotion of urbanization level, the gap of public service input among cities is gradually increased.

It can be seen from the analysis results of public service standard deviation in different urbanization stages that along with the promotion of urbanization level, the gap of various kinds of public services among cities gradually increase. In the aspect of urbanization stage, it can be seen that public service input gap among cities in relatively high urbanization stage is the largest. In the aspect of type of public service, it can be seen that the gap of medical system and education system input among different cities is the largest; in contrast, the gap of social security input among cities is the smallest.

Table10 Descriptive statistics of public service in different urbanization stage in our country in 2010 and result of single-factor variance analysis

		Average Value	Standard deviation	Minimum value	Maximum value	Fvalue inspection
Health care	Relatively low urbanization stage	21.31	14.15	1.59	69.71	30.49 ***
	Middle and low urbanization stage	27.60	11.93	5.95	58.36	
	Middle urbanization stage	32.27	14.63	0.00	100.00	
	Middle and high urbanization stage	36.51	14.08	0.45	72.98	
	Relatively high urbanization stage	50.19	18.16	8.60	91.10	
	Total	33.57	17.57	0.00	100.00	
Education	Relatively low urbanization stage	23.84	14.08	0.00	64.38	8.55 ***
	Middle and low urbanization stage	32.18	16.29	3.25	80.96	
	Middle urbanization stage	38.47	17.56	3.53	98.25	
	Middle and high urbanization stage	41.38	21.38	2.96	99.79	
	Relatively high urbanization stage	39.02	20.48	0.54	100.00	
	Total	34.98	19.11	0.00	100.00	
Traffic	Relatively low urbanization stage	6.65	4.38	0.00	17.97	18.15 ***
	Middle and low urbanization stage	10.81	6.77	2.03	36.01	
	Middle urbanization stage	13.56	6.71	2.76	29.62	
	Middle and high urbanization stage	14.49	6.10	5.48	33.95	
	Relatively high urbanization stage	20.03	15.08	4.29	100.00	
	Total	13.11	9.66	0.00	100.00	
Culture	Relatively low urbanization stage	6.47	4.30	0.00	22.43	17.67 ***
	Middle and low urbanization stage	7.13	4.62	1.76	25.64	
	Middle urbanization stage	10.34	9.23	2.33	54.93	
	Middle and high urbanization stage	11.13	7.05	1.99	38.34	
	Relatively high urbanization stage	20.89	18.83	3.77	100.00	
	Total	11.19	11.45	0.00	100.00	
Social security	Relatively low urbanization stage	1.83	1.16	0.00	5.02	33.67 ***
	Middle and low urbanization stage	3.07	1.33	0.51	6.32	
	Middle urbanization stage	4.57	2.04	1.70	13.02	
	Middle and high urbanization stage	6.78	3.30	1.67	15.63	
	Relatively high urbanization stage	16.87	16.83	3.90	100.00	
	Total	6.62	9.41	0.00	100.00	

Finspection is also called as homogeneity of variance inspection. Study assumption is that two parts of variance inside general body are not equal, while null assumption is that these two parts of variance are equal. If the F value calculated is greater than the critical value regulated under certain significant level, then it should deny the null assumption, indicating that the two parts of variance inside general body are not equal, i. e. no consistent or the difference is obvious; conversely it will accept null assumption, i. e. recognize that two parts of variance inside general body are equal or they are consistent. [1]

$p < 0.001$, indicate that the difference of average value is obvious on 99. 9% confidence level, i. e. The possibility of having significant difference is 99. 9%. Generally $0.01 < P < 0.05$ indicates significant difference, $P < 0.01$ indicates extremely significant difference. The same below.

5. 3 Empirical analysis of urban public service and urbanization

5. 3. 1 Model setting and variable description

This paper selects quantile regression model to carry out analysis on public service in the purpose of dividing different impacts of various factors in different prefecture-level cities and different urbanization stages on public service. The thought of quantiles regression was introduced into economic analysis by Koenker and Bassett(1978) [2], and it is a kind of extension of traditional general ordinary least squares(OLS). OLS is used to estimate the effects of independent variable on average number of dependent variable condition in the assumption that the effects of independent variable at different distribution points. But quantile regression is a kind of general estimation method, taking weighted mean absolute error as target function to carry out estimation on regression coefficient, so as to observe different functioning extent of independent variable on different quantile[3].

Comparing to least square estimation, quantile regression has two advantages. I. using least square estimation method to carry out estimation, its result

---

① Five points division method is a kind of analysis method in statistics. It is processed by arranging all data from small to big, and conducting segmentations at percentile of 20, 40, 60 and 80 to divide all data into 5 groups.

② Koenker, R. and G, Bassett (1978) Regression Quantiles, *Econometrica*, 46(3): 33 – 50.

③ Chen Zhenzhen, You Jiaxing (2009), Factor analysis on the income level of off – farm workers based on quantile regression, *Statistical Research*, 26(6): 79 – 84.

only reflects the effects of explanatory variable corresponding variable on average value of conditional distribution; but quantile regression allows the regression parameters in study to change according to different quantiles of dependent variable. It is no longer limited in relatively simple function formula, and it is conducive to carry out more detailed analysis on regression relation between phenomena. II. It does not carry out specific assumption on error term distribution; it has relatively strong resistance on non-normal distribution or abnormal value. Therefore, its estimation result is more stable [1].

This paper takes urbanization rate as independent variable, with GDP and industrialization rate as control variables. The regression is carried out on the quintiles of 20%, 40%, 60% and 80% of public service; therefore analysis could be carried out on different distribution positions of public service input condition. Through conducting more detailed description on difference of different quantiles of public service, we can understand the relation of public service and urbanization development level in deeper extent.

Where, for standard result of data of dependent variable public service is based on score aggregation of five subsystems including health care, education, transportation, culture and social security divided according to above public service, and its score threshold is within 0—100. Independent variable urbanization rate follows the result of prefecture-level city urbanization rate in above texts; the control variable GDP and industrialization rate are respectively regional total output value of all prefecture-level cities, and the proportion of second industry output value in total output value. The specific descriptive statistical analysis results are shown in the following table:

Table 11   The descriptive statistical analysis results of variable

Variable	Sample capacity	Average Value	Standard deviation	Minimum value	Maximum value
Public service	280	29.13	14.60	0	100
Urbanization rate (%)	280	0.50	0.15	0.14	1
GDP (one hundred million Yuan)	280	1520	2010	104.028	17200
Industrialization rate (%)	280	50.97	10.69	17.12	89.75

① Zhang Weiying, Zhou Li – an, Gu Quan – lin (2005), The growth of high – new – tech firms and its determinants: An application of the quantile regression model, *Management World*, 10: 94 – 101.

5. 3. 2 Model result analysis

Following conclusions are obtained through quantiles regression analysis of public service.

① Under the condition of controlling GDP of various cities and industrialization, urbanization level still has obvious positive impact on public service; along with the promotion of urbanization level, the input of public service appears rising tendency. This is consistent with above descriptive analysis result.

② Along with the promotion of urbanization level, the pulling capability of urbanization rate on public service appears "reversed U" type tendency. Generally the average value of pulling function of our country's prefecture-level city urbanization on public service is 32. 96, which has difference with the result of different quantile regression. Where, in 20%, 40%, 60% and 80% quantiles regression, the influence of urbanization level on public service are respectively 28. 73, 33. 57, 36. 00 and 35. 81. At 60% quantile regression of pubic service, i. e. it appears the turning point of public service around urbanization level of 51%.

Table 12   Quantile regression result of public service

	Quantile regression				OLS
	0. 2 quantile	0. 4quantile	0. 6quantile	0. 8quantile	
Ln(urbanization rate)	28. 73 ***	33. 57 ***	36. 00 ***	35. 81 ***	32. 96 ***
Ln(GDP)	1. 18	−0. 15	−0. 15	−1. 18	0. 46
Ln(Industrialization rate)	0. 30	1. 39	−0. 39	−7. 74	−2. 58
Constant term	21. 96	47. 79 **	61. 27 ***	112. 3 ***	56. 02 **
Sample capacity	280	280	280	280	280
Pseudo R2	0. 25	0. 28	0. 29	0. 30	0. 45

$^{*}p < 0. 01$, $^{**}p < 0. 005$, $^{***}p < 0. 001$.

5. 4   New requirements on public service in new urbanization development stage

5. 4. 1   Basic interpretation and current status overview

The general standard of evaluating modern city development level is urban development achievement that urban residents can enjoy, which is also called as quantity and quality of public service. UNCHS has provided out in the "Urban Management" declaration issued in Nairobi in 2001 that complete management must let all people whether male or female can obtain benefit of urban citizen. Through complete urban management, the citizen can display their talent and fully give play to their capabilities; therefore it can fully improve their social and economic status.

In above chapter it always emphasize on public service, which means to satisfy certain specific and direct requirements of citizen in narrow sense, such as basic necessities of life, production, life, development, entertainment, etc. It does not include some function activities included in broad sense public services engaged by government such as economic adjustment, market supervision, social management, etc, so it is more suitable to the concept of basic public service.

The "Twelfth five-year plan" has in the first time carried out concept demarcation on basic public service, which means public service that is built on the basis of certain social common sense and is provided by government, and also it adapts to economic social development level and stage, in the purpose of guaranteeing basic demands of all people's survival and development. Meanwhile, it is proposed on the basis that it should gradually improve the equalization of basic public service, i. e.. all people can fairly and possibly obtain roughly equal basic public service.

The realization of basic public service is firstly based on development level of current economic society; secondly it is based on government's current basic financial state and the available basic support. It can be understand from the point of government supply main body that the public service scope and level provided by government directly affect residents' benefit level and specific existing status.

In the scale of prefecture-level city and above level in our country, the comprehensive development level of city include economic strength and urbanization speed etc. , which affects the input of government on basic public service in many aspects and in large extent. On one hand, as stated in above analysis, for cities that urbanization rate reach 60%—70% and above, the expense and scale of government on social security, education, health care etc. are all obviously higher than cities in relatively low urbanization rate. We have also found that in these high urbanization rate cities that inputs are basically in relatively high level, however there are also some indicators existing many slightly high

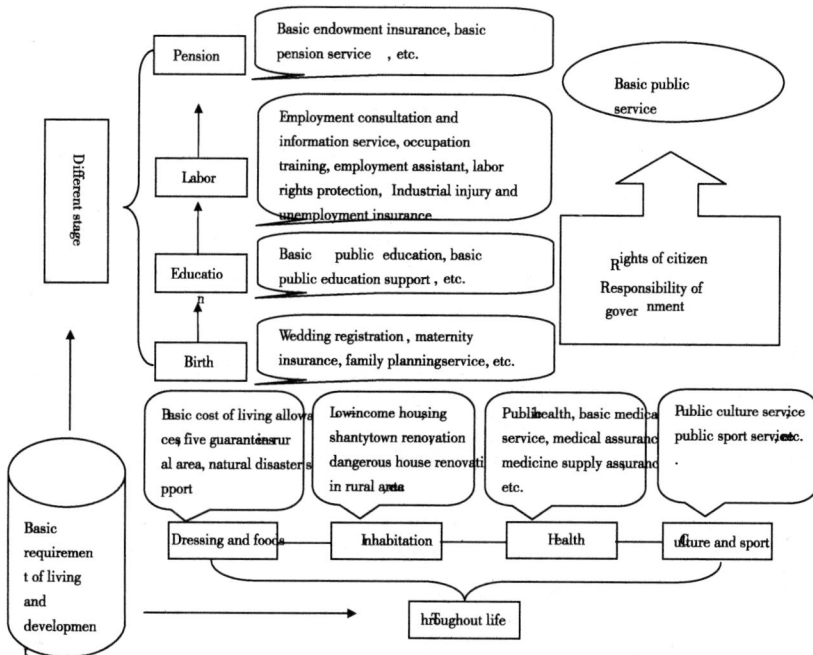

Different stage

Pension — Basic endowment insurance, basic pension service , etc.

Labor — Employment consultation and information service, occupation training, employment assistant, labor rights protection, Industrial injury and unemployment insurance

Educatio n — Basic public education, basic public education support , etc.

Birth — Wedding registration , maternity insurance, family planningservice, etc.

Basic public service

Rights of citizen
Responsibility of gover nment

Basic requiremen t of living and developmen t

Basic cost of living allowan ces,five guarantees,rur al area, natural disasters su pport

Lowincome housing shantytown renovation dangerous house renovati in rural area

Publichealth, basic medical service, medical assurance medicine supply assurance etc.

Public culture service public sport serviceetc.

Dressing and foods — Inhabitation — Health — Culture and sport

Throughout life

Figure54   Connotation of basic public service scope
of the "Twelfth five-year plan "

value and slightly low value, the difference among cities are quite obvious; but such kind of difference has no obvious performance on the aspects such as urban road area, number of buses, infrastructure construction and social insurance, etc. Along with the increase of urbanization rate, they all appear rising tendency in different extents. On the other hand, among economic growth (we usually u-ses per capita GDP indicator), economic development(we usually uses per capita disposable income indicator of residents in rural and urban area) and basic pub-lic service, a kind of mutual functioning relation also exists, especially in recent years, the economic growth and basic public service all appear high relevance, in contrast, the correlation with economic development is weaker. Therefore, the three items do not simply observe a kind of logical relation, i. e. once the economic development in one region or city is in good status, and the public fis-cal capacity increases accordingly, then the basic public service will rise accord-ingly, and vice versa . This has proved in one aspect that the growth of economy does not absolutely represent the development of economy. Under our country's current government oriented and urban management system, the central government does not has clear boundaries with local governments on fiscal transfer, demarcation and division of basic public service right and expense responsibility. If it wants to gradually shorten regional difference and realize the coordinated development among economic development and growth, economic strength and public service, there is still a long way.

5.4.2 Development requirement under new stage

In fact, the marketization and urbanization process of our country have provided out objective requirements on government transformation, i. e. transformation from economic construction type government after 1980s to modern "public service type government" [①], and this has already became the basic objective of our country's new round of government reform. The occurring of service type social management mode firmly will require changing of government function, in which public service has became the core value in service type social management mode, and its connotation and extension also should reach the level with richer contents.

Under the influence of western public goods theory, the demarcation of our country on public service is mostly based on material characteristic; it believes that public service is to provide public product and service. Current theory section prefers to define public service by behavior style, i. e. from the aspect of public management, the matters involving serving the public and the activity process of responding difference demands of public are collectively referred to as public service. It can be seen from this point that the boundary of public service and public management is not clear, and under the limitation of different standards and points of view, the two will show different relation.

America's administrative expert Denhardt proposed new public service theory, the core idea of which is to place the people into the center of whole management system. It claims to response on the benefits of society and public actively,

---

① The concept "Public service type government" is provided out during the process of our country's administrative reform in1998, replacing controlling type government model. In 2004, premier Wen Jiabao officially provided out the problem of construction of service type government in a speech of Central Party School, indicating that the theory discussion of service type government begins to turn to practice. Comparing to another China style theme "service type government", it pays more attention to the function of government providing public service.

timely and responsibly; it emphasizes that the government's governing role should be service rather than navigation; it believes that the mechanism of realizing policy objective should focus on establishment of union among public, individual and none-profit organization in the purpose of satisfing consistent requirements, i. e. the establishment of multi-center social management structure. Meanwhile it advocates and cultivates active citizen spirit, and emphasizes that citizen should actively participate into public affairs. Robert Rosenblum has proposed a kind of Multiple administrative concept, in which new public management and new public service are incorporated, they have either contrasting or mutual influence. His management route includes traditional management route and new public management route. He has proposed that the urgent task of current public administration is to carry out integration on value, structure, procedure management and technical method possessed by three kinds of different research routes: politics, management and law.

The development status of all countries have already indicated that even they are in different national conditions and systems, public services appeare their respect defects in three fields: Nationalization, marketization and socialization, and no independent organization or action can have sufficient resource and strength to solve all public problems. Under the background of being impossible to let informatization, globalization and government managing all public affairs, public service should emphasize on democracy of public affair management concept, diversity of management bodies and variety of management modes, aiming to solve public issues that can not be solved by independent market bodies. Its implied value judgment is that what things must be provided by government and what things should be completed by external subjects rather than government. Finally the public service subjects must cooperate to form a kind of complex and interactive social management structure.

6 Conclusion

No matter it is public service or public management, its essence should be serve public interests. The authority of government is from the assignment of public. The premise of this assignment is that the government should provide better service in order to better satisfy public interest; this process requires public to observe relevant laws and regulations, as well as various public policies stipulated by government according public interest at same time. Both shall form a kind of bilateral relation of social contract accordingly, they either can be constrained mutually or can be existed together. As the most important public department, government should play a role on regulating and coordinating when there is contradiction or conflict on public caused by satisfying personnel demand. ①

Our government always emphasizes accelerating construction of basic public service system covering all social members in recent years; it gradually realizes equalization of basic public service in the purpose of realizing above objectives and reducing unfairness in society, as well as narrowing the gap between rich and poor. But the public demands are changed along with the economic and social development, even in same time section; there should be large difference among rural-urban area, region, individual or group, so it is far from satisfying the demand of maintaining social stability if it only carries out improvement and promotion from the aspect of material production and provision. In fact, there were still a lot of aspects needed to be improved in current public management and service system, furthermore it has exposed various social problems due to this.

After entering 21 century, our country begins to entering developing type society. With the deepening of social reform and the readjustment of economic structure, interest pattern has changed dramatically. Objectively the public service of our country currently has not realized public. During this period, the contradiction among full and rapid increasing of public demands of social members, public goods shortage, poor basic public service is gradually prominent. The old income allocation system and uneven occupation of capital lead to continuously enlargement of gap between the rich and the poor. Some people is lacking of corresponding bearing capability, which causes imbalance social mentality, thus cause a series of social problems. Chongqing Wanzhou event happened in 2004; On July 1, 2008, the case of Yangjia entering Shanghai Chabei police office to murder 6 people; Menglian event happened in same year; Police and citizen conflict happened in the same year in Shanjiang town, Guangdong ; " Ancient lane event " in Chao'an county of Guangzhou in June, 2012; " 9· 21 Wukan village even" in 2011; On August 25, 2012, Large-scale conflict happened in Suining, Sichuan etc. for these so called social group events on hot layout of va-

---

① Xue Lan(2012), Serve is The Core of Public Administration[J], *Outlook Weekly*.

rious media, if you want to find out the reasons, the reasons include that in a series of social reform, their profits are damaged but they can not obtain proper compensation, the profits they deserved can not be obtained for some reasons, more direct factors should be that many people believe that the public service or interest they deserved have not been obtained or even have not been satisfied, such kind of dissatisfaction may be settled down, once any blasting fuse is touched, it may cause intensive contradiction and conflict.

The transformation currently in our country is transformation of government essentially; public management (service) is the soul of this major transformation. From central government to local government, all level of government must be able to actively and effectively response such kind of dynamic and various demands, as well as greatly improve public management and service innovation. Through promotion of public service supply level and capability, enhance the citizen and fair consciousness of public, train inclusive, self-discipline and dedicative behavior consciousness, so as to really realize social justice.

Given this, our annual report has prepared three special reports for relevant problems faced by government in the transformation process of public management and service field. It is expected to provide some reference for policy preparation during the transformation process of various level of government from point to area.

(Director: Yang Xu, Yuan Chongfa, Bai Nanfeng; Author: Zheng Ying, Ding Yu, Xiang Yizhi, Li Yan, Wang Ting, Wang Lu, Bai Nanfeng; Statistic Analyst: Li Yan, Zheng Ying, Liu Zhihe, Wang Ting; Data Processor: Liu Zhihe, Zheng Ying, An Di, Zhang Wenning, Tian Mei)

On the Development of Urban Community in China

1 Preface

Since reforming and opening-up, in addition to government institutions and large state-owned enterprises, the system of unit ownership has basically disintegrated. China has rapidly changed from unit society to individualized society. With China's rapid urbanization process, a large foreign population rushed into cities, which has accelerated this change. Then, the problems that urban public service and management faced with have become increasingly important, and the difficult position and transformation of basic society management is the focus of these problems. In some way, the benign development of public service and management relates to the prospect of urbanization, social harmony as well as economic growth and social improvement of the entire country, which is the non-negligible link in the system of reform and urbanization process.

As for the public service and social management of cities in new China, it focuses on system of unit with system of neighborhood committee's supplemented before reforming and opening-up. With disintegration of system of unit, it has naturally changed to system of neighborhood committee. Non-adaptability and limitation of system of neighborhood committee occurring during rapid urbanization process cause the generation of system of community. At present, the basic social management of the city is in the transition stage of system of neighborhood committee to system of community.

Every change is an institutional innovation. Institutional innovation is a process; with development and reform of the society, non-adaptability of the original system is increasingly outstanding, social problems and contradictions continuously accumulate to form the demand of institutional innovation. During the institutional innovation, due to the trial and error mechanism, social change as well as diversity and complexity of different interest groups, the new problems will continue to occur. It requires an continuous institutional innovation process in certain period, especially in the transition stage of these two systems.

Research on Urban Community task group of China Urban Development Academy has carried out preliminary investigation on the innovation situation of management system of urban basic society in China. It is believed in the research the system of neighborhood committee that was taken as auxiliary management method of system of unit that was not satisfactory when forced to become the mainstream social management system after disintegration of the system of unit ownership. With the progress of urbanization, the horizontal flow of population has increased largely, and people's separation between household registered and actual residences has become the normal conditions; the basic social management of system of neighborhood committee is increasingly difficult. At the same time, the emergence of commercial housing has created numerous owners, and property right consciousness and self-awareness derived from the property right are increasingly strong. All these have constituted the challenge to the traditional system of neighborhood committee. The central and local governments actively explore and reform the system of basic social management, thus system of community is generated. However, because of inertia of traditional system and thinking, current system of community still has many problems, and many aspects still follow the practices of system of neighborhood committee, thus to result in low public service and management efficiency and serious waste of resources. The channel for communication between residents and government is not smooth, which has unstable factors.

Only by continuous institutional innovation can constantly improve the new management system of urban basic society. We believe that innovation of community management system should have long-term strategic vision, while not only taking stop-gap measures, to avoid unilateral solution for problems. Therefore, we should base on the principles of service management integration, marketization, residents self-management, small government and big society and advancing with the times.

2 Changes in Management System of Urban Basic Society in China

After founding of new China, the management model of strong-government and weak-society is established, resulting in the government's undertaking and control of all the social life. Under this background, urban basic society in China had gradually established the *two-line* management system, which focuses on system of unit with sub-strict committee system (hereinafter referred to as system of neighborhood committee) . One line was *government-unit-worker*; the other line was *government-sub-strict office-neighborhood committee*. The public goods and services required by residents of working unit were mostly provided and mainly governed by the unit; while personnel without unit such as social idlers, housewifves, people with social special care and civil relief were included into the jurisdiction range of sub-strict offices and committees. The system of unit ownership and system of neighborhood committee constituted the basic framework of urban social management system, and thus to realize the strong control of national political power to urban basic society through the classified management of all the social members of the city. With formation of nationalization and planned economy system, basic social management system focusing on system of unit with system of neighborhood committee supplemented had been popularized and established in China to become the main component of urban social management system in China and play an important role in the maintenance of urban economic and social life.

After reforming and opening-up, China has experienced changes in economic system and the society, and the system of unit ownership is broken gradually. The unit management model tends to be failed. System of neighborhood committee is facing numerous realistic difficulties due to huge change in basic society, and thus to fall into the management puzzle. Therefore, urban basic society urgently requires a new organizational form and institutional arrangement to solve various problems and contradictions occurring in the society, and undertake the function of re-integrating the society. The occurrence of system of community has changed the concept and method of traditional urban basic society management, which will play larger and larger role in development of urban society in the future China.

2. 1　Origin of System of Unit and Its End of History

System of unit was an important institutional arrangement in urban social management in our country after founding of new China. The unit was a special organization form set to adapt to the planned economic system, which integrated the functions of politics, economy and society. ①. Under the planned economy system, the system of unit ownership played an important function in resources allocation, social mobilization, meeting people's needs and realization of social stability. It also seriously restricted the self-development space of social economy, social organizations and individuals, and limited the social mobility to form the highly dependent of social structure (*two in one* of social organization and unit society) , and made the nation and economy bear the heavy social load. After reforming and opening-up, the ownership structure changed, socialistic market economy system is gradually established, social mobility rapidly increases, and the function and position of system of unit are constantly weakened, and thus to finally result in basic disintegration of system of unit.

2. 1. 1   Origin and Development of System of Unit

2. 1. 1. 1   Development Stages of System of Unit

Being the main institutional form of urban management in China under planned economy system, the generation, establishment and development of system of unit can be divided into the following four stages②③:

(1) The exploration and initial formation period of system of unit (1948— 1953). During the revolutionary war, it gradually formed a set of special management system (i. e. public officers' management) in rural revolutionary base to execute the supply system for public officers focusing on Communist Party of China, including members in party groups, army, political institutions and public enterprises. This had accumulated referential system model for formation of system of unit after founding of new China. After founding of new China, to complete the socialist reform, establish the new social economic system, centralize scheduling and use the limited social and economic resources to realize the industrialization rapidly, the focus of work was transformed from village to city. Based on base experience and Soviet model, combining the specific conditions

①　He Haibing. Changes in Management System of Urban Basic Society in China: From system of unit, system of neighborhood committee to system of community[J] . *Management World*, 2003(6).

②　Tian Yipeng. Origin and Formation of "Typical System of Unit"[J] . *Jilin University Journal*, Social Sciences Edition, 2007, (4).

③　Zhou Yuhong. Study on Institutional Reform of Urban Community in China[M] . China Financial and Economic Publishing House, 2010(12).

in early period of northeast liberation and taking the lead in finding out a set of model and experience in receiving and managing cities and enterprises in Northeast China, the system of unit ownership society of state-unit-individual was formed, and thus to reconstruct the old society and realize the new social integration through re-systematization of the society.

(2) Formation period of system of unit (1953—1956). With completion of three great transformations of new China, China had gradually established the ownership structure in which the public ownership took dominant position and highly centralized planned economic system. System of unit had gradually developed to main form of urban management with its highly integrated society and resource control function, and since then, system of unit in China had been basically established all over the country. China had formed the social organization system of state-unit-individual and the economic system with large state-owned enterprises as the subjects, and thus to lay the foundation for socialist country.

(3) Comprehensive promotion period of system of unit (1956-reforming and opening-up). With advanced completion of socialist transformation, especially several hundred million farmers were quickly organized into the cooperatives and people's commune to start the expansion of system of unit to rural areas. The production brigade or production team of the people's commune was the basic unit of the rural social system, which organized the farmer organizations into the unit through the people's commune movement quickly, which is evaluated by the work-point system that is similar to unified wage system. The people's commune movemen has important impact on the urban management at that time, which incorporateed workers' families except those in public institutions and other idle personnel into the system of unit ownerships through district offices and substrict collective enterprises, and thus to form the completely institutionalized pattern of the urban city.

(4) Decline of system of unit and its period of walking towards disintegration (after reforming and opening-up). After reforming and opening-up, with transition from planned economy system to market economy system, the system of unit ownership faced the huge impact. The public services, welfare and management functions of the unit were continuously weakened and stripped, and the unit's control of its members was severely weakened. The unit was bankruptcy, restructuring and reorganization, and various non-public enterprises and social u-

nit were emerged which was beyond the system of unit ownership; thus, a large number of unit members flowed outside of the system, and the proportion of the increased population to the system is increasingly reduced. Foreign population flooded into the city with sudden increase in non-unit personnel. These changes eventually led to the disintegration of unit society.

2.1.1.2　Causes for Establishment and Development of System of Unit

System of unit was a special type form of social organization formed during the early period after the founding of new China. The reason was that it was related to political, economic, social environment and system at that time as well as Chinese traditional clan culture in essence. It was the highly centralization and organization in politics, planned system in economics and clan system in the history, and thus to provide demand and foundation for system of unit. [1]

First, system of unit met the requirements of promoting social integration with politics at that time. After the Opium War, the control of Chinese traditional society and integration mechanism successively disintegrated. After the overthrow of the Qing Dynasty, China not only failed to establish the strong, unified central or modernization oriented political system, but also fell into mess by warlordism and strong foreign powers' invasion. At the same time, with the introduction of the western democratic ideas, the integration mechanism of traditional society based on Confucian ethics was impacted continuously. Facing the prevailing severe social economic and military situation of home and abroad, one of the choices was to promote social integration by political integration, and change the social status of disordered situation depending on highly organized and centralized political system and its strong abilities in resource mobilization, allocation and scheduling. [2]The demand on social integration and control promoted the generation of system of unit, and the political system highly centralized in superior to subordinate level ranking provided the political basis for system of unit.

Secondly, the planned economy system is the economic basis for existence of system of unit. The destruction for many years due to war resulted in serious damages to Chinese economy order, especially after founding of new China, various problems appeared: budget deficit, inflation, mass unemployment and ram-

①　Zhang Rong. Disintegration of System of Unit[J]. *Social Sciences Review*, 2009(8).

②　Jie Aihua. The Unit: A Type of Special Social Life Scope[J]. *Journal of Zhejiang University*, 2000(5).

pant business speculations; thus, the resources required for modernization were scare and dispersed[1]. At that time, the government must consider how to realize industrial objective on such poor basis. In order to eentralize the social resource, China established the planned economy system oriented with public ownership and mainly featured with national powerful monopoly and control under the influence on Soviet model, , which provided the national basis for realization of resource allocation through the organization form of enterprises and institutions.

Thirdly, Chinese traditional clan system is social basis and cultural basis for generation and existence of system of unit. For a long time, Chinese traditional society, which provides not only basis for social system of system of unit but also the basis for cultural psychology. always depends on clan and ethics relations advocated by Confucian to define the social order, The unit has the responsibility for comprehensive management of unit members and obligations for life service of unit members, which owns the unit members' strong dependence and authoritative identity due to its resource allocation power and level order. This is extremely similar to functions and culture of traditional clan[2]. The inheritance between the two makes people accept the existence of system of unit naturally due to habit psychology.

It can be seen that system of unit was a type of social organization structure and institutional arrangement based on politics, economy, society and culture. And at that time it's correspond to the political, economic, social and cultural needs in China, which will change with changes in politics, economy, society and culture.

2.1.2 Advantages and Disadvantages of System of Unit

Being the social management mode once existing for a long time, system of unit played an important role in the situation from chaos to governance, and its ability in integration and management of political, economic and social resources is outstanding. However, it is like the two sides of a coin, and its advantages are just its shortcomings.

First, system of unit incorporates most urban individuals into the jurisdic-

---

① Zhang Rong. Disintegration of System of Unit[J]. *Social Sciences Review*, 2009(8).

② Jin Yuanjun. Discussion on Negative Impact of Social Function of System of Unit on Community Construction[J]. *Journal of Shanxi College for Youth Administrators*, 2003(1).

tion range of the unit to ensure high efficiency in resource scheduling and allocation, and ensure the effectiveness of management and social control. However,
this also caused limitations to the individual development and living
space. What's more, tiny possibility of the people's horizontal mobility, limited in
the unit before vertically mobilized to top leaders of the unit. While, improvement of political status, economic status and social status of each person mainly
depended on his own superior of the unit. As time passes, people have developed the psychological characteristics and behavior habit that they were only responsible for the superiors but not the personnel at equal level with poor self-discipline and self-management ability, and thus social negotiation, interaction
consciousness and ability were greatly affected. Some people were depressed in
personality at the unit, but defied laws outside the unit. This point has been still
obvious in today-many years since disintegration of system of unit, which also
leave difficulties in new social management mode established based on the market economy.

Second, the unit undertook most public services and social welfare functions in system of unit, and the unit was responsible for the illness and death of
staff. In the extra large state-owned enterprises, the staff could stay within the
unit at their birth, nursery, kindergarten, primary school, junior high school,
technical school, work, retirement, until his death. The public services and
welfare functions comprehensively included in system of unit, and the resource
allocation of the above limited mobility as well as the management functions were
integrated, and thus to ensure the coverage and average of public services and
welfare in the urban residents, and also causeed the strong personal attachment.
The result was serious weakening of people's sense of independence and independent living ability. In the economic reform, a number of large state-owned
enterprises did not adapt to the market and stopped the production (or half stop
production), and the cases in which tens of thousands of workers waiting for
government relief were common Ensuring the workers' life was the obligation of
the unit compulsory, so it was natural to find the unit for solutions. If the unit
failed to solve the problem, asked the government for help; thus some groups e-
vents happen this way. This behavior of wait, dependence and request is the dependence psychology that like a child would cry for the milk, which has also
formed the left problems in the social management after disintegration of the so-

ciety.

Third, the unit in system of unit was the government's embodiment and representative,. Unless the abnormal things like lawsuit. people are not directly dealing with the government, This results in flat social management. The management system of the whole society included only two levels-individual and unit (government delegate). At the same time, due to the unit's undertaking all things, the management system of the whole society was too narrow. For employment population, the unit was the unique leg of the government, and all the reports and assignations were completed through the unit. This ensured the simple and efficient social management and full overage of social mobilization, but seriously hindered the development of social organizations especially the intermediate organization. In fact, the government did not require intermediate organization, and everything could be completed through the unit. The social consultation and provision of service function of intermediate organization were taken by special agencies or personnel in the unit. This caused China seriously lacks social intermediate organizations, which had impact on the formation and development of new social management system based on the market system after disintegration of system of unit.

Either success or failure boils down to the same person. This is not the fault of system of unit, but the destiny of any one system replacing the old one. The non-adaptability of old system appears just because of changes in social and economic environment, and thus the new system emerges as required. While the previous advantages of the old system just cause the non-adaptability, which is the object to be changed by the new system. Therefore, for new system, advantages of the old system are often disadvantages. This will not obstruct the contributions the system of unit ownership has made in the history.

2.1.3 Elimination and Disintegration of System of Unit

With reforming & opening-up and urbanization, Chinese society has changed drastically, and the ownership structure has changed; thus, a large number of private enterprises and individual operators have emerged as well as non-state-owned units. Since then, people were no longer bound in the original unit, and many people escaped from the system, most of which went to other cities. In case of restructuring, reorganization or bankrupt of state-owned enterprises, the staff earned their own living and moved towards the society. A large number of farmers flooded into the city, undertook private enterprises, worked in non state-owned units, or held temporary posts in state-owned units. Social mobility has become to be more and more frequent, and more people had no u-nits or long-term fixed units. The de-unitization trend has become increasingly obvious, and system of unit has lost survival soil, whose position and function are increasingly weakened.

Since the mobility and combination of element are increasingly free after reform, the state-owned units lose its monopoly and control of resources, especially the comprehensive control of people. Two-way selection of employment has gradually become the social norm. On the other hand, the enterprise reform and market competition enable the state-owned enterprises to give up the mode of enterprises running the society. The state-owned enterprises have gradually become the pure economic units and get close to the real enterprises with the main objective of profits. Finally, in addition to those conditions remaining in government organs, institutions and large state-owned enterprises, the system of unit ownership has basically disintegrated for the entire society and become the history.

2. 2　Development and Dilemma of System of Neighborhood Committee

System of neighborhood committee constituted by government-sub-strict of-fice-neighborhood committee is another facet of basic management system of urban society in our country. During the planned economy period, the system of neighborhood committee provided management and service for non-unit personnel, mainly aiming at the social idlers, family women, people who need social special care and civil relief, which is the auxiliary system of system of unit. This made the system of neighborhood committee to become the main social management system after the gradually collapsing of the system of unit ownership, and fell into dilemma due to various non-adaptabilities.

2. 2. 1　Development History of System of Neighborhood Committee

2. 2. 1. 1　Before reform and opening-up: establishment and development of system of neighborhood committee

Organic Rules for Urban Sub-strict Offices and *Organic Rules for Urban Residents Committees* released in 1954 determined that system of neighborhood committee system of neighborhood committee was the auxiliary system of system of u-nit. Therefore, until the decline of system of unit, its development process was nearly identical to that of system of unit, which also experienced the initial exploration stage during 1949—1952, legalized stage during 1952—1958 and stable development stage during 1958—1978.

2.2.1.2 After reforming and opening-up: expansion of system of neighborhood committee

From early 1980s to 1990s, with continuous and further economic system reform and the consequent social transition, the system of unit ownership gradually disintegrates, which is replaced by system of neighborhood committee. It is transformed to the main management system of urban basic society from the original auxiliary system of system of unit.

However, this change is compulsory. After decline in system of unit, the public services and social management functions separated from the unit are transferred to the government in succession, many of which are left to the sub-strict neighborhood committee. Lacking the help of the unit, the government has to use the remaining sub-strict neighborhood committee to undertake basic social services and management.

With social mobility and sharp increase in unemployed population, unsuitability of system of the neighborhood committee appears rapidly. Large amounts of self-employed entrepreneurs, private enterprises, unemployed persons emerge in the society, with a huge number of peasant-workers flowing into cities. In housing reform and sales of commodity houses, huge amount of outside tenants run into old-style communities, leading to separation of owner and the house. System of neighborhood committee, on the basis of domicile control, is facing too many problems to handle because of its lack of managing personnel. Neighborhood committee, mainly organized by unemployed personnel such as housewives and retirees, bears the responsibility of managing registered population of the city as assigned by district government, while failing to meet the demand brought by huge change of grass-roots society. This, however, causes rapid expansions of the sub-district officer and institution, without considering the fact that above-mentioned situation remains to be an issue.

In such situation, Ministry of Civil Affairs proposed the concept of Community in middle and late 1980s. It is required to carry out community services and gradually propose the idea of community construction. However, it takes time. The community construction in this period is still carried out under the frame of system of neighborhood committee.

2. 2. 2　Development Dilemma of System of Neighborhood Committee

System of neighborhood committee has appeared congenitally deficient since it became management system of main basic society, which is originated from the objective and functional positioning of setting the auxiliary system at that time.

In the early setting period of system of neighborhood committee, the manning quotas and institutional positioning are definite. The sub-strict office is the government's dispatch agency, processing issues related to residents on behalf of the government, which does not have the nature of complete administrative institution. The number of full-time staff is 3 to 7 with main three work assignments: transaction of issues related to resident work assigned by the city and municipal district government, guidance of the neighborhood committee's work and reflection of the residents' opinions and requirements. The neighborhood committee is the autonomous resident organization of the mass with staff number of 2 to 4. The work contents include transaction of the residents' public welfare issues, reflection of the residents' opinions and requirements to local government or its dispatch agency, mobilization of the residents to respond the government appeal and abide by the law, guidance of mass security and safe-guarding work and mediation of disputes among residents.

This determines the non-adaptability of system of neighborhood committee after it became management system of main basic society.

The first is non-adaptability of the sub-strict. During continuous development in the future, the sub-strict has already broken through the initial positioning for a long time, not only completion in party or government group organization with increased departments and expanded personnel teams, but also the economic management function, such as neighborhood enterprises, whose nature is yet the dispatch agency of the government, not first-level government, with affair power but without decision-making power. In addition, resource scheduling and allocation capacity are extremely limited, owning no substantive management authority to each unit within the jurisdiction area. This is what we said that large responsibility but small power. If required to take over the public services and management functions transferred out after decline in system of unit, it is beyond its capability, which needs an adaptive and adjustable process. However, the history did not give it sufficient adjustment time and the contradiction still exists, even more prominent, after the transition system of neighborhood committee is developed to system of community.

What's more important is the non-adaptability of neighborhood committee members. During the period when the system of unit ownership was responsible for providing public service, social welfare and social management for majority employment population of urban residents, the number of objects that system of neighborhood committee had taken charge of management was few. In addition, due to the political and social environment at that time, its main functions referred to social control with few service functions because the public welfares and public products that non-employment population could enjoy were few at that time. Therefore, neighborhood committee in system of neighborhood committee mainly consisted of non-employment or retirement staff including family women, who were designated by sub-strict or the unit of the owner of real estate to accept the leadership of sub-strict (and sometimes also including ownership unit of the real estate). The neighborhood committee gets tasks from the sub-strict, besides reporting and informing, the daily tasks include supervising and knowing the social activity, public feelings and the family, member and relationship conditions of different families in the community, managing the community's security condition, coordinating dispute between neighbors, and charging for living service such as sanitation fee and bicycle keeping fee. The neighborhood committee is the leg of urban basic regime, which coordinates with the social control work of basic regime. After disintegration of system of unit, various public services and welfare functions are transferred to sub-strict, and the cultural composition of neighborhood committee's members is relatively low, many of whom have never worked within the system or enjoyed too many public services and welfares; thus, the work coordination engaged this aspect is of great difficulty. Therefore, the coordination of neighborhood committees in service functions to sub-strict is very limited, the sub-strict has to expand its staff and establish many special agencies, but still lacking "legs".

The dilemma of system of neighborhood committee determines the transition nature of system of neighborhood committee after reforming and opening-up. It is essential to strengthen the function of neighborhood committee, increase the functions of neighborhood committee, improve the quality of neighborhood committee's members, change its member composition, expand the jurisdiction area of neighborhood committee to reduce the sub-strict services and manage the quantity and blind area of objects. Under such circumstance, system of community emerge as required.

2.3　Development and insufficiency of System of Community

It is pointed out in many studies that management mode of system of community is a new type of community management mode to correspond to world trend in community construction and community development which symbolizes the gradual connection with basic social management mode of developed countries. In fact, the generation of system of community is first derived from the realistic demand brought by severe social changes after the reforming and opening-up. The rapid development of market economy has broken the original social basic management system, and the transition institutional arrangement after disintegration of system of unit-system of neighborhood committee cannot adapt to the social service and management requirement under market economy and free movement of population, in which the core problems and obvious weakness are centralized in the neighborhood committee. Therefore, the neighborhood committee with level upgraded-community neighborhood committee emerges and thus the system of community.

2.3.1　Generation and Development of System of Community

In 1991, Ministry of Civil Affairs proposed the concept of community construction. In March 1996, Jiang Zemin pointed out that strengthening the urban community construction largely and fully playing the role of sub-district offices and neighborhood committees. Shanghai city actively explored the urban management system under the new situation and result in the new system of *two-level government* (*city, county*) *and three-level management* (*city, district, county, sub-strict township*) ; after national promotion, it developed the *four-level* networks (city, county, sub-strict township, neighborhood committee & village committee). In 1999, Ministry of Civil Affairs formulated *Work Implementation Plan for National Community Construction Experimental Area*. In November 2000, General Office of the CPC Central Committee and General Office of the State Council jointly promulgated *Opinions of Ministry of Civil Affairs on Promotion of National Community Construction*.

In 2002, Jiang Zemin's Report at 16th Party Congress puts forward clearly that we will improve grassroots self-governing organizations, their democratic management system and the system of keeping the public informed of matters being handled, and ensure that the people directly exercise their democratic rights according to law, manage grassroots public affairs and programs for public good and exercise democratic supervision over the cadres. We will improve self-governance among villagers and foster a mechanism of their self-governance full of vitality under the leadership of village Party organizations. We will improve self-governance among urban residents and build new-type and well-managed communities featuring civility and harmony.

2.3.2　Features of System of Community

Compared with system of neighborhood committee, the most obvious change in system of community is to change the scattered neighborhood committees to community neighborhood committees. The jurisdiction area of community neighborhood committee includes multiple previous neighborhood committees. According to the Constitution, the residents' committee is a self-governing organization of urban residents elected by the residents. Current community neighborhood committee is still selected in procedure, but in practice, the responsible person of the community neighborhood committee is social workers (social-workers) appointed by the street. These social workers obtain the qualification through the exam organized by the government, and they are often not residents of the community, but professional managers, or occupational social workers, with certain administrative and social coordination capabilities. Their income is paid by the street, their daily tasks are arranged by the street, and their performance is evaluated by the street. They are actually engaged in the work of civil servants, but do not have civil service status, and do not enjoy the treatment and welfare of civil servants. Their education level, work experience, management and coordination capacity are much higher than the staff of traditional neighborhood committees.

Compared with previous committees, the largest feature of community neighborhood committee is to undertake part functions of public services, social welfare and administrative management, such as employment, social insurance, social relief, social security, family planning, sports entertainment and educational work. This cannot be realized by the previous neighborhood committees, which is also the largest feature of system of community to differ from system of neighborhood committee. This is the biggest reason why system of community is generated with disintegration of system of unit and insufficiency in system of neighborhood committee.

2.3.3 Development Status of System of Community

Under active promotion of governments of various places, system of community has made great progress, especially the extensive establishment of community neighborhood committees in relatively large cities. The number of community service organization increases rapidly, and the community practitioners team expands rapidly. Now take Beijing as an example:

By the end of 2011, the population of permanent resident in whole Beijing city is 20, 186, 000 and the population of foreign resident is 7, 422, 000, occupying 36. 8% of the permanent residents. There are 140 sub-strict offices, 2773 community neighborhood committees, 5411 community service institutions, including 180 community service centers, 5231 community service sites. There are 27376 community employees, 8012 community service volunteer organizations, 12490 urban civilian and community service spots. The total area of community service institutions amounts to 1, 238, 000m^2.

2.3.3.1 Advantages of System of Community

(1) System of community improves the ability of sub-strict to carry out public service and management.

System of community street office has a strong *leg*, which benefits the provision of public services and welfare as well as basic social management. System of community expands the service and management area of neighborhood committee, which can not only reduce the service and objects which streets are faced with, but also centralize and use the resources, good to development of funding, organization of resident sports and entertainment activities. Some community neighborhood committees of large cities have community centers and activity sites, in which various types of cultural & sports activities and educational activities are carried out all year round, thus to enrich the people's amateur life and improve quality of the residents.

(2) System of community benefits the elimination of blind spots in social management.

With rapid increases in housing commercialization and commodity house, a large number of neighborhoods of new styles emerge. Different to a majority of conventional neighborhoods assigned and managed by units or housing administration department, these new neighborhoods were developed by estate agents and managed by property management companies, and neighborhood committee organizations could be rarely found. However, certain neighborhoods have owner committees, though many more have not been founded. Pursuant to relevant laws and regulations, such owner committee with limited administration authorities shall not be entitled to conduct public services assisting the owner or responsible for supporting street administrative work like conventional owner, . Therefore, the blindness thereby comes. After foundation of community neighborhood committee, each neighborhood requires no neighborhood committee any more, and they can conduct close cooperation and communication with owner committees and property management companies. Thus, it puts new neighborhoods without neighborhood committees into social management and services.

(3) System of community benefits the development of social organization.

With regard to large jurisdiction, huge population, as well as encourage, organization, guidance and sponsorship of community neighborhood committee or workstation, system of community proves more beneficial to organization and development of the society. Various residential groups and volunteer organizations grow rapidly, with major characteristics of self recreation, temperament cultivation and body building. Many other organizations are founded to provide services for residents for example, *"Mutual Help among Neighbors"* workroom of Nanyang Community, Jiaxing City, Zhejiang Province, *"Club for Entrepreneurs from outside Beijing"* of Jinbaojie Community, Beijing and *"Sunshine Class"* of Xiangcaolu Community, Tianqiao Street, Beijing. To our extra surprise, certain management organizations of self-management, conscious maintenance for social order emerge, such as established spontaneously founded parking order management organization of Jianguomen Street, Dongcheng District, Beijing, *"City Woodpecker"* for safeguarding city appearance of Volunteer organization by residents of Jiangxing and Zhejiang, etc.

(4) Guiding ideology of *"Common Building of Community"* opens the door to residents and social organizations for participating in community related services and management.

Guiding ideology of *"Common Building of Community"* was put forward in building of the community, which is contrast to systems of unit and neighborhood committee, providing unprecedented possibility of self-management, discussion, supervision and positive participation in social service and management by the residents. Community residents nearby Beijing Union Medical College Hospital organized by themselves the Food Safety Picket along the Jianguomen Street, Dongcheng District, Beijing to help urban management officers and health department inspect and stop such person who peddles expired or fake food to those standing in line for registration at the gate of hospital. The effect of such behavior proves much better than simple management by urban management officers for the convenience of distance.

2. 3. 3. 2　Insufficiency in System of Community in Present Stage

(1) Sub-strict office begins to expose the disadvantage of large responsibility & small power the system of neighborhood committee after forced to be the system of main social basic management, which is more prominent in system of community.

After decline in system of unit, sub-district office plays an increasingly important role in lower management system of the city, and objectivity and reality require it to be stronger authoritativeness, capable of coordinating and organizing residents from different units and interest groups within jurisdiction during bottom-round management for the city. However, due to China's divided management system and self-legal status of sub-district office, functions of them over expand, form such strange pattern of managing all and fail in all. ①

Firstly, over expansion of the functions of sub-district office is getting worse. With establishment of "Two Levels of Government and Three Levels of management", functions of sub-district office expand rapidly. Loads of administration, law enforcement and district development are imposed on the sub-district office. After the disintegration system of unit, many public services and management functions emerge, the majority of which were shouldered by sub-district offices. Despite that, economic development and social changes give rise to new management fields as city appearance and floating population. Thousands of works and issues are waiting for settlement by one. Service and management functions of nearly all governments are sent to sub-district office for enforce-

---

① Ding Maozhan. Study on institutional reform of urban community management in China[M]. China Economic Publishing House, 2009.

ment, which holds liable for a combination of functions of administration, society, economy and district.

Secondly, large responsibility and small power in sub-strict offices are not fit with each other. In recent years, despite the fact that authorities of sub-district office were largely strengthened, such authorities are limited to rights of matters instead of decision-making, examination and approval and disposition powers. Main work contents involve achieving targets and finishing tasks issued by governments according to requirements of superior authorities. However, sub-district office is shouldering increasing load of tasks while failing to be granted respective guaranteed powers. As the end of administrative power chain, sub-district office is shouldering daily administration and management as well as law enforcement, while lacking resource distribution power and dispatching ability granted to functional sectors of government, therefore, lacking restrictive mechanism and supervision intensity. In addition, the absence of relevant supporting laws and regulations, current status of administration and law enforcement proves not optimistic. Under most circumstances, sub-district office can "see", but "fail to manage or manage poorly" the issue present, while functional sectors of government "have the power to manage, but fail to see and shoulder no responsibility" to such issue, leading to this situation of "Management without Power while Power Without Action".

Finally, the organization law system and legislation of the street offices are lagging behind with no legal support. "*Organic Rules for Urban Sub-strict Offices*" formulated in 1954, and "*Organic Law of the Local People's Congress and Local People's Governments of the PRC*" adopted in 1979 and revised in 2004 stipulate that "municipal district, municipal people's government with no districts, subject to the approval of governments of higher levels, can set up a number of street offices as its agencies". "*Organic Law of the Urban Residents Committees of the PRC*" adopted in 1989 summarily stipulates that the relationship between the street offices and the residents' committee is guidance and assistance. The organization law system of the street offices apparently lacks the support of the constitution law, the cornerstone of the organization law[1]. "*Organic*

---

① Wei Di, Li Xuhong (2007) Legal Principle and Perfect Selection of Two – level Government and Three – level Management in China, *Journal of Shanghai Polytechnic College of Urban Management*, 2, 8 – 11.

Rules for Urban Sub-strict Offices" adopted in 1954 is still the major legal support of current street offices. The starting point of setting up street offices then was to consolidate political power, and the main purpose was to strengthen the work of urban residents, maintain close ties between the government and residents, so its functional requirements was very simple. Obviously, the definition of street functions and administrative power and arrangements at the level of performance then is far from meeting the great social changes.

(2) The community neighborhood committee has a serious adminis-trative tendency, deviates from the nature of residents' self-governing or-ganizations stipulated by law and results in role disorder.

First is the administrative trend of the community neighborhood committee. With the active promotion of local governments, the community neighborhood committee plays an important role in community building, and community build-ing undergoes great progress. It is because that the development mode of China's community building is government promotion and streets domination and that the streets have urgent needs to separate and hand over the over-expanded public service and management functions to lower levels, the community neighborhood committee has, since its birth, assumed the administrative mission. It ensures the coverage of public services, strengthens the conveniences of the residents, and enhances the administrative efficiency, which is the biggest difference be-tween the community neighborhood committee and traditional neighborhood com-mittee. The community neighborhood committee is funded by the streets, its dai-ly work is arranged by the streets and it exercises the public service and admin-istrative power entitled by the streets. So the streets are, in essence, the "semi-government body" of grassroots society.

Second is the civil servant trend of the neighborhood committee staff. In or-der to ensure the quality and efficiency of the administration, the responsible person for the community neighborhood committee is "selected by the residents and employed by the street" in the form of election. Candidates are social work-ers designated by the streets, paid by the streets, and in essence, administrative staff appointed and dispatched by the streets, "quasi-civil servants" that do not enjoy the welfare of civil servants, whose sources of interests and evaluation mainly come from their superiors- the street, rather than residents. When there is conflict that they shall be responsible for the residents or the government (the street), they will naturally prefer the latter.

The Constitution clearly stipulates that urban residents' committee is a self-governing organization of grassroots mass in 1982, followed by the "*Organic Law of the Urban Residents Committees of the PRC*", which also stipulates that "residents' committee is a self-governing organization of grassroots mass for self-management, self-education and self-service". The current administrative nature in essence as well as the appointment system of responsible person in essence of the community neighborhood committee have greatly changed the self-governing and self-management nature of the neighborhood committee, weakened the consultation and supervision functions of the neighborhood committee, reduced the channels and platforms for communication between residents and the government and social participation, affected the enthusiasm of residents to participate in community building, and hampered more participation of individual resident and resident's organizations in community building.

(3) Lack of Attention to and use of the Rule of the Market and the Regulation Rules of Interests

Due to the traditional system and habitual thinking, public services and social administration of the system of community is still limited to administrative means. There is not sufficient knowledge about outsourcing selectively via the market means, procurement of public services and carry out public administration through the regulation means of interests, which is not conducive to further enhance service and management efficiency, lower service and management costs, reduce unused resources and waste, and not conducive to bringing all social forces and ingenuity to build and administrate the communities together, either.

Meanwhile, due to over-reliance on administrative measures and administrative systems, the government takes on all services and administration. As a result, the government plays a permanent responsible role, and often became a target of public discontent. The government gets the work done all in vain because it gets blamed for the work done.

(4) The Community Building Subject is Single, Lack of Diversity, and the role of Social Organizations, especially the Owners' Committee, is not brought into full play.

Development of the system of community leads to the progress of social or-

ganizations. But there is still a long way away from the diversification of community building subjects. Current development is still led by the street-community
neighborhood committee, and there is insufficient awareness of building and ad-
ministrating a community with the joint efforts of residents' groups, volunteer organizations, intermediary organizations, and non-governmental organizations.

It requires particular emphasis on the owners' committee and property management company. The former is the only true residents' self-governing organization, which determines the organization degree of the residents and the level of
supervision and guidance on the latter; the latter is the most important provider
of daily life services of the district residents, which ensures the life quality of the
residents. The functioning and the level of interaction between the two determine
the living environment and life quality of the districts. However, most commercial residential building areas have not yet established owners' committee, and
old-fashioned districts are left blank as well. The supervision management of the
community neighborhood committee on the property management companies
(and the developers) is also very weak. All above mentioned factors affect the
community building and management.

3　Development of Urban Community in China Faces Institutional In-
novation

To sum up, the community development in China is facing some problems
as well as some opportunities, especially the opportunities of institutional innovation. Considering about these issues, governments of various places should
dare to explore and actively practice to explore some models to solve the defects
of the above model and carry out institutional innovation in social management
practice.

3.1　Reform Exploration of System of Community

3.1.1　Reform Practices in Development of System of Community[1]

Since the late 1990s, Cities like Shanghai, Nanjing, Shenyang, Shenzhen,
Wuhan and etc. have carried out reforms of community management system successively, and actively explored new community management system that adapts
to the needs of the development of modern society. On the basis of absorbing re-

---

[1]　Theoretical discussion and practice innovation of management system of urban community. Source: *Xinhua News Agency*; Date: July 13, 2012.

form experiences across the country, the CPC Central Committee and the State Council General Office transmitted "*Suggestions on Urban Community Construction Promotion across the Country by the Ministry of Civil Affairs*" in 2000. The reform of community management system has sprung up from single spark to fire in cities across the country since then, and a few typical development modes have emerged.

3. 1. 1. 1　Administrative Guidance Mode in Shanghai

In the administrative guidance mode, the government is the subject of community governance, and administrative means is the major way of community governance. The most important feature of this mode is to integrate community construction with the city management system reforms of "*Two-level Government, Three-level Management and Four-level Network*", which not only strengthening the power, status and role of the sub-district offices, but also orientating the community at street, separating a considerable part of the management functions of the municipal and district government to gather at street level, attaching importance to the leading role of the government in community development, and building a street community management system combined with community management and leadership, execution and support system.

The administrative guidance mode in Shanghai affords us lessons that merit attention in terms of the transformation of government functions, the establishment of "Super-Ministry System" in sub-district offices, the creation of professional and occupational social work team, and the administrative operation mechanism of decision-making, execution, supervision and coordination and etc.

3. 1. 1. 2　Autonomous Model in Shenyang

Dominant Community Autonomous Model is a typical new modern governance model. Shenyang City explicitly proposes the basic principle of "People-oriented and Community Autonomous". Community party is the core of the leadership of the community, and the community committee is elected by and for the community member meeting or community member's representative meeting and shall report work to and subject to the supervision of them; Community Consultative Committee is the community consultative body, whose members are mainly community NPC deputies, CPPCC members, celebrities, residential representatives and residential unit representatives with one full-time director (a concurrent post hold by the person in charge of the community party), two deputy directors and several committee members by implementing the system of voluntary work.

Shenyang Mode is a major breakthrough in the construction of urban grass-roots democracy and autonomy, which embodies the principle of "Community Autonomous and Separation of Legislative and Executive Powers". This ensures the dominant position of the community's neighborhood committee from the perspective of the system, and thus makes the community become a real residential community of autonomy.

3.1.1.3 Model of *One Committee, Two Offices* in Shenzhen

According to the idea of "Separation of Legislative and Executive Powers", Yantian District of Shenzhen City established the community governance model of "One Committee, Two Offices" in 2005, which separates the administrative, autonomous and service functions formerly undertaken by the neighborhood committee in the long run, and transfers the government administrative and public service functions from the neighborhood committee to the community workstations; community workstations are the organizations dispatched by the street committee, whose work staff implement the contract system and are entitled to authorized size and fiscal wages; service function is transferred to the community service stations; meanwhile community committee is elected by the residents directly to implement autonomous functions in order to rationalize the relationship between the government and community. Community Organizations like the Community Committee, Community Workstations and Community Service stations and etc. are under the leadership of the Community party, and the Community Committee and Community Workstations shall cooperate on the same standing. The Community committee inspects and supervises the work of community workstations on behalf of the residents, and guides the work of community service stations, which are functional private non-enterprise organizations that provide a variety of social services for the community residents.

Fig. 3 – 1   Model Figure of "*One Committee, Two Offices*" in Yantian District, Shenzhen. ①

---

①   Wang Bo, Miao Yuexia, Liang Ying. Study on Innovation of Management System of Urban Community – Three – element System of Administration, Coordination and Autonomy. *http: //mzzt. mca. gov. cn/article/hxsqyth/zbkt/200810/20081000020653. shtml.*

Note: Solid line represents the relationship between the leader and his staff, and the dotted line represents the relationship between guidance and under guidance.

3. 1. 1. 4　Tongling Mode: Revoking of the Street Offices

Tongling City has revoked 10 street offices of Tongguanshan District and Shizishan District successively, integrates the former 61 communities to 23 new communities, adjusts the original "city-district-sub-strict-community" four-level management to "city-district-community" three-level management, and establishes a comprehensive architecture, with the community Party and Labor Committee as the core and community committees, community service centers and various social organizations as the support. The community party and labor committee is directly under the management of the district committee, mainly undertaking the responsibility of the overall planning and coordination within the community. The community service centers open seven professional service windows like General Affairs, Civil Affairs, Population and Family Planning, Comprehensive Satiability Maintenance and Petition Letter, Civilization Establishment, Social Security, Economic Services and etc.. The center isunder the unified leadership and management of the community party and labor committee and the community's neighborhood committee, and manages the community matters in the principle of *One-office styl*e approval and *One-stop* collective processing. Public administration, services and examination and approval functions related to the original sub-districts are transferred to the communities, and the original district authorities and work staff of the street offices are transferred to the communities as well. Meanwhile, grid management is implemented. One community management worker is allocated for 300 residents, and the workers' wages are directly linked to the satisfaction of the residents. All community work is put under the supervision of the masses.

3. 1. 2　Community Workstations: Highlights in the Reform[①]

"Suggestions on Urban Community Construction Promotion across the Country by the Ministry of Civil Affairs" transmitted by the CPC Central Committee and the State Council General Office greatly stimulated the reform enthusiasm of local governments. Community workstations became bright spots of the reform at

---

①　Xu Daowen. Reform and Development of Management System of Urban Community in China[J]. *Humanities & Social Sciences Journal of Hainan University*, 2009.

this stage, and many cities established community workstations one after another, especially after entering the 21st century.

3. 1. 2. 1　Three Modes of Community Workstation

(1) Mode of "Separation of Legislative and Executive Powers" Beijing Xicheng District carried out the reform of neighborhood management system in communities in 2003, adjusting the autonomous management mode of neighborhood community to a new management mode of *"Separation of Legislative and Executive Powers"*. The feature of Separation of Legislative and Executive Powers is to implement *"One Committee, Two Offices"*, that is, to establish community workstations and community service stations under the neighborhood communities. The neighborhood community, as the consultation organization, executes the decision-making and supervision power over the major events of the community and community management; and workstations and service stations, as the "execution" organizations of the neighborhood community, are to complete the administrative work commissioned by the government, attend to the community autonomous affairs and serve the people. Some urban areas of Dalian, Guangzhou, Hangzhou, Ningbo, Nanjing, Changzhou, Qingdao and etc. also adopt the mode of *"Separation of Legislative and Executive Powers"*. While Shenzhen's *"One Committee, Two Offices"* policy refers to *"Separation of Committee and Station"* instead of *"Separation of Legislative and Executive Powers"*.

(2) *Separation of Committee and Station* Shenzhen began to promote this mode in the community management in 2005. *"Separation of Committee and Station"* refers to the establishment of community workstations and neighborhood committees in grassroots communities simultaneously; both independent of each other, the former assumes administrative and service work, while the latter engages in the residents' autonomous affairs. According to *"Pilot Scheme of Community Workstations Management in Shenzhen City"*, community workstations are the service platforms of government in the communities, assist and cooperate with the government and other departments on the work in the communities and provide services to community residents. Community workstations start work under the guidance of the street party committees and the street offices and accept operational guidance from the municipal, district departments and other government work sectors; in principle, staff management is carried out with reference to the relevant provisions of the average employee management in Shenzhen government departments and institutions. According to these provisions, community workstations are similar as public institutions fully funded by the Government. The relationship between community workstations and the community committees is that of government agencies and the self-governing mass organization, supporting each other, cooperating with each other, each performing its own functions and each doing its own duties.

(3) *People-run Non-enterprise* **Mode Shanghai began to implement this mode in 2005.** So-called "People-run Non-enterprise" mode refers that the nature of the community workstations is a private non-enterprise unit, which undertakes social affairs decentralized by government and street offices, such as social assistance, investigations on relief objects and so on; undertakes social affairs spin off from the street offices, such as civil disputes mediation, social surveys assistance and so on; undertakes social welfare services, such as community services, service work related to enterprise retiree after community management and all kinds of services for the elderly and so on.

3.1.2.2 Evaluation of the Three Modes

(1) Mode of "*Separation of Legislative and Executive Powers*" transforms the traditional mode of "*Combination of Legislative and Executive Powers*" of the community's neighborhood committee. In the mode of "*Combination of Legislative and Executive Powers*", the autonomous function, management function and service function of the urban community is three-in-one, while the autonomous functions are actually relegated to the category of things wanting. In the mode of "*Separation of Legislative and Executive Powers*", management functions and service functions are relatively separated, but still under the guidance of the community's neighborhood committee. The system of "*Separation of Legislative and Executive Powers*" does not change the administrative characteristics of the community's neighborhood committee, it builds more organizations and employs more personnel in the neighborhood committee in order to complete more and more administrative affairs in the community and thus enhance the administrative color of the community's neighborhood committee to a certain extent.

(2) Mode of "*People-run Non-enterprise*" is in full compliance with the existing law. It differs from the mode of "*Separation of Legislative and Executive Powers*" in that the community service functions separated from the neighborhood committee is borne by the private non-enterprise units. This approach is consist-

ent with the popularized trend of social welfare reform among average people in the West, and is of great significance to breaking the situation of single administrative means rules all. Mode of *"People-run Non-enterprise"*, however, did not involve the reform of the community's neighborhood committee itself. It lessens the administrative color of the performance way of the functions of the neighborhood committee, but the functions of the neighborhood committee are not yet separated. From this perspective, mode of *"People-run Non-enterprise"* falls into the category of mode of *"Separation of Legislative and Executive Powers"* in essence.

(3) Mode of *"Separation of Committee and Station"* strips the administrative functions and service functions from the community's neighborhood committee and hands them over to the representative bodies of the street – Community Workstations. The neighborhood committee becomes a pure autonomous organization to execute the functions of consultation and supervision. This is undoubtedly the nature most in line with the legal provisions of the community's neighborhood committee, a sharp weapon to solve the current evils of the above-mentioned system of community, and the most noteworthy mode currently. But the fact that community workstations as the representative bodies of the street lacks a legal basis.

3. 2　Institutional Innovation of System of Community

3. 2. 1　Principle of Institutional Innovation

Considering the performance of the system of community till today and current existing problems, we believe that institutional innovation should have a long-term strategic vision instead of a short-term one to avoid the back-and-forth of institutional reform experienced in the past. To this end, innovation of management system of urban basic society shall depend on the following principles:

Principle of Service and Management Integration: Service contains management in that public administration is improved by strengthening the public service, management and coordination is achieved by taking advantage of the access to public resources. It is not recommended to pursue blindly simplistic means of administration.

Market-oriented Principles: Reduce the mandatory administrative means, and increase economic and interest regulation means. Outsource part of the service and management functions to economic agents in an open, fair and justice way selectively to enhance service quality and management efficiency, reduce the government burden, and at the same time to avoid putting the government as permanent direct liability at the finger of blame for undertaking all things.

Residents Self-management Principles: In the grass-roots management system composed of the street- the community's neighborhood committee (District Committee of Owners) -residents, administrative functions and supervision functions are separated and relatively divided. The community's neighborhood committee is further divided into community workstations, community service stations, and neighborhood committees (resident representative organizations, residents' meetings), each exercising its own administrative, service, consultation and supervision functions. It not only strengthens the residents' supervision of the community work, but also enhances residents' self-management and self-discipline, and enhances the level of residents' self-management and self-discipline. Establish owners' committee in suitable residential areas proactively to enhance the management, consultation and supervision functions of the owners' meeting and owner's committee and strengthen the self-management of the residents.

Principle of Small Government and Big Society: To attach importance to bring the service enthusiasm of the residents to the community and the surrounding areas into play, to strengthen the development of social organizations, encourage residents to establish residents' groups and volunteer organizations and intermediary organizations that are healthy, civilized and conducive to social progress, including not only sports and entertainment societies, but also service organizations and management organizations that possess social service and management functions, and strengthen guidance and management on those organizations. To carry out community construction and management through collaboration and joint efforts of the government and its dispatched institutions, residents' self-governing organizations, volunteer organizations, social intermediary organizations, non-profit organizations, non-governmental organizations and residents.

Principle of Advance with the Times: It is required to study the community service and management in the Internet age, such as the grid management promoted in major cities, the smart community concept and mode based on the Internet and IOT and which combines effectively the interaction of commodities service and information communication and so on.

3.2.2　Institutional Arrangement

(1) First, separate the current administrative functions from the community's neighborhood committee and hand over to the community workstations specially established by the street; separate the service functions and hand over to professional service institutions, better private non-enterprise units, like the community service stations. The nature of the community workstations is an agency dispatched by the street offices.

(2) The community's neighborhood committee is directly elected by the residents to execute the consultation and supervision functions and cooperate with and assist the daily work of the community workstations and specialized service agencies. The community's neighborhood committee and the community workstations are parallel institutions, and there is no mutual affiliation between the two. Considering that the communities now have a certain size with a large population, it is recommended to set up residents representative institutions or the advisory body of the community's neighborhood committee composed of public-spirited residents or retirees with management experience in larger communities to cooperate with and assist the work of the community's neighborhood committee.

(3) Outsource selectively part of the service and management functions through an open, fair and impartial manner, under the supervision of the community's neighborhood committees, optimize service quality, improve management efficiency and reduce costs, at the same time reduce the work burden of the community workstations and service agencies and promote the diversification of the community building subjects by way of government procurement of services. Some cities have gathered some successful experiences related to this, for example, Shenzhen has outsourced some urban management functions like the supervision of the appearance of the city to an enterprise, and the government reception vehicle service to a company. Beijing launched the home-based care coupons for the aged (disabled). The government procurement of services covers a wide area, including social welfare and relief, employment, medical care and health care, home-based care and disabled care, disability rehabilitation, household management, catering for the elderly, community order, conflict mediation, rights protection, psychological service, behavior correction, community corrections, youth and adolescent education, marriage and family, and so on.

(4) Allow social organizations like the residents' groups to join community development, and public service and management, promote the diversification of community building subjects, and promote joint efforts of the government, the neighborhood committee, residents and social organizations to manage the community. It is allowed to collaborate with residents' groups and volunteer organizations to perform some service and management functions. Social organizations should make use of regrouped social resources. There is a large amount of human and material resources in the society, the way that the government used to provide social service alone lost sight of engine on, integrate and make use of the various vital forces scattered in the society.

3. 2. 3 Supporting Institutional Arrangement and Policy Recommendations

(1) Enhance the functionality of the owners' committee. To actively promote the establishment of the owners' committee in the residential area, to strengthen the self-governing management of the owners, and to allow the owners to cooperate with the property companies and developers and safeguard legal rights in an organized and orderly manner. Existing laws and regulations on the owners' committees are relatively sufficient and clear. It requires further consideration regarding increase of the scope and function of the self-management of the owners' meetings and committees to cultivate the self-governing skills, social negotiation capabilities and self-discipline awareness. Clarify the relationship between the owners' committee and the community's neighborhood committee to strengthen the collaboration between the two.

(2) Encourage the development of social organizations, and strengthen the management and guidance on social organizations. Pay attention to, cultivate and bring into play the enthusiasm of residents to participate in community building and management, support, encourage and assist residents' groups and volunteer organizations conducive to the society, with particular emphasis on the development of service organizations and management organizations. Currently most participants of service and management groups are retired personnel, such as retired doctors impart knowledge about health care free of charge to community neighbors; retired teachers participate in the sunlight classroom for migrant children free of charge and so on. The coverage of social organizations should be further widened.

(3) Cultivate a team of professional and occupational social workers. Im-

prove their degree of specialization through the establishment and improvement of the training, examination, and certification system. Reduce the frequent turnover of social workers and the outflow of talent through the establishment and improvement of incentive system. In the process of system construction, it is required to face squarely the reality that social workers have low income, low status and low career expectations and make efforts to improve such a situation through institutional arrangement. Community building and institutional innovation would be empty talk if there is no sufficient number of qualified social workers.

(4) Strengthen the legislative work of the system of community. Work out supporting legal systems step by step according to the development of the street offices, the community's neighborhood committees, community workstations, community service agencies, social workers and social organizations and the maturity of the systems and make sure that they have legal support. Currently the government only has one level of branches, namely, the streets, no organs of state power are set up under the jurisdiction of the streets. Currently there is no legal basis for the emergence of this new thing the community workstations. It is required to work out supporting laws according to the needs and maturity in the process of social practice.

4 Conclusions

Social grassroots management and community development progress are gradually along with change and progress of the times.

Mankind has entered the age of the Internet, the concept and way of the community public service and management will continue to progress along with the arrival of the Internet age that has changed people's way of life significantly. "Smart Community", a concept of community life services and information interchange in the Internet age has been proposed and studied, and correspondent hardware and software platform has been developed. This point-to-point platform integrating cloud computing, IOT, mobile communications and various intelligent controls not only allows people to enjoy quick cheap life services, daily necessities purchase, as well as health care, etc. while remain indoors, but also helps realize seamless information concentration among the government departments, the streets, the neighborhood committees, the property industries, the owners' committee, non-profit organizations and the community residents and solve the last mile information service problem of the urban community. The idea of combining the logistics and information flow in a point-to-point way will provide an alternative solution to the establishment of new social service systems and the "intelligentization" of urban grassroots management and public service.

These are new issues that we face now.

(Director: Yang Xu, Yuan Chongfa; Author: Bai Nanfeng, Tian Mei, Zhang Wenning, Lang Lang, Xiang Yizhi, Wu Benjian; Document Manager: Zhang Wenning)

Reference

[1] Lv Fang. From system of neighborhood committee to system of community: change process and its deep meaning[J]. Fujian Tribune (The Humanities & Social Sciences Monthly), 2010(11).

[2] Cui Lixia. From system of unit to system of community-Exploration on Management Method of Urban Community in China[J]. Economic Research Guide, 2009.

[3] Xia Jianzhong. From system of neighborhood committee to system of community: Changes in Urban Community of Our Country for 30 Years[J]. Heilongjiang Social Sciences, 2008(5).

[4] Qin Bo. Evolution of System of Unit in Transition Period-Concurrent Discussion on the Necessity of Development of System of Community[J]. Gansu Theory Research, 2006.

[5] Ren Xueli, Li Cheng. Evolution of Relationship between Our Country and the Society Since Founding of New China-Based on Perspective of Changes in System of Unit[J]. Journal of Hubei Administration Institute, 2010(10).

[6] Yang Yue. Study on Management Subjects of Urban Community in China[D] Master Thesis of Nanjing Normal University, 2008.

[7] Ji Naiwang. Formation of System of Unit in Contemporary China and its Characteristics[J]. Economic Research Guide, 2011(30).

[8] He Haibing. Main problems in management system of urban community and its reform trend in China[J]. The Journal of Shanghai Administration Institute, 2007.

[9] Wu Junming, Gao Di. View of Changes in Social Organization Structure of our Country based on Changes in System of Unit in Transition Period(J). Journal of Heilongjiang College of Education, 2005(9).

[10] Wang Qiong. Elimination of System of Unit and Changes in Governmental Governance Mode [J]. Theoretical View, 2007(2).

[11] Yang Yue. Study on Management Subjects of Urban Community in China[D]. Master Thesis of Nanjing Normal University, 2008.

[12] Lou Chengwu, Sun Ping. Community Management Study[M]. Higher Education Press, 2006 Edition.

[13] Pan Xiaojuan: *Reconstructing of Basic Society in China-Community Governance Study*, China Legal Publishing House, 2004.

[14] Chen Jie. Evolution process of management system of urban community in China [J]. Administrative Management.

[15] Ding Maozhan: Study on institutional reform of urban community management in China, China Economic Publishing House, 2009.

[16] Pan Xiaojuan. On Issues of District Administration[J]. Journal of State Administrative College, 2007, (1).

[17] He Haibing. Main problems in management system of urban community and its reform trend in China[J]. The Journal of Shanghai Administration Institute, 2007.

[18] Zhan Chengfu, Huang Guanhong. Study Report on Setup Mode of Community Workstation [EB/OL](2006 – 0518)[2008 – 04 – 03]. http://www. mca. gov. cn/redian/shqgz/shequjs46. htm. 1.

[19] Wang Lian. On Construction of Specialized Community Workers Team[J]. Journal of Hubei University of Economics (Humanities and Social Sciences).

[20] Wang Ying. Analysis of Institutional Reform and Innovation of Urban Community Management in China[J]. Journal of Sichuan Administration College, 2007, Volume 6.

[21] Liu Yueping. Analysis of problems existing in management system reform of urban community and the reform measures[J]. New West, 2008.

[22] Zhu Yi. Management Theory and Practice Study of Urban Community[D]. Doctoral Dissertation of Wuhan University of Technology 2005.

[23] Huang Yan. Study on Management Model of Urban Community in China[D] Master Thesis of University of Electronic Science and Technology of China, 2006.

[24] Liu Ting. Preliminary Analysis of Innovation of Management Models of Chinese Communities[D]. Master Thesis of Jilin University, 2006.